From Saturday Night to Sunday Night

MY FORTY YEARS OF LAUGHTER, TEARS, AND TOUCHDOWNS IN TV

Dick Ebersol

SIMON & SCHUSTER

New York   London   Toronto   Sydney   New Delhi

Simon & Schuster
1230 Avenue of the Americas
New York, NY 10020

First Simon & Schuster hardcover edition September 2022

SIMON & SCHUSTER and colophon are registered trademarks of Simon & Schuster, Inc.

For information about special discounts for bulk purchases, please contact Simon & Schuster Special Sales at 1-866-506-1949 or business@simonandschuster.com.

The Simon & Schuster Speakers Bureau can bring authors to your live event. For more information or to book an event, contact the Simon & Schuster Speakers Bureau at 1-866-248-3049 or visit our website at www.simonspeakers.com.

Interior design by Wendy Blum

Manufactured in the United States of America

10   9   8   7   6   5   4   3   2   1

Library of Congress Cataloging-in-Publication Data has been applied for.

ISBN 978-1-9821-9446-8
ISBN 978-1-9821-9448-2 (ebook)

To Susie

The finish line is only the beginning of a whole new race.

—Teddy Ebersol, June 2004

Contents

Part Three

Part Four

Prologue

Just Another Great Day

The alarm went off around 6:00 a.m. in our hotel room at the Century Plaza Hotel in Los Angeles. My wife, Susan, and I were in a bedroom on one end of our suite, while our two younger sons, eighteen-year-old Willie and fourteen-year-old Teddy, were sharing the bedroom at the other end. It was the Sunday after Thanksgiving in 2004, and after a terrific week celebrating the holiday in L.A. with all five of our children and a collection of friends, we were heading back east.

As Susan got out of bed to pack the last few things in our suitcases, I went into the bathroom to get ready. Our trip would have a few stops. First, our private plane would land in Colorado and drop off Susan and her friend Rebecca—the wife of Susan's ex-husband, Tom (yes, you read that right; to this day, our family happily thrives off our unconventionality). They'd spend a few days prepping the house we owned in the mountains of Telluride for Christmas. Next, the plane would head to South Bend, Indiana, to drop off our older son Charlie, who was in the middle of his senior year at Notre Dame. Then, by early evening, the plane would land in Hartford, Connecticut, and I'd drop Teddy off at the Gunnery, a boarding school where he was a freshman, before I finally drove to our home in Litchfield, a small town in the bucolic northwest corner of the state where I'd grown up as a public school kid, never dreaming I'd be able to live this kind of life. Then, first thing the next morning, I'd take a car into New York City and go to my office at 30 Rockefeller Plaza, to continue working on one of the most exciting deals of my career.

As the head of the sports and Olympics division for NBC since 1989, I'd made big deals, taken huge risks, solved difficult problems, and built lasting relationships. I'd joined forces with NBA commissioner David Stern to create arguably the most successful partnership between a network and a sports league in history with the NBA on NBC; turned NBC into America's Olympic network through a series of deals with the International Olympic Committee that ensured the Games would be on our air through 2012; and through Super Bowls, World Series, major golf tournaments, Grand Slam tennis events, and more, lived out a career that I only could have dreamed about as a kid, watching ABC's *Wide World of Sports* on TV at home.

ABC Sports had in fact been where I'd started my career, as the network's first-ever Olympic researcher, working for the legendary Roone Arledge and traveling the world as a twenty-year-old kid who'd dropped out of Yale at the height of the Vietnam War to take the job. Not long after, I'd get promoted to be Roone's assistant, getting a front-row seat to everything he did, from sitting in on executive meetings in his place to delivering files to him at the 21 Club when he met at the restaurant with NFL commissioner Pete Rozelle to iron out the deal to create *Monday Night Football*. Then I'd left sports for a while, taking an offer from NBC to join its entertainment division to start a weekend late night comedy show, and finding an unknown producer named Lorne Michaels and co-creating *Saturday Night Live*. From there, I'd work in worlds as disparate as talk, music, and professional wrestling, but came back to my first love when I took the NBC Sports job in '89.

The full-circle nature of my path had also been on my mind throughout Thanksgiving week—especially given my tiny role in the creation of *Monday Night Football*. On my way to Los Angeles, I'd made a brief but important stop in

Denver. There, my number two, Ken Schanzer, and I had met with the owner of the Broncos, Pat Bowlen, the head of the NFL's television committee, to pitch him on a simple but seismic proposal: to reinvent pro football on prime-time television by moving the league's top prime-time game every week from Monday to Sunday—to essentially replace *Monday Night Football* on ABC with *Sunday Night Football* on NBC. We'd been out of football since I'd made the decision to walk away from our coverage in 1998—but I was excited to try to bring us back, which could be a huge boon to the network's struggling ratings overall. For his part, Pat was definitely intrigued; we'd been talking on and off about the idea for months, but that meeting just before Thanksgiving was the first time that money had come up as part of the discussion. Any time ten figures were thrown around with a straight face in a media deal, it was a definite sign that things were serious.

Back in our hotel room in Los Angeles, Susan and I very quietly woke up Teddy to tell him to get ready to head to the airport. Willie, a freshman at USC, was staying in California to finish out the semester. After years of fighting relentlessly as brothers do, Willie and Teddy had matured, and were closer than ever. They'd stayed up late the night before playing video games. Now Teddy dragged himself out of bed and put on his clothes as we tiptoed out of the room so as not to wake up Willie.

A half hour later, we arrived at the small airport in Van Nuys for private planes. Our plane was a Challenger CL-600, with two pairs of seats facing one another up front on either side, and then a couch and another four facing seats in the back. The pilots and flight attendant boarded the plane and briefly said hello. We'd been told the night before that a severe snowstorm in Telluride made it too difficult to fly there, so our first stop would be another small Colorado airport, at the lower altitude of Montrose, a longer drive for Susan and Rebecca to our house, but otherwise not a concern. Charlie, who'd been staying with a girlfriend in Los Angeles, went right to the back of the plane and fell asleep on the couch. Up front, seated facing backward, opposite me, Teddy turned on his personal video player and for roughly the twentieth time since he'd gotten the DVD just a few days before, he began watching the highlight video of his beloved Boston Red Sox's improbable journey to their first World Series title in eighty-six years.

I'd loved everything about sports for as long as I could remember, and my job took me to stadiums, ballparks, arenas, racetracks, and golf courses across the globe. At one point in the nineties, when President Bill Clinton had said to me, very sincerely, "You have the best job in the world," it was hard for me to argue with him. But while Charlie and Willie had always shared my passion, Teddy had only grown interested in sports over the last few years. I suppose part of it was normal childhood rebellion—wanting to forge a different identity than his dad. That might've also been why, when he did get into baseball, he chose the Red Sox as his team rather than the Yankees, who I'd rooted for since I was his age. But I didn't mind. Teddy's newfound love of baseball had bonded us more deeply than ever before, and as he got the DVD cued up, we talked about the uncertainty surrounding the upcoming free agency market for the Sox.

"Pedro just can't leave," Teddy was saying about his team's longtime ace, Pedro Martinez. "Not after they finally won!"

As Teddy and I analyzed how much money it would take to re-sign Pedro, on the other side of the small aisle, Susan opened her book and began reading. We'd just celebrated our twenty-third anniversary, which gave me another reason to be in a reflective mood. We'd met when she was the host of a *Saturday Night Live* episode in 1981, and I was the producer of the show. A few years later, when her hit sitcom *Kate & Allie* ended, she decided to walk away from her career to raise our kids. She never seemed to miss Hollywood, and loved being a mom, particularly to the youngest, Teddy. They were inseparable. But now that he had gone off to boarding school, it felt like a new phase of our life was beginning. And even more so with the prospect of the NFL deal and the exciting challenge that it posed. It was a deal that could shake up the television world, and change the landscape of the way millions of fans watched America's most popular sport every week during the fall. It had the potential to be the greatest achievement of my career—or the biggest failure. Either way, it could end up defining my professional legacy.

But at that moment, I wasn't thinking too hard about the intricacies of the deal points. There'd be plenty of time for that in the weeks and months ahead. Right then, I was just looking at my family and thinking of how lucky we were. All together, traveling in such comfort and luxury. Just us, with the flight attendant handing out some coffee and juice and letting us know breakfast would be coming soon.

The plane took off from California a little after 8:00 a.m. In Colorado, the snow was beginning to come down hard.

Part One

CHAPTER 1

The Decision

When I got invited to go on the most exciting adventure of my life, my first thought, honestly, was to turn it down.

I was sixteen years old and finishing up my junior year of high school. I had everything I thought I'd ever want: lots of friends, a loving family, and a small town where I knew everyone and everyone knew me. I was at the top of my class at Litchfield High School, had an eye on becoming class president, and was playing on a basketball team that had hopes of a state championship the coming season.

So then—why in the world would I have any interest in the letter that came to my house in northwest Connecticut in the spring of 1964, informing me that I'd been accepted into an exchange student program called the American Field Service, inviting me to spend my entire senior year of high school not in cozy Litchfield, but more than three thousand miles away in the Normandy region of France?

The truth was that I'd only applied for the exchange student program a few months earlier at the urging of my father—in part to please him, and in part, whether subconsciously or not, to impress him. But I'd never given much thought to the possibility that I actually might get accepted and have to consider missing my entire senior year. Then, though, came that letter.

The afternoon it arrived, I immediately got a pit in my stomach. I hopped onto my bike and rode into town and back to work off the stress, and then just kept stewing when I got home. All I could think about were the things I'd be missing.

My father was a lawyer in a small city whose office was just a few miles from our house—at least in my mind, he was northwest Connecticut's answer to Atticus Finch. He set his rates and kept them at an affordable level so locals from all backgrounds could hire him, and he also took a measure of quiet pride in his role as a town judge, meaning he would oversee small-claims cases and the like. He'd leave every morning by eight o'clock with his lunch in a brown bag my mom had packed for him, typically come home for dinner around six thirty, and then go back to work—clearing the dishes off our kitchen table and washing them himself, and then spreading out the papers he'd brought home in their place—not going to bed until eleven. But one night soon after the letter came, he put off work and sat me down after dinner to talk about my decision. It wasn't the kind of conversation we typically had. Charlie Ebersol was much more of a lead-by-example figure than a tell-you-what-you-should-do mentor. But that night was different.

"You have to examine what this opportunity is," he told me, sitting across the table, his eyes trained squarely on mine. "This is really something to think about, Dick—and think about hard. It's potentially an absolutely life-changing experience."

My dad never actually told me I had to go that night, but he laid out—just as a good lawyer would—a pretty unassailable case for heading across the ocean in the fall. How it would give me the chance to live, all expenses paid, in France for a year—and for a young history buff like me, right in Normandy, where the Allies had seized control of World War II. How it could give me the kind of education that wasn't possible in small-town Connecticut—an education that had nothing to do with books, but everything to do with life.

Senior year, student government, the basketball team—it all suddenly sounded remarkably small measured against what could await me. And so my father pretty much made the decision for me—a decision that turned out to be one of the best of my life. In part because, almost improbably, it would end up setting me on a course for my career. But more broadly than that, the year that awaited me in France would transform my view of the world, and how exciting it could be to embrace it.

The sheltered, comfortable existence I enjoyed as a kid was largely due to the efforts of my adoring mother, Peggy. She was born in 1913 in Main Line, Philadelphia, but hardly ever got to know her own father—he was a military man, a colonel who died in the final months of World War I in eastern France. Her mother, my grandmother, then married a man who ran through the family's money, leaving them struggling to support themselves, and forcing my mom to grow up quickly.

Eventually, my mom began supporting the family, first through modeling work, and then as a manager of a small chain of dress shops on the Main Line outside the city. She got married and had a son in 1939 named Josiah (nicknamed "Si"), but soon after got divorced. And so she was a single, working mother in her early thirties when on V-J Day in August of 1945 she went to a party in downtown Philadelphia celebrating the end of the war, and met a handsome naval intelligence officer named Charles Ebersol. They didn't need a lot of time to realize they were meant for each other—Charlie and Peggy were married by November. The union would last fifty-five years.

My father had grown up in Pittsburgh; his father was an investigator for the Carnegie Hero Fund, an entity that still exists today, doling out financial awards to individuals who save people's lives in extraordinary ways. My dad went to Haverford College outside of Philly, and then on to Yale Law School, where he was part of a class that included future president Gerald Ford, future Supreme Court justices Potter Stewart and Byron "Whizzer" White (the latter a Heisman Trophy runner-up), and Sargent Shriver, who later founded the Peace Corps. In 1941, my dad joined the navy, and became an intelligence officer with a torpedo boat squadron and won a Bronze Star before returning stateside to work as the head of naval intelligence at the shipyards in Philadelphia.

My father had figured he'd go to Seattle when the war ended; he'd spent two summers there during law school, clerking for a prominent firm. Instead, right around the time he got married, he got an offer from two older lawyers—a pair of brothers—who had a modest practice in the small industrial city of Torrington, Connecticut. The idea appealed to my father, and so he took his new bride and seven-year-old stepson (who he always treated like his own) to Torrington.

Just about a year later, on July 28, 1947, I was born—Dickie Duncan Ebersol. Dickie was the name of very close family friends of my father's who'd been particularly good to him after his mother died when he was in college, and Duncan was my mother's maiden name. My mother's best friend sent her a telegram from a trip in Spain when she heard, incredulous about the name and not afraid to say it. "Enough of this Dickie Duncan Donald Duck stuff," the telegram read. So, my mother flip-flopped the name from Dickie Duncan to Duncan Dickie. Regardless, what everyone has called me for as long as I can remember—Dick—was more conventional.

Torrington was very much a classic, mid-century, working-class, small New England city, anchored by several local factories. Our family of five—my younger brother was born in 1952—fit tightly into a split two-family home. We knew all our neighbors, and had to walk only one block to school, where we also knew all the store owners nearby on Main Street. That helped me as a nine-year-old when I decided it was time to get a job—and ended up with no fewer than three of them. The first was an afternoon newspaper route covering four nearby blocks. I also convinced the owners of a Main Street paint store to hire me when I walked in one day and pointed out all the dust on their paint cans; they agreed to pay me a quarter an hour once a week to dust the bins and polish the can tops until they gleamed. And then I also helped Sonny, our milk deliveryman, meeting him as early as 6:30 a.m. in the summers and lending a hand with his deliveries.

The only one of those jobs that made me anything close to essential was the newspaper route, which is why when I woke up one winter day with a horrible flu and couldn't get out of bed, I was upset that the good people on my route wouldn't get their papers. It was, by chance, the day of the governor's ball in nearby Hartford, an event my parents would be attending through my dad's connections. And by the time the papers were set to be delivered, in the midafternoon, there was a driving rainstorm. But even though my mom had already changed into her gown, there she was, heading off around the block to deliver forty-five papers for me in a veritable monsoon. And then she went to the governor's ball!

My brother Si, eight years older than me, was out of the house by then, at the first of a few prep schools he'd attend as a teenager. (Ironically, the boy who'd go on to a decorated career as a marine, Rhodes scholar, military officer, and educator got himself kicked out of a few of those schools for playing pranks.) In 1960, my dad saved enough money for the first time in his life to get his dream house—hiring an architect to build one from scratch five miles southwest, in the town of Litchfield, on Minerva Lane. It was a house all for ourselves, on a quiet street, with a yard. Today, our home is about eight football fields from that house. It would be impossible to calculate how many miles I've been lucky enough to travel in between.

We had one radio in our house in Torrington, and one of my earliest memories is when I was eight, coming home from school on a Tuesday afternoon to tune in to the seventh game of the storied 1955 World Series, when the Brooklyn Dodgers finally won their first championship, beating their longtime rivals, the Yankees.

Northwest Connecticut was one of the halfway points between New York and Boston, but it was an easy choice for me to pick the New York teams as my own: the Yankees, with Mickey Mantle, Yogi Berra, Whitey Ford, and company; and the football Giants, led by Frank Gifford and Charlie Conerly. When I was about ten, and their games started appearing on the television in the corner of our living room, even in black and white, the effect was magical. I quickly immersed myself in the endless details of my new obsession. Fifty-two home runs, 130 runs batted in, and a .353 average—the statistics in Mantle's 1956 Triple Crown season were like my lucky numbers. That was also the season Gifford won an MVP, the California kid who became the toast of New York. No one knew their stories better than me.

In Torrington, and then Litchfield, the town libraries were—like everything— just a walk away, providing an endless supply of stories, information, and records for my inquiring mind. I could read about sports, I could read about history—with a father who'd fought in World War II, and a grandfather who'd lost his life in World War I, there was nothing more fascinating to read than stories about soldiers, and the great leaders like Eisenhower and Pershing who guided them. I loved fiction, too, like the Hardy Boys mysteries, and the Chip Hilton sports series written by the legendary basketball coach Clair Bee. Reading was as natural to me as eating or breathing (at least after I donned the Coke bottle glasses that corrected my awful vision). Living in a small town in Connecticut, books could take me all over the world and introduce me to all kinds of fascinating characters. And back home, so, too, could my favorite show on television, which premiered late in the afternoon on Saturday, April 29, 1961—ABC's *Wide World of Sports*.

The show—initially conceived to run just a few weeks over the spring and summer before becoming a phenomenon and one of the network's most popular programs—was a window into sights American fans had never seen. Every week, different sports would be spotlighted—from big international events like the 24 Hours of Le Mans, the British Open, and the World Figure Skating Championships, to more random and overlooked competitions like powerlifting, rodeo, and logrolling. All the sports were fun to learn about, but what really hooked audiences were the stories the show told about the athletes competing. Years later, I'd often hear Jim McKay, the legendary host of the show, tell a story about walking through Idlewild Airport in New York City (before it was renamed for John F. Kennedy) to work on a skiing show and going on a flight with Billy Kidd and Jimmie Heuga, the two best American alpine skiers of the 1960s. They had their skis over their shoulders, and an elderly woman stopped them as they were walking out to their plane and asked, "What are those boards for?" It was a reminder, McKay always said, of how little the general American audience knew about Olympic-style sports and the people who played them, and how interested they would be to hear their stories.

McKay understood that was the heart of the show for audiences of all ages, including a kid like me in Litchfield, Connecticut, who did his best to never miss a telecast. But the figure who created the template, as I'd learn later, was the young producer who oversaw the show, a fearless thirty-year-old who had his own ideas about how to broadcast sports on television that would change the medium forever. To this man, it was clear how you grabbed audiences and held on to them: by telling them those stories they would fall in love with. It could be logrolling or it could be college football—to him, if you got an audience invested in an athlete's personal story, and gave them a rooting interest, you had their hearts, their minds, and, as we say in television, their eyeballs. This producer had an innate sense, too, of how to make an audience feel like they were really *at* an event—making sure the sound of the scene came through, and finding camera angles to make the experience of watching much more intimate.

As a fourteen-year-old, I didn't know the name Roone Arledge, but within just six years of the premiere of *Wide World of Sports*, he'd change my life.

I was never afraid of sharing my thoughts and opinions. At North School, my grammar school in Torrington, one of my teachers, Mr. Dreyser, once attached a large cardboard sign to my desk adorned with a single word in huge tall letters— "THINK"—to remind me to, well, think before I talked. I may have known all the answers, but the point was to get me to slow down and let the other kids in the class have a chance to talk, too. In junior high, I got the perfect job for speaking my mind, and my first job in sports media—a column in one of the oldest weekly newspapers in the country at the time, the *Litchfield Enquirer*. I wasn't going to win a Pulitzer Prize, but it was a great early way to see how my love of sports could be something more than just a passion on the side.

By the time I entered my teens, my father had taken over his practice and begun devoting much of his free time outside the house to civic and charitable causes. He was a leader at our local Congregational Church. He was the head of trustees at the local YMCA in Torrington for years, and spearheaded an effort to build a new swimming pool there, which was ultimately named in his honor. But his efforts with the American Cancer Society were the most extensive. His involvement initially began just after the war, going door-to-door to raise money, and from there he steadily grew to be a well known and respected voice in the organization. Later, a few years after I graduated college, he'd be elected its national board chairman. And after his term was done, international cancer groups in places as far off as Iran and Egypt would travel him to train their people on how to build similar organizations in their countries. Mind you, this was all entirely volunteer work alongside his job. With how hard my father worked, and how much he cared about what he did, he was my first role model—and the best one I'd ever have.

As for my mother, she would do just about anything to spoil me—including on many a weekend morning bringing me breakfast in bed in my room upstairs. And during the week, at Litchfield High, I had plenty of friends, and was a mediocre forward on the basketball team—a gangly six-foot-three presence primarily distinguished by my thick glasses and limited ability and strength in the paint. Life wasn't too complicated, and life wasn't too challenging—precisely why, in the fall of 1963, in my junior year of high school, my father began encouraging me to apply for that American Field Service scholarship.

Even after I accepted the opportunity that following spring, one of the biggest things I lamented leaving behind was a shot at the Connecticut small-school state basketball championship. My two best friends, Danny Fuessenich and Chris Korn, were the best players on the team, and there was a sense that we'd have a real shot at winning a title. Well, my departure from the lineup left an opening for a talented young sophomore, a kid named Jon Torrant, to take a bigger role on the team—and Torrant would be one of Litchfield High's stars as they won that state title. As I've claimed ever since then, the team "only could have won *without* me."

In any event, in late September, a couple of weeks after school had started in Litchfield, I headed to France for my year abroad. I had absolutely no idea what to expect.

Then again, as much as anything else, that was the point.

CHAPTER 2

Adventure

The American Field Service wasn't exactly swimming in cash, and so my path to France wasn't the most direct—a flight on Icelandic Airlines to Reykjavik (just the second or third airplane trip of my life), then a connecting flight to Luxembourg, a bus to Paris, and then finally a train through Normandy to meet the family I was going to spend the year living with. The father was the doctor in their small town, Verneuil, and they had four kids.

The trip hardly started off well—the first night I slept at the family's home, I had probably the worst stomach flu of my life. From there, my biggest problem early on was my French—I'd taken it for a few years at school, but it was nowhere near where it needed to be to understand more than a few words of what the teachers were saying. And then, not much more than a month after I'd arrived, I was hanging out with some new friends and decided it was time to turn in for the night. Unfortunately, we happened to be hanging out on the roof of someone's father's factory, and on my climb down the ladder attached to its side, I missed a rung and fell. The good news, I suppose, was that I didn't break my neck. The bad news was that I tore the medial meniscus in my knee about as violently as one can, and I soon found myself in the well-known American Hospital in Paris for ten days for the operation and recuperation.

I'd spend those ten days listening to as much of the 1964 World Series as I could on Armed Forces Radio, with the Cardinals prevailing over my Yankees in seven games. The surreal nature of the experience only grew when I learned that the then-biggest movie star in the world, Elizabeth Taylor—in town making a movie and felled by some sort of illness—was, at least briefly, in a room down the hall. Another neighbor was the premier of the then-Syrian government; his room was easy to spot when I was taking my therapeutic walks and came face-to-face with the guards armed with machine guns posted outside. It was the first time in my life ever seeing machine guns up close and personal. It wouldn't be the last.

Most of all, though, the experience was really defined by how alone I suddenly was. I had no visitors in the hospital, and only two phone calls. (Maybe my dad was still testing me.) But I got through it. And by early November I was back at my French family's home, finding my way through school with the help of the family as well as the friends I'd made. For better or worse, the rocky start had toughened me up and fortified my sense of independence. There was something liberating, I realized, about being an ocean away from everything I'd ever known—and managing, despite the early complications, to live. Yes, my mother continued to write me letters every day. But the trip was already exactly what my father wanted it to be for me.

After Christmas and before New Year's, I went to Paris with a friend from school whose family had an apartment there. At the last minute on New Year's Eve, they decided to head elsewhere, but invited me to stay at their place anyway. I was seventeen years old, an American kid alone in this amazing, historic city. I navigated the Metro and made my way to the Champs-Élysées, where I came upon a theater advertising a midnight showing of *My Fair Lady*. So I went in, bought a ticket, and spent the first few hours of 1965 with Rex Harrison, Audrey Hepburn, and a couple hundred Parisians all dressed up for the show. The Metro was open until 4:00 a.m., and I got back to the apartment with no problem.

It was far from a wild night—but for seventeen-year-old me, it was a night I'd never forget. Already, I was long past lamenting whatever I had left behind in Connecticut for the year. If there was a life out there that could take me to places like the streets of Paris on New Year's Eve, this was the life I wanted to live.

Once my knee was healed, I joined the town's local rec basketball team, the coach evidently thinking that my experience as a high school player, and my height, would be an advantage. But carrying barely 170 pounds on my six-foot-three frame meant that I spent games mostly getting banged up by burly French factory workers who loved having a skinny American kid to push around. It wasn't pretty, but you might say it was also another small thing that toughened me up a little bit more.

Looking ahead, I'd also begun realizing that I had a future to deal with. I'd applied to a handful of colleges, with my preferred choice being Yale. And starting when I was hospitalized in the fall, I wrote weekly letters to the school's director of admissions in New Haven. Even if this was going to be a year where I fell behind a bit academically, reminding the school of my story—that I was spending my senior year in such an unconventional way—seemed to be a path to standing out. It turned out I was also in luck in that Yale was turning a corner with its student body; the Class of 1969 would be the first ever at the school to include more kids from public schools than private prep schools. I don't recall getting any responses to my dispatches from France, but a letter did come at some point that spring to our house in Litchfield, welcoming me to the next fall's freshman class.

A couple of months after that, my parents took a long-awaited flight to France to visit me. They met the family I was staying with and spent some time touring, the highlight of which was a memorable visit to my mother's father's grave, near Verdun in northeastern France. My mom had never really known her dad—he'd died when she was just three—and this was her first trip to the cemetery, in this corner of the continent that had seen so much devastation in the First World War. I'll never forget going to a central building on the grounds that were so exquisitely kept, where we got a small card that told us where the grave was, amid the rows and rows of headstones. And after a walk through this beautiful cemetery, there was his name, Joseph G. Duncan, the grandfather I'd never met, a man who'd made the ultimate sacrifice for his country.

After my parents headed back to the States, I had a few more weeks before returning myself. And on one of my last weekends in Normandy, I joined my French host family on a trip that sounded very cool—three or four hours away to the town of Le Mans for the famous 24 Hours of Le Mans endurance sports car race.

Along with the Indy 500 and the Monaco Grand Prix in Monte Carlo, Le Mans was one of the most famous auto races in the world—and one that I'd learned about when I'd seen it covered on *Wide World of Sports*. 1965 would be the sixth straight year that a Ferrari won the race; fellow movie buffs might note that the next year came the events depicted in the movie *Ford v Ferrari*, when three Ford teams historically crossed the finish line together, breaking Ferrari's run of dominance. But for me, the winner of the race was overshadowed by the spectacle of the gathering. We went to Le Mans on a two-day trip, and from the start, it was fascinating to see—the eight-and-a-half-mile course that traced through countryside roads, with eight hundred thousand French fans having flooded into the town to see it. And after we'd walked the grounds for a while on the first day, I split off from the family to see if I could find where ABC Sports was headquartered. I wasn't entirely sure what a television setup would look like, but the idea of catching a behind-the-scenes glimpse of the show I'd grown up watching was a very cool chance to explore.

After a bit of wandering and asking the right people, I found the small ABC compound, identifiable by a tiny *Wide World of Sports* banner. Peeking inside and discovering two small trailers behind a fence, I struck up a conversation with a member of the ABC team sitting outside, who told me I could actually come back the next day to help them out; they could always use another "gofer," a person to help out the crew to "go for" errands. I was happy to take him up on the offer for no money.

So early the next morning, I came back and spent the day running in and out of the compound for whatever the production team needed—coffee, cigarettes, even ice cream at one point—as they worked in the trailers. Maybe the degree of difficulty wasn't high, but at the end of the race, the guy told me I had done a nice job. I'd mentioned to him earlier that I'd be going to Yale in the fall, and he told me that I should write so-and-so back in the network's office in New York and tell him that I'd be interested in doing more gofer work when ABC Sports came to New Haven to broadcast football games. (These were the days when Yale was routinely ranked in the top twenty-five.) I thanked him and headed back to find my host family. My television career had begun.

———

Before college could start, my trip home from France was its own adventure. In mid-July, the American Field Service brought us home on an ancient passenger ship called the *Seven Seas* that during the war had been turned into an aircraft carrier, and afterward used as the home of a "semester at sea"–type program for students abroad. About five hundred miles from Newfoundland, there was a brief fire in the engine room, and we were stuck without power in the middle of the Atlantic. Within a few days, a tugboat from Portugal would arrive to provide a very slow tow to Canada, but with a ship exclusively full of high school boys and girls, you can imagine how we found ways to occupy the time.

Then, a little more than a month later, it was off to college. North Street, which cuts right through Litchfield near our house, is Route 63 in Connecticut— a road you can take all the way, for a little less than an hour, south to New Haven, right through the Yale campus I moved into in September of 1965. I was a public school kid from prep school country. My year in France had changed me a lot, enhancing my confidence and sense of what the world could offer—but I had the same interests and passions as always: sports and history. And when Hank O'Donnell, the sports editor of the *Waterbury Republican* newspaper, a dean of Connecticut sportswriters, and the father of a schoolmate in Litchfield, told me to head to the department of athletics and say hi to an old friend of his when I got to campus, I quickly discovered just how much opportunity sports had to offer.

O'Donnell's friend was a man named Charley Loftus, a Yale legend who'd led the sports information office—essentially the public relations division of the athletic department—since the 1940s. Loftus was a colorful figure who always arrived at the Yale Bowl for football games with a police escort in tow. He also was great about getting eager students involved—and by my sophomore year, I'd been made the press box announcer every Saturday for home games, announcing official rulings and statistics to the assembled members of the media. Then, for road games, I'd get in a car with the local New Haven radio commentators, Dick Galiette and Tiny Markle, two wonderful men, and travel to schools like Penn and Cornell, where I'd help them on the air, minding the big spotting boards they used to identify the players on each team. When a tackle was made, it was my job to spot the defender who'd made the play and point as quickly as possible to his jersey number on the poster board, in case the announcer couldn't make it out. If it sounds a bit archaic, they still haven't found a better way; plenty of announcers today still use spotters.

Beyond that, looking to accumulate as many sports contacts as I could, in the winter, I got a small job as a stringer covering minor sports—like fencing, wrestling, and squash—for larger papers. I'd watch the meets and matches, get the results and the names of the key players, and then race back to my dorm, write up a few paragraphs, get someone to type them (I could never type), and dash off to Western Union a few blocks away, sending off one article to, say, the *New York Times*, and the other to the *Boston Globe*. As a stringer, I wouldn't get a byline, but it was a way to stay on the radar of those papers for maybe a summer job in the future.

If all the work I was doing was good for my prospects of working in sports and media, when it came time to decide what to do in the summer after my freshman year, I decided on something very different: taking a spot on the assembly line at the Chase Brass and Copper factory in Waterbury, a city about halfway between Litchfield and New Haven, then known as the brass capital of the world. It was hardly the obvious choice for a kid whose only manual labor experience was mowing lawns and shoveling snow, but a girlfriend's father was an executive there, and the idea of making a not-insignificant amount of money appealed to me.

My dad loved the idea; my mother was horrified by it. Working the 11:00 p.m. to 7:00 a.m. shift, wearing asbestos-lined clothing, my job was basically to man a long metal pole to maneuver buckets that poured steaming molten masses into huge cylindrical molds. If you got too close, the red-hot heat could burn right through the protective clothing; it happened to me once, and I can still recall the awful sensation today. But maybe the most valuable lessons that summer—other than don't get burned—came from an older man I met my first week at the factory, a lifer on the assembly line who carpooled with me every night on the way to work.

I can still see him turning to me in his car with an all-too-serious look on his face.

"You better realize what you've got there at Yale," he said. "Don't think this job is anything special. You do what you're supposed to do. Learn. And get a job that looks nothing like this one."

I wasn't of a mind to disagree. The fall couldn't come soon enough. And in the race to get going on my career, I didn't realize how far along I already was.

Both my freshman and sophomore years, the Yale Bulldogs had off years under their new coach, Carm Cozza, in the first two of his thirty-two legendary seasons at the job in New Haven. But there was real talent coming that would turn the team into one of the best programs in the nation over the next few years, including my classmates Calvin Hill, the future NFL Rookie of the Year and Pro Bowler and father of NBA star Grant Hill, and quarterback Brian Dowling, who'd be the inspiration for the character B.D. in the iconic comic strip *Doonesbury*, authored by another one of our classmates, Garry Trudeau. In the Yale Bowl press box, I made the official announcement of every one of their touchdowns to the assembled reporters.

In the lecture hall, as a history major, I loved my classes—the more I could read, the happier I was. And as my sophomore year came to an end, my summer plan was to try to capture some of the excitement of my time a couple of years earlier in France. One of my roommates and I decided we'd head to London, hoping to use a family connection of his to get jobs as gofers at the Time Life office there. The start of that summer happened to coincide with the first long vacation I can remember my parents ever taking, out to the Rocky Mountains and up into Canada by car. And so after my last final exam, my roommate and I headed to his family's house in Pennsylvania to spend a few days before returning to campus to grab our things and catch a flight to London. Only thing was, while we were in Pennsylvania, we got word that the London opportunity had fallen through.

So we decided to head back to school anyway and figure out a new plan there. The day we got back to New Haven, ever so serendipitously, I checked my mail, and had an unexpected note waiting for me, in an envelope marked with the ABC Sports insignia.

Inside was a letter explaining that the network sports department was looking to fill a new position, and fill it urgently. The title was Olympic Researcher, and the role was to work on preparations for the upcoming 1968 Olympics a year away—both the Winter and Summer Games, which back then were held in the same year. Evidently the sports department had put a collection of candidates together, and even though I was still in college, the work I'd done as a gofer had gotten me on the list.

While it appeared that taking the job would likely require me to drop out of school—and at the height of the Vietnam War at that—I didn't hesitate to let them know I was interested. A few days later, I took the train to New York for my first interview. The more I learned about the job, the better it sounded. Seven years earlier, CBS had broadcast the Olympics—the 1960 Winter Games in Squaw Valley and the Summer Games in Rome—on American television for the first time. Then, for 1964, ABC and Roone Arledge had bought the rights, figuring it dovetailed well with the growing success of *Wide World of Sports*. But during ABC's first Olympics, in Innsbruck, Austria, Arledge realized one of his biggest problems was that there was no way for his producers to really know the stories of the athletes they were covering. The United States Olympic Committee provided very brief biography capsules of American athletes, but nothing really about their personal stories; ABC would only learn those stories along with the rest of the world when someone won a gold medal and reporters asked them more questions.

But as Arledge had proven on *Wide World of Sports*, the way to capture audiences for unfamiliar sports was to tell the stories of the athletes competing; to pique their curiosity and give them a rooting interest. The Olympics were just a bigger example of that. If he could find a way to learn the personal stories of the athletes—both American and international—before they competed, rather than afterward, then he could tell those stories to the audience, give them that rooting interest, and get millions of people to care about sports like skiing and swimming and skating and track and field for two weeks every four years.

Still, that wasn't necessarily an easy strategy for ABC to implement. Remember, in 1967, there was no internet that allowed television producers to look up and read about Olympic athletes, particularly the international ones. They competed year-round in obscurity, often in far-off locales. And thus the completely original idea of the Olympic researcher was hatched: a young staffer who would spend the year before the Games traveling across the United States and

Europe to a wide range of events, becoming an expert on the best competitors—and the best stories—and communicating it all to the on-air broadcasters and key production people as they prepared to work the Games.

It was, in other words, just about the greatest sports adventure anyone could ever dream up.

Like a lot of sports fans, I'd certainly been taken with the Olympics as soon as I was old enough to know what they were. When I was thirteen, I'd watched the Walt Disney–produced Opening Ceremony of the 1960 Squaw Valley Games on CBS, and then followed the U.S. hockey team's stunning run to a gold medal—the original Miracle on Ice, twenty years before the Americans' win over the Soviets in Lake Placid. Now I had the chance to work on the Olympics, and have a real role that involved a lot more than getting cigarettes and coffee—it was almost too amazing to believe.

I'm not sure exactly how many candidates for the job there were, but my first interview went well, particularly when ABC found out I spoke French—important considering the Winter Games would be held in Grenoble, France. So I got called back the following week, and had my second interview with a senior producer by the name of Chuck Howard, one of Roone Arledge's top lieutenants known, among many other things, for giving sports trivia quizzes when he interviewed potential new hires. It was pretty much what it sounded like: Chuck sat across from me and drilled me about my sports knowledge for the better part of an hour. Baseball, football, basketball, college sports, the Olympics, and more. It wasn't cursory stuff; he asked what I knew about the ace of the Cardinals, the quarterback of the Bears, the coach of the Lakers, and the gold medalist in the marathon at the 1960 Olympics—all questions designed to weed out people who didn't really know sports, and who didn't really love sports. But it was as if the *Jeopardy!* categories were made for me—I nailed the test without breaking a sweat.

The next day, I was formally offered the job. My parents, meanwhile, had been on their trip out west the whole time, pretty much unreachable. I knew they'd be surprised, and even disappointed, by my decision to leave school. For me, the risk wasn't really connected to the idea of dropping out; I always intended on going back to finish. The issue was the time period—it was the summer of 1967, and the draft was a distinct possibility for any young man who wasn't in school; college was a deferment from the burgeoning Vietnam War. But between my bad knee and weak eyesight, I was willing to take the chance that I wouldn't be sent to the jungles of Southeast Asia. Hopefully my parents would understand when they found out.

By the last week of July, I was on a plane from New York to Winnipeg, Manitoba, in Canada for the Pan American Games, an Olympic-style competition. I had my first two credit cards ever, courtesy of ABC—one specifically for air travel, the other for everything else—and an incredible year ahead of me.

I hadn't quite yet turned twenty years old.

CHAPTER 3

Tell Me a Story

The first lesson I ever got in television came in Montreal, on my second remote production event. We were at a track meet in the middle of the summer, just a few weeks into my new job, a competition billed as "The Americas vs. Europe," featuring joint teams from each side of the Atlantic competing against one another. The event was set up on a small island in the middle of the St. Lawrence River that would eventually be one of the venues for the Olympics held in the city in 1976.

The main reason I'd been sent to the meet, at least I thought, was for research: to interview the athletes and learn as much as I could about their personal stories, their family backgrounds, anything and everything that would be of interest to the much larger television audience that would watch them compete a year later at the 1968 Olympics in Mexico City. But as I quickly found out, another massive benefit to my job was that the production people at ABC Sports were going to make me as useful as possible to them wherever I showed up. So I'd be pulling double duty: working as a production assistant while we were taping segments for *Wide World of Sports* (in those days, we were rarely broadcasting Olympic-type sports live), and then I'd also be expected to find time for my research work when I could.

The day before the competition in Montreal, the small ABC team gathered at our tiny production compound to go over the plan for our coverage. While I'd gotten a tiny taste of the unique flow of a sports TV production in Le

Mans, and then at a few events I'd worked as a gofer for ABC during my time at Yale, and on my maiden trip as a staffer to Winnipeg, this weekend in Montreal was really the first time that I would have any responsibility. Of course, I wasn't necessarily now any more qualified to have that responsibility. Yes, the research thing, talking to athletes, getting their stories—I'd been prepping for that since I was nine years old, reading every sports book I could get my hands on in the Torrington public library. But television production was a whole other bag entirely.

The show's director, Lou Volpicelli, was addressing the team. To give you a sense of the dynamics: the director of a sports television production is not the same as the director of a Hollywood film. In sports TV, a director is more the technical wizard of the broadcast; the producer is the head of the entire operation. And so, in this meeting, Volpicelli—who had been with *Wide World of Sports* since its beginning—was giving the technical rundown of what he was expecting from us during the production, using television jargon that to my ears might as well have been in another language.

The opening of the show would be pre-taped. Or maybe it was post-taped. Wait, maybe the tease would be post-taped? The APs and TD had to be ready, and everyone had to listen to the AD. Or was it the other way around? All of it made my head swim.

But after he ran through it quickly, Lou doubled back to me, sensing a look in my eyes that betrayed something less than full cognition.

"Ebersol," he said to me, interrupting himself. "Do you understand what I'm saying?"

I could only reply honestly.

"No, sir, I don't," I said.

He softened a bit.

"Okay, then. Make this the most important lesson you ever learn in this business. Do not ever be afraid to ask a question when you don't understand something. Never be hesitant about it. Never be embarrassed about it. And if the first person you ask doesn't want to give you the answer, then find someone else who will help. Because it's always on you to figure it out and get it right."

He paused for a second, and then went on.

"So, then—what don't you understand?"

A few minutes later, I'd figured out what he was talking about. And I was never afraid to ask a question again.

I'd officially started at ABC Sports on a Monday, and by that Wednesday, I was on my way to Winnipeg for the Pan Am Games. The Montreal track event was a week after that. And so, rather than figure out where I was going to live in New York City, I became something of an urban vagabond. At first, I lived in a hotel on West Fifty-Seventh Street that had a thriving roach colony in the kitchenette, but then quickly began rotating between the apartments of new-found friends at ABC Sports who were traveling just as much as me. It was a great arrangement, even if I almost blew it a few months in. While I was away on a trip, a producer whose apartment I'd been staying at came home, only to be confronted angrily by his girlfriend holding a pair of colorful underwear that were definitely not hers and that she'd found buried in the sheets of his bed. If memory serves, he was eventually able to convince her that the under-garments in question belonged to a guest of the young researcher he'd been letting stay there. Guilty as charged.

I was growing up quickly. And thankfully, I had my parents' support. When I'd gotten in touch with them during their vacation to tell them that I'd taken the job, it turned out that they were just a few hours away from Winnipeg and the Pan Am Games. So they'd diverted their trip to come see me. When they arrived at the ABC compound, they were intrigued by what they saw; the only thing was, it was clear they thought I'd only taken a summer job.

"So just to clarify," I said to them as we sat down for lunch in the catering tent, "this is a bigger job than you may think it is. I'm working as the researcher all the way through both Olympics, next year."

My father didn't miss a beat.

"You realize what you're exposing yourself to, don't you?" he asked, immediately recognizing that I would lose my deferment from Vietnam by leaving school.

"I do," I said. "But my knee will never be totally right again, and we know how terrible my eyesight is. It's a risk, I know, but a risk I'm willing to take for this job.

"And no matter what—you have my absolute word that when the job is over, I'll go back and graduate."

Looking around, it was hard to argue that I wasn't in the middle of something exciting, and with a lot of potential. They never questioned me about it again.

Meanwhile, if "Never be afraid to ask a question" was my first big lesson—the kind of insight I'd take with me pretty much everywhere I'd go after that, on the job and beyond it—the TV education came fast and furious from there. Sports television is inherently a teaching business; by definition, every moment you're on the job, you get new chances to learn from the people alongside you. For me, the insights could come in any number of ways. An afternoon spent with a production assistant, for example, was a schooling in the basics of how the graphics operation worked—how to prepare all the lettering that would appear on-screen during an event to identify athletes, their background information, their statistics, and so forth. It was an education that would prove critical when I was eventually called upon to man the graphics station myself, and have the graphics ready in the production truck when the producer called for them to be inserted on-screen.

Then there could be hastily scheduled interview tapings—like the first one I "produced" on my own, in October of 1967. An Olympic sprinter from Poland named Ewa Kłobukowska, who'd won a bronze medal in the 100-meter dash and a gold in the 4x100-meter relay in Tokyo a few years earlier, had just become the first athlete to fail a controversial gender identification test; she'd been found to have a rare genetic condition, and banned from competing in the next Olympics. This was eons before transgender athletes became a big story, but Kłobukowska was a world record holder—this was definitely real news at the time. When the story broke, and the producers decided they would cover it that weekend, I was sent uptown from our Sixth Avenue office to Columbia University to ask a doctor there about the test and the science behind it. I'd never done anything like it before—interview someone for television, set up the lighting on a shoot, all of it. But that was all typical of how ABC Sports worked. No one would say, "Don't bother Ebersol, he's just the researcher." Rather, it was "Ask the kid to do it—he'll figure it out."

There were harsher lessons, too, like the time I approached one of the most senior producers at an event and asked him if there was anything I could do for him. "Yeah, you can go take a piss for me," was the answer. The lasting, burning sensation of humiliation that day was enough to ensure that I'd never let frustration, cynicism, or the stress of the job turn me into a pompous bully who used seniority as a lame excuse to be nasty.

Still, all told, the job was awesome—and not least because, whatever I was doing, I was working for a department that was changing the course of sports media forever, thanks to the greatest visionary the business has ever seen.

Before anyone had ever heard of *Wide World of Sports*, Roone Arledge was just a kid who grew up in the 1940s dreaming of being a sportswriter. He went to Columbia, and then broke into television in the late fifties, originally working in New York as a producer for a children's show starring the ventriloquist Shari Lewis and her sock puppet Lamb Chop. The show won a local Emmy Award.

A short time later, Roone impressed a star ABC executive named Edgar Scherick, who among his other duties was heading up the network's expansion into sports coverage. Roone began working as one of a handful of sports employees at ABC, and in 1960, wrote a now-famous memorandum to Scherick proposing an entirely fresh approach for broadcasting college football games. To supplement the standard stationary cameras up in the press box, Roone argued for a new way to cover the games: with additional cameras mounted on risers to capture new angles, plus roving handheld cameras on the sideline, as well as huge boom microphones to capture the sounds of the action. He had a vision—to give viewers the sense that they could almost touch the game as they watched it. He wanted the audience to see and hear the cheering in the stands, players celebrating their touchdowns on the sidelines, coaches screaming at referees for bad calls. Most important, every game would be an epic story to tell. As he wrote in the memo, in all caps, "WE ARE GOING TO ADD SHOW BUSINESS TO SPORTS," and concluded his proposals boldly, stating that "we will be setting the standards that everyone will be talking about and that others in the industry will spend years trying to equal."

Roone worked on the memo over a weekend, Scherick loved it, and quickly put him in charge of the production of ABC's college football coverage. It was a huge success, and just the start. Soon after came *Wide World of Sports*, and in 1964, ABC's first Olympics, the Winter Games in Innsbruck. Through every broadcast, the mission of ABC Sports was constant: tell the viewer a story. And as the sixties continued, the network's advances and innovations on the technical side enhanced that storytelling. Roone's top engineering lieutenants, most notably the executives Julius "Julie" Barnathan and Bob Trachinger, were pioneers, improving the quality of handheld cameras, refining the technology behind slow-motion instant replay, developing underwater cameras, and more. At ABC Sports under Roone, everyone was encouraged to be bold and creative, and the environment led to incredible achievements. While ABC was the number three network behind NBC and CBS when it came to entertainment and news, conversely, it was far and away the gold standard when it came to sports coverage.

When I showed up for work at ABC in the summer of 1967, I quickly found out that Roone was not an easy person to get to know—or even glimpse. That was the way he liked it; he was not a very visible presence in the ABC Sports offices on Sixth Avenue, and it was never easy for those who worked under him, alongside him, or even above him to simply find Roone to talk to him. On a day-to-day basis, Roone was largely an invisible figure, notorious for often not coming into the office, or coming in extremely late.

But as it happened, the small office that I was assigned to wasn't far from Roone's suite, and when I quickly made it a habit of staying late pretty much every night working, when he did come in, he'd spot me with the light on as he walked by to go to the elevator. We'd exchange a few words, as he'd be curious about the athletes I was researching. Sometimes it's about the simplest things: you just have to be there.

As I got to know Roone just a bit, I also became the rare young staffer welcomed to meet with the "talent"—the broadcasters who appeared on the air and formed something of a kind of elite caste floating above everyone else in the production power structure. While the main purpose of my research was for use at the upcoming Olympics, the talent also wanted it in real time, to use on their *Wide World* shows as the Games approached. Working with hosts and broadcasters as they prepared to go on the air could teach you how they thought before they spoke, and what kind of information best served them. And their biggest need was always the same, simple thing: stories.

The greatest storyteller at ABC Sports—and in the history of sports television for that matter—was Jim McKay. As the host of *Wide World of Sports* from the show's beginning in 1961, he was the face of ABC Sports—not to mention a huge star to a kid like me who'd been watching him on TV in my house for years. What Walter Cronkite was to news, McKay was to sports. So, one of the most exciting things about my job was that at the actual Olympics, my primary role would be assisting McKay—shadowing him, almost—to make sure he had all the research he needed on demand, for whatever story he was covering.

One of the first occasions I really got to spend a bit of time with McKay was on a trip to Mexico City in October of 1967, a year before the Summer Olympics. The city was staging some preliminary events, almost as a dry run for the actual Games, and ABC sent a small crew to cover it for *Wide World*. The city was incredible to take in: a modern metropolis built on top of ancient ruins that was the most crowded place I'd ever seen, with a 7,500-foot altitude that you could feel even just walking around.

To make sure McKay really grasped how much that thin air would impact the athletes, a producer got it in his head to prove it to him. So one day on that trip, we all went to the empty Olympic Stadium track for a demonstration. McKay and a producer would run half a lap, and—maybe as a bit of an initiation for the kid—I would have to run a whole lap, four hundred meters. I made it around the track, half-dead by the time I met a just-as-out-of-breath Jim at the finish line. The point was made, and a year later, the viewing audience would hear plenty about the effect of the altitude.

The struggle to catch my breath in Mexico City might as well have been a metaphor for the entire experience of prepping for my first big assignment: the Winter Olympics, coming several months before the Summer Games. That said, all the initial events that I attended in my first few months at ABC were for the Summer Games, and a big part of the challenge of the job over the course of the fall of 1967 was catching up with the research that needed to be done on winter sports without really being able to go to any events to meet the athletes until their seasons began. I spent many of my days and late nights that fall putting together what were in effect large reference books for the talent and producers, detailing the histories of the different winter sports, the rules, major records, and so forth. There were individual media guides put out by the international biathlon association, the international speed skating federation, and the like, but organizing them all together in ways that would be useful for the producers and talent was something else entirely. Then, as soon as the winter season got going, it was off to Europe to chase the athletes.

Flying back and forth over the Atlantic on ABC's dime, in a golden age of air travel, was one of the most exciting parts of the lottery ticket I felt I'd won by getting the job. One of the most memorable trips I took was on New Year's Eve, when two or three other colleagues and I constituted just about the only passengers on a Lufthansa flight to Germany to head to the first women's World Cup skiing event of the season. One of the people traveling with me was a guy named Jay Michaels, whose son Al was a young aspiring broadcaster fresh out of Arizona State. Jay was the top executive at Trans World International, the production company founded by the legendary sports agent Mark McCormack that did a lot of broadcasting of international sports alongside ABC. The flight was into Munich, but then it was a drive to the tiny ski town of Oberstaufen, which didn't have a hotel big enough to house both skiers and media. Instead, as we got there, we were taken to an enormous stone building that evoked the feel of a castle but didn't look to be a hotel. I asked our translator where we were, and he told me it was a summer asylum for the mentally ill, and a facility where people came for "the cure"—to rehabilitate from tuberculosis. It was otherwise totally empty while we in the media stayed there for the event.

In the end, on that trip just like every other, I didn't spend much time in my room, instead doing everything I could to track down the skiers from the American team, as well as the more competitive French and Austrian teams. Particularly for the foreign contingents, it was a multistep process; before I could even open my notebook to interview the athletes, I had to make sure there was an English speaker I could rely on, and then explain to the coaches and officials what my job was—there had never before been a network researcher assigned to do background work like this, and the teams were instinctively skeptical of the media. But once the message was gotten across that we weren't looking for any deep, dark secrets, I was able to spend time with the athletes—many of whom were right around my age—and learn their stories and write them up in the research manuals that the producers and talent were waiting on.

Barely a month later, we were in Grenoble for the X Olympic Winter Games, as they were officially known. The temporary stadium built for the Opening Ceremony was at the end of a long avenue, and it took place in the afternoon, with Charles de Gaulle, in the final year of his presidency, opening the festivities as per tradition. And while I was in the stadium for the entire ceremony, seeing the aging de Gaulle raise his hand to salute the crowd was just about the last thing I'd see—at least with my own eyes. Soon after that, the main part of the ceremony began, and I had to find a spot to park myself in ABC's tiny broadcast booth. There was simply no room in the cramped space for me to stand behind or sit beside the two more important people there, McKay and his broadcast partner, Chris Schenkel. So, in a bit of improvisation, I folded my now six-foot-four body under their desk and spent the ceremony—which marked the first time the Olympics were being broadcast live in color back to the United States—following along on a tiny black-and-white monitor on the floor, and handing up to the announcers various cards I had meticulously prepared, one per country, as the delegations made their way in for the Parade of Nations.

While most people think McKay hosted the Olympics for all of ABC's Olympic telecasts dating back to 1964, it was actually Schenkel—a great broadcaster in his own right—who played the traditional role of "studio host" in Grenoble and Mexico City. It made sense: while Schenkel was as good as anyone of his time with college and pro football, McKay was the versatile, master storyteller, and an expert on international winter sports. So Jim joined Chris for the Opening and Closing Ceremonies, and then handled play-by-play for much of the competition, including, most notably, alpine skiing and figure skating.

Jim's best qualities on air—his authenticity and warmth as a storyteller—doubled as his best qualities when the cameras turned off. He was smart, he was considerate, and he was a wonderful man to work for. I had to earn his trust, but once I did, he treated me as essential to his preparation. In fact, one of the only times I remember him getting even just a little cross with me happened when he was concerned about that preparation.

It took place a couple of nights before the Opening Ceremony, when I was having an early dinner at our hotel with Curt Gowdy. That in itself was a thrill—Curt was a broadcasting star who'd been the voice of the Red Sox for years, and worked for Roone Arledge at ABC in the early sixties, calling football. Though he'd signed with NBC a few years earlier, he was still close with Arledge, and continued to host *The American Sportsman*, an outdoor life show, on ABC, and also had a clause in his deal allowing him to work the Olympics for his old friend, doing hockey play-by-play for the Winter Games. As I'd found out quickly, Curt was also one of the nicest, most generous, easygoing figures in the business, and that night, he'd asked me to go with him after the early dinner to Geneva, Switzerland, about an hour-and-forty-minute drive away, to watch the American hockey team's final warm-up game before the Olympic tournament. But when McKay walked into the restaurant and came over to say hello and I mentioned my plans, he made it clear that wasn't going to fly.

"You're not going anywhere tonight," was the matter-of-fact but very direct response. "The Opening Ceremony's forty-eight hours away. You're working with me tonight on prep."

I was momentarily frozen. But thank goodness I was dealing with the saintly Curt Gowdy, and he swiftly told me to stick with McKay, the message clear: go with the flow.

While that encounter definitely rattled me a bit, once we got to work, I soon forgot about it. I learned more discipline from my association with McKay than with any other teacher I ever had in my life. As a journalist who'd began his career as a newspaper reporter, his instincts were totally geared toward storytelling. McKay loved the information I brought him, but taught me how to present it to him; like a great freshman history teacher, he drilled it into me. He didn't want things in full sentences; he just wanted facts, laid out in bullet points. He never wanted to sound like he was reading anything; it was more natural to turn the shorthand into a lyrical spoken-word cadence. He knew that would also help him to convey what he wanted to the audience succinctly, and in a way that they would immediately understand. And he could use the pictures the audience was seeing to enhance the words he delivered.

"We're behind the Iron Curtain," he said at the beginning of one famous *Wide World* broadcast as a group of people stared at the lens of the camera. "And here on Paris Street are the people of Prague—as curious about us, apparently, as we are about them."

There was a certain kind of tone—a combination of personal touch and precise yet natural wordsmithing—that TV called for, and whether it was on *Wide*

World of Sports, the Olympics, or anywhere in between, McKay unlocked that code better than anyone. Watching live television wasn't like reading a book—the audience couldn't go back and read a passage again to make sure they got it. So, our job was to tell stories in easily digestible ways, highlighting the most important points, and finding ways to make sure the people watching at home were compelled by them.

The Winter Olympics were much smaller in 1968 than they are now; only thirty-seven countries participated over eight days of competition. The nightly ABC telecasts, led by McKay, told America a novel's worth of stories. One of the best was about Eugenio Monti, the forty-year-old bobsledder who, four years earlier in Innsbruck, had selflessly given his British rivals a bolt off his sled to repair their broken one—and then watched them beat him out for gold. Now in Grenoble, Monti returned and won two golds of his own, in the two-man and four-man sleds.

Then there was Jean-Claude Killy, the French skier who won three gold medals, including a controversial one on the last day of the skiing competition in the slalom. I watched that race from the mountain with Roone himself; Arledge had decided that he'd go watch the final races in person, and he decided to take me in case he had any questions about the competitors. So there I was with the head of ABC Sports, at the bottom of the hill, when confusion broke out as an Austrian contender named Karl Schranz claimed (without any way to prove it) that a patrolman on the course had crossed in his path, forcing him to stop in the middle of the race. Unlike what would have happened today, there were no cameras to corroborate his story, and Killy was awarded the gold with the fastest time. In any event, on the mountain, Roone wasn't bothered at all—as far as he was concerned, more drama made for a better story.

The last day of the Games, I was also on site for the drama that unfolded at the Palais des Sports, the arena that held the figure skating competition and the Closing Ceremony. Going into the event, the U.S. team had won just six medals, and no golds—but had one last shot in the ladies' event. Peggy Fleming had been born on a farm outside San Jose, California, and was the reigning world champion. Her story was also inseparable from a tragedy seven years earlier, when much of the U.S. figure skating team had been killed in a plane crash on the way to the 1961 World Championships. Peggy's coach had been on the flight, and *Wide World of Sports* had chronicled her improbably rapid ascent to the top over the previous few years—a small-town girl who radiated elegance and poise on the ice. Now, in Grenoble, she turned in a virtually perfect performance to win the gold, a triumphant ending to the story that turned her into one of the biggest American Olympic stars ever, and the catalyst for a boom in American figure skating. I watched Peggy skate from just off the ice, alongside Jim McKay and Dick Button calling the event.

When I returned to the U.S., I dealt with a swift return to reality—as I had to immediately head back to New Haven. No, not to Yale, but to my draft physical. When the doctor went to test my knee, he hit it from the side, and it knocked out of place. I'd never been so relieved to fail a test. The Summer Games were just eight months away.

I'd eventually be part of twelve Olympic television broadcasts. The historical significance of the Mexico City Games in the fall of 1968—not just competitively but culturally and politically—was as large as any of them. Not that I had any time to appreciate the magnitude of what was transpiring. The Summer Olympics were many times the size of their winter counterpart, with so many more countries, so many more athletes, and so many more stories. That all meant that Mexico City, more than anything else, was a two-week blur for me, working in the broadcast center around the clock, dashing from the control room to edit rooms to McKay's side at the competition venues and back.

The one thing in my favor, at least in terms of my preparation going in, was that those Olympics weren't held until October, owing to the heat of Mexico City in the summer. Today, that would have been a prohibitive TV ratings disaster—going up against the NFL and college football. (They actually began right after the World Series that year.) But this was long before the billion-dollar rights deals that I'd be in the middle of decades later, and American television didn't have the leverage it does now with the International Olympic Committee. I definitely benefited from the few extra months to write biographies of the athletes and histories of the sports. And while ABC couldn't benefit from summer viewership, Roone Arledge was able to get the network to put every night of competition in prime time, which had never been done before for an Olympics or with big-time network sports at all. The move ended up being a precursor to the success of *Monday Night*

Football two years later—giving Roone the confidence that sports in prime time could work in a big way.

The 1968 Games were also defined by the tumult of the time. In Mexico, they'd been preceded by student protests that led to the awful, infamous Tlatelolco massacre, with the country's armed forces killing hundreds of civilians just before the Games. Meanwhile, in the U.S., the climate of protests and upheaval had made a boycott by African American athletes a very real possibility leading up to the Opening Ceremony. We'd followed the story on *Wide World of Sports*, including the month before the Games in Echo Summit, California, near Lake Tahoe, for the track and field trials. There, in the high altitude that created thin air comparable to Mexico City's, John Carlos and Tommie Smith, two members of the Olympic Project for Human Rights, the group threatening the boycott under the leadership of a brash young professor at San Jose State named Harry Edwards, dueled in the 200-meter sprint, with Carlos beating Smith in a world-record time that wasn't recognized because of unapproved cleats that Carlos wore.

On a Wednesday night in Mexico City in October, there was plenty of anticipation when Smith and Carlos squared off again, and plenty of excitement when Smith crossed the finish line first in an official world-record time, with Carlos finishing third. When it came time for the medal ceremony, the two walked out shoeless, and then, famously, each put a black-gloved fist in the air as the American flag was being raised, and kept them there as the national anthem played. (Peter Norman, the Australian who won the silver, wore an Olympic Project for Human Rights badge in support of the Americans.)

Watching from the back of the control room as it all unfolded, there was one voice guiding our coverage, and one voice only: Roone Arledge's. Roone instantly knew what was happening as Smith and Carlos stepped onto the medal stand, and made sure our director stayed zeroed in on the shot of them. There was no sense of running away from the story, or trying to minimize it. In a time of political and racial upheaval, Roone knew exactly what was happening—and the future head of ABC News was going to cover it like the extraordinary news story it was.

In the days after, of course, an uproar ensued, and Avery Brundage, a reactionary American who was then the head of the International Olympic Committee, rushed to banish Smith and Carlos from the Games. On TV, we continued to cover the controversy in full, Arledge's dictum—follow the story—guiding us the whole way. And when it came to this story, along with the reliable McKay, Roone had the perfect reporter to chronicle the narrative—the singular verbal force that was Howard Cosell. Mexico City was Howard's first Olympics, and he conducted the first interviews of Smith and Carlos on television after the race, and later offered a blistering commentary when they were sent home, supporting the athletes and lashing out at the officials who'd shunned them.

Watching the whole thing unfold up close, alongside Arledge, McKay, and Cosell, was another incredible chapter in my education. Right there, right then, there was no doubt in my mind: this was absolutely what I wanted to spend the rest of my life doing.

CHAPTER 4

Wide Wide World

The idea was always that I'd go back to Yale to graduate, and then begin my career, but in the world of sports television, there's a long tradition of trying to make the impossible somehow work. So while I did go back to school for the spring semester of 1969, I had a side job. Nearly every weekend, I'd fly off to an ABC Sports production somewhere, work the event as a production assistant, and then make it back in time to get to class on Monday. I knew college was supposed to represent the best years of my life, but really what could be better than spending every weekend at a sporting event? And as a history major, most of my classes were reading intensive—and books were the best way to pass the time on long flights.

So over the next year and a half, the airline timetables—the comprehensive booklets that airlines would print for passengers to see every flight scheduled on every day of the year—became my best friend. There were weekends when I'd leave school on a Thursday afternoon, drive a rental car to New York, catch a flight across the country (or occasionally even to Europe) for an event, and make it back onto campus just in time for my first class on Monday in the early afternoon. In the fall of '69, the first regular weekly series that I was assigned to work on was ABC's coverage of the Professional Bowlers Tour, with Chris Schenkel as the main commentator. I was in charge of the graphics for the show. I'd hardly been much of a bowling fan growing up, but it turned out to be a fun series to work on. The best bowler on tour that season was a guy from Alabama named Billy Hardwick, who

41

bowled in an unconventional style because his middle finger, injured in a machine shop accident in high school, wouldn't bend. Bowlers like Hardwick were happy for the attention that national television gave them, down-to-earth and friendly both during the telecasts and behind the scenes.

From bowling I went to basketball, as, back in those days, ABC was the home of the NBA. Televised games on the East Coast were most frequently in Boston, Philadelphia, and New York, making them easy to get to from New Haven; actually, sometimes, when the seasons crossed over, I'd even work a bowling event on the West Coast on a Saturday, catch a late-afternoon flight back east, and make it to a Sunday 1:00 p.m. Knicks or Celtics game to work graphics there, too.

These were the early days of pro basketball, an early ancestor of the thriving global force that the NBA has become today. And that meant covering the games on TV was very different from today as well. One of the top producer-directors for NBA games at ABC was a guy named Chet Forte, a true character in sports television history. Forte was undeniably talented, but also could be incredibly difficult to work with, a mercurial personality with a massive sports gambling habit. He'd also been one of the best college basketball players in the country for Columbia in the 1950s, despite being just five foot six, leading the nation in scoring, and even beating out seven-foot-one Wilt Chamberlain as the UPI Player of the Year. Before games that he directed for ABC, Chet would often shoot around with his crew, forty-five minutes before tip-off. Today, it would be impossible for a television crew to do anything close to this, but back then, it was no problem for me to head out onto the Boston Garden's iconic parquet floor to join a game of HORSE with Forte, or another young guy on the crew from Chicago who was a few years older than me but quickly became one of my best friends. His name was Don Ohlmeyer.

Shooting around did become a bit of a problem one afternoon when, during one of those games, I went up for a shot—and split my pants right down the seam. Fortunately for me, standing on the sideline watching us was John Havlicek, the future Hall of Famer and a Hall of Fame human being. Smiling, he took mercy on me as I stressed about what to do.

"Just head down to our locker room," he said. "My wife is sitting in the hallway—she can sew them up for you in two minutes."

As I said, it was a very different time.

Of course, when I made my way to the locker room, Beth Havlicek was nowhere to be seen, and as I wandered around inside, trying to find my way, I instead found myself face-to-face (or, really, face-to-chest) with one of the most feared intimidators of all time in sports.

"What the hell are you doing in my locker room?" said Bill Russell, calmly but ominously, as he stared me down.

I meekly replied that I'd split my pants and Havlicek had sent me back here to find Beth to help me.

Russell paused, and then broke out into his famous, singular cackle. He was just messing with me.

It turned out to be the beginning of a great friendship with both legends. Yes, back in those days, long before the sports world was the multibillion-dollar industry that it would become, it was that easy for a production assistant to get to know two of the greatest players in NBA history.

But the job wasn't all about hanging out with legends. There were more stressful tasks to be in charge of, like the "escape"—the term for the broadcast crew's quick exit from a venue, most important at college football games, where tens of thousands of people packed the stadium. The objective was to map out a plan to always get the announcers and producers in a convoy of cars within just a few minutes of getting off the air to beat the traffic across a city or town to the airport, knowing we'd be stranded if we didn't catch the last flight out in time. It was standard practice to pay a local police department for a motorcycle escort to the airport. One time, an escort somewhere in Kansas was not going fast enough for Don Ohlmeyer, and Don simply flew by him at eighty-five miles per hour on the freeway. When we got to the airport, Don handed the stunned officer a twenty-dollar bill, thanking him for his assistance nonetheless.

Back at school, I worked my ass off to finish the final two years' worth of my credits in three semesters and graduate just a year behind my class, in June of 1970. That spring, the turmoil of the era hit New Haven hard, and protests led the government to call in troops to the city, causing my final exams to be canceled. All I had to do was hand in my senior history paper, which was about IOC president Avery Brundage, liberally citing interviews I'd done as part of my job. Then, no more than a few hours after I got my diploma, I was on a flight to Europe for 24 Hours of Le Mans; this time I'd be working the event as its associate producer. A few weeks later, I was back in New York looking to find an apartment of my own at last, moving into sports television full-time for good.

Sometime in that fall of 1970, I got a message from Roone's secretary asking me to go to lunch with him.

The reservation was for 2:30 p.m., after rush hour, since Roone always ate late, at a steak place not far from ABC called Mike Manuche's. We stayed for about two hours, not walking out of the joint until 4:00 or 5:00 p.m. Roone liked his wine, and I was a lightweight drinker, so by the end of it, the only thing keeping me upright was all the water I had drunk on repeated trips to the bathroom to keep up with the cabernet glass that kept getting refilled at the table. But despite the difference in our alcohol tolerances, we definitely had a connection, which had been slowly but gradually forged in fits and starts during our encounters over the previous few years. The foundation of it was simple: I was loaded with questions, and he had a huge appreciation for curiosity and an infinite supply of stories.

At the end of that lunch, he asked me a question: Was I interested in becoming his assistant? It would be a job on top of working as an associate producer; I'd now be fully immersed in everything Arledge worked on, getting a graduate-level education on the business side of the industry, while continuing to maintain a hand in production. The answer was obvious.

To be an assistant to any top executive is nearly always a fantastic education and experience, but with Roone, it was uniquely exceptional. First, since Roone was so often not in the office, I would sit in on meetings, representing him in absentia with executives from all across the company. I didn't talk, but I got a chance to absorb everything I could by observation. I'd go through all of Roone's mail, marking what was priority and handling what I could take care of on my own. Then I'd spend afternoons in his office if he came in, or if he didn't, I'd head over to his spacious apartment in Columbus Circle, overlooking Central Park, going over whatever was on the agenda.

Evenings, though, were the best part, as I'd often meet him at P. J. Clarke's, the famed burger joint and bar on Third Avenue, for long nights in the back room alongside some legendary figures of the time. We'd sit at the center table, often joined by *Sports Illustrated* writer Dan Jenkins and the former New York Giants superstar Frank Gifford, the liquor and the stories flowing. It might have been the greatest place in the world for a curious kid in his mid-twenties to hang out. I didn't necessarily always need to stay at the table with Roone all night, but I stayed regardless, often till two o'clock in the morning. If there ever was an instance in my life where simply "being there" was its own reward, this was it. No one else had this kind of access to him—no one else had this kind of relationship with him.

Sometimes Roone's eclectic network of connections put me in situations that I'm not sure I'd believe if I didn't experience them myself. Like the time I got a call in the office from Ethel Kennedy. Ethel was throwing a birthday party for a cousin—and she had the idea that it would be great fun if an animal showed up as a surprise guest. How to make it happen? Well, call her friend Roone Arledge's capable assistant, of course. Which is how I ended up going to the far west end of Fifty-Seventh Street on a freezing-cold Friday night, picking up a donkey from a stable, and walking it all the way across town, and then up to an address at Eighty-First Street and Fifth Avenue, where the doorman agreeably let us in and took us up in the elevator. Everyone thought it was hilarious when the surprise guest showed up—and then afterward, I had to walk the damn thing back to the stable.

For his part, whomever he was with, wherever he was, Roone was always thinking, always asking questions, always seeking the next new creative idea. As I came to discover, that was the reason he was all but a ghost in the hallways. He'd deal with the meetings and obligations when he had to; he knew the most valuable use of his time was to always be focusing on ways for ABC Sports to innovate. Roone believed in exposing himself to as many good ideas and as much intelligence as he could to stretch his mind, and he was always the most well-read, well-informed person in any room, as passionate about news and politics as he was about sports.

I felt like I was there to learn and, if I could, find ways to improve the department. One early project I came up with was to see if I could help Roone cultivate a better relationship with the staff. Being that he wasn't always around, and didn't communicate with everyone, people may have idolized him, but they didn't really feel connected to him. So I proposed an idea: every couple of weeks, I'd draft letters to four or five key people who'd done good work of late, Roone could sign them, and it would be an acknowledgment that he'd been watching and paying attention to them. He agreed to it. The week after I sent the first batch of letters, one came back from Andy Sidaris, the funny, very talented director of ABC's top college football game every Saturday. It was the letter addressed to him, still in the envelope that I'd sent it in from Roone's office, all marked up with red ink. On top it read "Dick, do you really think that I'm going to believe that Roone wrote this letter? You wrote it, you little S.O.B.!"

Other projects went better. In the spring of 1972, at the Olympic trials for track and field in Eugene, Oregon, Roone assigned me to help Erich Segal, who he'd hired to be a commentator along with Jim McKay for our marathon coverage. It was a classic Roone move—Segal was a Harvard scholar and professor known for his best-selling novel *Love Story* who also happened to be an avid marathoner. Erich had never been a marathon commentator, but Roone had seen him on television talking about his books, knew how well-spoken and emotional he could be, and knew he would be a natural. He was right. In the Olympic marathon, when a man wearing a West German uniform, posing as an actual runner in the race, ran out in front of the leader, American Frank Shorter—who, coincidentally, Erich had actually taught at Yale—Erich memorably screamed into the microphone, "That's not Frank, it's an imposter! Get that guy off the track! It's a fraud, Frank!" The call is still played almost every year on highlight tapes.

Now weeks before that, while we were in Eugene for the track trials, Erich spent nights regaling me with his knowledge of the Ancient Games in Greece, and we came up with an idea to produce a film based on that history that could air during our coverage in Munich. Roone, always intrigued by creative ideas, told us to check it out and develop it further.

Without wasting any time, I flew to Greece. The problem was that at the time, the country's government was under military control—but I got lucky when I was connected with an experienced Greek motion picture producer there who was willing to help me. She put me in touch with the right colonel, who agreed to let us shut down for a few days the ancient stadium that remained intact at the top of the ruins in Delphi. Within a couple of weeks, the idea was fully formed: I would invite Rafer Johnson and Bill Toomey, who'd won gold medals in the decathlon in 1960 and 1968, respectively, to come to Greece to be the stars of our show. Initially, Rafer said he couldn't do it; he was scheduled to go on his honeymoon. I responded, "What better place to go on your honeymoon than Greece?" His new wife happily came along.

And so there we were: the athletes, me, Erich Segal, and Lou Volpicelli, our director, along with a crew, to put together a film showing Johnson and Toomey competing just as the ancient Greeks did: the same events (many of which were comparable to decathlon events—the long jump, discus, javelin throw, a sprint, etc.), in the same clothes (or lack thereof—they wore more conservative versions of a loincloth). There was no crowd, and with Volpicelli's direction and Segal's narration, the thirty-minute show felt almost like a dream sequence. As a young producer, it was great to have everyone's trust, and we were able to edit it all together in a harried week in New York before heading back over the Atlantic for the modern Summer Olympics in Munich. The idea was that the film would be a standby element for any weather delays for the track and field coverage the second week; if a night of action was postponed, we could air the film to give the audience something else original to watch.

I never could have imagined the circumstances under which it would air.

CHAPTER 5

Unfathomable

The first week of the Munich Olympics were as joyous, triumphant, and idyllic as any Olympics I've ever been involved in. The '72 Games were viewed by the West Germans as their way to reintroduce themselves to the world, separate from East Germany, as a home of progress, democracy, and openness. And with beautiful venues and weather, impeccable organization, and plenty of drama in the competition, the first week of the Games went just about perfectly.

That went for the ABC broadcast as well. Which was in large part due to the most valuable asset we could have hoped for: terrific stories. Mark Spitz was a lanky twenty-two-year-old who'd grown up in California and Hawaii and become a superstar swimmer at Santa Clara High School. He'd gone to Mexico City in 1968 as a teenager holding ten world records, and boldly proclaimed he'd win six gold medals—only to fall short and be part of just two winning relays. But he'd gotten only better as 1972 approached, and came to Munich, again looking to win six golds. Well, he'd do one better—and actually win seven. And even better than that, he set a world record in every one of them.

Then there was Olga Korbut, the tiny seventeen-year-old gymnast from the Soviet Union who, as Jim put it, looked "like a little kid playing in the sun" as she competed. She was actually a last-minute replacement for the Soviet team, but her spirit brought her sport alive to the audience like no other gymnast before her. Even if she was from the land of our Cold War enemy, her charisma transcended borders, a quintessential example of the power of the Olympics to bring the world closer together in ways nothing else really can.

With both Spitz and Korbut, we had not just great stories but stories that progressively built all week long, keeping the audience hooked. With every night of the Games broadcast in prime time, Roone was in the control room every evening, carefully monitoring every minute of our coverage. Taking advantage of the six-hour time difference from the East Coast, we were able to edit just the way we wanted to perfect our storytelling to the audience. In a pre-internet age, few people watching back home knew the results as we showed them hours after they occurred, and ratings were sky-high, delighting everyone, most of all Roone, who was completely in his element.

The middle Monday of the Olympics, the last night of the swimming competition, our night ended extremely late, with the time difference keeping us at the broadcast center until four o'clock in the morning as we edited various parts of the prime-time show right up until we had to feed them onto the air via satellite. Because the next day was a light one on the schedule, Roone and I stayed after our nightly postproduction meeting to talk about other matters on the ABC Sports agenda. Right after the Olympics, we were scheduled to go to Kansas City for a negotiation over college football rights, and we worked on a letter to send to Walter Byers, the executive director of the NCAA.

Once Roone was satisfied, he decided it was finally time to leave, and we walked out the back door of our compound at the International Broadcast Center. It was close to five o'clock in the morning, still more dark than light, the sun just making its first faint hints of reemerging, and the most glorious full moon you could imagine hovering straight above us. Just off in the distance, we could see the lights in the Olympic Stadium were on, and on the other side of the driveway, over a short fence, was one side of the Olympic Village, where the athletes were living. To Roone, there was no better, more beautiful place to be in the world, and he was clearly riding the high of being at the center of one of the biggest television successes of all time. His vision of how the Olympics could be a TV phenomenon really was playing out just as he had pictured it. And as we stood there in the driveway, he reflected, poignantly and poetically, about the whole experience.

"Have you ever seen a more beautiful night?" he mused aloud. "It's just perfect, the world coming together here. We're just lucky to be part of it all."

As we soaked it all in, the other man standing there with us, a wonderful guy by the name of Kurt Fuchs, a German who was a regular driver for ABC at all our events in Western Europe, was a bit less emotional.

"Roone," Kurt said in his German-accented English. "The kid and I are tired. Let's go home."

So we got in the car—me in the front seat with Kurt, Roone in the back—and we drove down the driveway to make a left turn out to the road leading to our hotel.

As we'd later find out in the investigations to follow, no more than five minutes later, eight men from the Palestinian terrorist group Black September, who'd been hiding in the trash bins just about fifty feet from where we'd been standing, emerged and hopped the six-and-a-half-foot chain-link fence, alongside athletes who were also sneaking in after breaking curfew that night. The terrorists were carrying duffel bags full of assault rifles, pistols, and grenades. They headed toward Connollystrasse 31, the dorm where the Israeli delegation was staying, and stormed inside. In a struggle, an Israeli coach and weight lifter were killed, with nine others taken hostage, including an American weight lifter named David Berger from Shaker Heights, Ohio, who was competing for Israel.

I'm not sure what would have happened had we lingered a few minutes longer in the driveway that night. Maybe with the delay, the eight Palestinian terrorists would have been scared off by the daylight. Maybe they would have shot us. We'll never know. An hour and a half or so after we got to the hotel, Roone was awakened by a call informing him what had happened, and he headed right back to the broadcast center. Though Chris Schenkel was, as he was in 1968, the prime-time studio host, Roone knew McKay was the figure he wanted in his anchor chair. Famously, when Roone reached Jim, he was doing morning laps in the swimming pool, and Jim was so stunned that, when he returned to his room to get dressed before heading to the studio, he forgot to take off his wet bathing suit. He'd have his wet trunks on underneath, not even realizing it, all throughout the long ordeal to follow that day and night.

I awoke, heard the news, and got to the broadcast center later that morning, heading straight for the control room. The mood in the room had a heaviness to it, but as always with Roone, it was calm. There was no yelling, not even any loud voices. Just a steadiness to every decision being made, anchored by a plan that

Roone formulated virtually on the fly. For years, I'd heard him critique (and often criticize) the decisions of ABC News as big stories unfolded. Now, with one of the biggest news stories of our time unfolding in real time, he was fully in command, and his team was rising to the challenge.

We sneaked walkie-talkies into the Olympic Village, and Howard Cosell, taking off his yellow ABC blazer and convincing officials he was a shoe company representative, and Peter Jennings, then a foreign correspondent, got themselves just a few hundred yards from the hostage situation. A production aide named Gary Slaughter posed as a member of the U.S. track team and started carrying film and supplies in and out of the village. A producer named John Wilcox got closest of all, taking a borrowed uniform and making his way to a balcony just about fifty feet from where a terrorist was standing watch at Connollystrasse 31. All of them would be constantly relaying information back to the studio as the day unfolded.

Today, networks broadcast from all over the world constantly, all at once. Back then, satellite access was much more limited, and as soon as the news came, Roone had our engineers "block-book" it, setting up ABC to go live at 1:00 p.m. local time (7:00 a.m. back in New York); we'd be the one American television source covering the story live all day long. Roone had our tech crew wheel two studio cameras down the hallway to point them out the same back doors from where we'd been leaving every night; that was the angle America saw as the ordeal would continue to unfold over the next several hours.

It would be a surreal, torturous experience sitting in the back of the control room watching the situation unfold. Gofers quietly brought in food and snacks. Other producers and aides quietly came in and out as needed. Just in front of me, Roone was at his very best, the best live producer I've ever seen, quarterbacking a story he never could have imagined telling. Information was constantly coming in from our correspondents in the village, sources in and out of Munich, and the wire services doing their own work. He was in McKay's ear the whole time, guiding him through the latest reports, never letting anything get on the air that our reporters weren't one hundred percent sure was accurate. As for Jim, he was completely in control, and yet completely human; journalism and empathy molded perfectly and naturally. Walter Cronkite would send a telegram the next day to McKay lauding ABC's work throughout the ordeal.

The hostage situation carried on all day. In the afternoon, when updates from people spread around the grounds became scarce, Roone put on a few events of competition; Avery Brundage hadn't initially suspended the action, even as the entire Games seemed to be in a state of shock. Then Roone put on *The Ancient Games*, my film from Delphi. Probably 50 million people saw it. I would have given anything for it never to have been seen in exchange for the crisis to end without any more lives lost.

As nightfall approached, the story seemed to eerily get darker. The terrorists had proclaimed deadlines, threatening to execute Israelis if their demands weren't met; those deadlines were getting pushed, but there was no real sense the Germans had any plan. At 6:00 p.m., we briefly lost our satellite time to CBS, who'd prebooked the hour; Roone smartly and quickly got someone to accede to CBS's demand to take our feed. A few hours later, Cosell came into the control room; as a Jew, he'd grown increasingly emotional about the story, and was insisting he go back on the air from the studio. Roone stood fast; Howard was in no condition to go on, and getting told no only enraged him further.

Late in the evening, after negotiations had stalled and resumed multiple times, an agreement was made to let the terrorists go with the hostages in helicopters to the airport, and fly them to Egypt. The helicopters flew right over the broadcast center; I got a lump in my throat as they flew away. If the day had been defined by a feeling of helplessness, hearing them head out was the eeriest part. The Israeli athletes weren't much younger than me; I couldn't get the feeling of terror they must have been feeling out of my head.

The agreement to fly them to Egypt, as it turned out, of course, was a ruse; the West German police were secretly planning an ambush. Tragically, it was an operation they were ill-prepared to pull off. Though initially others reported that the operation was successful, things in fact went awry quickly, and in the ensuing firefight, all the hostages were killed. After Roone waited and waited for the confirmation he could trust, at 3:24 a.m. in Munich, I watched from my seat as he gave Jim the final word through his earpiece. Jim then broke the news to the country, thinking, as he'd explain later, of David Berger's parents in Shaker Heights, Ohio.

"You know, when I was a kid, my father used to say, 'Our greatest hopes and our worst fears are seldom realized,'" Jim said into the camera. "Our worst fears have been realized tonight. They've now said that there were eleven hostages.

Two were killed in their rooms yesterday morning, nine were killed at the airport tonight. They're all gone."

We were all crushed. Not long after, I finally left the control room. Roone sent me and another producer, Terry Jastrow, to the stadium to set ourselves up to record a memorial service that the IOC had planned. We were completely hollowed out emotionally. But somehow, there was still work to do. The full story had to be told.

CHAPTER 6

Surprises

If the Munich massacre was at once our worst nightmare and finest hour at ABC Sports, it was just one unforgettable moment in the decade that certified Roone Arledge as one of the most significant production figures in the history of television. After completely revolutionizing the idea of how sports could be brought to the masses in their living rooms with *Wide World of Sports*, there were more innovations yet in store. And the biggest of them was undoubtedly the genius of *Monday Night Football*.

Originally, scheduling one game a week every Monday night was NFL commissioner Pete Rozelle's idea, but *Monday Night Football* became a phenomenon because of Roone. He'd first seen the potential of sports in prime time at the Mexico City Olympics, and with ABC the number-three-ranked network in prime time behind CBS and NBC, he didn't have much competition convincing his boss Leonard Goldenson to buy the package from the NFL. That was just the start of his plans, however.

Roone had revolutionized college football with more cameras, better audio, and other technical innovations; now *Monday Night Football* could be an even bigger extension of that. Like everything else Roone did, it was about storytelling, and the best broadcast technically, but even more than that, it was an entertainment spectacle. And at the heart of that spectacle was the brilliant pairing of the erudite, bombastic Howard Cosell and the laid-back country boy and former Dallas Cowboy quarterback Don Meredith in the announcers' booth.

Cosell, much like Jim McKay, owed his success to Roone; he'd risen to fame in the 1960s with his appearances on *Wide World*, most notably his series of interviews with Muhammad Ali, who was then widely shunned for his refusal to fight in the Vietnam War on religious grounds, but supported by Howard. Still, when Roone put Howard on *Monday Night Football*, it was an entirely new perch. Howard wasn't an experienced play-by-play caller like Keith Jackson, nor was he an expert analyst like Meredith. But Roone put him in the booth as a third figure—then, an unprecedented idea—to be entertaining. To pick fights with "Dandy" Don, as he called him. And in Cosell's unique, grandiloquent style, every week he'd take shots at Meredith, at players, teams, and coaches, and do it all in a way that infuriated a large portion of the audience. Complaints flooded the switchboard, and even Henry Ford II, the chairman of the show's biggest advertiser, called Goldenson, the president of ABC, demanding Howard be taken off the air. When Goldenson related this to Roone, Roone's response was to ask to call Ford himself and explain to him why he was being shortsighted. Roone understood that while millions of people hated Howard, they also loved to hate him—and they wouldn't turn off blowout games late, just to hear him continue to spar with Meredith, perfectly cast as America's surrogate. Roone got his way—and ABC continued to get Ford's advertising dollars.

It was yet another element of Roone's vision—his realization that personalities like Howard could compel the audience along with the drama and narrative of the sporting events themselves. Today's "hot take" culture? Even if no one today is in Howard's class, nowhere near as completely original, or intelligent, it's a descendant of that vision.

Behind the scenes, Cosell was just as colorful a character as you'd hope. I first got to know him well in Mexico City at the '68 Games, when after aggravating my bad knee, I got a special pass to go in and out of the Olympic Village to get treated by the U.S. team doctor. When Howard had gotten word of this, he'd realized he could use my injury to get himself into the village, and potentially get to talk to athletes when no other reporters would have access to them. He didn't have a pass, but that wasn't going to stop him from talking—in butchered Spanish—his way past the front gate with me. He pulled it off, too.

On the air, Howard was a broadcasting virtuoso; blessed with total recall, he could walk into an audio booth and record a report for his ABC radio show, *Speaking of Sports*, error-free, without a single note in front of him. He was never not in character, he loved referring to himself in the third person, and he was unendingly obsessed with what was going on in the office when he wasn't there. For a while, I bore the brunt of this, as he knew how much time I spent with Roone, particularly late at night. So I'd be in my apartment at six thirty in the morning, asleep, when my phone would ring, and it would be Howard, loudly articulating in his rhythmic, heavy-stepped staccato.

"Dickie Boy, it's Howard Cosell calling, good morning to you. As you were no doubt the last individual to be in the company of Mister Roone Arledge last night, I ask you—*you*—what he might have said about the broadcast plan for next Monday night."

After these calls became daily events, I complained to Roone, asking him what to do.

"Just tell him that you've moved beyond the point in your career where you should be fielding these phone calls," Roone said, "and he can't treat you like this."

I tried the next morning. Howard's response was apoplectic.

"Dickie Boy, how *dare* you claim that you are *too big*, too *progressed* in the course of your meager professional advancement, to greet the dawn with a call from *me*, Howard Cosell, the most *provocative* voice in all of television *history*? How dare you!"

And yet, as always was the case with Howard, there was the slightest hint of a smile in his voice. Even he got the joke.

After the first season of *Monday Night Football*, even with the ratings and popularity sky-high, Roone did want to make one replacement. He'd grown close with Frank Gifford in New York all those years at P. J. Clarke's, and decided in 1971 to put him in the booth as a replacement for the play-by-play man, Keith Jackson—this despite Gifford, the former player, having no experience whatsoever doing play-by-play, a more difficult role. To me, the exchange made no sense— Keith had done nothing wrong in his one year on the job, he was a star in his own right as the voice of ABC's college football coverage, and a regular presence on *Wide World* and the Olympics. To replace him with Frank would be the ultimate case of fixing what wasn't broken. And so for two or three months, I made my case to Roone, and he listened, postponing his decision. That is, until one day, sitting in my tiny office just outside Roone's giant suite, I sensed a figure materialize at my door. It was Frank. He and I were friendly, but this, it was clear, was a serious visit.

"Dick," he said, "you've got to stop this. He's going to make this move, and by stalling him, you're just postponing the inevitable and making it harder on everyone. Get out of the way."

Soon after, the move was made. Frank would be the play-by-play announcer of *Monday Night Football* until Al Michaels joined him in the booth in 1985. He'd learn on the job, at times painfully, but the attention that Cosell and Meredith absorbed from the audience gave him ample runway. As for Keith—his fame would only take off as the greatest voice of college football ever. At ABC Sports in those days, the machine was so strong, there could be no losers.

My relationship with Roone Arledge was as valuable, rewarding, and influential as any relationship in my career. Roone was my original model of what a leader and innovator looked like in the media world. As a boss, he could be both charming and elusive, inspiring and maddening. As a visionary, he was brilliant and ambitious, forever hungry for the next great idea, ever unwilling to compromise. And just as important, as a manager, he was always willing to rely on the star members of his team to see his plans through. Along with telling stories, Roone's goal—with *Wide World of Sports*, with the Olympics, and with football—was to take the audience to the sports in ways that television hadn't done before.

In early 1973, on a trip out west, Roone and a few of us got stuck in a ridiculous stretch of rainy weather that canceled a string of flights. While we were waiting it out, Don Ohlmeyer and I hung out for a long night in Roone's bungalow at the Beverly Hills Hotel, and he told us that he had begun to form a plan for the future to make the leadership of his group younger. He was going to put Don in charge of production, and me in charge of programming. We just had to give him a bit of time to put all the pieces in place.

It was all completely out of the blue; Don and I were surprised, and obviously thrilled. We were still only in our twenties, and the man that we idolized was going to officially make us his top deputies. So we continued to work, and have plenty of fun doing it. One night in the fall of 1973, ABC broadcast the Muhammad Ali–Ken Norton rematch at the Inglewood Forum in Los Angeles. Norton had upset Ali several months earlier, breaking the legend's jaw in the process; this second fight, Ali refused to sit in his corner between rounds, looking to show off his stamina by standing. He'd win back his title through a split decision. I sat ringside with Roone, and just a few seats down from none other than the Chairman of the Board himself, Frank Sinatra. Sinatra was a huge boxing fan, and after the fight, as we lingered ringside, he said offhandedly to me, "Hey, kid, we're going to the Beverly Hilton, table's in my name. You should come." I didn't know him, but he knew I was with Roone, and I didn't want to question the invitation. A few hours later, after a stop at the hotel, I found myself following Frank to a party a publicist was throwing, and standing by a window talking to him.

"So what do you do with your free time, kid?" he asked me.

"I read as much as I can." I couldn't think of anything else to say.

Well, it turned out that Frank Sinatra was a bookworm, too. And so we talked books for a while, and then—improbably—he asked me for a ride home. So I drove him to his house at the top of Coldwater Canyon on Mulholland Drive, at which point he asked if I wanted to see his library. It was, as you'd think, pretty impressive. At the end of the night, I went back to Roone's same bungalow at the Beverly Hills Hotel, where the night owl was still awake, wondering where I'd been, and for once, jealous of a night I'd gotten to have without him.

A few months after that, about a year after the meeting Don and I had with Roone about our careers, I got a call from someone else, a man named Herb Schlosser. Schlosser was the president of NBC, and he wanted to speak with me about the possibility of interviewing to become the head of NBC Sports. It was a huge offer, but I never seriously considered it. As much as I'd learned over the previous four years at Roone's side, I knew I wasn't ready to run a network sports division—and particularly not in competition with my mentor. So I turned it down. I did, however, soon after tell Roone about the offer, and that I'd passed on it, and asked him about what he'd said a year earlier about promoting me and Don. His answer wasn't definitive; it was clear that even after he'd told us his intentions, he was—understandably—struggling to find a way to part with the top executives who'd been with him since basically the beginning of ABC Sports.

Then, soon after that, as summer began, I got another call from Schlosser, asking me to come spend a day with his family over the July Fourth weekend at his home on Fire Island, just off the coast of Long Island. It was a bit of a cryptic request; all he said was that he wanted to talk to me about something that had nothing to do with sports. Curiosity got the best of me, and I agreed to go.

During a long walk on the beach that weekend on Fire Island, Schlosser explained to me why he'd wanted to talk.

"We've got a problem to solve on the weekends," he said. "Saturday nights, to be specific."

Johnny Carson, whose *Tonight Show* had been the gold standard in late night television for thirteen years at that point, had told NBC that he didn't want the network airing his reruns on Saturday nights anymore. But NBC didn't want to simply give the lucrative Saturday late night time block back to its local affiliates to program.

"So I need a new show," he said. "And I think you can be the executive who can help me find it."

I was stunned by the offer. I didn't have a minute of experience on the entertainment side of television, but here Schlosser was giving me a chance to create a whole new show. If the sports job at NBC seemed like the obvious wrong move, the unexpectedness of the entertainment challenge intrigued me. Yes, I'd had my dream job for the better part of seven years, but as I thought about the delay in my promotion, it felt like I'd stopped moving forward. Working for Roone and observing him up close for all that time had been a priceless experience. But this offer had put things in a new perspective. I knew I was going to come to a point where I didn't just want to be an assistant, even if it was the assistant to the most admired and successful executive in television. Maybe that time was now. And while it wasn't sports, the world of entertainment was a new horizon.

After an agonizing few weeks of deliberating, I decided to take the job.

When I told Roone, he was blindsided. He didn't really have much to say—it was almost like he realized belatedly that he'd left Don and me hanging for so long, never thinking we might leave for another opportunity. ABC Sports just wasn't a job a lot of people left.

My last day there was the same day Richard Nixon resigned from office, August 9, 1974. With a few weeks' gap before I started at NBC, I drove up to Boston to stay with Curt Gowdy and his family for a week or so, to try and make sense of the whirlwind decision I'd just made.

And then, it was time to explore a new world.

Part Two

CHAPTER 7

A Whole New World

Just after Labor Day 1974, I showed up for my first day of work at NBC.

There weren't many more magical places to start a new job than 30 Rockefeller Plaza. The building's legacy went back to when it was built in the early 1930s alongside Radio City Music Hall as the broadcasting home of the Radio Corporation of America—better known as RCA—and its biggest subsidiary, the National Broadcasting Company, or NBC. By the time I was growing up in the 1950s, NBC was a television network, and 30 Rock was where dozens of legendary shows were produced, from *NBC Nightly News* to Jack Paar's *Tonight Show* and, for its first ten years on air, Johnny Carson's edition of the program. It was also, of course, where the most famous Christmas tree in the world was lit every December, overlooking that picturesque skating rink. If you watched TV when you were a kid, and I certainly watched plenty, the words "30 Rockefeller Plaza" had a mystique to them, and every time over the next thirty-five years that I'd walk through those revolving doors into the art deco lobby to go to work, it never stopped feeling special.

Sports may have always been my first love, but that's not to say they were the only way the television set entertained me as I grew up. You name it, I watched it—the Warner Bros. shows on ABC like *Maverick* and *77 Sunset Strip*; *This Is Your Life* and *Bonanza* on NBC; *The Ed Sullivan Show* on CBS.

From Saturday Night to Sunday Night

Once I moved to New York in the seventies, late nights in the office meant turning on the TV when I got home to see Carson, and that of course was a window to see pretty much every great entertainer in America. Johnny wasn't just a world-class humorist; he was a world-class broadcaster who could put all his guests at ease more effectively than any other host—or, if he had to, go toe-to-toe with anyone on his set, about any topic, from movies to politics to sports. All of it was entertaining—so entertaining that the audience would put off sleep to keep watching, afraid of missing a great moment if they turned off the TV too early. In that way, it wasn't so different from people not wanting to turn off *Monday Night Football* to miss what Cosell might say. Or even more fundamentally, not wanting to turn off a game for fear of missing a great dramatic ending—or to put it in Roone's terms, missing how the story would end. I'd learned all that from Roone, I talked about it with Herb Schlosser, and I suppose that understanding of what appealed to viewers was what appealed to Schlosser when he hired me for my new, very-much-non-sports job at 30 Rockefeller Plaza that fall. It wasn't the Olympics or the NBA or *Monday Night Football*, but it still sure didn't feel like work.

Of course, there was still a lot I had to learn—and at the top of the list: what you ask for when taking a new job. The big office and secretary I'd been expecting were nowhere to be found when I showed up on my first day; instead, my new professional home was a tiny, closet-sized windowless enclosure with no assistant in sight. So I quickly realized that the fastest way to make an impression was to get a concept for a show prepped as soon as possible. And I wouldn't be in the office that much anyway. After all, figuring out what the show could be meant traveling all the time, scouring the country for talent.

Since the show I'd been hired to find was going to be replacing Johnny Carson reruns, the obvious place to focus was comedy. In New York, Catch a Rising Star had just opened on the Upper East Side, and Billy Crystal and Andy Kaufman were frequent performers there. In Los Angeles, the hottest club was the Improv on Melrose Avenue—Richard Pryor was among the regulars. And in Chicago, the place to see comedy was the famed Second City theater. I crisscrossed the country dropping in on these venues, and "taking meetings," as I quickly learned it was called in Hollywood, with talent managers and agents. I may have been new in the entertainment world and just twenty-seven years old, but once the word got out that NBC was looking to put a new comedy show on Saturday nights and I was the executive looking for the right concept, my phone wouldn't stop ringing.

I felt like I had a good sense of what the show needed to be. First, it had to be a show that would appeal to a young, hip audience; a show that my generation wanted to watch. We weren't going to find another Johnny Carson, and besides, it was the start of a golden age of comedy, with so many different voices and fresh talent. And to take advantage of the breadth of that talent, my initial idea for a format, which came to me almost as soon as I started forming a concept for a show in my head, was for a "wheel." I was too young to really remember *The Colgate Comedy Hour* on NBC in the early fifties, but the show had been hosted by a cast of four comedians, working in a steady rotation. I envisioned something like that being the foundation of the new show. Rotating the hosts would keep the show fresh, and the format would also make it more likely to get big names to be part of it, considering they only had to work once a month. And in a perfect scenario, the biggest name in the rotation would be one of the hottest comics at the time: Richard Pryor.

The ambitious idea felt like it was gaining momentum when I met with a writing and producing team, Bob Einstein and Chris Bearde, pitching a show centered around Pryor. I also talked to two other great talents who would appeal to a younger crowd, George Carlin and Lily Tomlin, both of whom were interested when they heard Richard might be involved. Though not as far along in our conversations, I had also been in touch with Steve Martin's manager. The show felt like it might be coming together—the plan would be for each comedian to do one show a month, totaling eight or nine shows a year each, with the other three months in repeats. I had follow-up meetings with Einstein, Bearde, and Pryor in NBC's offices in Burbank to talk more about the concept. Everything was going perfectly—until I got a call from a lawyer in Atlanta named David Franklin, telling me he was Richard Pryor's new representative, and that there was no way Richard was going to do network television, because Richard's whole act was based around things you couldn't say on network television.

"You know the National Broadcasting Company," I still remember Franklin saying to me on the phone, "will never allow Richard Pryor to be Richard Pryor, at eleven thirty on Saturday nights or at any other time."

I would have argued harder with him—the problem was, he was exactly right. It was close to the end of 1974. Without Pryor, I had nothing. But I had also met someone else—someone who didn't have a name anyone in the mainstream would recognize, and who didn't even have any interest in appearing in front of the camera himself. Yet he had the genius and vision to change comedy on television forever.

Compared to a lot of crusty old managers and producers I typically found myself meeting with that fall in Los Angeles, thirty-year-old Lorne Michaels was a welcome change of pace. He'd worked as a writer for the comedienne Phyllis Diller and on *Rowan & Martin's Laugh-In*, the NBC prime-time sketch comedy show, among other places. He'd also written and produced a handful of well-received, Emmy Award–winning specials for Lily Tomlin. When I met with him at his agent Sandy Wernick's office, high up in a building on Sunset Boulevard, he was partnered with an older variety show director, but being that we were roughly the same age, we immediately seemed to connect. I wasn't interested in the idea they were pitching, but afterward, as the meeting broke up, already seeing that we'd get along, I quietly sidled up next to Lorne.

"Why don't we grab coffee after this?" I asked him. "I'd be curious to talk a bit more."

Over a drink nearby, we had a great conversation, talking about comedy and show business, and as we were wrapping up, he had another idea.

"You should come check out this show I'm going to tonight. You might like this act for what you're looking for."

A few hours later, Lorne came by the Beverly Hills Hotel, where at this point I had a locked closet in a room where I could leave my clothes, since I was spending at least half of every month there. Lorne was driving a Volkswagen convertible, and sitting in the back was a woman with dark curly hair whose relationship to him wasn't quite made clear to me. We were heading near the Fox lot in Century City to see something called Kentucky Fried Theater, a comedy troupe that was the brainchild of two brothers, David and Jerry Zucker, and their friend Jim Abrahams, who years later would become comedy legends with *Airplane!*, *The*

Naked Gun, and *The Kentucky Fried Movie*. The show that night was funny, though I didn't see anything that would necessarily help with a new NBC series. As for Lorne, in almost typical fashion, all throughout the night, he never told me that the mystery woman in the car with us was his wife. Rosie Shuster was the daughter of Canadian comedy royalty, Frank Shuster, half of the famous Wayne and Shuster comedy duo with Johnny Wayne. Lorne and Rosie had met on the thriving Toronto comedy circuit, and had moved to Los Angeles a few years earlier, where they'd separated but stayed close.

After the show, the three of us went back to the Beverly Hills Hotel and into the Polo Lounge off the lobby to have a drink. As we sat in our seats, Lorne nodded in the direction of the other side of the restaurant.

"Aren't those some old friends of yours?" he said.

I looked across the room. Improbably, seated in a booth having a late dinner and drinks, were none other than Howard Cosell and his wife, Emmy, and Roone Arledge and his wife, Ann.

I hadn't seen either Howard or Roone since I'd left ABC a few months earlier—and, of course, Roone hadn't taken my departure well. But with some encouragement from my new friends, I went over, said hello, and any sense of tension quickly dissipated.

"Well, if it is none other than Mister [pause] Dick [pause] Ebersol," Howard intoned with a sly grin on his face, "our former compatriot who has chosen to consort with the competition—and in the entertainment space no less!"

All was evidently forgiven; they were happy to see me, and excited to hear what I was doing. And I knew—through Don Ohlmeyer—that the irony of the whole encounter was only boosted by the fact that they, too, were developing a variety show, produced by Roone, and hosted by Howard, to air on Saturday nights. The concepts weren't identical—theirs would be in prime time—but beyond the similarities, what sticks with me about that night as much as anything else was the real sense that Roone was rooting for me to succeed at NBC—and how great that felt. Somehow, on the very first night I ever went out with Lorne, Roone had been there—my professional past on one side of the room and my professional future on the other. It's almost too improbable to believe.

If Roone had taught me anything, it was to appreciate real talent when I saw it. And Lorne Michaels was definitely like no other mind I had met during my first few months in comedy. We talked deep into that night at the bar, and I had a real sense that something could develop out of this. Lorne was young, he was hip, and it was clear that he had a true vision of what the next generation of comedy could look and sound like on television. Like me, he wanted to create a show that appealed to young people. He talked about his vision in vivid, thoughtful terms— how the show would need to be in the "language" of the way people really talked. He didn't mean cursing or anything like that; it was more about embodying the attitude of how young people thought. The number one comedy on television was *All in the Family*, about a working-class American who spoke the language of millions of middle-aged viewers. Lorne wanted a show that did the same for the next generation.

Back in New York, after the news of Richard Pryor falling through, Herb Schlosser had taken the setback well, and made clear that he thought we could do a show without a built-in star. In a memo he sent to me sometime around New Year's, he'd even suggested bringing the show back to New York—and specifically staging it in one of the original 30 Rock studios, Studio 8H. It would be not a show that NBC bought, but rather that NBC owned and produced in-house in its headquarters.

Lorne and I spent the first few weeks of 1975 in Los Angeles continuing to brainstorm what the show could be. We'd meet for late lunches day after day, and then continue talking late into the night either at the Polo Lounge or over at the Chateau Marmont, the famed hotel and bungalow colony where he was living. Generations of writers and artists had lived and worked there, from F. Scott Fitzgerald to Jim Morrison, and now, over our long, even epic conversations, an idea was taking shape—of a variety show that would feature a guest host and guest musical acts around a regular repertory cast performing sketches. It would air live, an idea that would need to be part of the show's identity, keeping it on the edge. And just as important, the show would reflect the language of young people, the language of college campuses and city streets. The audience watching would know that it was expressly intended for them. A show that would look, sound, and feel different is easy for anyone to say in a pitch, but in this case, it was clear to me that Lorne really understood how to get there.

Schlosser and Lorne had a great rapport from the start, but he wanted him to meet with some other, older top figures at the company. At ABC Sports, if Roone liked an idea, it was a total green light. At NBC Entertainment, with a stodgier culture, and a large roster of old-school, old-time executives, things moved slower. So a breakfast meeting was proposed for Lorne and me to meet with the head of talent and the head of prime-time programming—which sounds simple enough if not for the fact that Lorne was, and is today, one of the world's great night owls. I convinced him that it was important enough for him to come, and he got up early (or maybe just stayed up all night) for the 7:30 a.m. breakfast with these two execs—who were each close to twice our age. They were, certainly at least to Lorne, a pair of old stiffs, but he said enough of the right things to gain their approval, and NBC was able to sign him to a deal, an agreement negotiated by his manager, Bernie Brillstein, who would come to play a huge role in the early years of the show himself.

(Along with Lorne as producer, my original hope was to bring in Don Ohlmeyer to direct the show, but Roone wouldn't let Don out of his contract. Still, a few years later, he'd come over to NBC as the executive producer of the sports department, and eventually follow me into the entertainment side of the business as well.)

A few weeks later, further indicative of the way the network ran, we flew to New York to meet with a larger group of NBC executives known as the "programming council" to outline the show to them. The "council" had been a cohort that Schlosser—a lawyer by background—had created to delegate the supervision of all programming at the network. They'd all been there for years, and were defined as much by their territorial ways as any creative tastes. Just before the meeting, one of the execs came out to speak with me.

"Here's the thing," he said. "It's really not appropriate for Mr. Michaels to address the group. He's not an NBC employee—he's a contracted producer. This is really an internal meeting."

"So what are you saying?" I asked. "You just want me to go in and explain the concept?"

"It really would be better."

So, as totally ridiculous as that was, I reluctantly went in on my own to explain the concept. Schlosser wasn't there for the beginning of the presentation (nor for the moment when I was told to keep a bemused Lorne downstairs), but he walked into the room about two-thirds of the way through my pitch. When I was finished, he spoke up.

"Hey, Bill, what do you think of the show?" he said to the network's ancient head of research.

Without missing a beat, relying on the infinite wisdom he'd gained over decades in the ratings business, the exec gave his response.

"The audience for which this show is designed," he said pompously, "will *never* come home at eleven thirty on a Saturday night to watch it."

Fortunately, Herb Schlosser didn't see it that way, and with his support, we had the green light. But it would be an all-out sprint to get it done. The timeline for taking the Carson reruns off the air was unchanged, and if the network didn't have a show ready, affiliates all across the country would fill the time slot with local programming. We had six months to put all the pieces together. We had to hire writers, talent bookers, and a musical director; design a set; and most important of all, figure out who was going to be in the cast. We weren't looking for names that would be recognizable to the general public. Rather, the idea was to find a bunch of rising comedic talents who could play in a variety of sketches every week. If we succeeded, they'd become stars.

The cast came from many different corners of the comedy universe Lorne knew well, among them repertory clubs and troupes from L.A., New York, Chicago, and Toronto. But, owing to the era, and their lack of exposure, there wasn't really any useful video of the candidates, so they'd have to audition live for us, many of them in a rented space on West Fifty-Seventh Street just up the block from the hotel where I'd first lived when I'd moved to New York. They lined up in the hallway outside our makeshift studio, dozens of hopefuls who'd read about the show in the entertainment trade publications and saw it as their big chance. Everyone who came in showed up with their own material, some with partners, many by themselves, auditioning with characters they'd created, and bits and comedy songs adapted from improv work they'd done. The key, as Lorne knew, was to find people who would be at their best performing live—who could, in the moment, with no safety net, summon a certain kind of genius to not just make an audience laugh but thrill them as they did it.

There would be callbacks, and then one-on-one meetings on both coasts—whatever it took to get everyone on board with the choices. For me, as the executive in charge, it was a delicate balancing act, and an adjustment from my creative days in sports, trying to keep my mouth shut as long as possible, resisting sharing my thoughts until I felt like I really had to. In the end, in every case, the decisions needed to be Lorne's—he would be the producer who had to function with the talent; I knew he needed to have the final say.

The first two performers we hired were women: Gilda Radner, a twenty-nine-year-old from Detroit who'd worked in Toronto with the Second City comedy troupe there, and who was clearly an incredible talent; and Laraine Newman, just twenty-three, from the Groundlings in Los Angeles, who'd worked with Lorne the year before on his Lily Tomlin special. Jane Curtin, who came from the Boston comedy scene, would be the third woman in the cast; immensely talented and hilarious and, further, she somehow seemed more sophisticated in her demeanor than the rest of us. As I figured out what Lorne was building, it seemed important to me to have a woman who could remind the audience of their girlfriend or young wife—a woman who, when she needed to, could play the "straight man"—and that was Jane. On one of the few occasions where I really opened my mouth, I lobbied hard for her to get a spot, and she'd appear in more sketches than almost anyone else in the show's early days.

With so many of their fellow future costars, what's probably most remarkable is how close so many of them came to not being hired. Dan Aykroyd originally showed up with Gilda at her audition; he'd given her a ride on his motorcycle. But he was just twenty-three years old, and though he'd been successful in Toronto and Chicago as part of Second City, Lorne initially had concerns about whether he was experienced enough. After multiple auditions, he was finally hired, and Dan and Lorne would end up forming a close creative partnership in the lead-up to the show. His future Blues Brothers partner, John Belushi, meanwhile, was clearly a talent, but was also going to be a handful—it was no secret in those comedy circles even then how much John could party, and how much he seemed to thrive from living on the edge. He also had it in his head that TV wasn't for him, with his focus already on movies—and, predictably, he wasn't shy about telling everyone, even

Lorne, just that. John had to be encouraged to come to the auditions by friends like Gilda, and then even when he did, Lorne had to be assured that his talent outweighed the risk of relying on him. A few of the writers Lorne had brought on and trusted pushed for John, and at one point, I even offered to be personally responsible for him. And of course, ultimately, despite the reluctances on both sides, Belushi came on board.

Two other members of the cast were originally hired as writers. Garrett Morris, the one Black member of the cast, officially made the transition a few weeks before the first show. Chevy Chase, whose résumé included writing for the *National Lampoon* radio show, had met Lorne in line at a movie at Cinerama in L.A., of all places, and was hired to be the head writer. Chevy, though, wanted to be in the cast, seeing himself as a physical comedian—the master of the pratfall. Though I left the creative direction of the show in Lorne's hands, there were times when I'd speak up as the executive—and this was one of them. With so much inexperience on the show, I thought it was hugely important that the show had a dedicated head writer, purely focused on the task of managing the ninety minutes of comedy we needed written every week. If Chevy was also wrapped up in performing, who knows how far off the tracks the writing could get. Well, at some point after Chevy was hired as head writer, he, Lorne, and I went to a comedy show in New York to see a potential performer who I'd been touting to Lorne for weeks. The comic's name was Billy Crystal. It was a rainy night, and as we left the club after Billy's stand-up, trying to avoid getting drenched, Chevy went ahead, hurrying without an umbrella, ostensibly to find us a cab. As we watched him half walk and half run, about twenty-five feet in front of us, he suddenly—and purposefully—fell head over heels into a giant pothole filled with water.

As Chevy tried to shake off the water, Lorne turned to me.

"Now, c'mon, if he's willing to do that to perform on the show, we can give the kid a chance, can't we?"

It felt like we were all kids being allowed to play in a grown-up's world. But we did need some adults in the room. Davey Wilson was in his early forties, and a veteran director whose experience working on live TV specials would be huge. Audrey Dickman, originally from England, is a name that doesn't get mentioned in a lot of early histories of the show, but as associate director, she would play an essential role in terms of the fundamental task of actually getting us on the air every Saturday night. Another important grown-up was Herb Sargent, a well-known comedy writer who'd worked for both Steve Allen and Johnny Carson on *The Tonight Show*. He was also president of the East Coast Writers Guild. Herb may have been from another generation of comedy, but something drew him to Lorne, the sense that Lorne had a real respect for writers, and even bigger than that, the opportunity to work with a group of kids who had nothing to lose. Herb would be the guiding voice of *Weekend Update* for years, and become one of the true behind-the-scenes legends of *SNL*.

Both Herb and Davey decided to come to work with us over offers from ABC and Roone and Howard's prime-time show. And throughout the months of buildup, through my friends at ABC, I kept track of their development as we raced one another to the fall. A few of our cast members had auditioned for them, and they'd actually hired Bill Murray, who plenty on our staff wanted to bring on to the show. Still, the hallways of 30 Rock would soon be filled with some other characters who never would have appealed to Roone and his co-producer, Alan King, one of the deans of the established comedy world. Like Michael O'Donoghue, a dark character who wore smoked glasses with wire rims and often seemed to be on the edge of an explosion, but who was also a genius comedic mind. "The Prince of Darkness" was initially hired to be a cast member, but ended up on the writing staff. Alan Zweibel, Al Franken, and Tom Davis were other young, unknown writers who came on board as part of a Writers Guild apprentice program that Herb was instrumental in creating, and who would contribute some of the show's best material in the years to come.

From the beginning, I did everything I could to put Lorne in a position to succeed. Whether that meant keeping some distance between the out-of-touch network executives and him, consulting on difficult hires, trying to make the budget work, or prepping the censors for what was coming, I saw my role as a facilitator and organizer much more than a creative force. The whole lead-up to the show felt like a race, with the clock always ticking down toward the fall and our premiere. And with NBC filled with figures in power who had no understanding of what we were trying to do, and no real interest in seeing a young upstart show succeed without their involvement, I had to keep up as big a buffer as possible. My relationship with Lorne was different from anything I'd had at ABC. Years later, I'd return to the creative stuff in sports. Here, though, I wasn't a comedian, I wasn't a writer—but I could do everything in my power to make sure that Lorne and his writers and cast could see their vision come to life.

Part of that job occasionally involved being a little subversive myself. Barbara Gallagher was an associate producer who Lorne had hired to do a lot of dirty work in terms of organizing and budgets, working directly with the network managers. At one point, Lorne and I found out that one of them had been exceptionally rude to Barbara. We also learned that he'd recently been promoted, and was crowing about getting a new office with a nice rug. So Lorne and I went outside, caked our shoes in mud, and then paid him—and his rug—a visit, where we let him know that it wasn't all right to treat our people without respect. He never bothered her again.

Another great example of what needed to get done came in the summer, when Lorne was worried about the set. We'd hired Eugene Lee, a Broadway set designer who'd won a Tony the year before. The set Eugene had designed looked fantastic, but was going over budget. My solution was simple. I told Lorne to grab one end of the large, fragile model of the set sitting on his desk, I grabbed the other, and we carried it together from his office on the seventeenth floor (where it still is today) down the hall to the elevators and the fourteenth floor, and then transferred to another elevator to the executive offices, which were then on six. All the while, we ignored the strange glances we were getting from people wondering what we were carrying.

By that point, I'd gotten to know the security guard on the floor, as well as Herb Schlosser's secretary, and we just walked in and laid the model on his desk.

"Herb," I announced excitedly, "have a look at your new set!"

Schlosser may not have had the creative vision of Roone Arledge, but he had supported us every step of the way, and seemed to really enjoy the process himself. So as I figured, he couldn't have been more delighted to check out the set, alone in his office with just the two of us, asking questions and musing on its possibilities. And once Herb was excited, it was a lot easier for me to mention that, oh by the way, we'd need several thousand dollars more than we'd thought to build it. He immediately agreed. And nearly fifty years later, that set design, created by Eugene Lee, is still pretty much what audiences see when the show comes on the air.

While the set would be a constant for decades to come, the format we envisioned for the show would go through some evolution. When Lorne and I went back to Los Angeles to address a group of affiliates at the Century Plaza Hotel a few months before the premiere to sell them on the concept of this show, what got the biggest reaction from the middle-aged affiliate executives was hardly the promise of a live, edgy show with fresh sketches from a young, unknown cast. Instead, many in the room seemed most intrigued by the deal we'd made with Albert Brooks to produce short films that would appear on the show. That idea had originated a few months earlier, when Lorne and I had been driving in his convertible in Los Angeles and saw Albert next to us in traffic. He and Lorne knew each other, and we'd pulled over to talk and tell him about the show; out of that conversation came a deal to make half a dozen films. The affiliates seemed to like the concept, and they were also drawn to another one we'd developed with Jim Henson—like Lorne, a Bernie Brillstein client—to have a group of "grown-up" Muppets appear on the show. All in all, the affiliate meeting went well enough, and they were willing to take a chance on the new show.

More memorably, after we were done, we found out something else: We'd been summoned over to *The Tonight Show* compound at NBC's Burbank lot a half hour away. Johnny Carson himself wanted to meet us. It was quite a feeling heading over to see him, and when we got to his office, he was behind his desk, dressed in an undershirt and slacks, with Fred de Cordova, his longtime producer, also there. They had a few questions for us, mostly centered around our booking of the guest hosts. Essentially, it seemed like they were concerned about us stepping on their toes in terms of who they wanted for their show and when they wanted them. In that sense, it was encouraging; as much as ever before, the meeting was clear evidence of the level we were playing on if *The Tonight Show* was worried about who we were bringing on. We made clear that we'd give them fair warning of who our hosts would be, and if they had any issues, we'd change our plans.

Before we left, Johnny, who was businesslike but encouraging in the meeting, gave us a piece of advice.

"So you're going to be live in New York at eleven thirty, and then on tape three hours later at the same time in L.A.?" he asked.

We nodded.

"That's fine. But understand this: You have to think about this show, and build this show, for everyone else. For the rest of this country. Chicago, Des Moines, Kansas City. They're going to be watching at ten thirty. That's when they watch me. That's still prime time. A lot more people, a lot more televisions. If you can convince all of those folks, between Trenton and Reno, to keep their TVs on, that's how you'll be a success."

It might not have been the sexiest piece of advice you'd think of coming from a comedy icon like Johnny. But I never forgot it, in all my years to come producing late night TV.

CHAPTER 8

NBC's Saturday Night

Saturday Night Live premiered on September 20, 1975. The show was immediately panned by critics, and would only run eighteen episodes before being canceled forever, becoming just a footnote in the annals of television.

Fortunately, NBC's new show was destined for better things, to say the least. Confused?

You see, because they got on the air first, *Saturday Night Live with Howard Cosell*—ABC's version of the show, airing in prime time—took the title that we wanted. So, the original *Saturday Night Live* on NBC instead came on the air three weeks after Cosell, with the title *NBC's Saturday Night*. In the end, the shows had little in common, other than their names; the ABC show had much more of a Gilbert and Sullivan variety bent, while we were—as Lorne intended—totally original. Our first host, long in the works, was George Carlin. During rehearsals the week of the show, one of the stodgiest executives at NBC (and he had tough competition) came in and asked what Carlin was going to be wearing. To reflect the sensibility of the show, we'd planned to have him just wear a T-shirt. The network couldn't believe it—this was NBC, he had to wear a suit. And so, somewhat annoyingly, but with a slice of perfection, George Carlin walked onto Studio 8H just after 11:30 p.m. eastern time on October 11, 1975, wearing a three-piece suit—with a T-shirt underneath.

Beneath the bleachers that lined the set for the live audience, less than an hour earlier, we'd narrowly averted something of a labor crisis. NBC was insistent that no one go on the air without a signed contract, and the night of the show, we were still one short: John Belushi hadn't signed his deal. Even though we'd made it all the way to the premiere, there was still a part of John that worried that signing up for a TV show would hinder his career—and working without a manager or any real representation, he'd just procrastinated dealing with this last detail. While dress rehearsal went on, I worked every angle I could to try to get him to sign it. Finally, something I said must have clicked, or he just decided enough was enough, and John pointed at Bernie Brillstein standing ten feet away under those bleachers and said, "All right, I'll sign it, but only if that guy manages me." Bernie said fine, John had a manager, I had a signed contract, and a few moments later, he was in the cold open of the show.

The ninety minutes of television that ensued only partially represented the elements of what would define *SNL*. Carlin did four separate monologues—really four sets of stand-up—and there were two musical guests, Billy Preston and Janis Ian, who played two songs each. There was also an Albert Brooks film and an appearance by Andy Kaufman, the totally original mind who I'd first seen at Catch a Rising Star in New York the year before, and immediately had seen as someone who could be part of our premiere. Andy did one of his classic bits, singing along to the *Mighty Mouse* theme on a record player. The cast—the Not Ready for Prime Time Players (a friendly shot at Cosell's show, which had announced its cast as the "Primetime Players")—had a few highlights, most memorably the "Wolverine" cold open with Belushi playing a foreigner learning English, and specifically ridiculous, nonsensical English terms, from teacher Michael O'Donoghue. When O'Donoghue (and then Belushi, imitating him) keeled over as if he had a heart attack, Chevy Chase came out onto the set looking like a confused stage manager, and then uttered for the very first time those immortal words, "Live from New York, it's Saturday Night!"

One performer who didn't appear in the premiere that night was Billy Crystal, who had prepared a sketch to perform solo at the end of the show. The problem was that—as would be typical in the years to come—Lorne had, on purpose, approved too many sketches to fit in a ninety-minute show, the theory being that he could cut the ones that didn't work after the run-through on Friday night or the dress rehearsal on Saturday. It was a complicated puzzle to make work, and the day of the show, Billy's sketch got cut for time, and he was left to head home to Long Island on the train. It was disappointing, even if years later he'd have the last laugh, becoming an *SNL* legend.

Now if you watch that first show back, you'd probably be surprised how little sketch comedy was in it—though there was the first *Weekend Update*. But it was live, and it was funny, and we'd pulled it off. After we got off the air, I remember there being a real sense of achievement and celebration—people hugging and shaking hands, congratulating one another for making it. Then, in the control room, I got a call—the NBC switchboard had received a complaint from the Catholic Archdiocese of New York about Carlin's last monologue of the night, on religion. It was tame by today's standards, but George apparently had gone too far for the cardinal. I decided not to tell Lorne, and let him and everyone else go off and enjoy the first of hundreds of *SNL* after-parties, this one at a club called One Fifth Avenue. Instead, all hyped-up on adrenaline, and probably foolishly thinking I could solve the problem directly at one forty-five in the morning, I walked over to the back entrance of St. Patrick's Cathedral on Madison Avenue, only two blocks away, went to the back and right up to the door of the cardinal's residence. But just when I was about to press the doorbell, I thought better of it and decided to figure it out on Monday. It was the right move—considering it turned out the call had been a prank, and the cardinal had likely gone to sleep long before we came on the air.

In the weeks to come, I came up with a solution to NBC's concerns about more complaints lighting up the switchboard: when they weren't in a sketch, a few of the cast members, often the amazing Gilda, would go into a room off the control room and make calls to the switchboard using different voices, raving about how great the show was that night. They had fun with it, and it seemed to keep the stodgy executives who didn't get the show at bay.

That kind of stunt reflected what it was like to be working on the show in those early days. When it came on the air, I was just twenty-eight years old. Lorne was thirty-one. Nearly the entire cast and writing staff was under thirty. The crew—guys in their forties, fifties, and sixties who'd lived and worked through the live, variety, and playhouse theater era of television—fed off our enthusiasm, and became a part of the extended family that somehow made everything we wanted to do every week happen.

As for the material every week, the show's voice became clearer, funnier, and often more daring. Dealing with the network censors was a part of my job, trying along with Lorne to convince them that something was okay to air while also trying to manage the frustration of the writers, cast, and Lorne when something had to be tweaked. The instinct, always, was for the creatives to push back against the network, and sometimes, that became a great opportunity for material in itself; the audience understanding that part of the joke was taking it right up to, or even just past, the edge. Behind the scenes, though, every week was a struggle, and there was no single way to get the material we wanted on the air. It could be about rewriting a line just a bit, or changing a camera angle just so. It could be about going up the byzantine chain of different executives in the NBC Standards department, all of whom had their own standards, and many of whom could be surprisingly reasonable and supportive. Occasionally, it could just be about going ahead with what we wanted to in the live show, and begging for forgiveness afterward. Through it all, Lorne became maybe the best producer at dealing with censors in television history.

As the executive in charge, it was probably inevitable that I'd find myself caught between the creative and business sides of the show—though one of the first times that happened ended up having a pretty great comedic reward. In the first show, one of the sketches that bombed featured Belushi and a few others dressed as bees, in costumes that took up a significant piece of that part of the budget. As the show was written the next week, the bees were nowhere to be seen in the list of sketches, which concerned my executive side; the whole reason we'd paid for the expensive bee costumes was because they were supposed to be a recurring bit. I worried aloud to Lorne that the costumes would go to waste; this was going to be a problem if it kept happening. Not to worry, he told me—and sure enough, in that second show, the bees showed up, with the host, Paul Simon, complaining, "Wait a second, these guys weren't funny last week, why are they here again?" And they'd be back the next week, too, with Rob Reiner as host, in a sketch that featured Reiner and Penny Marshall in a restaurant, the bees showing up, and Reiner breaking the fourth wall and complaining about these totally unfunny bees, who had been terrible in their first two appearances, being alongside him. John Belushi, speaking for the bees, responded by complaining that he and the rest of the cast didn't have writers like Norman Lear on *All in the Family*, which got huge laughs. It was the first of many instances of the show going meta—joking about the joke itself.

The hosts during those first several weeks included Reiner, Candice Bergen (twice), Lily Tomlin, and then, in mid-December, Richard Pryor. A little more than a year after I'd been unable to hire him to star in the show, he was the guest host. Richard had actually called me after his lawyer had turned me down, saying that if he ever did television, he'd do it with us. And though it wasn't easy for our bookers to pin him down, they did a great job of getting him for our seventh show. That week, the network insisted, for the first time, on a seven-second delay in case Richard used a word not fit for television. Richard was hilarious that night (I guess for one night, at least, he could be Richard Pryor on network television), the delay wasn't needed, and, predictably, the episode got our best ratings of the season.

The show's format was continuing to evolve as the writers found their voice, and a sense of what would work for TV. In those early days, sketches would come in that involved three or four different setups, all kinds of different characters, and any number of elements that simply wouldn't be possible in a live TV show. So it was a challenge to produce and revise enough material for Saturday nights. Albert's films (there would be eight of them in all) were often some of the funniest stuff on the show—if also, as I recall, very expensive. The concepts ranged widely— from spoofs of news stories like a blind New York City cabdriver; to mockeries of midseason replacement shows on NBC; to one that ran thirteen minutes featuring Albert "following his dreams" and becoming a heart surgeon for a day. It was great, even if Lorne almost refused to run it because it ran so long; only Rob Reiner, hosting that week, convinced him to put it on the air. The Muppet sketches from Jim Henson, on the other hand, were a tougher fit; as Michael O'Donoghue complained, "I don't write for felt." Together, though, they're each part of a kind of "pre-history" for SNL.

Then came the show's break for Christmas. Over the few weeks off, Lorne convinced Chevy and O'Donoghue to stay in New York. They worked right through the holiday, writing and writing, day and night, and building for the first time a stockpile of sketches they could use to get ahead of the punishing weekly schedule. Those few weeks were pivotal and productive. The first show of 1976, hosted by Elliott Gould, with the Canadian singer Anne Murray as the musical guest, was the first that really felt like Saturday Night Live. There was still an Albert Brooks film, his last one as it turned out, but the show was now truly an ensemble comedy, with the cast front and center. Sure enough, that episode would be submitted for the Emmy Award the following year for best writing in a variety series, one of the remarkable three Emmys the show won in its first season, with Davey Wilson winning for directing and, most important of all, Lorne being honored for producing the best comedy/variety series in all of television.

The show was thriving in every which way. After initially only issuing a half-review of the second episode (in which, outrageously, the reviewer admitted that he'd missed the start of the show because his Saturday night dinner had run long), the *New York Times* had given *SNL* a glowing rave on Sunday of Thanksgiving weekend, calling it "the most important and most exciting development in television comedy since *Your Show of Shows.*" The format had worked itself out, with the best material coming in the first half hour, carrying to the musical guest and then *Weekend Update*—always crisply written by Chevy and Herb Sargent, always highly anticipated by the audience, airing just after midnight to keep viewers awake, and the ratings as high as possible as the night went on.

The cast was on the cover of magazines, with Chevy becoming the biggest star, in large part because, as the host of *Update*, he went by his own distinctive name ("I'm Chevy Chase, and you're not," he introduced himself), and essentially had his own weekly monologue—really, a second monologue for the show. Belushi was second, with his early classic sketches like "Samurai Man" always getting huge laughs, including one when he nearly decapitated guest host Buck Henry with his sword. "He hit him!" I can still remember someone saying from the front of the control room. And a few seconds later, sure enough, on the monitors, we could see blood dribbling down Buck's face. Ever a gamer, he'd continue the rest of the show bandaged, leading the rest of the cast to don bandages in hilarious solidarity as the night went on.

More than anything else, the show was a realization of the vision Lorne had expressed to me when we'd first met. It was written in the language of a new generation—offering a commentary through laughs of the world seen through fresh eyes. It was the opposite of predictable, and the epitome of original.

SNL's cultural currency grew so much so quickly that in mid-April, Ron Nessen, then the White House press secretary, came to New York to be the host. Early that week, Lorne, Chevy, and I went to Washington to tape a cold open with President Ford, who Chevy had lampooned, playfully, in his signature bits, poking fun at Ford's predilection for clumsiness (despite being probably the greatest athlete in the history of the American presidency) with his classic prat-falls.

The president was a great sport—we just needed three lines from him—the classic "Live from New York, it's Saturday Night" that followed the cold open, an introduction of Nessen right before the monologue after credits, and then, the biggest and easiest line, "I'm Gerald Ford, and you're not," to play against Chevy's signature line. As we prepped him, I couldn't help but think how surreal it was that barely eighteen months after my taking the job at NBC, here we were in the White House with the leader of the free world.

It took a few takes to get him to say it right, but with Lorne directing, it was pretty painless. Then, in a twist you almost couldn't make up, just as we wrapped taping, he got up from his chair in the Cabinet Room just outside the Oval Office without disconnecting his microphone and pulled down one of our cameras in the process.

Mixed in with the success of the show was, undeniably, a wildness that embodied, even defined, everything behind the scenes. Putting a ninety-minute live comedy show together every seven days was an almost impossible task to complete. That weekly achievement was one of the things that endeared SNL to its audience, not only because the audience appreciated the effort but also because the audience could imagine what went into making it all happen. Combine the feverish intensity with the young cast and, sure, you had a good deal of drugs, sex, and whatever else you could imagine unfolding everywhere from 30 Rock to the after-parties every week.

Drugs had never been my thing, but for the cast and writers, whether they turned to it all to spur creativity, deal with the pressure, or somewhere in between, it was, as much as anything else, part of the culture that this new generation of comedic minds embodied. As the bridge from NBC to the show, as always, I did whatever I could to keep it all afloat. Some of the solutions were incredibly simple. For example, with NBC's executive offices on the sixth floor of 30 Rock, from the beginning, I made sure to have our show's offices on a much higher floor that was accessed through a different elevator bank in the lobby. And so, the likes of John Belushi and Michael O'Donoghue could enter the building and head up to the seventeenth floor, Monday through Saturday, without incident.

Then there were more delicate dances to get through. Like the time in those early months when I got word that that same aging talent relations executive who just couldn't understand the show had met with Bert Convy, the actor and game show host, and offered him a spot hosting *SNL* later in the first season. Convy didn't fit the profile at all for what Lorne was looking for, and I had to call Michael Ovitz, Convy's agent, to find a graceful way out of it. Then, just a week after that, it happened again—though this time with Buck Henry, which presented a different situation, since Buck did have a match with the show's sensibilities. But I knew Lorne would nonetheless hardly take well to NBC higher-ups telling him who should host his show. The solution was to connect with Buck myself, and have him come in to meet with me and Herb Sargent, who he'd known for years in the New York comedy writing scene. Herb and I connected Buck with Lorne, and Buck, who'd actually been living in England and hadn't yet seen the show, would go on to become an *SNL* legend, and host the show twice that first season.

Sometime in the spring, in the midst of the show's burgeoning popularity, Lorne brought up an idea. By now, *Saturday Night Live with Howard Cosell* was canceled and off the air. What if he sent Roone a lighthearted letter, asking him for our title back?

My old boss was happy to oblige.

CHAPTER 9

Go West

As fun as it was to celebrate the success of the first season of *SNL*, by its halfway point, I was already no longer working on the show full-time. The fact that I moved on pretty quickly from developing the show to other things was probably inevitable; ultimately, the job that Herb Schlosser had tasked me with was finding a show, and once it lifted off into success, there were always going to be other new projects to tend to. Nevertheless, leaving the show so quickly wasn't something I was ever actively looking to do. And my unexpected departure had its roots in the mercurial nature of the genius I'd brought on to make the series happen, and the corporate politics that had quickly engulfed our success.

It started with just the fourth show. That night, Candy Bergen's first time hosting, there was a technical breakdown when an engineer in NBC's master control room, not realizing that a parody commercial was in fact a parody, had cut out of it for a local break. Afterward, Lorne lost it, ranting and screaming, and announcing that he quit as he stormed out of 8H. I didn't see him lose it, but when I heard about the fit, I didn't think too much of it. Over the course of the year we'd been working together, there had actually been plenty of times where he'd threatened to leave; it had become almost a code for him reaching his limit with, as he saw it, inflexibility or unreasonableness from stodgy network executives. In this case, I absolutely understood his frustration, if not the extremity of his reaction, but figured we'd get to the bottom of it, and start anew on Monday once the postshow emotions had cooled. After all, we were just getting started.

Instead, that Monday afternoon, I got a call from Bernie Brillstein, confirming that Lorne meant it this time—he was done. If I was still not a hundred percent convinced we'd never see him again, I also knew we had a show to produce, with Robert Klein ready to host. So I called all the writers, explained the situation, and said everyone just had to keep on working and get set for the next Saturday night.

Then on Wednesday, I got a call from a senior NBC executive telling me that Lorne was coming back, but that I was no longer the top executive responsible for the day-to-day operations of the show and its budget. I would still be involved, but not in charge.

It was ridiculous; the technical snafu had had nothing to do with me, or anyone in *SNL*'s control room. Still, I was told, NBC was going to announce the next morning that I was being promoted to vice president, which would make me—as they would include conspicuously in the announcement—at age twenty-eight, the youngest vice president in the entire history of the National Broadcasting Company, going back to the RCA days in the 1930s.

I was smart enough to know there was no way out of the box they were building for me, but to have my job diminished was still a blow. And looking back, as much as it felt sudden in the moment, the change was the result of months of machinations behind the scenes that had begun as soon as *SNL* had shown itself to be a success. All those executives who had been unable to see the show's potential, and unwilling to do anything to help us as we tried to get it on the air—once it did, and once it became nothing less than the hottest show on the entire network, they'd quickly reversed course and done whatever they could to get involved. Within barely a month, whether they were suggesting hosts or musical acts, or finding paths more arcane, people who'd had no involvement in the show were inserting themselves into its hierarchy, and at some point, I was destined to be cast aside in the process.

The reality was that I didn't really go anywhere; I stayed very close to the show all the way through the first season and halfway into the second. But while we continued to work closely together, my relationship with Lorne had undeniably changed, and gotten more complicated. After working so closely building the foundation of the show, there was no doubt that the swamp of figures at NBC we both resented so much had wedged their way between us. Maybe Lorne thought that fighting the network alone would be better than having me help him out. Maybe he had no say, and it all happened above his head. I didn't press the issue then, and too much time has passed to press it now. Besides, there would be a lot more twists and turns to our shared story and shared lives—at *Saturday Night Live* and beyond—in the years ahead.

The episode was also my first real experience with the strange ways the entertainment world could work. But I'd have to get used to it, because the impact of me moving off *Saturday Night Live* full-time was that I'd be spending more time in L.A., working as the executive in charge of *The Tomorrow Show* with Tom Snyder, the talk show that followed Johnny Carson, as well as *The Midnight Special*, the concert show that aired late on Friday nights and was created and produced by Burt Sugarman, a terrific character who'd become a great friend.

By Halloween 1976, about a quarter of the way through the second season of *SNL*, the appeal of staying involved with the show while spending half my time in L.A. dealing with other series had worn off, and I moved full-time to California. Though, if I was feeling a little lonely and let down by the way everything had worked out, I quickly got a lifeline to go back to the world I'd left behind just two and a half years earlier.

No more than twenty-four hours after I landed in L.A.—taking a flight with Chevy Chase, whose last show before heading off to a movie career coincided with mine—I got a call from Roone. He'd just landed in Los Angeles from an ABC affiliate meeting in Hawaii and wanted to talk to me. I went over to his bungalow at the Beverly Hills Hotel, and he explained that he'd gotten the job he'd long wanted; he'd been appointed president of ABC News in addition to Sports. It wasn't a surprise; I'll never forget being with Roone in the Watergate days when the Saturday Night Massacre took place, and him eviscerating the ABC News coverage, explaining how he'd do it better. Now he had the job, and he was asking me if I wanted to come back and be his number two.

We talked it over all night, but in the end I decided that for all the tumult and unknowns of my situation at NBC, it didn't make sense to go backward and return to working for Roone. Even if heading back to New York, and back to ABC, felt safe, I hadn't quite lost my faith in what could come next.

My new official title at NBC was Vice President of Specials, Variety, and Comedy. It was a new role, made up especially for me. I made a deal with Dick Clark for a series of music specials. I worked with my old friend Don Ohlmeyer, creating a show called *US Against the World*, similar to *Battle of the Network Stars*, featuring celebrities from the U.S., England, and everywhere else competing in various athletic competitions. With *The Tomorrow Show* and *The Midnight Special*, I was in charge of all of NBC's West Coast late night operation, save for *The Tonight Show*, though I'd frequently go over to watch Carson and got to know him better and better. Johnny was famously shy, but if he liked and respected you, he could be, as you'd expect, loads of fun to hang out with on the set. One time, in fact, I was backstage when he got into a whipped cream fight with Burt Reynolds with the cameras rolling. When Johnny ran back to get some more supply, I handed it right to him.

Meanwhile, though *Saturday Night Live* had given NBC a huge hit in late night, the network's prime-time comedy lineup was a mess. By the summer of 1977, the cupboard of funny shows was just about completely bare, and I needed to make a move to restock it. A few years earlier, I'd met with a young guy in New York who'd been a year behind me at Yale, and who'd pitched himself as a sketch writer who could work on *Saturday Night Live*. The sketches weren't too good, and I'd sent the writer back to Chicago, where he was working in the promotions department at the ABC-owned station there. But I'd never forgotten his enthusiasm, and we'd stayed in touch as he'd gotten promoted to a job in programming and moved to work in ABC's network offices in L.A. Now, that summer, I hired Brandon Tartikoff to come to NBC to run comedy development. My instincts were right: not only was Brandon terrific at the job, working at my right arm, but within just a few weeks, he became my best friend in Los Angeles.

Like me, Brandon was originally an East Coast guy, having grown up on Long Island. As a teenager, he'd formed a double-play tandem with future rock star Huey Lewis on the baseball team at the Lawrenceville School, a prep school in New Jersey. Now as a young executive, Brandon had the passion—and patience and tolerance—to deal with the Hollywood-scripted development process. He loved meeting with writers, and encouraging and tweaking their good ideas. Even more than that, Brandon was a natural when he met with a writer whose idea he was turning down. He was never dismissive, and didn't focus on the rejection; rather, he made a real effort to talk about how an idea could be improved, or someday resurrected. As a result, writers wouldn't get frustrated with Brandon—much to the contrary, they couldn't wait to go back to him with other pitches. Over the many years to come, that would mean that the best writers always brought him their best ideas. Then, and forever more, there was virtually no one who didn't love Brandon, and I was the biggest member of his fan club. Hiring him was the most important move I made in that job. And add to that the friend for life I got out of the deal; we were inseparable, both in the office and on weekends, hanging out at my house in Mandeville Canyon or the one he shared with his wonderful wife, Lilly, nearby.

In the spring of 1978, we got a new boss, as Fred Silverman was hired as NBC's president and CEO to replace Herb Schlosser, who'd been bumped up to a bigger job at RCA. Silverman had a well-earned reputation as a programming wizard: he'd created a collection of hits at CBS in the early seventies including *All in the Family*, *The Mary Tyler Moore Show*, and *M*A*S*H*, and then promptly moved to ABC, where as president of entertainment, he'd lifted the network to the top of the ratings with shows like *Charlie's Angels* and *Laverne & Shirley*. Now the expectation was that he might do the same at NBC. But it wouldn't turn out so well.

Fred came for a whirlwind set of meetings in our offices in Burbank, and in a span of three days, immediately ordered something like twenty comedy pilots and another ten variety pilots, a healthy amount that was all well and good—except he wanted them all developed and executed for that November. I didn't know Fred well at all, but if I'd learned anything, it was that there was no better way to deal with a boss than honestly.

"I have nothing but respect for your track record, sir," I said to him in one meeting, "and am under no illusions that I have anything close to your years of experience. But you know as well as I do that no established comedy and drama producer is available to create and turn around a pilot this quickly. They're all busy putting together the shows they've already sold! And even if they are available, none will agree to put on shows with that accelerated schedule."

Silverman wouldn't hear anything of it, and insisted we find a way to make it work. But as we launched into a frenzy to get his orders accomplished, our relationship would quickly deteriorate further.

That summer, among the rushed productions on his misbegotten agenda was a variety show featuring two singers from Japan who were sensations at home, and a comedian named Jeff Altman. Silverman had a friend in the record business who'd raved about the singers but neglected to tell him one key detail: neither could speak a word of English. I ordered the show because I had to, but after watching a day or two of disastrous rehearsals, I shut it down. There was no way we could go forward. That quickly got back to Silverman at his office in New York, and as he was wont to do, he lost it. There were a few other similar snafus in the weeks to come with more shows headed for failure, and it was clear something had to give. After working for Roone, and then succeeding with *SNL*, I had by now plenty of confidence that I knew what I was doing—and that blindly executing Silverman's crazy orders would only make things worse. That said, I also knew the alternative could be painful as well.

I was sitting in my office one morning when Brandon popped his head in.

"You're going to hear something in a few minutes that you won't like," he said. "I'm not going to tell you what it is, but I'll be waiting outside in the parking lot in my car for you if you want to talk about it afterwards."

Sure enough, a few minutes later, I got called down to another office, where I was told that Silverman had promoted Brandon, who he'd first gotten to know from their days together at ABC, over my head as the new head of NBC on the West Coast. They asked if I still wanted to stay, even if in effect I'd been demoted beneath my former number two, not to mention best friend. I said I'd think about it.

I went straight out the doors, hopped in Brandon's car, and we drove away to talk things through. We were probably gone for six hours, trying to make sense of what had happened. Immediately, being the ultimate mensch that he was, Brandon said that we could both quit and start our own production company together, or he would just tell them he wasn't going to accept the promotion. I told him there was no way he was going to do that; this was a great thing for him, and we were going to figure it out. In the end, we resolved that Brandon would go back and accept the job, but he'd insist that they had to draw up a new contract for me, and Silverman had to agree to have a face-to-face meeting with me to discuss his reasons for the change. (Which did happen, and was one of the more uncomfortable, and fruitless, twenty-minute meetings of my career.)

Still, what could have been a much more uncomfortable situation between Brandon and me was never an issue; that's how strong our friendship was. Regardless, I think I knew my days were numbered at NBC, and sure enough, at the beginning of 1979, I was summoned to New York for another meeting with Silverman—only to be pulled into the office of another executive, who actually took care of the task of formally firing me.

When I got back to L.A., again Brandon offered to leave with me, and again I told him he had to stay; he was barely thirty years old, and even with Silverman as his boss, he had a chance to build NBC's entertainment portfolio, an incredible opportunity. Then, at the end of the week, the administrative people came back with a terrible offer to barely pay out any of my contract. I refused—and that's when things got really weird.

They told me that I could have an office for the time being, even though I no longer had a job. So I went into that office for a few days, and then was told to go to another office, which had no furniture at all—just a phone sitting on the floor. It was clear that in their own passive-aggressive way, they were trying to basically wait me out until I agreed to their low-ball buyout offer. But I wasn't going anywhere. I swiped a pillow from someone else's office to use to lean against the wall, and sat down on the floor and started making calls. For a week, this went on, with different actors, actresses, and independent producers stopping in to say hi after their meetings with the woman who'd replaced me, oddly marveling at the bizarre limbo in which I found myself.

Finally, about two weeks into this craziness, Ron Howard came into the building for some meetings. I'd gotten to know Ron, who at that point had been a star for years on ABC's *Happy Days*, by going over to hang out at the set occasionally—with a great cast and crew, it was always a fun, happy place to visit. Then Ron had set up a deal to direct some TV movies and specials on NBC as he transitioned to working primarily behind the camera, and we'd had some great meetings talking about ideas. But no one had told Ron that I'd been fired, or at least put on the cooler, so that day, he innocently asked a few people where I was when he couldn't find my office, and eventually located me, literally on the floor. We'd built up a nice relationship in the short time we'd been working together, and Ron was courteous enough not to ask why I was on the floor; instead, he just sat down next to me. At one point, a senior executive poked their head inside, offering to escort Ron out, but Ron made it clear, amicably, that he was here to meet with me. Not long after, another executive poked his head in the door and asked if I could step outside to talk to him. There was a new deal on the table: the network would pay out my contract in full.

The next day, I began what Brandon affectionately termed "nine months of back-packing in my Porsche." I'd been in the business, working nonstop, since I'd been in college. I was still getting paid. There was no rush to jump into another job—particularly a corporate job, which, as I'd learned, could put me at the mercy of someone like Fred Silverman.

Not more than a few weeks into my break, I decided to see if I could drive from the Beverly Hills Hotel to the St. Francis Hotel in San Francisco in less than five hours—a crazy idea that I'm lucky didn't end with me in a heap of metal alongside the road. On Route 5, somewhere north of the Bakersfield cutoff, I came up on a Volkswagen absolutely flying up the highway. I passed it on the right, but a second later, it was back alongside me, and weirder than that, as I looked inside, I couldn't see anyone driving it. We were both going over a hundred miles an hour, and soon, the Volkswagen-without-a-driver began honking at me. Just as I wondered if I was hallucinating, a face leaned forward, looking over at me through an open window. It was, improbably, a familiar face and one of the greatest athletes in history: Bill Russell, smiling widely, his signature cackle in full effect. Ten years after we'd become friends during my time as a production assistant on NBA games, he still recognized me, going a hundred miles an hour up Route 5.

We pulled over by the side of the road and caught up as cars whizzed by at high speed.

"How were you even able to keep up with me in that little car?" I exclaimed.

"Because of what's inside," he said, pointing at the hood. "Check it out—it's got a Porsche engine. I got it custom-installed in L.A."

He also showed me the special driver's seat he'd had installed to accommodate the long legs on his six-foot-ten frame, effectively letting him drive it from the back, and making it look like it was driverless as he made his way home up north.

We had a few more laughs by the side of the road, and then parted ways. The stop meant I wasn't going to make it to San Francisco in less than five hours. But the trip served as a reminder, then and now, that you never, ever know what part of yesterday might appear in your story on the road ahead.

CHAPTER 10

Live Again

"Would you do it?"

Sitting side by side on the patio outside my house at the top of Mandeville Canyon and turning my head to look right at him, I knew Brandon Tartikoff well enough to know he was very serious. He wanted to know if I'd come back to NBC in New York and try to save *Saturday Night Live*.

It was January 1981. About eight months had passed since Lorne, exhausted after steering *SNL* for five seasons, had decided to leave the show. He'd departed on terrible terms with NBC—not with Brandon, mind you, but, almost too predictably (like me), with Fred Silverman. The show's collective feud with Silverman had hit a peak late in the 1979–'80 season, when the show had lampooned him in a brutal Al Franken sketch called "A Limo for a Lame-O." Leaving 30 Rock late every night for months, Franken had always seen a limousine waiting outside for Silverman, idling in front of the building for hours, unused. The constant sight came to annoy him to no end. Being Franken, he'd hold nothing back, and go right up to the driver.

"How about you just drive me home, and then come back for him?" he'd ask.

The driver, not surprisingly, would turn him down. So instead, Al wrote a sketch making fun of the premise of the executive who had a car at his beck and call—which absolutely enraged Silverman, who watched it live at home. Franken couldn't have cared less; the entire cast and writing staff were following Lorne out the door after the last episode. They were just as burned out as Lorne was, and uninterested in taking on the challenge of trying to keep the show successful without him.

In response, Silverman had personally decided to promote Jean Doumanian to become the show's producer. Jean was the show's talent booker; her job had been working for Lorne to book the host and musical acts each week. It was a big job, but not a creative job, and besides, with all the cast and writers leaving, she was destined to be working with second-level talent. It was no way to put together a winning show. Which made it no surprise when the "new *SNL*" didn't measure up.

By the end of 1980, the show—with a replacement cast, and all new writers—was struggling badly. The cast, headlined by forgotten names deeply in the shadows of the original departed stars, were backed up by writers whose concepts were caught between trying to imitate what the old staff had done and struggling to come up with new concepts that were original, let alone funny. At its best, it was plagued by obvious attempts for easy laughs; at its worst were ethnic and racial jokes with no purpose. "Whatever Happened to TV's 'Saturday Night Live'?" read the headline of a scathing *New York Times* review, going on to note that "the key missing ingredient was the very quality that made the old show so special: an innovative vision." The *Washington Post* said the show had "no compensating satirical edge," and "was just haplessly pointless tastelessness."

But for all those problems, NBC couldn't just let the show die away. Regardless of Silverman's lack of respect for Lorne, and lack of respect for his talent, *SNL* had been a landmark success for the network, and losing it would be a dark mark on Silverman's ever-diminishing résumé. And then of course, there was Brandon, who was a different matter entirely. Remember, he'd once dreamed of writing for the show—but even more than that, he cared about creative television, and was always in love with its possibilities.

Even after I'd left NBC, Brandon and I had stayed extremely close, keeping our routine of spending weekends together, especially when he moved to New York for his job but frequently came back to the West Coast for meetings and stayed in my house. So I'd heard plenty about the problems at *SNL*, and offered bits of advice where I could. But on this day in early 1981, the issue had taken on a new urgency, and a new relevance to me.

"What if you produced the show yourself?" Brandon was saying to me. "You take over, complete control, and see if you can save this thing."

After my several months of wandering up and down the West Coast—but really more importantly catching my breath after a wild first ten years of my career—I'd been really happy with the transition I'd made into independent production. For the first time in my professional life, I wasn't in a hurry. There was time to figure out what came next. Burt Sugarman had hired me to produce the show that I'd previously overseen for NBC, *The Midnight Special*, which was fun. Producing the show's weekly television concerts kept me in late night, and also in the music world, which I enjoyed. I'd produced a handful of other variety specials with Burt, and had found myself comfortable not being in the executive suite. After my quick rise, I'd made a discovery: I could make money and have fun without having a boss in the corner office. It was a very freeing idea.

But the idea of producing *Saturday Night Live*, and trying to keep the show alive, was hard to get out of my head. I'd be in charge, and it was a chance to produce, not simply return to being an executive.

I didn't give Brandon a straight answer that day, but we'd keep talking about the idea over a number of weeks, in a series of phone conversations and get-togethers.

"The way I see it," he said to me bluntly at one point, "there are only two people who can save the show—you or Lorne. And since Lorne won't come back, you're our only shot."

I was obviously concerned about going back to work—even indirectly—for Silverman, but Brandon, one of the greatest salesmen in TV history, had convinced even him of the potential of the idea. And so, after getting more and more intrigued by it, in early March, I agreed to go to New York, quietly, without anyone knowing. I'd meet with Silverman, but also do something else: sit in a back office at 30 Rock, nowhere near the studio, without anyone seeing me, and quietly watch rehearsals on an internal video feed over the course of a few days leading up to the show. Eavesdropping on the active creative process would give me a sense of the quality of the writing, and the abilities of the cast. With a copy of the script, I could see what on paper got laughs, and what was improvised dialogue. And overall, I'd see not just what was wrong with the show but the roots of what might signal hope for a turnaround.

What I saw overall wasn't promising. Just a few weeks earlier, the signature low of the "new" *SNL* had come when Charles Rocket had said "fuck" in a sketch, enraging executives. The show was clearly too often trying to imitate its previous incarnation; straining to be original and edgy when it just wasn't. Still, despite all that, I couldn't deny the undeniable excitement of the challenge potentially in front of me. Since I'd left NBC, sure, I'd been having fun and enjoying success—but the stakes weren't all that high. If my career had taught me anything, it was that the only way to achieve something fantastic was to take big chances. The adrenaline was pumping through my veins again. The sense of what could be was inescapable and intoxicating.

Brandon and I talked late into the night after that episode of *SNL* aired, and the next day, the conversation continued with my meeting with Silverman over at his sprawling apartment on Central Park West. No matter how much faith and trust I had in Brandon, I wasn't going to sign on until I saw Silverman and got him to agree on a few key terms to me taking the job.

We were way past any awkwardness when I arrived; we both knew how we felt about each other, which almost made it easier to be blunt as we spoke on couches facing one another in his living room.

"We need to take the show off the air for six weeks," I told him. "We need time to change things. Hire new cast members, and definitely find some new writers."

It was the only way to give the show even a prayer. Silverman blanched.

"We can't take the show off the air in the middle of the season! That's crazy. It'll lose its audience, and people will forget about it."

"No, they won't," I calmly explained to him. "We'll put on reruns that people remember, and it'll actually warm the time period up again. It'll remind the audience what the show was."

We argued throughout the afternoon, and eventually he came around—though in typical fashion, at the last second, he had to feel like he won the argument, and made the break five weeks, not six.

I had another surprise for him, too: I asked for a pretty low salary, considering the job. I could tell he saw a catch coming.

"All I want is a simple reward for succeeding," I said. "For every year I keep *Saturday Night Live* on the air, I get a pilot commitment that can lead to a series that I will own."

I'd gotten the idea from a few friends. A deal like that meant that the network would back the production of another show I could create independently. If I was going to take a risk, I might as well do everything I could to bet on myself, and ensure the payoff was as big as possible.

Silverman was fine agreeing to that. Which left just one more thing to do: I wasn't going to officially sign a deal until I could talk to Lorne. In my head, the only way the show could not just continue, but recapture its success, was if Lorne wanted it to. He had to be on board with me taking over, and he had to be on board with me approaching the only people who could save the show—the old writers. They wouldn't come back unless they knew Lorne was okay with it.

To his credit, Silverman was okay with this when I told him, even though those writers had completely roasted him just a few months earlier. I guess even the most thin-skinned executives could have a short memory. I had called Lorne when I arrived in New York to let him know I was in town, and after I left the meeting with Silverman, I called him again to let him know I wanted to stop by. He lived only a few blocks away from Silverman on Central Park West, and I walked over to his place, where we'd spend the rest of the night talking.

It had been a little more than six years since we'd first met. For all the twists and turns in our relationship since then, our connection and understanding of one another was still strong. Lorne had gone into independent production since leaving the show, but even then, at just thirty-five years old, *SNL* was already his legacy. He was—at least for the foreseeable future—done with the show, but now the question was: Did he want the show to live? And did he agree that if anyone was going to revive it, it made sense in a lot of ways that I should be the one to try?

We talked about the pluses and minuses of me taking the job, what I was up against, and what I'd need to do to succeed. It was, like so many of our conversations years earlier, hours and hours long. We talked about NBC, and the support I'd need—creatively, and financially, from Brandon; the budget that Jean had been working with had been shrunk substantially. We talked about writers that I should hire, and the ones he knew who would jump at the opportunity to return to the show. In the end, I left his apartment just as dawn broke on that Monday morning knowing that he had, in effect, blessed it. The word would soon go out to agents and managers that he was okay with his old staff coming back, and with that staff now refreshed and eager to get back to work, the calls started coming in before we even announced that I was coming back to produce the show.

The next five weeks would be a whirlwind. Hiring back writers, including, as Lorne encouraged me to, Michael O'Donoghue, hunting down new cast members like Tony Rosato and Tim Kazurinsky, doing whatever I could to inject as much creativity back into the staff as possible. One of the best memories was just a few days into my return to 30 Rock, when a few visitors swung by. Dan Aykroyd and John Belushi had been in Asia traveling together, and when they landed, had picked up a newspaper, read that I was back, and decided to come right in for a visit. It was good to be among old friends again. I told John I was headed to Chicago the next week, and he ended up recommending some potential cast members, including Kazurinsky, who I hired on the spot after meeting him.

Five weeks later, I'd be back in Studio 8H, getting ready to bring the show back on the air. The Friday before my first show, as we were going through rehearsals, I had an unexpected visitor: Lorne's girlfriend. She was carrying a small box and told me Lorne wanted me to have something for the next night. When I opened it, I found the small duck pin that he'd worn on his lapel as a good-luck charm for every *SNL* show he'd ever produced.

Then and now, Lorne Michaels was far from a sentimental guy. As much as anything he'd said in his apartment, the symbol of that gift revealed just how much the show meant to him, and, after everything we'd been through, how much our relationship still meant to him. And whether it was the duck pin or not, three huge strokes of luck were headed my way.

One of them would come quickly, giving me more time to try to keep fixing the show.

The other would end up as the most significant thing to happen in my life, ever.

The third, of course, was Eddie Murphy.

CHAPTER 11

Eddie

The first thing the audience saw in our first show back was a familiar face: Chevy Chase, wandering under the bleachers in Studio 8H, looking for recognizable signs of what he'd left behind years earlier. He heard a rustling in a trash can, and found Mr. Bill, the tiny clay figurine of the show's old short films, sitting there. The two "reminisced" about the old days, and we were off and running. Chevy wasn't the host of that first show per se—the staff wasn't ready to put together enough material for an outsider—but he was as close to one as we'd have, also hosting *Weekend Update* that night. There was a cameo from Al Franken, too, announcing that he was going to host the next week. And yet, it was all thankfully not meant to be.

Literally at midnight on Sunday, April 12, in the middle of the show, a national Writers Guild strike that had long been feared began, meaning that we wouldn't be able to produce the show the next week, or at all until the labor dispute was resolved. And in the days to come, as it became apparent the strike would be an extensive one—ultimately three months—we knew our season was over. While NBC might not have been happy, it was a gift from the television gods as far as I was concerned— I now had time to fully rebuild the writing staff and recast the show.

I'd make some good decisions, and some bad ones. Lorne had thought it would work to bring back Michael O'Donoghue as head writer. But *SNL*'s Prince of Darkness had a nihilistic vision of the task in front of him—he openly proclaimed to me that his real fantasy was to "kill the show" and give it a Viking funeral; in essence, put together something so unairable that NBC would have no choice but to cancel it. Alas, he also knew he needed a job, and agreed to come on, but as all that background indicates, he was as unhinged as ever. He made a performance out of the first writers meeting he led, spray-painting the word "*DANGER*" all over the wall, in reference to what he thought the show had been lacking in his absence. For all Michael's talent, it was never going to work, and I'd have to fire him later in the fall.

Michael leaving meant promoting Bob Tischler to head writer. Bob—who before his time on *SNL* had been one of the top record producers in comedy—would guide the staff for the next several years. For starters, unlike Michael, Bob wanted the show to succeed, but more than that, he was exactly the leader the writers' room needed—steady, calm, and respected. I also hurried to scour the comedy world for new cast members, and hired two new women, Christine Ebersole and Mary Gross.

But on top of the key personnel changes, the biggest item on the agenda was to take the show back to its basics: focusing on getting the funniest sketches into the first half hour. Johnny Carson's advice still applied. The beginning of late night was 10:30 p.m. central time and 9:30 in the mountains—between Trenton and Reno. There, a lot of people were still up when the show started, and if you got them to keep watching, you'd win. So the goal was to put together a great first half hour, capped off by a strong *Weekend Update* segment—in effect, as it had always been, a second monologue—just after midnight. Just like that, you'd be almost halfway through the show with a big audience, and you could keep millions of people awake longer and longer.

Was it that simple and easy? Yes—but only because of the secret weapon I'd been gifted.

Sitting in 30 Rock before I even took the job, those first few days when I'd snuck into the building to watch the feed of rehearsals and evaluate the state of the show, it hardly took a producing genius to see that Eddie Murphy was the funniest person in the cast. I had the scripts in front of me as I watched the monitor so I could see which performers were getting hamstrung by poor material, or which ones were failing good material. In Eddie's case, what I saw was how he could take whatever material he got and find a way to make it funny—almost regardless of its quality.

Eddie was still only a few weeks shy of twenty years old when I saw him, but an absolutely mesmerizing talent—and one of only a few cast members I knew I had to keep on. He'd started the season as a "featured player" in the cast—a designation for junior members who had been instituted a few years earlier—and had been promoted to full cast member about ten episodes in. Then, once I took the job and got to see him work, I saw even more how in every which way, not just in front of the camera but behind the scenes, Eddie was a natural. The characters he created were completely original, and yet, as he performed them, there was always a sly wink directed at the audience, letting them know he was having as much fun as they were. He had a twinkle in his eye, and an ability to keep everyone guessing about how far he'd take a performance. That gave every appearance he made an unpredictability, and an electricity, that was just irresistible to watch.

Maybe the best place to see the genius of Eddie was to sit in writers meetings, where he'd all but give birth to characters right there on the spot. As he riffed with his great writers, Barry Blaustein and David Sheffield, Eddie would sit with them for about forty-five minutes, fooling around with a new character or concept, and then leave, with Barry and David knowing what to do to finish a sketch. From Buckwheat to Gumby to Velvet Jones to his Stevie Wonder and Bill Cosby impressions to so many other one-off sketches that viewers still remember today (many opposite his favorite sidekick, the talented Joe Piscopo, the only other cast member we kept on from the previous regime), Eddie's work was absolutely singular.

More than ever before, and arguably ever since, Eddie Murphy gave *Saturday Night Live* a regular anchor for the show to build around. And so, as soon as we began producing regular shows in the fall of 1981 after the writers' strike ended, my rule was simple: Eddie had to appear three times in the first half hour of the show. It wasn't revolutionary—it was just logic. Eddie, almost instantly, once we put him at the center of the show, was the reason people would stay up late. So give them what they want, get them laughing, and they'd want to stay up, and stick around to see more.

With Eddie as such a powerful star presence, we had wide breadth to take other chances with the show. We might not have been making the same creation that Lorne had envisioned, but trying to do that would have been a mistake anyway. There was only one Lorne. That said, there were other ways to achieve the fundamental goal of the show: entertaining the audience. One thing I'd always lobbied for in its early days were mainstream, star musical acts. That hadn't always been easy; back in season 1, I'd pushed for ABBA to be the musical guest, and Michael O'Donoghue had staged a revolt, writing a sketch (called "S.O.S.," like their song) in which they drowned on a *Titanic* set. (Michael thought he was being a saboteur, but ABBA were such pros that they played it straight and had the last laugh.) Now, years later, in large part through the music connections I'd made producing *The Midnight Special*, big acts came on week after week, from Rod Stewart to Elton John to Queen to Stevie Wonder and more. Lorne would later joke with me after one of the big *SNL* anniversary specials that all the music in the special came from my years producing the show.

With the sketches, there was plenty of talent behind Eddie who added to the show's success. Tim Kazurinsky, with his "I Married a Monkey" sketches, was a flexible, versatile star—who somehow kept it together when his chimpanzee "wife" started pleasuring himself right there next to him in the bed onstage one night. I also added variety acts to the format. My agent, Marty Klein, recommended we look at another client of his, a colorful young comedic magician. That's how Harry Anderson was introduced to America, and his appearances got him a starring role on *Night Court*—showing that Hollywood was still very much watching *SNL*. We featured Andy Warhol in short films. There was a juggler named Michael Davis who performed half a dozen times. To me, it didn't all have to be the edgy comedy that Lorne pioneered, all the time. If the audience didn't know what was coming, and was excited about the possibility of being surprised, that was another way to keep them awake, and keep them watching.

As for the comedy, while I was never shy about weighing in on what I thought was funny and what I thought wasn't, I also trusted the best people in the writers' room. As the writers got to work after I started the job, I asked them what I could do to support them. Their answer was unequivocal: the most important thing they needed was protection from outside interference; a buffer from the network. And so, more than anything else, as the show's producer, I saw it as a central part of my job to protect the people creating the comedy from the people who didn't know anything about comedy. You could think of me as the bridge between executives and creatives, or the moat separating them—but either way, the mission was the same: give the funny people the freedom to be funny.

Still, that's not to say writing on *SNL* was easy. The process could be difficult, and emotions could run high. The brilliant Larry David, before he found his voice as the co-creator of *Seinfeld* and the star of *Curb Your Enthusiasm*, struggled in the *SNL* writers' room when we hired him for season 10. He just couldn't get a sketch on the air, and on more than one occasion, had to endure me cutting his material in dress rehearsal. Well, after one of these cuts one night, just about five minutes before the show went on the air, an enraged Larry found me underneath the bleachers.

"This show stinks!" he started screaming, with a few more expletives thrown in. "It stinks! It stinks! I'm done. I'm done. I quit!"

Again, there were a few more expletives thrown in. And off he went out into the hallway. As for me, it was only roughly the thousandth such explosion I'd seen from a writer or cast member over the years, and so I kind of shrugged, and put my headset back on.

Well, when our production meeting Monday morning came around, there was Larry sitting with the rest of the writers, who were all snickering. When I turned to Audrey Dickman and asked what was going on, she told me that everyone thought he had actually quit, and were waiting for me to respond. And of course the best response was to go along with it, and let Larry stay. Television can be an emotional business with emotional people. You're best off understanding and even appreciating that notion if you want to make something great.

Of course, years later, in a *Seinfeld* plot, when George Costanza famously got so angry at his boss about something that he quit on the spot, only to later regret it and try to act as if the whole episode hadn't happened, it didn't quite work out so well for him.

As for the people who did drive the material on the air, I felt strongly about rewarding them. In the early days of *SNL*, the idea of "favored nations" when it came to paying the cast—ensuring that every cast member made the same salary—sort of defined the ethos of the show. Now, in this new age of *SNL*, the reality was that the show's success was being driven by a breakout star, and that star absolutely deserved everything we could give him in reward, including a much larger salary. Then again, the money we could pay him was only so relevant, because almost as soon as he became a sensation on *Saturday Night Live*, Eddie's movie career took off as well. Halfway through my second season on the show, Nick Nolte—Eddie's costar in his first movie, *48 Hrs.*—was supposed to host. But when Nick bailed midweek, realizing after a few nights of partying that he wasn't up for doing the live show, and called me from the airport that he was going back to L.A., I gathered everyone in my office and announced that Eddie would host that week. He'd famously open his monologue yelling, "Live from New York, it's the Eddie Murphy Show!"

In a lot of ways, Eddie was beyond his years. His success hadn't happened by accident; he'd been doing stand-up since his mid-teens, with dreams of making it big. And so, when he did, he had the poise of a veteran star. He didn't ever have any trouble with the load we placed on him, and he was generous; he'd look at sketches written for him and often ask how we could get other members of the cast in it, to give them a star turn.

There were also altogether different signs of Eddie's fame behind the scenes, too—like the afternoon in 1982 when I got a nervous call from one of the assistants on the show that was hard to believe.

"Umm, I'm not sure you were expecting him," she said, "but it sounds like Mr. Rogers is downstairs. And he's looking for Eddie."

It was true. Fred Rogers himself had come to 30 Rock for an appearance on David Letterman's late night show and had decided to go looking for the man who'd done his own version of his act. A few moments later, I was face-to-face with him in my office. He was as kind and benevolent as you might expect, but also, it was clear, he had come to express his discomfort, at least to an extent, with "Mr. Robinson's Neighborhood."

"I do think Eddie is very funny," he told me in his quaint, deliberate manner of speaking. "But it just always needs to come from a good place."

After about ten minutes of conversation with this friendly but firm fellow, I figured the best thing to do was deal with this head-on, and so I walked him down to meet with Eddie himself, alongside Barry Blaustein and David Sheffield and Bob Tischler. If there was going to be any awkwardness in the room, it was immediately dissolved when Eddie saw who'd come for a visit.

"The *real* Mr. Rogers," Eddie exclaimed with a giant smile. And he immediately went in for a hug.

They had a friendly conversation, and in the end, Eddie and Mr. Rogers posed for a picture, which Mr. Rogers proudly showed to Letterman later on the air that night. And when our show aired that weekend, there was a "Mr. Robinson's

Neighborhood" sketch that played. Really, as the man himself wanted, it may have been a funny caricature, but it was also a loving portrait.

The following summer, Eddie and his friends lived in my house in Mandeville Canyon in L.A. while he filmed *Beverly Hills Cop*. His movie career was absolutely exploding, and it was going to be impossible to keep him on the show much longer. But we were able to make an unusual deal with his representatives to get him to appear in ten episodes, taping a good deal of his material ahead of time on a few concentrated days that worked with his schedule. Eddie was worth making those compromises for; and plenty more iconic bits came out of those shoots, including "James Brown's Celebrity Hot Tub Party," an idea that came to Barry Blaustein one time when he himself was stepping into a hot tub and let out an instinctive shriek when he dipped his toe in the scalding water. Eddie, of course, took it to another level—as he did with everything.

Eddie wasn't the only star who deserved rewards. Behind the scenes, his writers Barry and David were a huge part of his success. (They even came back in the fall of 2019 to work with Eddie when he made his long-awaited and tremendously successful return to the show as a host with Lorne producing.) Barry and David first started writing for him when he was just a featured player in his earliest days on the show, overlooked by everyone else. As soon as I saw how much great work they were doing when I took over, I made them the highest-paid members of the writing staff.

The show's ratings were up, the reviews were great, and a buzz had returned to *SNL*, just the way Brandon Tartikoff had dreamed it up. And even better than that, I'd found a new kind of partner—the greatest partner I've ever had by far—in the process.

CHAPTER 12

Susie

The first show in the fall of 1981 was my second show as producer, five months after the writers' strike had cut short the previous season. The episode was supposed to be hosted by James Caan. But just days before we were to start rehearsing, Caan called and said he needed to drop out because of a family health emergency. It was hardly an auspicious way to start my first full season, but Rod Stewart was still a strong musical guest, and through an Australian manager I knew named Roger Davies, I got Tina Turner to join him for a song, and the rest of the show went fine without a host or monologue. The after-party was at Studio 54, going late into the night as usual, and when I woke up in the early afternoon on Sunday, I was quickly reminded of the unforgiving rhythm of the show when I realized that I had to meet with the next week's host, to introduce myself and prepare them for the fun, relentless schedule that awaited. So I quickly showered and got dressed, and walked over to the Berkshire Hotel on Fifty-Second Street.

Susan Saint James had begun her career as a model in Paris as a teenager, become an actress at age twenty, and a star by the time she was twenty-two. In the late sixties, she won an Emmy on the series *The Name of the Game*, and soon after took a starring role opposite Rock Hudson in the hit crime series *McMillan & Wife*. By 1981, she was thirty-five, starring in movies, and had been booked for *SNL* because she was promoting a film called *Carbon Copy*, a romantic comedy that also featured an actor named Denzel Washington in his movie debut.

Susan's agent, Ron Meyer, years later to become the head of Universal Pictures and a friend and colleague of mine at NBC, booked her on the show, telling her that the old producers had come back, and the show was going to be good again. Not giving it much thought, Susan expected to be working with Lorne, and so she was surprised when I turned up at her hotel. Later she'd tease me that when she had been on *US Against the World*, the reality show featuring network stars that Don Ohlmeyer and I created in the seventies, I hadn't even bothered to introduce myself on the set as the NBC executive in charge. But in this meeting, we got along great, talking for a few hours about the show and what was in store for the week.

The next day, Monday, she came in for a tour of 8H to get her bearings and meet the writers. They were headed back to their offices to begin writing for the week, but being that the best thing I could do as the producer at that point was to leave them alone to work, I asked Susan if she wanted to grab dinner. We went to Elaine's on the East Side, and a connection and spark was definitely in the air as we learned more about each other's lives. We actually had a lot in common in terms of our backgrounds; while she'd been born in California and raised in Rockford, Illinois, her parents were both from Connecticut. We even discovered a near encounter in an unlikely time and place: Paris in the fall of 1964. The American Hospital there, where I spent two weeks recovering from my leg injury, was one street over from where Susan lived as an eighteen-year-old model; we later figured out that the window in my room looked out onto the back of her apartment building.

All these years later, the woman I was having dinner with clearly wasn't just beautiful—she was wickedly smart. She understood the entertainment industry, and not just from a star's perspective. She was completely fearless about speaking her mind, and for as unlimited as her talent on-screen was, she was much more than just a fantastic actress. She was passionate about politics, and music, too—several of the Doobie Brothers were among her closest friends. She even loved sports. And she was a mom to two children, her son, Harmony, and daughter, Sunshine, from her previous marriage, which had ended a few years prior; she shared custody in an amicable relationship with her ex-husband.

I hadn't asked her to dinner with romantic inclinations. But as we took a car back to Midtown, even though it was after midnight, I didn't want the night to end, and had a good sense she didn't, either. So I suggested we go to Xenon, a disco club on West Forty-Third Street that in its day was a competitor to Studio 54. There, we got a table, watched some dancing for a while, then danced ourselves, and eventually, as two people rapidly falling for each other are wont to do on an evening like this, began making out on the dance floor. I remember the lights seeming like they were flashing brighter around us as the night went on, but didn't think much of it—nor, in a bit of a delirious state, did I think much of the horde of paparazzi that began firing off photos as soon as we stepped out of the club.

The next day, in a two-page spread in the New York *Daily News*, there we were. The headline: "When Dick Ebersol Books a Host . . ." and then, continued beneath it, "He Doesn't Fool Around." And then at the bottom of the page: "Or on Second Thought, He Does." I was sort of amused by the whole thing, and Susan, accustomed to being in the tabloids, didn't seem to be bothered much at all. Things were just too perfect to really get in the way of how we were feeling.

On set, the week went well, though on Friday she began losing her voice, and I had to find her a throat doctor to bring it back just in time, especially considering the show's cold open featured Susan singing in a sketch with Joe Piscopo. That went off without a hitch, and the rest of the show was a success. We went to the after-party, and then back to the Plaza, where I was living at the time, for a long, lazy, happy Sunday, which even then felt like the start of something amazing in our lives. She was heading back home to L.A., but we were going to make this work, one way or another.

For all the mystique of falling in love with a star like Susan, it was by far the easiest, most natural relationship I'd ever found myself in. And whether I saw it then or not, the parallels to my parents' own marriage were there, as my mom had had a child—my brother, Si—from a previous marriage when she met my dad. And they'd wasted no time in getting engaged and married.

Well, after Susan and I met the first week of October, it wasn't even Halloween when we began talking marriage. One afternoon in November, when I was in California during an off week for the show, I asked her if she wanted to call Marcus Welby for some blood tests. There may have been more romantic ways to propose, but she got the reference to the old TV show, and loved it. We were married the Saturday before Thanksgiving—barely six weeks after meeting, and barely beating my parents in terms of speedy courtships.

Over the course of the next year or so, as much as she could, Susan would spend a week with her kids in California, and then come back and spend the next week with me in New York. When *SNL* wasn't in production, I'd go out west to visit her and the children. It worked for both of us. Susan was fiercely independent, which was not only important as a foundation of the marriage but something I found very attractive. We loved each other passionately, but neither of us needed each other every moment of every day. That would be central to the success of the marriage as the years went on and our life together evolved.

In the summer of 1982, with Susan pregnant with our first child, we all rented a house together back in Litchfield, not far from the home I'd grown up in. Susan fell in love with the area, and in the fall, she and Harmony and Sunshine moved east, as we bought the home that we still live in today. I kept my apartment in New York, and when we were in season, would come up as much as I could, usually on Sundays after the show.

The *SNL* writers, of course, had watched my head-over-heels romance un-fold up close from the beginning. The week after Susan hosted, they passed around a piece of paper in the writers' room, asking for predictions on when in the week I'd start a romance with our next host—the venerable middle-aged actor George Kennedy of the *Airport* disaster movies.

I may not have been a comedian. But I did have a sense of humor. Life was too good—all I could do was laugh along with them.

CHAPTER 13

Stars and Legends

Susan was hardly the only memorable host who came on *SNL* over my years producing the show. Stevie Wonder (working side by side with Eddie imitating him), the great Johnny Cash (who told incredible stories of his famous prison concerts), my old friend Ron Howard, entertainment legends like Sid Caesar and Jerry Lewis, the list goes on and on. Every week, some new star would come in and become part of the massive challenge of putting a funny ninety-minute show on the air by Saturday night.

In November of 1982, on a night when we had the youngest host ever, a seven-year-old Drew Barrymore, the show also featured one of many appearances by Andy Kaufman, who if you remember, had appeared on the very first *SNL* singing the *Mighty Mouse* theme back in 1975. Andy and I had been friendly ever since I'd met him performing at Catch a Rising Star in Manhattan, and I'd always admired his completely original and unique brand of humor. And even if he seemed to play slightly deranged characters on-screen, there was absolutely no one easier or more professional to work with. But on that night, things got complicated, because Andy had pitched an idea that I thought would doom him. After a sketch of his had gotten cut in dress rehearsal a few weeks earlier, Andy had, as always, been totally professional about it, but he had the idea to stage a fight between him and me that would result in a vote—via a 1-900 number—whether Andy should keep performing on the show, or be banned from the show forever.

The "fight"—a screaming match between Andy and me—was staged in the control room, with him screaming at me about the sketch getting cut, and demanding that I let the audience decide. It wasn't on camera, but only a few of us were in on the joke, with the rest of the staff thinking it was real. As we knew it would, that led to the gossip columns unwittingly writing that Andy was actually feuding with *SNL*, and the world being fooled into thinking that Andy's demand to "put it to a vote"—and my decision to go with the 1-900 number—was all authentic. The idea was totally on-brand for Andy's kind of humor, with his total commitment blurring the line between what was real and what was a joke, but as the plan played out, I had second thoughts.

"Andy," I told him and his manager, George Shapiro, "you realize that the audience is paying to make these calls. We can't just forget about this thing. We know the feud is made-up, but if they vote you off, we're going to have to abide by their choice."

He was totally unbowed. Whether he didn't think he'd get voted off or simply going to the edge was the point of the bit, Andy wanted to go ahead with it, and sure enough, when the votes were announced at the end of the show, about 190,000 had voted to "dump" him, and 160,000 to keep him. Andy was gone. And, in real life, he was crushed.

Still, we were able to stage a "paid announcement" a few weeks later to give him one more appearance. And when the next season started, we came up with another idea: that an odd, tall female extra would start appearing in sketches here and there all season long, in progressively more prominent ways. Eventually, it would be revealed as Andy. But sadly, we'd never be able to make that happen, because later in 1983, Andy was diagnosed with cancer. He died tragically at the age of just thirty-five the following May.

Of all the hosts that we had during my years on the show, probably my favorite was an instance that proved how much of a relief comedy can be when life hands us heartbreak. You see, in 1983, Brandon Tartikoff was now the head of all of NBC entertainment—prime time, daytime, and late night—thanks to the wise support and confidence of Fred Silverman's successor, Grant Tinker. He'd developed some huge hits, like *Hill Street Blues*, *Cheers*, and *Family Ties*, with *The Cosby Show* and *Miami Vice* soon to follow. But Brandon was also in the midst of a relapse of the non-Hodgkin's lymphoma that he'd been fighting since he was in college. Outwardly, to people who didn't know him well, Brandon hid the situation well. He only scheduled his weekly chemotherapy treatment on Friday afternoons, so he could spend the weekends recovering and be back at work by Monday without anyone knowing. Wearing a wig and fake eyelashes didn't help with the ruse, but it was still a symbol of how determined and brave he was in his fight. (He also somehow found humor in his ordeal—like the time he called me delightedly to report that he'd discovered that the guy who made his wigs also serviced the great Charlton Heston—who he'd run into at the shop.)

Still, even if there were laughs to be had, I had no doubts about how much of a toll the disease and the treatment were taking on him. At one point, his wife, Lilly, who was just as close a friend to me as Brandon was, called me up while he was in the hospital and asked if I had any ideas on how to keep him engaged and upbeat. I thought about it, and then came up with something that excited me. Brandon was the biggest ham that any of us knew. He'd always been a *Saturday Night Live* fanatic. What if we put him on the show as the host? Sure enough, he loved the idea, it gave him something to look forward to, and in October of that year, the season premiere of *SNL* was hosted by the network's head of entertainment. Brandon was wearing his wig, and surely far from feeling a hundred percent inside, but he had a wonderful night, and acquitted himself pretty well as a host, highlighted by one sketch that had him go out in the streets begging people to watch NBC shows, and another in which he wore a body-fitted thin black leather jacket and pants, with nothing underneath, as he pitched ridiculous show ideas for NBC's new season to the man who'd originated that outfit, Eddie Murphy.

That season was Eddie's last on *SNL*—his movie career had skyrocketed into full flight—and with Joe Piscopo and others departing as well, the show had reached another crossroads as it celebrated its tenth anniversary. Rather than scour the country for more unknown talent, I had a different idea that I pitched to Brandon: go after proven comedy stars who could become the new anchors of the show. Brandon gave me the go-ahead, calling it my "Steinbrenner" year as producer, a reference to the Yankees owner who signed expensive big-star free agents from other teams to massive contracts.

My "big signings" included Martin Short, who'd become a star on *SCTV*, the Canadian sketch comedy show that came out of Second City; and also Christopher Guest, who was breaking out as a star with the cult hit *This Is Spinal Tap*. But the biggest name I wanted was Billy Crystal, who'd shined brilliantly when he'd hosted the show twice earlier in 1984, a triumphant return after the launch of *SNL* had been stained with such disappointment for him, getting his sketch cut at dress rehearsal.

In the years that followed, Billy had, of course, become a TV star through his specials and his role on the sitcom *Soap*, and moved to Los Angeles. But I'd seen how much he loved being on the show when he'd hosted the previous season, and how great a match the show was for his performing and writing talents—not to mention his passion. So I went out to L.A. to meet with Billy and his managers about him coming to *SNL* on a one-year deal.

Sitting in the Polo Lounge at the Beverly Hills Hotel with Billy and his reps, I laid out the idea—only to have it dismissed out of hand by his team. The message was that Billy was past television, and his future was solely in movies. These were some of the most powerful representatives in comedy—I knew Billy thought he should listen to them. But as I looked at his face while they talked, I had a feeling this didn't have to be the end of the story. And I had a plan to use a back door to try to get him to agree to the deal.

I'd become friendly with not just Billy but also his wife, Janice, when he'd hosted. In one conversation at a wrap party, Janice had said to me that, as much as she loved their life in L.A., she lamented not giving their daughters a taste of New York, where their parents had both grown up. So right after that meeting with Billy's agents, I wasted no time. I went up to my room and called Janice, and filled her in on the situation.

"Here's my pitch," I said to her, "and I don't want you to say yes or no until you let me finish.

"I want Billy to come and be the star of *SNL* for a year. We will pay him really well, and you can spend the year together in New York as a family. I know you want to do that, and Billy can get to do something he really wants to do as well. One year."

Janice said she'd think about it, and I could tell she really meant it.

The very next day, Billy agreed to come.

The tenth season of *SNL* may have been different from all the others before or since, but it was definitely a success. Billy has called it his favorite year in his entire career, and I'm not sure he gets the credit he deserves as one of the great performers in the history of the show. The characters that he and Marty and Chris Guest created and inhabited—from Fernando to Ed Grimley (who went back to Marty's *SCTV* days) to Frankie and Willie (the friends forever bemoaning the insanely painful situations they put themselves in) and far beyond—were as popular and funny as anything that's ever appeared on *SNL*. We had a great season of hosts as well, from the returns of George Carlin (remember, the first host ever) and Eddie Murphy to Mr. T and Hulk Hogan to "Mr. Baseball," Bob Uecker, and, in the season finale, my old friend Howard Cosell. It was the end of Howard's career, and Billy and I walked just up the street to the old ABC offices on the Avenue of the Americas on the twenty-eighth floor to ask him to do it. In the best skit of the night, Howard and Billy played Morris and Rose Cosell, Howard's parents, at his bar mitzvah in 1930, with Freddie Koehler, the kid who played Jane Curtin's son from *Kate & Allie*—the new hit sitcom about two single moms living together that she starred in with Susan—playing young Howard. The skit was finished off by a full kiss on the lips from Billy, in full drag, to Howard.

At least symbolically, that night brought my time at *Saturday Night Live* full circle. Ten years after our competition with Cosell as we each launched our own Saturday night variety shows, now he was onstage for my last show as producer. Four-plus seasons in the middle of the weekly massive challenge to get the show on the air had been a lot. When Brandon asked me late in the season what it would take for me to come back, I jokingly told him, "If we taped the show on Fridays, I'd be willing to do it." (Somehow, over the years, people have categorized that as a serious suggestion.) The real answer was that Susan and I were growing our family—Sunshine was thirteen, Harmony was almost eleven, our son Charlie was three, and Susan was pregnant with his brother, Willie—while *Kate & Allie* had taken off on CBS. With both of us shuttling in and out of Connecticut and New York, it felt like we were missing the chance to make memories together. As for the show, it had been on life support when I'd returned, and now Lorne, after five years off, was finally willing to come back. It would take a while, but his original vision for *SNL* would be restored, and the next thirty-five years of the show and counting would birth dozens of stars, and countless entries into the canon of American comedy.

All these years later, *Saturday Night Live* and Lorne Michaels are truly synonymous. How he's continued to run the show well into his seventies is an absolute marvel. Lorne is one of the seminal names in the history of comedy, a genius also responsible for the careers and legacies of so many of the most popular performers over the last half century. No other show of its kind on television has lasted this long. None has inspired the kind of passion from its fans. The young people who were the show's target audience when it launched are now grandparents. They can reminisce about when *SNL* spoke their language, and they have been able to pass down their love of the show to their sons and daughters, and now even grandchildren.

For my part, I couldn't be prouder of my role in the story of the show. And on the occasion of one of the show's anniversaries, in a conversation we were having, Lorne put it simply to me.

"You hired me to create the show. You saved the show when it was about to be canceled six months after I left and didn't want to go back. And you put together one of the best casts, if not the best cast, in the show's history."

I'll take that.

And besides, when I left that seventeenth floor office at 30 Rock in the spring of 1985, I had plenty of other things going on to keep me busy.

CHAPTER 14

No Sleep

I named my first production company in tribute to one of my favorite people in entertainment, Don Rickles. Rickles's show, *CPO Sharkey*, taped right across the hall from *The Tonight Show* on the Burbank lot, a fact well remembered from the famous "cigarette box incident," when Carson—after discovering that guest host Rickles had broken the cigarette box on his desk—took cameras onto the *Sharkey* set and mock-confronted Rickles in front of his live studio audience. I got to know Rickles by hanging around *The Tonight Show*, and became delightedly familiar with his assortment of favorite insults. One frequent example was his derision of "network guys," as he called us.

"You can never find them," he'd say. "They're always taking a cab."

In tribute to Don, when I stopped being a network guy, I called my first production company Take a Cab Productions when I did a few specials in the late seventies in L.A.

When I went to *SNL*, I called the entity through which I produced the show No Sleep Productions, and that would stick through the creations to come as the eighties went on. Because, remember, the most significant element of the deal I made with NBC to return to produce *SNL* was that for every year the show stayed on the air while I was producing it, I was guaranteed commitments from them to produce pilots for other show ideas I had. And so at some point in late 1982, in the midst of Eddie Murphy mania, I went to Brandon with a super-simple music-based show concept to replace *SCTV*, the Friday night Canadian sketch comedy show that was going off the air.

"So you want to produce a pilot?" he asked as soon as I told him I had an idea.

"Let's make it easier than that," I said. "Why don't I just come over to your apartment in New York and we can watch this new cable channel called MTV for twenty minutes?"

Friday Night Videos was about as basic an idea as anyone could conceive. In the summer of 1981, MTV had famously launched at midnight on a Saturday by airing "Video Killed the Radio Star" by the Buggles. A year or so later, the new channel was clearly popular with young music fans—but as a cable network in the early eighties, it was only available to about 20 percent of American homes. So, *Friday Night Videos* would bring this exploding new genre of music videos to the masses by airing ninety minutes of videos once a week in late night on a network.

The idea was so simple, it was almost too good to be true, especially considering that at that point, record companies were producing videos themselves, and then releasing them for free as promotional devices. That meant, in effect, the show would be virtually free to produce; the only costs would be in editing the videos in a row together for a given episode. I didn't even want a host; my thought was to give the audience simply the music, with no frills attached. Still, as we went ahead with the show, the idea of just taking the videos for free and putting them on the air—as MTV was doing—didn't sit right, or feel particularly safe. Knowing the unpredictability of the music business, there had to be a chance that lawyers would chase us down at some point to retroactively pay the artists and video directors, and bury anyone that aired them financially.

The risk of the exposure actually scared me so much at one point that I considered abandoning the idea entirely. But for the first of many times, Susan was my best counsel, urging me to figure out a way forward, realizing the concept was too good to pass up. Eventually, like everything else with *FNV*, the solution ended up being simple: I did an interview with *Variety*, the Hollywood trade publication, and in it revealed that *Friday Night Videos* would pay for the videos we aired. It was such a change in precedent that they put the interview on the front page. Relatively speaking, it wasn't a lot of money at maybe $1,000 a video, and $2,500 for "world premieres," but it protected us from potential damages later on, and also led the record companies to favor us over other outlets like MTV that didn't pay—nor reach the number of homes that NBC did.

Friday Night Videos premiered at the end of July in 1983, airing after Johnny Carson at 12:30 a.m. The series would be a ratings success, and even win an Emmy Award for our graphics and title design. I actually would end up dealing with litigation eventually with the show after all, as I was sued by someone who claimed I stole the idea from them. My defense was simple: I *had* stolen the idea—but I'd always been very clear about who I'd stolen it from: MTV. I even had my neighbor and friend in Litchfield County, Bob Pittman, the head of MTV, write a letter vouching that I'd indeed taken it from him. The suit was dismissed without merit.

As for the format of the show, the producer I hired to handle its day-to-day operations, a talented former CBS Records executive named David Benjamin, was connected all over the music business, and was a big reason we were ahead of MTV in showcasing R&B acts along with straight rock. We had all kinds of different hooks for viewers, including "Video Vote," which let the audience dial 1-900 numbers to cast their votes in head-to-head battles for videos of the week. Eventually Brandon would prevail upon us to add celebrity hosts, which—no surprise, considering it was his idea—made the show even better. We had musicians, comedians, actors, athletes and, maybe most memorably, Yoko Ono, who took us to her apartment in the Dakota so we could film a tour of where she had lived with John Lennon. The show largely otherwise retained the same structure until it finally went off the air in the early 2000s. By then, I'd long since sold the show to NBC as part of my deal when I took over the sports division. But the original light-up model of the logo still sits in my home office in Connecticut, and I still like to remember the show ending with the No Sleep Productions logo, a bloodshot eye, blinking open and shut, trying to stave off exhaustion to keep watching for a bit longer.

The more I worked in late night, the more potential I saw for programming in the window, and the more possibilities I was willing to explore to chase creative ideas. Still, in early 1985, as I got set to leave *SNL*, when my friend and agent Marty Klein told me there was someone I should meet to talk about a show, I wasn't interested.

"I'm telling you," Marty said in a meeting in my office one day. "You will love Vince McMahon. And he's got some ideas you should hear about."

Honestly, I had no interest. Vince McMahon? The pro wrestling guy?

But later that day at 30 Rock, I ran into none other than David Letterman in the hallway, by then three years into his great run in late night. Dave and I shared Marty as an agent, and as we talked while crew guys walked past us, I mentioned Marty's strange idea to have me meet with McMahon. Letterman immediately lit up.

"You should absolutely meet with him," he said. "Trust me, you'll love him."

McMahon, it turned out, had been in a sketch for Dave's New Year's Eve show that year, where he and a sportscaster named Bob Costas had been stationed as "correspondents" at two different hospitals in New York, covering the maternity wards to determine who would be the city's first "New Year's baby." Letterman had loved how McMahon played up the role.

And so, a few weeks later, I found myself welcoming Vince McMahon into my office at 30 Rock. On the surface, you'd think Vince and I couldn't have been less alike—in our backgrounds, our dispositions, and our interests. But sure enough, we hit it off immediately. What I remember thinking as Vince told me his story in our first meeting was how smart he was, and also how gutsy he was. As a kid, Vince hadn't met his father until he was twelve years old, but when he did, he'd immediately become transfixed by the family business: professional wrestling. The industry, such as it was, was a collection of independent traveling circuses, with different outfits in different regions all across the country, staging shows for modest crowds headlined by various local stars. Vince looked at his father's syndicate, the World Wide Wrestling Federation, as it was called then, and saw tremendous possibility. Vince's dream was to build a company that would unite the different regional promotions into a single, dominant, national, or even international attraction. He bought his father's company, which was based in the Northeast, in the seventies, and then began taking over other "associations" and "alliances"—as pro wrestling companies called themselves—and growing his own World Wrestling Federation, as it was now known.

By the mid-eighties, when we met, Vince had a rapidly growing company with an expanding national reach, spearheaded by an unrelenting schedule of live events and syndicated television productions. The biggest event yet, called Wrestle-Mania, set to take place in late March 1985 from Madison Square Garden, airing on closed-circuit television (essentially a telecast of the show piped into movie theaters across the country), was approaching. And now here was Vince in my office at NBC, talking about what we could do together.

For all of his outsized public persona, Vince was genuine, soft-spoken, and thoughtful one-on-one in conversation. Like a lot of kids, I'd watched wrestling from time to time growing up. But it wasn't until I met Vince that something important occurred to me: at the heart of the success of his operation was storytelling. Wrestling was, in effect, a live-action cartoon—with pretend heroes and villains, and rivalries and feuds, best delivered with a dose of humor and fun. Every one of those elements of the show was part of a story.

I suggested our lawyers get together and hammer out a development deal. But a few weeks later, when the lawyers were taking too long and making an agreement too complex for his taste, Vince and his wife and partner, Linda, came back to me with a different idea. Why don't we just shake on a fifty-fifty split, and get going on figuring out a show already?

Saturday Night's Main Event premiered about six weeks after the original WrestleMania. (In no coincidence, the night before WrestleMania, the stars of the main event, Hulk Hogan and Mr. T., hosted *SNL*.) *Saturday Night's Main Event* was the first time that pro wrestling appeared on network television since the 1950s, and was typically programmed into *SNL*'s off weeks, airing roughly once a month. The show was ninety minutes long, just like *SNL*, showing matches that had been typically taped the night before, along with sketches and interviews around them. Originally, the media questioned NBC's decision to get into business with the WWF, questioning Grant Tinker about NBC's self-proclaimed interest in "quality programming." The network president had the perfect response: this was "quality wrestling." And from the first episode in May 1985, the audience responded—the ratings were huge.

As for my working relationship with Vince, it was as seamless as any partnership I've ever had. The plan was clear: Vince would handle the wrestling, and I would handle the television. Since I had a shorthand with Brandon, handling the network was easy. But I also produced all the non-ring segments of the show: the interviews and out-of-ring interactions that set up the plotlines that viewers followed—often fanatically. I'll never forget coming home to Connecticut one weekend, and Harvey, our longtime family chef and an absolute saintly teddy bear of a human being, was ecstatic to talk to me about a WWF plot twist that involved an evil-twin referee.

"Harvey," I said, laughing. "You heard me talking to Vince about it on the phone in the kitchen last weekend! You know it's all scripted!"

It was more fun for thousands—no, millions—of fans to go along with pretending that it wasn't. And the storytelling worked best when it was planned out over months and months, letting *Saturday Night's Main Event*, which all fans could watch on NBC, set up narratives that would pay off on pay-per-view events like future WrestleManias, compelling fans to buy in. The show stamped the WWF as the country's premier wrestling company, and thanks to the charisma of the stars, and the quality of the storytelling, the "sport" became a national phenomenon. (A few years later, Linda McMahon would stun the world by testifying in front of the New Jersey state senate that wrestling wasn't, in fact, real competition. It was the break of decades of tradition of keeping up the ruse for fans like Harvey, but it was also a brilliant stroke to avoid needless regulation by the state athletic commission.)

Working with Vince and Linda was a wild, unpredictable, and absolute joyous way to spend the years after I left *Saturday Night Live*. It was the world's greatest education in storytelling and event staging, a giant, never-ending circus where no challenge was too big and no job too small. There was one night at the Meadowlands Arena in New Jersey when André the Giant was due in the ring—but nowhere to be seen. At *SNL*, there would have been ten production assistants looking for him. At the WWF, there was no hierarchy like that—it was on me to find him, racing through the bowels of the arena into the locker room to grab him. It couldn't have been more fun.

On Sunday mornings, I never could have imagined getting calls at home the way I did from Randy "Macho Man" Savage, but they came after pretty much every show, in search of the first overnight ratings report.

"*Ebbberrsoll*," came his signature, hoarse baritone over the phone. "Have you gotten the *oooovernights* yet?"

Savage, Hogan, André the Giant—the roster of stars grew with the popularity of the WWF. *Saturday Night's Main Event* was where Jesse Ventura debuted as an announcer, the first stop on his path to becoming an actor and eventually the governor of Minnesota. I got to know Jesse best when he, Vince, and I took a crazy spur-of-the-moment trip from Detroit into the jungles of southern Mexico to try to convince Arnold Schwarzenegger, filming *Predator*, to be a guest referee for WrestleMania III at the Pontiac Silverdome. Jesse had a role in the movie, and he thought we might have a shot at getting Arnold to do it. So we went to a University of Michigan apparel store to buy a change of clothes, chartered a plane, and landed on a dusty, dirt field, practically blowing over the tiny shack that doubled for an airport terminal. When we finally found Arnold, he was blown away that we'd come to see him, but regretfully declined because of his schedule. After a brief visit, we went back to the plane, slept in our seats till dawn, and then went back to the States the next morning. WrestleMania III went on to be Vince's biggest success yet, featuring the largest crowd ever for an indoor sports or entertainment event.

Vince and I never signed a contract. I would send him 50 percent of the production fee from NBC that we got for the show, and figured that was that. But nine months after our first batch of shows had aired, I got a surprise: the first of many checks in the mail at my house in Connecticut for half the profits of everything else that came out of *Saturday Night's Main Event*, like T-shirts and hats, and profits from international syndication. No business managers necessary; the McMahons had been totally true to their word.

If working independently for most of the 1980s was a chapter of my career that took a sharp turn from the executive track I'd put myself on in the 1970s, the rewards were more valuable than I ever could have imagined. In media, so many wonderful careers unfold linearly, with smart men and women working their way up an invisible ladder. For me, the biggest benefits came when I hopped off that ladder. Stepping out on my own forced me to take chances with every opportunity that came my way. As a producer, out there on my own, I had to take chances; I had to believe that my ideas could work.

Soon after I'd been fired by Fred Silverman, one of the meetings I'd had was with Sam Weisbord, the longtime head of William Morris. I barely knew Weisbord, but he reached out and asked me to meet. Weisbord was something of a Hollywood legend, who had represented Frank Sinatra and Marilyn Monroe, and he told me something that had stayed with me as a piece of advice as I headed out into producing on my own.

"Television, entertainment, movies—all of show business," he said, "isn't about shows and programs; it's about relationships."

"So go out and grow your own television family."

It may have been the best piece of advice I ever received.

By the end of the decade, it had been just about ten years since I'd had the good fortune of being fired by Fred Silverman. And after churning out *Friday Night Videos* and *Saturday Night's Main Event*, my production company had another new show that was premiering on NBC, airing after Johnny Carson and *Late Night with David Letterman* on weeknights. I'd originally gone to Brandon with an idea for a show I called *Last Call*, envisioned as a panel discussion of guests about whatever had gone on during the day—in news, culture, sports, and the like. My pitch for the host was Bob Costas, who'd become a young rising star at NBC Sports. I'd scouted Bob and gotten to know and like him, and he was game to try to expand his portfolio. Bob had come up as something of a broadcasting prodigy, leaving Syracuse before graduating to become the play-by-play voice of the ABA's St. Louis Spirits, and getting hired by Don Ohlmeyer at NBC Sports before he turned thirty. But while being the next Vin Scully or Marv Albert might have been Bob's original dream, it turned out he was much more versatile. He'd become the host of NBC's NFL studio coverage, and as we'd gotten to know each other, it was clear he'd be a great host of an intelligent talk show like *Last Call* that went beyond sports as well.

Right when we'd gotten ready to announce the show, it turned out that the network's owned and operated stations across the country had bought a show to air in that time period, and it had to take priority. But when that show failed, a year later, NBC came back to me, asking if we could resuscitate my idea. By now, Bob had moved his family to St. Louis, making it impossible for him to tape a show every night in New York. So I came up with another, even simpler concept.

Later . . . with Bob Costas was inspired by a show I saw when I was a kid, called *Biography*, that featured Mike Wallace interviewing figures of note. The modern version was envisioned as a half-hour conversation between Bob and an actor, musician, athlete, commentator, or really any public figure—not promoting a project, but rather talking about their career and their personal lives on a wider level. No music, no audience, just a conversation, in two old-fashioned comfortable chairs, airing after Letterman at 1:30 a.m. Bob could tape several episodes at a time when he was in New York, typically on Mondays after working in the sports studio on a weekend. And it would, in fact, be an interview in the first few months of the show with none other than Mike Wallace himself that epitomized just how appealing the show could be.

The taping was in the afternoon, and as Bob walked Wallace back through his life and career, at one point he asked a question about the battle with depression that Mike had spoken about only sparingly in a few magazine articles, and never on camera. After a slight pause, Mike responded, and began talking, and talking some more, and more. And talking not just about depression but about his reasons for talking about it.

"Who's watching this show right now, at one thirty in the morning?" Wallace said to Costas, almost rhetorically.

"Well," Bob responded, "some people who work late, so they're up now, but also people who just can't sleep."

"Ah," Wallace said. "My people. So that's why I want to talk about this. Because there are people out there watching right now, having a rough time, dealing with their own sense of angst or dread, and I want them to know my story. If they see what I've been through, they'll know they're not alone."

The whole exchange was eye-opening. We could see the space that the show could have—with the guest feeling comfortable with Bob, and no audience and no distractions. And also, we saw that the twenty-two-minute format for the half-hour program didn't have to be limiting. A conversation with a guest like Wallace could actually be spread over several nights—the audience would be happy for the multiple parts.

There would be hundreds of great conversations that Bob would have over the next several years, with everyone from Paul Simon to Jerry Seinfeld to Robert Duvall to Marilu Henner to Bruce Springsteen to Mickey Mantle and far beyond. Bob was the perfect host for the show; he was youthful, he was curious, he had a great wit that played late at night, and he had such a head for so many different facts that he could always take the conversation in smart places—the show was never stilted. *Later* would have a huge following among night owls for years to come, and be a great, successful change of pace in late night for NBC.

In 1989, if someone had asked me to reflect on my life as I approached the age of forty-two, I would have told them I was pretty damn happy. No Sleep Productions was humming along, and Susan was about to finish her highly rated run on *Kate & Allie*. Before we'd met, Susan had a home in Telluride, Colorado, and on a trip out there, we'd realized that pretty soon, with Harmony and Sunshine now teenagers, Charlie and Willie growing up faster than we could believe, and their youngest brother, Teddy, soon on the way, we wouldn't have too many more chances to live together under one roof as an entire family. So with Susan's sitcom set to stop in May 1989, we decided we would move our family out west to Colorado for at least a year. I'd be able to keep an eye on the shows from there and travel when I needed to, and she'd do the same for a few select acting jobs, but we'd be together, and take another collective breath from the wild ride we'd been on.

But then the decade ended the same way it began. With another bold idea from Brandon Tartikoff.

Part Three

CHAPTER 15

Perfect Fit

Where I was sitting was no accident. I was a few feet in front of the stage in Studio 8H in 30 Rock, on a stool looking out toward a group of about a hundred or so people. I knew a few of their names and recognized some of their faces, but for the most part, this was an introductory gathering for all of us. They were meeting their new boss. And their new boss—me—was there to tell them how excited I was to be working with them. I was in the setting that best epitomized how I'd spent the last decade and a half, but now my career was taking another sharp turn and coming full circle. I was back, suddenly and thrillingly, with my first love, as the new president of NBC Sports.

The truth, of course, was that I'd never really left sports behind. Whether I was working on *Saturday Night Live* or *The Midnight Special* or *Friday Night Videos* or anything in between, I'd never stopped reading the sports pages first when I picked up the newspaper in the morning. I'd followed the business side of sports as well, and stayed in touch with many of my old friends in sports TV, like Roone Arledge and Don Ohlmeyer. And that lasting connection to the passion I'd first harbored as a kid in rural Connecticut was the central reason why, when Brandon had broached his latest idea with me in early 1989, he knew I'd listen.

"I've got some news for you," he'd said to me one day in his typical enthusiastic, excited way over the phone. "Arthur Watson is retiring."

Arthur Watson, I knew, was the longtime president of NBC Sports.

"So," Brandon continued, "what if you came back to NBC to run sports?" He paused to let it sink in.

"Think about it—it's the absolutely perfect fit."

I was surprised by the idea, and I was intrigued. Almost a decade and a half had passed since I'd worked in television sports. Now, all of a sudden, I was getting an offer for one of the best jobs in the industry. Even if it wasn't something I'd thought about in years, it was hard not to immediately get excited about the possibilities. Still, Brandon's call had come no more than forty-eight hours after Susan and I had made up our minds to move to our home in Telluride, and spend more time together as a family there. In its own way, that plan—while I could continue to enjoy the freedom of being an independent producer—was exciting, too. But as Brandon laid out the details of why he saw the job as an ideal match, it was hard not to get more and more attracted to it.

Brandon went through the situation as he saw it. Arthur Watson's replacement would clearly be taking over a business in transition. NBC was exiting a longtime rights deal for baseball, and General Electric, which had bought RCA and NBC a few years earlier, was looking for someone to set the course for the network's sports group going forward. The cupboard was by no means bare, though. There was a contract with the NFL to broadcast all its AFC games every Sunday, and the Super Bowl in a rotation every third year. But even more attractively, NBC had secured the rights to broadcast the next Summer Olympics, in 1992 in Barcelona— meaning twenty-five years after leaving college to become an Olympic researcher, I could be returning to lead a major network's coverage of the Games. Yet with baseball going away, there was definitely ample room to define NBC Sports for the decade to come.

By now, as NBC's entertainment chief, Brandon was not just one of the network's top executives—he was also arguably its most successful. Even beyond that, he was liked and respected across the company, and the industry. So he definitely had the ear of the network's president, Bob Wright, and GE's chairman and CEO, Jack Welch, when he told them that I was the perfect person for the job. I'd met Wright once; he had made a point of coming to a press conference I'd once had with Vince at the top of 30 Rock to announce a wrestling event. He loved the shows and wanted to let us know he was a fan. As for Welch, a few years earlier, we'd actually spoken on the phone once about Brandon, when he'd been in the midst of a difficult contract negotiation, and Brandon's wife, Lilly, had called me, upset that he was going to leave the job. It was right around when GE was purchasing the company, so I'd reached out to Don Ohlmeyer, who I knew golfed with Welch, and then made a call to impress upon the already legendary businessman what a terrific human being Brandon was. The deal had worked itself out, and now things had come back around, putting the possibility of me working for Jack on the table.

Within a few weeks of my initial conversation with Brandon, he and I and Lilly and Susan were on a helicopter from New York City to Fairfield, Connecticut, where GE was headquartered, for dinner at Wright's house nearby. Suzanne Wright, Bob's wife, made a wonderful homemade meal, served unpretentiously at the kitchen table, and we talked all night, getting to know each other better. On the helicopter ride back to Manhattan, looking out over the Statue of Liberty, Susan turned to me.

"You have to take this job," she said. "You just have to."

She herself had come from a family of sports nuts—her older brother played minor league baseball, and her dad was a lifelong golf fanatic. Already her mind was turning about how much fun the whole family could get out of this. But there was no denying what kind of change it would be. Forget about Colorado—we'd be going from a scenario where we'd all pretty much be together all the time to me being away constantly, particularly on weekends when most sporting events took place. Neither of us wanted to raise our kids in New York City, but with our home in Litchfield a hundred miles away and too far to commute from on a day-to-day basis, I'd largely have to live in our apartment in the city during the weeks, and get back to Connecticut when I could. With *Kate & Allie* ending, Susan would be committing to a lot more of the parenting now on her own. But the backbone of our marriage, from the very beginning when we lived on opposite coasts, had been how much we both valued our independence, and how much we both loved adventure. Without a second thought, she wanted me to go on this new journey, and wanted it to be the next chapter for our family. To this day, I'm not just thankful for her full support; I know I couldn't have done the job without it.

The next morning, I met Welch in Wright's office at 30 Rock. GE was one of the world's most successful corporations, making everything from airplane engines to refrigerators to lightbulbs, and running dozens of businesses through its massive

GE Capital division in between. That meant joining NBC would be like joining the Yankees in terms of the resources that would be made available. Even more than that, as a public-facing, fun, and glamorous piece of GE's portfolio, Welch took a particular interest in NBC and its sports division. I knew from Brandon how much Welch backed the executives he believed in; and in those first few meetings, it was clear that Wright and Welch both really wanted NBC Sports to succeed, and were going to be bosses who would empower me to input a real vision for the department. But honestly, even then, I'm not sure if I could have dreamed just how much that would be the case.

We negotiated and came close to a deal pretty quickly. As part of the agreement, I would no longer be involved in *Saturday Night's Main Event* with Vince—wrestling, remember, wasn't a sport but part of the entertainment division. The business side of that separation was, as always with Vince, extraordinarily simple—no paperwork or lawyers needed.

"We've never had a contract, and it's worked out perfectly," I told him over the phone as I filled him in on my plans. "So let's keep it simple: the only thing that I want to continue is our great friendship. I'm giving up any financial interest in all this going forward, and you just take it from here."

I'd also no longer actively produce *Later*, even though I'd get to work even more frequently with Costas on the sports side. *Friday Night Videos* was the only part that got a little complicated. The best course forward seemed to be to sell the show directly to the network, but a lawyer in NBC's West Coast entertainment offices balked at the figure I wanted. When Bob Wright got wind of this, he stepped in, calling me directly to work out the deal to buy the show from me. It was another good sign of what was ahead, and how much trust there'd be on both sides. We came to an agreement soon after. I was going corporate again, and in early April, I was back at 30 Rock, addressing my new staff in Studio 8H.

I still remember that first meeting well. I wanted to give it a casual feel, and it lasted no more than twenty or thirty minutes. There were a few familiar faces, including Costas, as well as Marv Albert, who had actually appeared on the second episode of *Saturday Night Live* alongside streetball hoops legend Connie Hawkins. As I looked out into the crowd, I spoke about the great memories I'd had in the studio.

"This is where we started *SNL*," I told them. "It's where I met my wife. And now I'm talking to you here because I think today can be the springboard for more big things. Really big things."

As I continued to talk, I wanted to let them know that for all the entertainment work I'd done, my passion for sports was as strong as ever, and I was energized to get back into the game and lead a large, talented group like themselves. I told them another truth as well: I had a ton of respect for what they did in their live television work, but I was looking forward to putting an imprint on another skill— their storytelling. To succeed, and to be the gold standard of the industry the way ABC Sports had been in the 1970s, we had to tell stories better than anyone else.

But I also knew another truth. To even earn the chance of telling those stories, you had to be able to make the right deals for the right sports at the right time.

To really appreciate the challenge facing NBC Sports in 1989, you have to understand how different the business of sports television—and the world of sports—was then from the way it is today. ESPN was still just coming into its own, a rising force, but not a major player yet in terms of actually televising the biggest events. There was only one way to watch big-time sports on television—and that was on either of the three networks, CBS, NBC, and ABC. Even Fox was still a few years away from emerging as an equal player.

Like today, but even more intensely, the identity of each network was very much tied to the sports they broadcast. CBS was best known for its NFL coverage— they'd been broadcasting games since the league's beginnings, and with the irrepressible John Madden and unflappable Pat Summerall at the microphones, and the NFC package featuring the biggest markets and best teams, the biggest matchup on football Sundays was almost always on CBS. And though Roone Arledge had long since moved to ABC News by 1989, ABC Sports was still a force, with *Wide World of Sports* and college football remaining the flagships of its weekend coverage, and *Monday Night Football* an institution now almost two decades old.

Sports gave these networks some of their biggest ratings, with advertising revenues counteracting huge rights fees, and opportunities to promote their other programming providing less measurable but very significant benefits on top of the pure dollars. In other words, sports could be profitable for sure, but also an effective loss leader if they lifted the performance and profile of the rest of the network. Pat Summerall telling the audience what was coming up next on *60 Minutes* and *Murder, She Wrote* represented just as much of the identity of CBS to many viewers as Mike Wallace and Angela Lansbury themselves. (Though it was no coincidence that those Sunday night shows were the network's highest rated, with the football games as lead-ins.) The point is: sports mattered to both the bottom line and the brand in the business of network television.

As I jumped into the job, it was a complete whirlwind. Arthur Watson had been completely hands-off when it came to production, just focusing on the business side. (In fact, several years earlier, Don Ohlmeyer had been Watson's executive producer, running NBC Sports' production operation.) Here, Wright and Welch, as well as Brandon, saw me as not just someone who could shape and improve the specifics of what went on the broadcast but who could handle the strategy of what to put on the air. Years later, when asked about why he wanted to not just coach a team but also act as its general manager, Bill Parcells would say, "If they want you to cook the dinner, at least they ought to let you shop for some of the groceries." Now, just like Roone had years earlier, I was getting a rare shot to do just that.

Still, as much as my years apprenticing with Roone, alongside my experience in production, made me worthy of both jobs, I also knew what I didn't know. I'd never actually participated in a big-time negotiation with a league or governing body alongside Roone; I'd just watched him do it. In our very first conversation, before I was hired, Jack Welch said he figured that I'd want to get rid of Watson's top lieutenant so I could start fresh. I said absolutely not; I'd need that person to let me know what I was getting into and where things stood. And that's how my great friend Ken Schanzer started as my number two. He'd still have the same job when we left together twenty-two years later.

So there were events to attend and a staff to get to know and, just as important, any number of commissioners and owners and agents and executives to meet, all across the country and even the world. Some of the meetings were total thrills, like on just my second day of the job, when Pete Rozelle, the legendary NFL commissioner, came over to 30 Rock with Tex Schramm, the president of the Dallas Cowboys. The last time I'd crossed paths with Rozelle was when I'd delivered papers to Roone during their meetings to start *Monday Night Football* decades earlier. Now Rozelle was in the last year of his tenure, and had come to NBC's offices for the first time ever to see if the network was interested in taking an ownership stake in the World League of American Football, later to be renamed NFL Europe.

Our meeting that afternoon had a warm feel, but we weren't interested in the deal. A football league in Europe would never have any enduring stars—any talented players would jump right to the U.S.—and without stars, it wouldn't be able to sustain its popularity. As much as I admired Rozelle, the investment didn't make sense. But the meeting was a reminder nonetheless of how quickly I had to figure out what the next move for NBC Sports would be. Now that baseball was going away, I had to find a way to fill the void and fill it fast. Yes, the NFL was the foundation of NBC Sports on Sundays in the fall. And our golf coverage also took care of a number of weekends. Other events—like the French Open and Wimbledon, and of course the Olympics—were central parts of the portfolio, but only came in a contained burst of days, once a year or even less frequently than that. The loss of baseball, though, had left a glaring hole in the schedule from April through October; weeks upon weeks of regular, reliable advertising revenue that made real money for the company. For all the good vibes surrounding my hiring with Wright and Welch, if we couldn't find a way to get back that money, the very future of NBC Sports would be in jeopardy.

And as if I needed another reminder of how quickly I had to act, just a few weeks into taking the job, I went to San Francisco to address the network's affiliates from all across the country. They were a key group to keep on my side; if they sensed the network wasn't going to fill the hole left by baseball, they had the right to sell off that time in the schedule to syndicators; at least that would guarantee them advertising revenue. Because I couldn't guarantee anything, I decided to put on a show, and onstage, I listed some fictional, fantasy projects to almost amuse and distract the executives assembled. The first-ever television movie to premiere on a weekend afternoon, *Joe D and the Blonde*. And a touch football exhibition between the Dallas Cowboys and Oakland Raiders, titled *The Super Bowl You Never Saw*. It was the last time I ever gave a speech from prepared notes in my life; I remember realizing how reading my speech was interfering with the connection I needed to make with the audience, particularly in a case where I needed them to trust me. In any event, the "ideas" got some laughs, and on the side, I confided in some major affiliates that I did have a plan and was already working to enact it.

In our initial meetings, Ken Schanzer told me that he and Arthur Watson had been exploring bringing the NCAA tournament and Final Four back to the network. (NBC had been the original home of college basketball's signature event in the seventies.) But the tournament didn't make much sense as a major investment for the network. It was only a month of action, with only a few weekends in March of huge games, and the sport's appeal wasn't actually as broad as it might have seemed. To make a deal that would keep the business of NBC Sports successful, we needed something bigger. And I had my eyes on what I saw as a much bigger and better possible play: to make a deal with a league that was on the rise in exciting ways, and could fill the many weekends of programming that were going away with the loss of baseball's famed "Game of the Week." As I envisioned it, this league could become the new signature partner of NBC Sports. And best of all, its rights deal was coming up for renegotiation.

The National Basketball Association had been on CBS since the early seventies, after the network had grabbed the league from ABC, where I had worked on games. The league had declined in popularity the rest of that decade, plagued by a reputation that its players were drug abusers—a reputation that certainly had an element of racism to it.

CBS often failed to show the NBA Finals live in prime time in those years, instead often putting it on tape delay in late night. But then, as the eighties began, things changed. Lifted by the rising stardom and rivalry of Magic Johnson and Larry Bird, pro basketball started to grow tremendously. Through every single year of the decade, either the Lakers or the Celtics made the finals, with the teams matching up head-to-head three different times. The "Bad Boys" Pistons made for great villains alongside them. Tape-delayed finals would no longer be tolerated by fans.

And if the average fan saw Magic and Bird as the faces of the league, there were other stars emerging around them—and the NBA was clearly building itself on the back of marketing those stars. Michael Jordan, as a one-man highlight film, was the biggest of them, but all throughout pro basketball were big talents with nicknames and personalities that the league clearly saw as their best asset for growing the game. From Patrick Ewing in New York to Charles Barkley in Philadelphia to Isiah Thomas in Detroit to Hakeem Olajuwon in Houston to Karl Malone and John Stockton in Utah and more, the NBA had stars—and was using those stars as the foundation of its marketing strategy. And from everything I'd been told, that strategy all went straight back to the figure in charge, the NBA's commissioner, David Stern.

Making a deal and bringing the NBA to NBC immediately became my top priority. It was a pursuit that would set the course for my entire tenure at NBC. And the backbone of it all would be my bond with the man at the top of the league.

The day after that introductory meeting with the staff of NBC Sports in April 1989, I set up a breakfast meeting with Stern at the Berkshire Hotel on Fifty-Second Street, right across the street from the NBA's offices at the time. We set the breakfast for 9:00 a.m., after the room cleared out from the morning rush. We'd never met or even spoken before, but I knew that with CBS's deal ending after the 1990 season, conversations about the next deal were surely well underway with CBS to renew. ABC was likely having conversations about getting back in the mix as well. So I had two objectives for the breakfast: one, for David and I to get to know each other; and two, to let him know what else NBC could bring to the table—besides money—as a potential new network partner.

The first part would be easy—we hit it off before the coffee even came. David was five years older than me, and had a sharp sense of humor and a curiosity about the world that went far beyond basketball. Sitting there in that largely deserted dining room, we talked about a lot of things over breakfast—our careers, our lives, and the state of sports—which, of course, eventually turned the topic to the NBA. He was proud of his league, and had big ambitions for it, ambitions he'd been growing ever since he'd been named commissioner five years earlier after serving as the league's top lawyer. Very quickly, there was no question in my mind that this would be someone I wanted to work with and get to know better. Beyond how bullish I was about the league's future—this was one of the smartest and most impressive people I'd ever met.

"To me," I said to him, "the NBA has all kinds of potential, and it feels so unfulfilled right now. The game is just so damn entertaining—if you could have a network partner willing to air more games for you on weekends, later in the day closer to prime time, that will get more viewers, and can be the foundation of real growth."

He nodded—I wasn't telling him anything he didn't know. David was endlessly frustrated by CBS's coverage, from taped games to the fact that they regularly paused their NBA coverage in March while they aired the NCAA tourney.

"It just comes down to a network willing to partner with you in the fashion the league deserves," I told him.

I brought up another idea, too. At the time, the FCC had very stringent rules about what kinds of programming the networks could install on Saturday mornings. Because children were the main audience watching, the shows—even the cartoons—had to be educational in some way.

"So what if we were to do this," I pitched him. "What if we produced a weekly basketball highlight show geared toward young people in one of those slots?"

There would be profiles of players, instructive segments—I was laying out all the pieces for the show that eventually became *Inside Stuff*. David loved it. He knew as well as I did that there was nothing more valuable in growing the NBA's audience than getting young fans excited about the game. (I'd eventually also share the idea with NBC's lobbyist in Washington to confirm the concept could satisfy the FCC's requirements for educational programming.)

Our conversations picked up from there in the weeks and months ahead, lending a real urgency to my first few months at NBC Sports. Every day we came to work, every meeting I had with people in my group, I felt stronger and stronger that the NBA was a bet we couldn't afford to not make. I was under no illusions, though, what the real key would be: money. As great as my first breakfast and subsequent conversations with David Stern had been, and as much of a connection as we'd made, you can never deny the importance of the bottom line to a negotiation. And so I had to make a solid case to Bob Wright and Jack Welch that the NBA would be worth a big investment.

Making the scenario trickier was the undeniable sense of how significantly the tectonic plates of the business were shifting. CBS had just paid $1.8 billion for the rights to broadcast baseball's entire postseason, the All-Star Game, and the Saturday game of the week. It was a massive deal that had blown NBC (and ABC, which also had a deal with baseball) out of the water. But the truth was that Arthur Watson had been wise not to go anywhere close to that number. Within two years, CBS would incur a massive write-down on its deal, upward of $800 million as reported. It was a complete disaster for the company, illustrating the risk that a sports rights deal could be. As for ABC, while the Olympics had been arguably the network's most prominent sports showcase during Roone's golden years, ABC's new parent company, Capital Cities, had had a rude awakening the year prior when the Calgary Winter Games had been upended by weather, with a brutal financial fallout. Dan Burke and Tom Murphy, now running ABC, had been buried on their way in the door, and had no interest in taking a risk on a new sports deal again anytime soon.

Like anything, making a good deal in sports television was about reading the climate, and to me, this was the perfect time to make a big bet when everyone else was contracting. It was really clear that the NBA was a league on the rise. Plus, the league's calendar—with potential weekly featured games starting in January and then continuing on through the playoffs and finals into June—was an even better fit than baseball had been with our schedule. So I felt confident about making the case for a big investment in the NBA. And even better, I had a big ace up my sleeve, thanks to NBC's sports advertising department.

In an early meeting in my first few months on the job, the executives in that group had presented me an ingenious idea that had the potential to reap tens, if not hundreds, of millions of additional dollars in revenue for a possible NBA deal. For years, ad buyers had operated under the general premise that in any given game, brands would get "exclusive" placement with their commercials. That is to say, a car brand, like Chevrolet, would have the domestic exclusive in a given game—as the only domestic car to advertise. There would be a domestic exclusive and a foreign exclusive in each game, and companies would pay for that exclusivity. The problem was, it limited the number of advertisers a given broadcast could have. Well, just as I came into the job, NBC's very smart head of sports sales, Jim Burnette, came up with an idea to change the rules. If we could secure the rights to the NBA, Jim was proposing selling "multiple exclusives" to the automakers. Yes, it sounded like a contradiction, but that was essentially the point. Forget about every game—every *quarter* would have its own domestic and foreign exclusive. With as many as eight different sponsors, there would be more money to be made in every game—meaning it would be financially feasible to pay more in a rights deal.

The idea would have to be sold up the chain to Bob Wright, as well as NBC's longtime head of finance, Don Carswell, and his top analyst, the wonderfully named Ed Swindler (who, even more unbelievably, had a key lieutenant named Sue Costley). Their concern surrounded how odd the idea of "multiple exclusives" sounded; would the autos really go for the idea? But Burnette had done his research, and done it well, and he knew how eager automakers were to advertise in the NBA's games for its huge youthful audience. Just like us, they saw the league's potential for growth. With these "multiple exclusives," if we could land the league as a partner, we absolutely had a way forward to make a profit on even an expensive deal. And with Carswell's enthusiasm for the plan, when we presented it to Wright and then Welch, they bought in. We had the green light to make a big bet on the NBA.

We also had some luck: it was just a matter of time until CBS—already over-extended deeply with their new baseball deal—blanched at paying the big increase in a rights fee that the league wanted. ABC, as I said, was out of the picture. And so, on the afternoon of November 10, 1989, I sat in my office with Ken Schanzer and Arthur Watson (who'd helpfully stayed on, at my request, as an adviser for a year), waiting for the official word that CBS passed on their option to renew. The call came from David Stern himself, asking if we could meet. I told him we'd be over to his office in ten minutes, and walking by St. Patrick's Cathedral on Fiftieth Street and saying one more little prayer from the street, we were there in five. No time was wasted from there: we knew what their asking price would be, and were comfortable with it. After a brief meeting with David and his top deputies at the time, Russ Granik and future NHL commissioner Gary Bettman, the deal was done. It was hardly even a negotiation; the trust was already there between the league and the network.

Before dawn the next morning, Schanzer and I arrived to hang NBA hats on the doors all across the offices of NBC Sports to surprise the staff when they got in. They were thrilled—after spending several months after the loss of baseball concerned about their jobs, now they suddenly had a ton of work to do.

It was a four-year agreement for $644 million—almost four times what CBS had paid in its previous deal, but to us, it was totally worth it. Our calculations told us that with the multiple exclusives in place, we could make so much money on ads that we'd potentially be at a break-even point each season before the playoffs even started. Even better for the NBA, to hit our financial marks, we were excited to do everything we could to support the league's growth. We'd be televising more games in the regular season, with scheduled doubleheaders, and also more games in the playoffs. We'd be adding a more extended, and potentially lucrative, big pre-game show to our coverage. *Inside Stuff* would be airing on Saturday mornings. If the NBA on NBC was going to succeed, we needed to be all in.

There would be other highlights ahead for NBC Sports over the next decade. But that agreement with the NBA was absolutely the foundation of every other deal—and every other success—that followed. Not to mention, it would also be what you could arguably say was, to that point, the greatest partnership between a league and a network in television history.

Though, in the fall of 1989, a little less than a year out from the start of the NBA on NBC, we knew we were on the hook to make it all work.

CHAPTER 16

I Love This Game

The day after our deal was announced, Neal Pilson, the president of CBS Sports, professed not to be upset about losing the NBA.

"The future of the NBA," he was said to have told his staff, "is in Cleveland and Utah."

His point was clear: He didn't see the league flourishing in big markets, which would lead to poor ratings in the years to come. He didn't see any great teams and great stars in the NBA's present or future.

I couldn't have disagreed more.

First—and I was hardly the only basketball fan thinking this—if you had to bet on anything, it was that Michael Jordan was on the precipice of being the biggest force in the league. I certainly couldn't have predicted that he'd eventually win six titles, or become the singular marketing icon that he did, but to dismiss his significance out of hand was to ignore everything that any fan paying any attention could see. He was playing in the country's third-biggest city, and with Magic Johnson in Los Angeles, and Patrick Ewing in New York, plus a strong Pistons team in the auto-town city of Detroit, the league was actually loaded in the biggest markets. But even beyond that, going into business with David Stern, it was clear that no matter how the future went, the way the league marketed its players could transcend the profile of the cities they played in. And that notion would bear itself out in years to come when teams from Portland, Phoenix, Houston, Orlando, and, yes, eventually, Utah would develop stars that the audience was excited to watch play in the biggest games.

Still, not everyone saw it that way, and in the weeks and months following the announcement of the deal, the headlines swirled about the risk NBC had taken with the NBA. What if it flopped? they were speculating. How would NBC and GE deal with the fallout?

I didn't waste my time with what a few columnists wrote; from the beginning, I had so much fun as a basketball fan being close to the action I didn't have time to worry. Our coverage that first season, 1990–91, began with games in Barcelona for McDonald's-sponsored exhibitions featuring NBA teams playing European clubs. Then, as the season would go on, it was just like anything else in sports TV—we were telling the audience a story that would unfold over the course of the regular season and all throughout the playoffs.

I loved meeting the players, coaches, executives, and owners when I went to games—off and on during the regular season, and then routinely in the playoffs. It was an entirely different landscape than when I'd been a production assistant for ABC a few decades earlier, but the thrill of getting to know the stars at the center of the action was the same. Jordan was every bit the alpha you'd think he was, and took to calling me "Dickie Boy," Howard Cosell's old nickname for me, after we'd met a few times before and after games. Charles Barkley was the funniest player in the league, even then; a natural for television. Over the next few years, we'd talk plenty about his future as a broadcaster. Patrick Ewing was smart and curious, even if he didn't show it outwardly to the press. The coaches, like Phil Jackson and Pat Riley, who was the original analyst for our pregame show, *NBA Showtime*, before returning to the sidelines for the Knicks, were great characters in their own right.

Behind the scenes, a ton of work went into making the coverage so strong and the partnership so successful. Starting that first season, there was a nonstop collaboration between two dedicated staffs at the NBA and the network in New York. Every week, we had regular working lunch meetings with the league, either at our offices or theirs. Top production people, business executives, the PR staffs—being that we were just a few blocks apart in Midtown Manhattan, getting together for all of us was easy. The meetings were designed to keep an ongoing conversation going: what players we were focusing on in the weekend's matchups, what issues we might be having in the production of games, what we might need from teams in upcoming weeks, and so forth. It was a total and complete partnership, and rising executives in the league like the great Adam Silver, Stern's eventual successor, and the wonderful Val Ackerman, the future Big East commissioner, were regular presences at the table alongside our top producers.

Meetings like that had never happened before in any partnership between a league and a network, as far as I knew. The constant exchange of ideas, the completely open lines of communication, and the sense of shared mission that grew out of them really defined the relationship. And one of the central keys to its success was that everyone on both sides knew just how close their bosses—that is, David and I—were.

David was a magnetic personality—curious, brilliant, passionate, and at times explosive. Even his greatest admirers would tell you that he wasn't easy to work for. Like I've said, our personalities were a great match, but sure, like a lot of passionate people, we both had moments when our tempers got the best of us. I remember in one of our early meetings, angry about something forgettable, David's temper found me as its target. He screamed at me, in front of both our staffs right there in a conference room. I could have easily screamed back, but I let it go. A few hours later, I called him, and we talked it out. We just got along too well, I said, and saw the world too similarly, for us to go at each other like that, in front of our staffs. He agreed. And honestly: there was never another blowup between us—in either direction—again.

There had been that initial spark at our very first breakfast, but our relationship grew the old-fashioned way: spending time together. In 1991, with the McDonald's preseason exhibition, we were both in Paris. With the first Olympics featuring NBA players a little less than a year away, David had worked hard to shore up a strong relationship with FIBA, the international basketball federation, but didn't have much of a connection with the International Olympic Committee and its leader, Juan Antonio Samaranch, to whom I'd grown close (much more on that relationship in a bit). So I proposed that after the tournament ended, we could drive together from Paris to Lausanne, Switzerland, the headquarters of the IOC, and schedule a dinner with Samaranch. We set off on a road trip—David driving the rental car, me riding shotgun, our wives in the back. In Lausanne, the dinner went great, and before flying home to the States, David and Diane proposed stopping for a visit at the Matterhorn. Susan and I had never been there, and with some hastily purchased parkas to deal with the chill, we took a cable car up, and had a great lunch in what was billed the highest restaurant in all of Europe. It may sound like a random few days all these years later, but the trip was the kind of experience that solidified our connection.

Once the season started, there were the weekends when the dialogue would continue. Every Saturday and Sunday over the course of the season, David and I would have what amounted to a running conversation from our respective dens in Scarsdale, New York, where he lived, and Litchfield, when I wasn't at the games. He'd pick up the phone to good-naturedly complain about a comment one of our announcers made. And then I'd call him back five minutes later to point out a bad call from one of his refs.

"You've got to get a life! Get outside!" he'd tease me by the tenth phone call.

"Oh, come on," I'd respond. "I'm your dream—all you've ever wanted is someone who cares as much as you do."

The truth was that all throughout those meetings and those conversations, all the way to our game coverage, if there was one operating principle I wanted our team to abide by, it was the idea that the league—the partner—always came first. Every idea we had, every innovation we wanted to consider, every decision we wanted to make, had to first be run through the prism of: Is it good for the league? The league came first in everything; after all, it was "the NBA on NBC." That approach didn't mean we wouldn't cover tough stories, or have our announcers or reporters pull punches when commentating, interviewing, or analyzing. The audience would see through it if we did, and losing our credibility wouldn't be good for us or the league. Not to mention, occasional controversies stoked interest. But balancing the journalistic part of our coverage with our role as a partner—I didn't see that as a conflict, but rather just two parts of a living, breathing relationship with the league.

Having that attitude was a surefire way to maintain David's trust, and to make the partnership an ever-expanding collaboration. We willingly promoted games that were airing on Turner Sports, even though that was unheard of at the time. And as the league's ratings grew, we of course wanted to air more games ourselves, which is how Sunday doubleheaders became triple-headers, with one game tipping off at 12:30 p.m. eastern time, another at 3:00, and another at 5:30, guaranteeing the NBA would be seen in prime time every week, on the most widely watched night of the week. Christmas Day had long been a day to feature a great game on a network; we turned it into a network doubleheader. It was all a total contrast from the NBA's prior deal with CBS, when the league had to fight to get more games on, and even more unbelievably, fight to get their finals simply to air live.

Our strategy paid off with any number of benefits. At one point, for example, we talked with the league about getting more insight into how the schedule was done. David agreed, and soon I was getting brought into the process with the NBA's longtime scheduling czar, Matt Winick, able to advocate for the kinds of matchups we knew rated well on Sundays. I was able to work with Matt and give input into the schedule for David to give his final approval, offering an invaluable inside track.

The constant willingness to keep pushing actually started at our very first NBA Finals, a dream matchup that was the culmination of a terrific first season working together. With all due respect to Cleveland and Utah, nothing could have made us happier than when Jordan's Bulls finally toppled the Pistons to advance to their first NBA Finals, where they would face none other than the league's other top star, Magic Johnson and the Lakers. L.A. won a close first game before the Bulls came back to take Games 2 and 3. With Game 4 coming on a Sunday, I saw an opportunity, and went to David.

"What if we moved the game into prime time?" I asked him. "The audience could explode in size."

Of course he agreed immediately, but he cleverly turned it into a bargain.

"Great," he told me. "But if we're doing it for this series, we've got to do it for every series, every year, whether it's Bulls-Lakers or any other team."

I had no problem saying yes. It was clear how important this was to him; if a finals wasn't as competitive down the line, and putting a future game in prime time cost us a ratings point, it was worth it for the bigger benefit to the relationship. Again, it was just one of many instances where we each pushed the other to take chances—and just one of many instances where that kind of gamble paid off. Higher ratings in prime time meant more money for advertising. And when the Bulls won that series in five games, cementing Jordan as the face of the league, it was pretty clear we were going to be in great shape moving the finals into prime time.

Everything with the NBA on NBC seemed meant to be in those first few years—even our theme song, composed by John Tesh, became a beloved part of our coverage. Tesh, then hosting *Entertainment Tonight*, had had a side career creating music for sports television for years, going back to his time at CBS Sports working alongside David Michaels, Al's younger brother and a terrific producer who'd join NBC in 1990. When Tommy Roy, our NBA producer, received half a dozen tapes from composers auditioning for the job, Tesh's song, which he titled "Roundball Rock," just stood out. It wasn't like all the other sports themes airing for other networks that were dominated by classical sounds. It was much fresher and had more energy—almost like a musical expression for the adrenaline and sense of joy embodied by basketball at its best. When Tommy passed it along to me, I knew we had something great, but Tesh had recorded it on an electronic keyboard—this after he'd woken up in a hotel in the middle of the night with the tune in his head, and called his answering machine back home in Los Angeles to sing it to himself.

I called John with a bunch of producers in the room to tell him we'd chosen his theme.

"Congratulations!" I said. "We're going with your theme. It's just terrific. And I think it can be even better. So here's what I want you to do: go record it with an orchestra. Make it as big as you can. We love it, and the bigger it'll sound, the better."

I don't think it's a stretch to say that "Roundball Rock" is one of the most iconic sports soundtracks in TV sports history. We'd even bring it back during Olympic basketball coverage, years after our NBA deal was over.

As for the editorial part of our coverage, CBS hadn't had a pregame show, but we created *Showtime*. Originally hosted by Bob Costas along with Coach Riley, the show seamlessly led into our games, the biggest of which were called by Marv Albert, who established himself as the unquestioned voice of the NBA, working with Mike "The Czar of the Telestrator" Fratello and, later, Doug Collins. Our other top announce team, Tom Hammond, Bill Walton, and Steve "Snapper" Jones, was always a joy to listen to, with old friends Bill and Snapper sniping at each other, Jones never shying away from calling out Walton on an outrageous comment.

As for *Inside Stuff*, when David asked me at one of our early weekly joint staff lunches who I wanted to host the show, he loudly scoffed when I mentioned who I was considering.

"What about Ahmad Rashad?" I'd said. Ahmad, the former star wide receiver in the NFL, had been part of our football coverage for a few years, but we had bigger plans for him.

"Ahmad Rashad!" David shouted. "Didn't he play football? How is he going to host a basketball show?"

"You're not getting it!" I replied with a smile. "Ahmad is as charismatic as anyone we have working for us. And the players see him as one of them—as an athlete. Trust me."

It took a few more conversations, but eventually David relented, and Ahmad ended up not just being a huge success on the weekly show, but of course our star sideline reporter, becoming close friends with Jordan along the way—closer than anyone else in media to him.

It all contributed to big ratings, and with the "multiple exclusives" working just as we'd hoped, our sales team reaped millions. And as much as that was the ultimate way to measure our success, there was something even more fundamental. Very quickly, to fans everywhere—and in some ways even to us behind the scenes—it felt like the NBA had always been on NBC. The melding of the league with our presentation was so seamless that it felt like we were two parts of the same whole, instead of two different entities that had come together. And beyond that, the NBA's status as the hottest league in sports melded together with NBC's identity as the top-rated network in television. "I Love This Game" and "Must See TV" felt like different parts of the same whole; the NBA on NBC and *Seinfeld* and *Friends* were almost cousins who were part of the same family.

Both were immensely popular. Both were incredibly entertaining.

Like so many others, I remember where I was when I first heard one of the most stunning stories in NBA history. It was early November 1991 and I was in Dayton, Ohio, on a layover to South Bend, Indiana, heading to a big Notre Dame game, when I got a message to call Russ Granik, one of David Stern's top deputies, as soon as possible.

"I know what I'm about to tell you is shocking and will be hard to comprehend," Russ said when I reached him. "But Magic Johnson just tested positive for HIV. David's already on his way to Los Angeles for a press conference this afternoon."

The news was hard to comprehend—completely out of nowhere. But just hours later, there was David on a dais next to Magic in L.A. as he shared it with the world. That night, we worked with NBC News to produce a half-hour tribute to Magic that aired in late night. Not enough can be said about the grace and courage with which Magic handled his illness, that day and ever since—but David, it's important to note, was right there with him, steadfast in his support. He was concerned about Magic, but through his own anguish, he immediately realized how impactful the NBA's response to the news could be. In 1991, AIDS was an illness that came with a huge stigma. People suffered in secret, in silence. Even in the six years since Rock Hudson, Susan's good friend and former costar on *McMillan & Wife*, had died from AIDS, there was still a tremendous amount of fear around the disease. Together, Magic and the NBA would change all of that. From that very first press conference Magic held in Los Angeles, David was more than just right at his side. He did his own research, talking to all the experts, and supported Magic as he quickly emerged as the face of the disease. It would be hard to imagine any other commissioner making such a personal effort, and taking such a stand.

By the beginning of 1992, even though he was retired, Magic was still on the All-Star ballot and the leading vote getter. He called David and asked him if he could play, and Stern said yes, knowing the backlash it would engender. Many players spoke about being afraid to get on the court with him. Being that the All-Star Game was one of our biggest telecasts of the year, I was talking to David daily about it. He sent medical experts to every locker room in the league to explain to them the lack of risk. Whatever he had to do to convince players that it would be okay for Magic to play in the game, he did it.

That Sunday in Orlando, I left the production truck to watch the pregame introductions from the floor. It was like we were broadcasting a movie. It started with Magic going down the row of All-Stars standing on the court, the dramatic sight of him hugging every single one of them when his name was announced. Then, once the game started, came his splendid MVP performance—twenty-five points, nine assists, and a majestic turnaround three-pointer late in the fourth quarter. That All-Star Game was as magical as any NBA game we ever broadcast—and, of course, got massive ratings. And then, the tale continued that summer with Magic's appearance on the Dream Team alongside Jordan, Bird, Barkley, Ewing, and their fellow superstars. Serendipitously, of course, we had the Olympics, and to the audience, it was a seamless chronicle of hope—improbable hope that Magic would somehow be able to survive this disease, a hope that, all these years later, has so wonderfully proven true. It wasn't always easy; Magic would have to cut off a return attempt the next season when too many players voiced concern. But he and David stayed close, and taking their lead all throughout, we gave people a real understanding of AIDS for the first time—what was a risk, what wasn't, and what kind of life was possible, even then, with HIV.

In the middle of it all, in 1992, we even hired Magic to join our color commentary team for the NBA playoffs. That famous shot of Michael Jordan shrugging his shoulders as he jogged back down the court, as if to say that even he didn't know how he'd drilled six three-pointers in a row against the Trail Blazers. He was shrugging at his buddy Magic, catching his eye at the broadcast table. Magic was great to work with, and also fun to play with. That's right—play with. One of the fun parts of those early years of our NBA coverage was an occasional production staff game on an off-day morning. Of course, I didn't miss a chance to relive my not-so-glory years as a high school player, and I'll never forget the feeling of the ball hitting my fingers from one of Magic's warp-speed passes on a fast break— hitting my fingers, and almost going through them, that is.

As for Jordan, chronicling his first three-peat with the Bulls, sandwiched around the Olympic gold medal in Barcelona, was just about as good as any story we could have written ourselves. On the NBA on NBC, he became the most famous athlete in the world, and a marketing phenomenon. I met his father a few times, talking to him as we sat in the empty stands during pregame shootarounds in the midst of the NBA Finals. He liked to say that we were both "GE men," since he had once been a supervisor in a company factory in North Carolina. But just a few months after the last of those conversations, shortly after the 1993 finals, tragically, James Jordan was murdered. A few months later, I got another call from David's office.

"I'm going to Chicago," the commissioner said over the phone. "Michael's retiring."

I couldn't believe my ears—but I figured the only thing to do was get on a plane myself and be there for the press conference. It was surreal to be there as Michael walked away from the game. But from there, it was just a matter of working as closely as ever with the league to keep the audience engaged with the narrative that had to take Michael's place; namely, finally, the other stars were going to have a chance to win a title themselves. And sure enough, it would be the Knicks and the Rockets—led by Patrick Ewing and Hakeem Olajuwon—facing off in a close, seven-game finals in 1994.

Then the following spring, rumors started growing out of Chicago that Michael was considering a comeback. As always, I stayed in close contact with David and his team, as we all waited to find out if it was real or just smoke. And then, on a Wednesday at about noon in my office, I got a call from David Falk, Michael's agent.

"Michael wants to talk to you," he said.

I told him I was available anytime, and sure enough, a moment later, my assistant told me Michael himself was on the line.

"Dickie Boy," came the familiar voice on the phone. Falk was also listening in.

"I want to explore something with you," Jordan said. It was immediately clear I was talking to Michael the businessman, as opposed to Michael the basketball player.

"We think me coming back has some value to NBC."

Even if it was unheard of, his point was not hard to see through: he was calling to see if NBC would be willing to pay him in some way to return.

"Well, maybe it does, Michael," I replied, "but you *not* playing had *no* value to NBC. In fact, you were a big part of the value that we agreed to when we signed our new [rights] deal before last season. And we haven't come close to making the numbers we anticipated without you playing. So you've got to consider that side of it, too."

The call ended quickly but pleasantly, and as soon as I hung up, I called David to brief him on what we'd talked about. I never heard from Michael about it again. Several days later, I was sitting in a control room at CBS of all places (thanks to an invitation to observe them producing the first afternoon of March Madness), when I got a message to call David. It was official: Michael was coming back. Surrounded by my friendly rivals, I had to maintain a straight face, knowing that three days later, the following Sunday, with Michael's first game, we would obliterate CBS's NCAA tournament numbers. In fact, that Bulls-Pacers game would be the highest-rated regular season game in NBA history.

And Michael's comeback would be defined by three more championships in 1996, 1997, and 1998, each of them unfolding on NBC.

It wasn't all good times. Probably the most complicated juncture of the NBA on NBC was in 1999, when the league struggled through a lockout that lasted several months and threatened to cancel the season. By then, we were well into our third deal with the league—we'd originally extended our contract in 1993, and then again in 1997. Very clearly written into the deal, the league was well protected by a clause that ensured that we still paid them even in the midst of a job action. All we could do was be patient and supportive, and hope for a good outcome as soon as possible.

As the work stoppage bled into what was supposed to be the start of the season, it was stressful, but we had some breathing room because our broadcasts didn't begin until Christmas. Then, though, Christmas came and went, and after New Year's, prospects for the season weren't looking strong. David could report no progress, even behind the scenes. Meanwhile, Bob Wright, still the CEO of NBC, was getting more and more nervous about writing checks to the league without any games to show for the money.

Fortunately, David and I came up with a solution together in Gordon Gund, the owner of the Cleveland Cavaliers, and the then head of the league's governing board. Gund, who'd lost his sight years earlier to an eye disease, was a terrific man and one of the most widely admired and respected owners in all of professional sports. He was also a personal friend of Wright, and bringing him into a meeting with Bob placated the situation.

By mid-January, prospects for a season were looking dimmer than ever. Then, almost out of nowhere, while at a GE management meeting in Florida, I got a call from David—there had been an unexpected breakthrough. Word was that Shaquille O'Neal—then at the peak of his prime—had played a huge role in getting the players to come back to the negotiating table at the eleventh hour. I immediately flew back to New York, ready to put the wheels in motion with a season perhaps suddenly starting—meaning new scheduling, new promotions, and more. I went straight from the airport to my office to wait for word. The phone rang, and my wonderful longtime assistant, Aimee Leone, picked up, and a moment later yelled for me.

"Dick, it's Shaq on the phone for you!"

Sure enough, when I picked up, the familiar baritone of Shaquille O'Neal came through some loud noise that sounded like a jet engine in the background.

"Mr. Ebersol, it's Shaq! I'm at the airport about to take off, can you hear me?"

"Yeah, Shaq, I can hear you."

"I just wanted to tell you, everything's fine! We're gonna play again. Did I do good?"

"You've done great!" I exclaimed.

And we were back in business.

That abbreviated 1999 campaign would be the first season after Michael Jordan's second retirement, and ratings wouldn't be great, but the following year, Shaq started his own three-peat, with Kobe Bryant and the Lakers, the beginning of a new story to tell. By then, we were in the final years of our partnership with the league. The landscape of television sports had changed drastically in the decade since we'd gone into business together. But even then, we were very much still reaping the benefits of our partnership, and not just with respect to ratings and ad revenue.

Because, much more than that, the huge success of our big bet on the NBA had given NBC Sports a long runway with the network and General Electric. Bob Wright and Jack Welch saw what we'd made possible, and believed in the idea that we could do more. The NBA on NBC had laid a foundation for the rebirth of NBC Sports.

And from there, the potential felt absolutely limitless.

CHAPTER 17

Olympic Dreams

The rhythm is somehow both unforgiving and invigorating. Every day, for upward of seventeen days, you work to your absolute limit. Far from home, away from your family and friends, it's a complete commitment, fueled by passion, day after day, night after night. I'm sure in other kinds of work, there are comparable experiences. But no matter how much someone else might love their job, I just can't imagine that there's anything more fun, more exciting, and more rewarding than working an Olympics for a television network.

When I was lucky enough to start my career going to my first Olympics as a twenty-year-old, the experience started a lifelong love affair with not just the Games but the unparalleled challenge of putting them on television. And so, another of the early highlights when I started my new job at NBC came at the end of May 1989, when I made a trip to Europe. I took Susan along, as well as Ken Schanzer and his wife, and Arthur Watson, still working with us as an adviser, and his wife. The trip started in London, where we had a dinner with our partners at Wimbledon, which NBC had been broadcasting for two decades, and then we flew to France, where the French Open, another network property, was approaching its concluding weekend. The champions at Roland-Garros that year were great stories, with two seventeen-year-olds—American Michael Chang and Spain's Arantxa Sánchez-Vicario—winning the singles titles. Chang's victory was great for ratings back home, while Sánchez-Vicario's championship was particularly auspicious considering who we were headed to meet with next.

Juan Antonio Samaranch had been the president of the International Olympic Committee since 1980. Samaranch, a longtime Spanish sports official and diplomat who'd served at one point as his country's ambassador to the Soviet Union, had taken over the IOC at a low point, soon after the 1980 Moscow Games, which were boycotted by the United States and dozens of other countries. The IOC was saddled with bankruptcy concerns, and struggling to manage its relationships with the many international athletic federations that wielded huge influence in its sports. Though the Soviet Union would lead their own boycott of the next Summer Games in Los Angeles in 1984, Samaranch would do a masterful job of reining in the federations, and solving the IOC's money woes largely by overhauling the organization's sponsorships and television deals. Those L.A. Olympics, thanks in large part to their chief executive, Peter Ueberroth, had illustrated how the Games could be a sponsorship and marketing bonanza, making a profit of more than $230 million in an era when the Olympics were infamous for leaving host cities with brutal debt. And now the IOC under Samaranch was no longer an organization in peril; much to the contrary, the Olympics were a more popular and valuable property than ever before. In the midst of all this, Arthur Watson had successfully negotiated to bring the 1988 and then 1992 Summer Olympics to NBC, and now, in Paris, I'd be meeting Samaranch for the first time.

Dealing with the IOC is more complex than managing a relationship with an American sports entity like the NBA or NFL. That's partially because of simple geography, with the organization based in Europe, but also because it's a body with more than a hundred members from all over the globe, all of them with their own agendas, persuasions and, at times, as history has occasionally borne out, corruptions. To maintain effective communication with the important figures at the IOC, it's essential to have someone on the ground in Europe, able to stay connected with the goings-on in Lausanne, Switzerland, where the group's headquarters have long been located. At ABC, Roone had used a Frenchman named George Croses as his conduit in Europe. For NBC, that role was originally filled by Geoff Mason, my old friend who'd come up at ABC under Roone, and who for years lived in Europe working as the lead producer of *Sportsworld*, NBC's answer to *Wide World of Sports*. Then, when Geoff had decided to move back to the United States, he found someone else to do the job, a colorful and charismatic man from Israel by the name of Alex Gilady. Alex was a TV executive in Israel who was so well respected that when Israel and Egypt had signed their landmark peace treaty in 1979, the Egyptians had been so impressed by Alex's coverage of Anwar Sadat's visit to Israel that they hired him to produce their own coverage when the visit was reciprocated soon after. So Alex knew production, but more important than that, he understood relationships. He lived in Europe, remaining a leader in Israel's own Olympic sports scene, while also cultivating connections all through the IOC. He was rarely seen not wearing one of his trademark double-breasted suits, and was a perfect fit for us as a consultant.

It was Alex who set up the dinner for all of us in Paris that Saturday night in 1989, just hours after Sánchez-Vicario—like Samaranch, a native of Barcelona—had shocked Steffi Graf to win the French Open. The dinner was to be in the Plaza Athénée, one of the chicest hotels in Paris. And I went there with a good-natured but stern warning from Alex.

"Remember," he said to me more than once before the dinner. "When Samaranch goes to dinner, it always ends in exactly an hour and a half. An hour and a half, no more. Okay?"

When I'd raised my eyebrows at this odd time limit, Alex's response was simply that this was just the way Samaranch was.

"It won't be a point of contention," he said. "It's just what it is. It's the way he lives his life. An hour and a half in, it'll be over, and he will simply get up to leave. So make sure you get accomplished what you need to get accomplished in that time."

To me, though, I didn't see the ninety minutes as any kind of restriction. Much to the contrary, it would be a way to make a point about the kind of connection we could establish. And I knew it wouldn't be that hard. Because I didn't want to even really discuss business. I just really wanted to get to know the guy.

From the moment we sat down, a lifetime of curiosity about the Olympics, fortified by my experiences in 1968 and 1972 with ABC, came flowing out. I pumped Samaranch with questions about the Games, about the IOC, about athletes, delegations, federations, and more. I was honestly just fascinated to hear how it all worked. At a certain point, when he got a sense of my background, he started asking me questions—about my experiences in the sixties and seventies, and working for Roone as the first Olympic researcher. I only glanced at my watch once—just before the two-hour mark of the dinner. And Samaranch was happy to stay even longer from there.

I'd like to think that out of that dinner, and out of my enthusiasm, came a realization for Samaranch that he wasn't dealing with someone who looked at the Olympics as just a piece of television business. I loved the Olympics, and believed in the Olympics, just as much as he did. And there just weren't a lot of people who he dealt with who could say that. From that point on, I made a point of always going to Lausanne at least two times a year, if only for a night at a time, to have dinner with Juan Antonio. These weren't set up to be negotiations, but rather just check-ins to keep the relationship flourishing, the dialogue ongoing, and, perfectly candidly, to ask him more of my endless supply of questions. I might be headed to England for golf or France for tennis; whatever it was, I would alter my itinerary to get a one-on-one meeting with Samaranch on the schedule.

Three years after we first met, it would then be especially fun to give him a tour of the NBC compound in Barcelona—an Olympics that were particularly meaningful to him, taking place in his home and native city. And over those two weeks, those Games were the perfect stage to show him how our nightly prime-time shows were a clear contrast from the way NBC had formatted the Games four years earlier in Seoul, before I had gotten there.

Because of the extreme time difference in South Korea, it had been possible in 1988 to put a lot of events taking place in the morning on-site in prime time live back home. But while the network had seen that as an asset, the problem was that a lot of those events didn't appeal to the broad, mainstream, and substantially female audience that, dating back to the advent of the Olympics on television, has always tuned in at prime time. Live or not, women had no interest in watching nightly doses of boxing, for example. But it appeared every night from Seoul when they turned on their TVs, and sure enough, two-thirds of the audience would vanish every time the sport came on.

In Barcelona, by contrast, there were no live sports to show in prime time anyway, considering that 8:00 p.m. on the East Coast in the U.S. was the middle of the night in Spain. So we could handpick the sports most popular with the audience—gymnastics, swimming, and track and field—to air, and then on top of that, we could surround the action with feature pieces introducing the Olympians to the audience, and giving them a rooting interest. Roone's old formula still worked. Two decades earlier, I'd watched him sit in the middle of ABC's control room, overseeing the network's coverage every day and night. Now I was running the operation, and living out a TV producer's dream.

Every day and night in Barcelona was spent in the International Broadcast Center, the giant convention space where all the networks and broadcasters from around the world were headquartered. I'd regularly shuttle between my office, which had a wall of monitors showing ongoing action from venues across the Games, and the control room, where we produced NBC shows to air in the morning, afternoon, and in prime time back home. As each day developed, a different puzzle would need to be solved: how to format our various shows and tell our viewers the most compelling stories. With the time difference meaning we didn't come on the air in prime time until 2:00 a.m. local time, the workday didn't end until four, five, or six o'clock in the morning.

The late nights weren't the only challenge. Before I'd taken the job at NBC, the network had made a deal with cable operators, led by Charles Dolan's Cablevision, to launch a special pay-per-view service alongside our regular network coverage. It would be called the "Triplecast," and offer viewers the chance—for a sizable price tag somewhere between $100 and $200—to watch the entire Olympics live on three different pay-per-view channels, as opposed to on tape delay, like much of our coverage. In some ways, the Triplecast, using the "world feed"— coverage of events produced by the International Olympic Committee's own TV arm—was ahead of its time; these days, viewers can use NBC's digital app to stream world feed coverage of live sports that NBC doesn't televise. The bare-bones live coverage is great for badminton lovers or field hockey fanatics, but the reality— then and now—is that the vast, vast majority of the American audience simply doesn't want their Olympics covered that way. Some fifty-plus years after Roone pioneered it, they still love the storytelling; they love learning about the athletes, their backgrounds, and finding a reason to cheer for them.

I knew the Triplecast was a doomed idea from the day I got to NBC, and tried at one point to get the company to bail on it. Pay-per-view was a tricky business, which I knew well from my days with Vince McMahon. In this case, the audience simply didn't want the product. They didn't want to readjust their schedule to watch endless hours of the Olympics—they wanted to watch it in prime time.

Sure enough, because of that preference, not to mention any number of technical complications with the cable providers, the Triplecast was a pretty big failure in Barcelona. While it didn't occupy a lot of our time on the production side—it was basically just world feeds coming through our wiring—it did overshadow, at least from media reporters writing about our coverage, the great job that our team did in prime time.

As a setting, Barcelona was a classic example of how an Olympic Games can raise and even redefine a city's global profile. Going in, the Opening Ceremony was hounded by the question of whether the Catalonian crowd would boo the king of Spain (they did not). Then came the memorable show—capped off by the unforgettable image of the Paralympic archer Antonio Rebollo Liñán shooting a flaming arrow over the cauldron, igniting it to officially begin the Games. Meanwhile, behind the scenes at the stadium that evening, we had done everything we could to get the Dream Team and its basketball superstars to march in the Parade of Nations. They were (rightly) concerned they'd be recognized by other athletes and end up at the center of a mob scene in the holding area, where athletes traditionally wait for hours before the parade. But we knew that seeing them march would be a huge highlight for our audience. So instead, we found a way to arrange for them to join the parade at the last minute. Randy Falco, our CFO, was at the stadium that night, and we tasked him to serve as their "executive escort" along with security, guiding them through the bowels of the stadium to a special entry point. Well, Randy would be pretty surprised when, as a joke, Scottie Pippen and Karl Malone locked his arms between them and began carrying him out onto the track. They only let go just before Randy would have been swallowed up by the crowd of U.S. Olympians wearing the team's Opening Ceremony uniform of blue sports jackets and white panama hats.

Once the competition began, stars like Carl Lewis, Jackie Joyner-Kersee, and Janet Evans headlined thirty-seven U.S. gold medals. Then, of course, the Dream Team were the Beatles of the Games—with both fans and fellow athletes mobbing them wherever they went; their popularity was unlike anything I've ever seen in sports. The stars chose to stay in a hotel rather than the Olympic Village, essentially sequestering themselves and spending most nights in their rooms hanging out playing cards—with the notable exception of Charles Barkley, who loved walking out at night in Barcelona and interacting with fans. Charles did coax his good friend

Michael Jordan to join him for golf at a course in the Pyrenees Mountains where NBC sponsors were playing—golf even then was one of Michael's great joys. But between the time they quietly showed up to play their round and the eighteenth hole, a crowd of several hundred people gathered to surround them.

Back on the court, the love for the Dream Teamers was unaffected even when Barkley threw an elbow at an Angolan player who'd made the mistake of trying to guard him. David Stern, ever the marketing genius, played the whole story brilliantly, and at the height of the NBA's popularity, the dominance of his superstars would inspire the growth of basketball globally for all the generations that have followed since. We're still feeling the impact of that team today.

For all of us working the Games—a team of several hundred in Barcelona—the experience of telling all those stories to millions of Americans back home every night was exhilarating. We finished editing the Closing Ceremony in the early hours of a Monday morning in Barcelona, just in time to feed it back via satellite to the United States, where it was still Sunday night. Heading home in mid-August, anxious to reunite with my family, I was exhausted but elated.

And really, my mind was already squarely looking ahead—because, four years away, the next Olympic Games were going to be in Atlanta. With a domestic Olympics, the potential for a ratings bonanza was massive. I knew that we'd impressed the IOC with the collective passion and skillful storytelling our team had brought to Barcelona. Samaranch, through his own observations, as well as the ratings, could see that in NBC's hands, the Olympics were being presented the best way to the American audience, which in no uncertain terms was his most important audience financially. American television money contributed far more to the IOC's budget than any other rights deal, and for the Olympics to continue their growth under Samaranch, retaining their popularity in the U.S. would be paramount.

But we had a lot of work to do to get organized for a deal to retain the Olympics ourselves.

CHAPTER 18

Gold Medal Deals

The negotiations for the Games of the XXVI Olympiad—better known as the 1996 Atlanta Olympics—would take place in the summer of 1993, almost exactly a year after Barcelona. For much of that year, preparing for the negotiations would be a huge priority. Because of the Triplecast, NBC had lost money on the Barcelona Games—close to a hundred million dollars when the accounting was complete (though Cablevision, the network's main partner, had eaten half of that). That wasn't a surprise; we had known before the Olympic cauldron was lit that the pay-cable idea had backfired. But making sure that everyone at NBC and GE understood that Atlanta could be a very different story was the goal internally. For generations, domestic Olympics, with the sense of patriotism and excitement they generated, not to mention time zones that afforded live events in prime time, always were the highest-rated Games. We knew that, and did everything we could to make sure everyone else at the company knew the potential the rights held.

We worked on what we planned to bid for the Games for months. Internally, the effort was led by Randy Falco, who would become an essential lieutenant as our sports CFO, as well as Ken Schanzer. Ed Swindler, who'd played a central role in our successful deal for the NBA, was again also in the center of these deliberations. The process involved the IOC and the Atlanta Organizing Committee as well, and shuttling to Atlanta many times to meet with Billy Payne, the head of the committee, to discuss the schedule, sponsors, and more.

Then there was also the game theory analysis we had to make about what our rivals would bid. In 1992, CBS had paid $243 million to wrest control of the Winter Olympics from ABC for the first time in two decades, and had the rights locked up to the 1994 Lillehammer Games as well, paying $300 million for that event. I knew CBS favored the Winter Games over the Summer, and the ratings they could grab during the lucrative advertising "sweeps period" in February. ABC, meanwhile, had suffered big losses during their last Olympics, the weather-plagued 1988 Calgary Winter Games, and the problems had alarmed the network's then-new owners, Capital Cities. I was confident that Cap Cities was still smarting from those losses, and would limit the ability of ABC executives to go big in a bid.

At NBC, though, we had momentum, and had already earned something priceless: Jack Welch's faith in the job I could do. We were at the absolute height of the success of our NBA deal, with Michael Jordan winning his third championship, against Charles Barkley and the Suns, just a few weeks before the bid process commenced. No one had any sense that Jordan's retirement was imminent. The NBA deal was greatly exceeding our profit predictions to GE, with the playoff ratings off the charts. Jack loved sports, he loved winning, and he loved backing a team that he thought could win. Those three truths meant that we could offer more money than any television network in the history of the Olympics, and we would be the favorite to win the bid.

Like virtually everything else with the Olympics, the bid process would be its own dramatic production, taking place over a single day that blended ceremony with strategy. After months of study and preparation, and back-and-forth with the IOC and the host city's management team, the interested players—in this case, each of the then three major networks—would come to a law office in Manhattan, and present envelopes with sealed bids for the rights. The networks then would get the opportunity to present their plans to the gathered IOC, USOC, and Atlanta officials. After the submissions were reviewed, the networks—still not knowing where they stood—would get a chance to rebid, one more shot to sweeten the number just a bit before the decision was made.

We spent the Sunday before the submission in a suite in the Carlyle hotel—myself, Randy, Ken, and Ed—finalizing our strategy. Two mornings later, on Tuesday, July 27, the day before my forty-sixth birthday, we got to the iconic Citicorp building, a few blocks from 30 Rock, at ten o'clock. Inside the envelope we were carrying was a letter with our bid. Six months earlier, at a dinner with Samaranch in Lausanne, he had asked me what I thought the winning bid for the Atlanta Games would be.

"I think it's more important what *you* think," I'd responded.

"Four hundred and fifty million," he'd said after thinking for a moment.

"Not a chance, sir," I'd said with a sincere and confident smile.

So much for my confidence—the combination of ad revenue math and gut instinct had in fact brought me to the figure Juan Antonio thought it would. Though, since I'd decided at some point that we shouldn't submit a round number, we ended up bidding $456 million. It was $55 million more than the network had paid for the Barcelona Games.

After laying down our envelope on the table alongside the others, we waited for about forty-five minutes, and then took our turn, along with ABC and CBS, in formally presenting our plan of how we were going to broadcast the Games— how many hours of coverage, the structure of that coverage, and so forth—to a group that included the aforementioned Billy Payne; Dick Pound, a Canadian lawyer and the longtime head of the IOC's broadcasting committee; Harvey Schiller, the head of the United States Olympic Committee; and Barry Frank, the veteran IMG agent who was advising the IOC with the negotiations. They asked a few questions, and then we were ushered out, heading back to 30 Rock to brief Bob Wright on how it had gone.

Around two o'clock, we were called back to the Citicorp building to make another bid; the IOC essentially communicating, as we expected, that they wanted even more money than any of the initial offers. But expecting this going in, we knew how we were going to respond; the strategy that we'd finalized in the Carlyle was that $456 million would be our first and only offer. So our second envelope contained the same number as the original one. It was a bet that the other networks wouldn't aggressively sweeten their offers, even when they realized they had a shot.

About an hour and a half later, we were called back in from the windowless conference room we'd been waiting in to another room that had a spectacular view of the Manhattan skyline.

"We must have won," Kenny said. "We have a window."

When Payne and Pound alone walked in, they had good news and bad. We had the highest bid, they said, but they needed more money to close the deal.

By now, I knew both of these men well, and liked them—which made it easier to be frank with them.

"None of us at NBC will have a job by sundown if we put another cash dollar in this deal, guys," I told them. "We're not going to negotiate against ourselves."

So instead, I got creative. Essentially making it up as I went along, I presented a collection of other incentives that would hold additional value for both the IOC and the Atlanta Organizing Committee, and no risk for us: a revenue sharing plan after we hit a certain amount of advertising dollars; promotional time in our other sports telecasts for the Olympic committee to run free commercials for tickets and high-end souvenirs; and an hour block for their own Olympic promotional show leading up to the Games on the biggest day in TV we could offer, Super Bowl Sunday in February 1996.

They went to discuss the deal one more time back with their group, and we called Bob Wright again to keep him updated. Then, around five o'clock, they came back inside. We'd won the bid to the Atlanta Games.

It would later be reported that CBS had bid $405 million in the first round of envelopes, and then, when it came time for a second bid, had dropped out. ABC, meanwhile, had tried to find money through a proposal that included partnering with Turner Sports for coverage on cable. Reports said they bid $440 million in the first round, and then went up to $450 million in the second. To this day, I don't believe either of those numbers were anything close to accurate; agents have always been notorious for exaggerating losing bids in negotiations to make it seem more competitive. Either way, the end result was the same—and the Games were ours again.

We celebrated that night in New York with our new partners from Atlanta at a restaurant a few blocks from where we won the bid. NBC was still in the Olympic game. Though it turned out we were still just getting started.

Less than a year after we won that bid, a week before Christmas 1993, the biggest change to network television sports in a long time unfolded when Fox created their own sports division, splashing onto the scene out of nowhere with a stunning $1.6 billion deal to televise the NFL's NFC package starting with the 1994 season.

That move, knocking CBS out of their signature sport, was a seismic shift for pro football rights, and there was no doubt among any of us on the scene that this new network wasn't finished with their shopping spree. Rupert Murdoch, Fox's chairman, was well known in everything he did for his willingness to take on risk, and go to whatever means necessary to get what he wanted. And so you could say that we were all on alert, wary of all the ways Murdoch might strike next.

In truth, NBC was really an outlier of stability with the television business in extreme flux in the mid-1990s. In the summer of 1995, within the span of a week, the Walt Disney Company bought ABC from Capital Cities, and the Westinghouse Electric Corporation bought CBS. You could say a new age of media was dawning, with Disney and ABC merging to create the world's largest entertainment company, and CBS ending its long era of independence by coming under a large manufacturing conglomerate. Of course, the GE era at NBC, almost a decade in at that point, had been a model of tremendous success. Jack Welch's management philosophy of focusing on hiring the best teams across his businesses, and then letting them do their jobs, had worked brilliantly all across his company, making GE arguably the world's most successful and admired corporation—and NBC was no exception. Six years into my time there, I'd benefited from that philosophy, and the results bore that out undeniably.

In the spring, I had one of my meetings with Juan Antonio Samaranch, connecting with him in Geneva, and he invited me to fly with him to Sarajevo, the host of the 1984 Winter Games that had been devastated by civil war in the former Yugoslavia. Looking out over the ruins of the once-beautiful city was simply tragic; he was heading there for a meeting at a neutral site to discuss future Olympic representation with both sides. Samaranch, meanwhile, was in a struggle in the always dodgy waters of the IOC, with a group of members seeking to institute age limits and term limits on the presidency that would spell the end of his time atop the organization. A few months later, at the end of June, I went to Wimbledon, where as usual Juan Antonio had come to see his favorite player and fellow Catalonian, the "Barcelona Bumblebee," Sánchez-Vicario. We had lunch along with his wife, and then on the middle Friday night of the championships, I set up a small dinner in the garden of my ground-floor suite at the Inn on the Park with the Samaranches as well as a handful of other senior IOC leaders with whom he was friendly, including Keba M'Baye of Senegal, Kevan Gosper of Australia, as well as our IOC liaison, Alex Gilady, and a few others. They were all in town to see the tennis. It was a social dinner, but as usual, I had questions for Samaranch; I wanted to hear what had gone on in a recent IOC meeting in Budapest, specifically about the campaign to institute the age-limit rule.

Samaranch had won the power struggle, but as I asked question after question about other topics, at one point, the subject of Rupert Murdoch came up. Apparently, back in Australia, his company had made a controversial move on rugby TV rights, making it very difficult on the governing bodies in the way they'd structured the deal. The aggressiveness had alarmed Samaranch and the IOC. Murdoch might have had money, but the committee didn't want to cede control of their product to someone they didn't trust. I filed it away; any information about Murdoch and Fox was interesting, particularly with the next summer Olympics after Atlanta five years away in 2000 set to be in Murdoch's native Australia, in Sydney—and a potential bid process for those Games about a year away as well.

As that summer of 1995 went on, the sense that Fox was going to make a move into the Olympic television sphere continued to grow. I'd gotten a call from Dennis Swanson, the head of ABC Sports, who had been trying to find ways for his company to get back into the Olympic broadcasting game. He explained that he'd looked into the idea of a joint bid by ABC and NBC to broadcast the 2000 Games. He knew there might be antitrust concerns with such an arrangement, but he'd gone to Dick Pound, the head of the IOC broadcasting committee, and confirmed that the organization wouldn't have a problem with it, which made the potential for the deal legitimate. It was intriguing. As much as I wanted to keep the Summer Olympics on NBC, the problem with Sydney as a location was the massive time difference between the U.S. and Australia. Because of the fourteen-hour time difference between Sydney and New York, competition was potentially going to be tape-delayed more than half a day for prime-time shows. Plus, the Sydney Games were scheduled to take place in September, and would have to battle both pro and college football *and* the powerful competition of the brand-new entertainment prime-time season in the ratings. It wouldn't be anywhere near as viewer-friendly as Atlanta was expected to be—but we knew the IOC would want more money nonetheless. I relayed the conversation to Randy Falco, and asked him to start meeting with Swanson and ABC to see how a joint proposal could come together.

At the end of July, the very same week that ABC and CBS were sold, I was in Atlanta. The 1996 Olympics were exactly a year away, and we'd come down for a series of production meetings. It was a perfect time for our technical people to check things like how weather and lighting could impact our plans at the various venues, and also to gain a new sense of momentum with the countdown to the Games really beginning. But the night of August 1, in what already was a tumultuous week of change on the business side of the broadcast industry, word started to get out that, sure enough, it was happening—Fox was getting in on the Olympic action, and they were doing it before the formal bid process could begin. The company had sent, in person, a delegation of executives to Dick Pound's office in Montreal, where they handed the head of the IOC's broadcast committee a letter. It was short, and to the point.

"Fox hereby offers to license the exclusive United States rights to the Sydney 2000 Games for $701 million."

Apparently Rupert had a thing about staying away from round numbers just like I did. But more significantly, $701 million was more than 50 percent more than we'd paid for the Atlanta rights—a domestic Games at that. Even in an age of ever-expanding television deals, this was a massive shot across the bow, preempting the IOC's traditional bid process, and making clear how badly Murdoch wanted Fox to broadcast the Games taking place in his home country.

In the world of Olympic television rights, this definitely classified as an emergency. Yes, the bid process typically unfolded deliberately and on the IOC's terms, but a check for $701 million was something the organization wouldn't be able to take lightly. After talking it over with Bob Wright from Atlanta, Randy Falco and I decided to immediately come back to New York to figure out what our response should be. We didn't tell the Atlanta folks why we were leaving town earlier than expected, only leaving word that something had come up that had to be dealt with back in the office. My assistant, Aimee Leone, chartered a plane to pick us up after dinner with the Atlanta Organizing Committee, and we landed in New York after 2:00 a.m. Randy spent the night at our apartment in the city so we could go in and meet Bob as early as possible at 30 Rock.

When we got to the office, Ed Swindler joined us, and we handed over to Wright a nine-page working financial analysis of what a joint bid with ABC would look like from NBC's perspective. Wright wasn't enthusiastic about it, and the truth was that as the financial guys, Randy and Ed weren't, either. It would be hard to promote, and hard to break down the coverage in a way that wouldn't be confusing to the audience, and wouldn't program the Olympics against itself with one big event against each other. That would kill the advertising premium we got for the Games as a show that would crush the competition, and thus significantly devalue the concept of broadcasting them.

As we sat there, Bob took a call—he was in the midst of a deal to buy a group of local stations for the network. While we waited, we talked among ourselves about the difficulty of the situation. The obvious move would be to make our own offer to the IOC, and make it as soon as possible. But this would mean walking away from ABC, and I knew that Dennis Swanson was on a long vacation in Europe; there was no real way to reach him quickly. I was hesitant to burn a bridge so abruptly with Dennis, who I'd known and respected for a long time.

Then Randy said he had an idea.

"What if we went for two?"

The 2002 Winter Games—scheduled to be held barely sixteen months after Sydney—had, just six weeks earlier, been awarded to Salt Lake City, Utah. Set to be the first Winter Games on American soil since 1980, they were sure to be a ratings slam dunk. The IOC had always awarded Olympic television rights one Games at a time. But already, Murdoch was trying to upend precedent, trying to preempt the bid process. We had to innovate right with him on the fly. This was a hell of an idea, and when he hung up the phone, Wright quickly agreed. Not only would a primarily live-in-prime-time Salt Lake Games offset the difficulty of a taped Olympics in Sydney but the ad sales team could combine the two properties in selling sponsorships.

Randy and Ed started working on some numbers immediately, with legal pads and calculators. By lunchtime, we'd come up with a figure: $1.25 billion for a combined bid for the 2000 and 2002 Games. It was a massive amount of money— the biggest sports rights deal NBC had ever done—but it made sense. And we'd have to move on it immediately. Even though I knew Samaranch and others at the IOC were leery of getting into business with Fox, we had to inject ourselves in the process before their offer was deemed too good to pass up.

As we talked it over, Wright turned to me to ask about Dennis and ABC. I'd be doing what I didn't want to do, potentially going around Dennis to make a secret offer on our own, but it was a different offer than I'd been discussing with him.

I told Wright we should go ahead. When Swanson came back into the office the following week, I'd talk to him, however this worked out.

The last step before submitting the offer was to call Welch, who was in Nantucket, recuperating from heart surgery. This was Jack's kind of deal: outfoxing Murdoch, and doing whatever was necessary to get the win. We ran him through the numbers quickly. His last question was to me.

"Dick," he said on the speakerphone. "I know you're setting this up to make money. But worst-case scenario: How much could we potentially lose on this, over both of these Olympics?"

I thought for a second on what Ed, Randy, and I had figured on our legal pads an hour earlier.

"I'd say fifty million dollars apiece for each one, Jack."

There was the briefest of pauses.

"Fifty million?! Fifty million?! That's a pimple on the ass of GE! Go get this done!"

That's a real quote, I swear. Jack Welch was one of a kind.

After we left Wright's office, my next call was to Alex Gilady. A year earlier, Alex had been elected as a member of the IOC, making him more connected than ever to the inner workings of the organization. Because of that, we couldn't tell Alex the number we were going to bid, but he could still lay the groundwork for us to connect with Samaranch. Every piece of the communication needed to be handled delicately; Juan Antonio could be hard to reach with how much he traveled, and this being the days before cell phones, I couldn't afford for any messages to get leaked or misconstrued. Alex, still in Atlanta, where we'd left him the night before, found out that Juan Antonio would be leaving the next day for Gothenburg, Sweden, for the World Track and Field Championships. Maybe we could head there to meet with him in person. Though, when we spoke, Alex was as candid as ever—he told me he didn't think the idea had a chance. The IOC would never award two Olympics at once. But he was still up for joining the adventure.

About five hours later, Randy, Alex (who'd quickly caught a flight to New York), and I were on the GE Gulfstream IV, headed to Gothenburg. Just before takeoff, I called Susan; she was on a boat off the coast of Cape Cod with the kids, and I was supposed to join them that weekend. Something had come up with the IOC, I explained. She wished me a bon voyage, and I was on my way to Europe.

When we landed in Sweden around lunchtime the next day, we went straight to the Sheraton Hotel, where all the executives and officials were staying for the event. Our biggest concern was being seen; the Track and Field Worlds were being televised in the States on ABC, and we couldn't risk getting spotted by people who would know who we were and might wonder what we were doing there. Randy and I hustled to the elevators after checking in, while Alex ran off to connect with his mysterious world of Olympic assistants and operators.

Ten minutes later, he returned with an update. Samaranch wasn't in Sweden yet, but he was arriving later that afternoon for the opening ceremony. He added that Dick Pound, who by that point had started to have a complicated relationship with Samaranch, thanks to Pound's role in the battle over instituting term and age limits, was home in Canada. Not having them both there wasn't ideal, but we'd wait for Samaranch, and get an audience with him when he arrived. Making the best of the delay up in my room, we lit up some cigars we'd brought. After a few hours, we'd smoked so many that Alex—the only person I've ever met who actually inhaled when he smokes cigars—made a run for replacements.

By late afternoon, when Samaranch arrived, Alex was able to connect with his people and tell them that I was in the hotel and I'd come with a proposal. Coming unannounced to speak to Juan Antonio felt like a positive thing—the surprise visit communicated my sense of urgency better than anything else could. With dozens of ABC executives and international sports officials all in the lobby getting set to go to the opening ceremony at the track, we made a request to the hotel to let us use the freight elevators to go up to Samaranch's suite before he had to leave for the stadium. The stealth mission was successful, and he greeted us warmly. But I knew this wasn't a time to dawdle. Right after we sat down, I outlined the pitch for the $1.25 billion total for the two Olympics. It wasn't just about the money, I told him. It was a deal that could cement NBC's status as America's "Olympic network." For the first time in history, the Games would have what felt like a permanent television home, and be part of the network's identity, ensuring constant promotion, year-round, and for years to come. As I spoke, I added a small sweetener that I knew he'd like, and would only come from us: an idea for NBC to produce a weekly show on Olympic athletes to begin after Atlanta and continue all the way to Salt Lake City. The show could be international in focus, and shared with the IOC's other rights holders all over the world. It was a small thing, but it was part of the story I wanted Juan Antonio to appreciate.

After he listened to my pitch, he paused a moment, and then spoke.

"Dick," he said in his Catalonian accent—which sounded more like "Deek"— "I am very, very impressed by this. But I have to get to this opening ceremony. Can you wait for me, and we'll talk more here in the room over dinner when I get back?"

A few hours later, we were back in the suite with more time to talk, and it felt like his enthusiasm for the deal had only grown as it had sunk into his mind. It didn't hurt that he was predisposed to be skeptical of a deal with Murdoch after the way his company had dealt with that rugby TV agreement. But more than that—he knew us, and he knew what kind of passion and organization we brought to the Olympics.

"We're excited, too," I told him. "But we need to have an answer by tomorrow. We can't have this get out there as a rumor. Our competitors will respond, and the whole thing will get out of hand. This is a big commitment that my company is willing to make to the IOC."

Samaranch responded by immediately picking up the phone. He was calling Montreal, where it was late afternoon in Dick Pound's office.

"Deek," he said into the phone—this time to Pound. "Mr. Ebersol and his company have just made me a very impressive proposal. I would like them to discuss it with you as well. I want to send them to Montreal first thing in the morning to sit down with you and finalize this deal."

It was a master stroke: after the tension of the previous several months after the age-limit dispute, Samaranch, forever the diplomat, was bringing Pound into the process, set to let him close the particulars of the deal on behalf of the committee. Pound would realize that he could maintain a sense of influence by closing the deal, remaining relevant in the never-ending dance for power at the IOC. In the midst of everything else, I was struck by Samaranch's brilliant playing of the chess match.

At dawn the next morning, we went down to the lobby for the first time since we'd arrived, to check out and head back to the airport for another long flight on GE's Gulfstream IV. The lobby was largely empty—except for a driver holding up a huge sign that said "EBERSOL." I thought about tackling him to the ground; I didn't want to take a chance that some ABC executive getting an early coffee would spot us. So we got out of the lobby faster than Carl Lewis. I half slept for much of the flight, anxious about what was going to happen next. Maybe Alex Gilady had originally deemed us having little or no chance, but the truth was that in Wright's office the morning before, I felt we'd had no more than a one-in-five chance of striking the deal. Now, improbably, it felt like it was really in reach.

When we arrived at Pound's law offices at about 10:00 a.m. Montreal time, he was initially frosty, unhappy that we'd gone around him, straight to Samaranch. We explained that we thought he'd be there for the track championships, too, and he softened. And then, a moment later, softened even more when we outlined the deal for him. He was impressed, and after we spoke for no more than a half hour, he called Samaranch in Sweden.

"I think we should take it," he said into the phone.

We'd traveled four thousand miles in less than twenty-four hours to hear the beginning and ending of their two-part transcontinental conversation from both sides.

They hung up, and Dick ushered us into the law library at his firm—the one room in the office where smoking was permitted. Randy and Dick lit up another round of cigars, and they got right to work on a deal memo, hunched over a computer. Watching them hash out the details, I looked out the window of the library and could see the Olympic Stadium from the 1976 Montreal Games. Only a few miles away was the setting where I'd taken my second trip for ABC Sports for a track meet as a twenty-year-old, and Lou Volpicelli had taught me to never be afraid to ask a question. Now if the question was "How did I get back to Montreal?" the answer epitomized everything I'd learned since then, a journey that started with my regular meetings with Juan Antonio, continued on to my dinner with him at Wimbledon, and was made possible by the faith and trust that Jack and Bob had in NBC Sports, in me, and in Randy Falco. All these connections, all these relationships. And now the last question was, could this ten-figure deal that would define so much of the future of the Olympics on television get to the finish line?

The only thing to resolve was how the money would get divided up. With respect to the Fox bid, Sydney would have to get at least $700 million; they ended up with $705 million—almost exactly a billion dollars in Australian currency. That left

$545 million for Salt Lake City; nearly twice what CBS had paid for the previous Winter Games in Lillehammer, but again, as a domestic Olympics, the payoff could be huge. The Salt Lake Organizing Committee was eager to grab it immediately. It wasn't quite yet 4:00 p.m. on Friday when the last cigars were lit. The deal had been made a little more than forty-eight hours after it had been conceived at 30 Rock. It would be announced in a press conference on Monday.

We flew back to New York that afternoon. That weekend, running on pure adrenaline, I went into the office on Saturday, and then Sunday, took a quick trip to Cleveland, where our new top NFL broadcast team—Dick Enberg, Paul Maguire, and Phil Simms—were working together for the first time in a preseason game. Back in my office early Monday morning, the first item on my agenda was to swing by 8H, where the press conference to announce the deal would take place early that afternoon. I had the stagehands dress up a set with an Olympic theme, even building a mock cauldron to sit alongside us on the stage. Then, back in my office, the next thing to do wasn't easy: a call to Dennis Swanson at ABC.

"Dennis," I said, "this isn't easy to tell you. In two hours, we're going to announce that we've made a deal for the Sydney and Salt Lake Olympics."

He was silent for a moment, and then asked when this had happened.

"It all transpired very quickly, on Thursday and Friday, in Sweden and Canada. It was an opportunity we saw and had to jump on. I'm very sorry."

Dennis, always classy, offered his congratulations, and we hung up.

The press conference set off fireworks across the media landscape. Never before had a network secured the rights to two Olympics at once. Fox—and Murdoch—had been shut out; CBS's brief reign as the home of the Winter Olympics would end after the Nagano Games in 1998; and Disney had not been able to make a big strike after buying ABC.

After all the press calls, and the celebrations with our staff back at 30 Rock, that Monday afternoon in my office, I called Samaranch to let him know how great the response had been. He sounded thrilled.

"Deek," he said, "this is so good. So, so good."

And then he paused once more slightly, as he was wont to do, the hint of a smile evident even over the phone.

"Perhaps we should do this again."

That same afternoon, when I called him from my office, Jack Welch couldn't believe what I was saying to him.

"He's open to it, I could tell what he was hinting at on the phone," I was telling my boss. "If we think that getting two Olympics is a great deal for the company, why not go for even more, with a willing partner on the other side?"

When I told the same thing to Wright, he burst out laughing—he couldn't believe it, either. But to their everlasting credit, both Jack and Bob told me without hesitating to investigate the idea of extending the deal even further, adding more Olympics beyond 2002. And a few weeks later, Alex Gilady called with a message. He'd floated the idea to Samaranch, who was enthused by it. At the start of his IOC tenure he'd brought the organization out of near-bankruptcy; now he could put it in a position to have a stream of steady income for more than a decade. With big money guaranteed to be streaming in from a U.S. television partner, the IOC could manage their future budget—and future Games—in ways they couldn't have dreamed of before. The money would pre-determine a big portion of revenues before even a city was awarded the Games, meaning that host cities wouldn't ever have to haggle with the IOC about what their share of the TV money would be; instead, they could know how much guaranteed money was coming in. That would make that bid process—to determine where the Olympics would be held—much more enticing for the candidates.

We spent several weeks drafting our proposal—a little less pressure than the half hour we'd had in Bob Wright's office earlier in the summer. Then, in late September, I flew from Rochester, New York, where the Ryder Cup was being held, to Lausanne for a ceremony formally signing the deal for Sydney and Salt Lake. In Samaranch's suite afterward, Randy and I made our initial pitch for the rights to the 2004 and 2006 Games—the locations of which had not yet been determined. Once again, Samaranch was into the idea, and once again, he turned things over to Pound to take it from there. This time, though, Dick was with us in Lausanne, and after an initial conversation, we decided the best course of action would be for each side to draw up memos—he referred to them as "term papers"—on how the new deal extension could work. As part of the commitment to secrecy, Pound gave the whole venture a code name, the "Sunset Project."

"This will be our last deal," he quipped. "We'll ride off into the sunset after this."

Several weeks later, in early November, we got together again, and Pound had some news. He wanted to go even further. It made more sense for the way the IOC sold their commercial sponsorships in quadrennials, he said, to make a deal through the 2008 Games. We were now talking about an absolutely staggering amount of money for GE to invest in the Olympics, but Jack Welch wasn't afraid. This was one of the strongest brands in all of sports, and GE—as the most profitable company in the world—had the money.

Eventually, the number that we settled on with Pound was $2.245 billion. It was all set—until it wasn't. Samaranch called me unexpectedly a few days afterward with one last request. Could we make it an even $2.3 billion?

What could possibly be the significance of an extra $55 million? It was important to him, he said. Maybe there was some powerful IOC member who needed to know that Samaranch had gotten everything possible out of NBC. Maybe the number meant something to some federation. Maybe he just knew he could get it.

I had to go back to Welch. But I knew what he thought of $55 million, and he gave the go-ahead for the increased fee.

The deal was announced two weeks before Christmas, shocking the media all over again. Critics complained about both sides of the deal, which was a good sign to me. NBC, the complaints went, had cozied up to the IOC to get the inside track. As big as the number was, others railed, the IOC had left hundreds of millions on the table by agreeing to a rights fee for Games that were more than a decade away.

They could bemoan the deal all they wanted. But everything went back to the relationship that had begun at that first dinner in Paris with Samaranch in 1989. GE's massive purse had obviously made it possible, as had the ability of both sides to innovate on the fly, and see the possibilities that surrounded doing the kind of deal that neither side had ever done before. But it all came out of the sense of trust, and faith, that each side had in the other.

NBC was now absolutely set to be America's Olympic Network for the next dozen-plus years. A fantastic ride was still just beginning.

CHAPTER 19

Lighting the Flame

A few days after the press conference to announce the Olympic deal extension, I went to Atlanta for another meeting with Billy Payne to go over a variety of topics, chief among them the Opening Ceremony of the 1996 Summer Games. The talented Don Mischer, who's directed many Opening Ceremonies and Super Bowl halftime shows, was there, along with Ginger Watkins, who was the executive in charge of the ceremonies under Payne, and a few other people. A little more than halfway through the meeting, I brought up something that had been on my mind.

"One of the things we haven't really tackled yet," I said to Billy and the group, "is how you're going to deal with lighting the Olympic cauldron in the show."

As an Olympic nut, I knew going back decades that lighting the cauldron was the dramatic climax to the Opening Ceremony. As the last big moment in the show, it would always be its most lasting moment, something for the audience to remember as the competition kicked off. Most typically, the job tended to go to an Olympic star from the host nation. In 1984, Rafer Johnson, the decathlete who'd been the star of my 1972 *Ancient Games* film, had lit it in Los Angeles. In Seoul in 1988, a South Korean schoolteacher and dancer had joined a young Olympic marathoner. And in Barcelona, organizers had done a great job of amplifying the drama with archer Antonio Rebollo Liñán's role in shooting the arrow. I felt like that had upped the ante in terms of the statement that an organizing committee could make, and now in Atlanta, Payne and his team had to make the most of that opportunity.

"I actually have thought about it," Billy said. "And I'm thinking it'll be Evander Holyfield."

Holyfield made some sense as a choice. He was an Atlanta native, had won a medal at the '84 Games, and then had become the heavyweight champion of the world for two years.

But to me, there was a far better choice, someone who'd been in my head as the perfect figure for months.

"I really think you should ask Ali," I said.

My memories of Muhammad Ali went back, like most people of my generation, to when he'd burst onto the scene in the early sixties, after winning a gold medal at the Rome Olympics. As a young sports fan, I'd watched him rise as Cassius Clay, shocking Sonny Liston to win the world title. Then, after he'd refused to enter the army on religious grounds as a Muslim, Ali's boxing license had been stripped. His title belt and his livelihood were taken away, and he was sent into sports exile for three years. When he came back, after his case had gone all the way to the Supreme Court—even a conservative bench had unanimously ruled 9–0 in his favor—he was almost thirty, his prime taken away from him.

But the second act that followed—his epic victories over Joe Frazier and George Foreman—had transformed him from one of the great boxers and most colorful characters of all time into the most famous athletic figure on earth, beloved by millions. Along the way, I'd met him a few times through his connection with Howard Cosell, and even went down to Miami a couple of times with Howard to cover his training camps at the 5th Street Gym for *Wide World of Sports* reports. In the decades since, all those years in the ring had taken their brutal toll, and Ali had revealed that he had Parkinson's disease. It had quieted what often seemed like the loudest voice in the world, but at the same time, that softening had made him a different kind of icon. A legend known throughout every corner of the globe, a man of faith and peace, and, to so many now, a true American hero as well.

But even when I laid all that out to him, Billy Payne wasn't so sure of the choice.

"I'm going to have a hard time selling a draft dodger here," he sadly lamented to me.

"A draft dodger? He's not a draft dodger!" I tried to tell him. He was missing the point—the potential wonder of the moment that Ali could create. But if that was his argument, I was ready to counter.

"Respectfully, let me just make sure that you know the history correctly," I said. "He was willing to go through the legal process. He was willing to forgo the massive amount of money he could earn in the ring for all this. He was found guilty, and he was on his way to prison, but the federal court of appeals in the state of New York threw it out. And the Supreme Court also agreed fully with that decision three years later, and he was cleared of all charges. He did it all despite sacrificing almost four big-money-earning years. And he didn't run away from the country. He didn't go to Canada. He was willing to stand on his principles."

I made my case a bit longer, and got Billy to promise to at least consider it. Then, after the holidays, I went to work further on it, on two fronts. First, I had our top feature producer, Lisa Lax, start working on a long film on Ali to present to Payne. The film would tell the whole story—from his days as an Olympian to the stand he took on Vietnam to his ascendance to legend. I also called a wonderful man named Howard Bingham, a friend and photographer who had been one of Ali's closest friends for years. I needed to find out if Ali could even physically do what I'd dreamed up, and if he could do it, would he do it?

As Lisa got to work, Howard got back to me quickly with a message from Lonnie Ali, Muhammad's wife. If we came up with the right way to do it, Ali was in.

The second week of May, I knew that Billy was having surgery, and would be recuperating at his lake house north of Atlanta. I called him and told him I was going to send him Lisa's film to watch while he was resting. A few days later he called.

"Okay, I see what you're saying. That was a fantastic film. I'm seeing what you're seeing. He'd be a popular choice."

Chalk another one up for storytelling.

"But I still have my misgivings, Dick. Do you even know if Ali would be willing to do it?"

"Do you really think," I said with a smile, "that I would have gone through all of this if I didn't know the answer to that question?"

I arrived in Atlanta on the last day of June, almost three weeks before the Opening Ceremony. While we had plenty of other sports business going on in the States and overseas—Wimbledon, and the upcoming baseball All-Star Game among them—the Olympics were by far the biggest few weeks of the year, and with our commitment to the IOC solidified for the next twelve years, we were all going to do everything we could to make sure everything went as perfectly as possible.

It was like the beginning of summer camp, as members of our staff and favorite freelancers trickled into Atlanta, checked into their hotels, and got to work at the International Broadcast Center and the venues. There were a lot of hugs, and a real sense of excitement with the start of the Games just days away. And, of course, the biggest thing on my mind was the Opening Ceremony.

I'd had to call Andrew Young, the former mayor of Atlanta and the only African American member of the executive committee of the Games, to convince some holdouts in the group even after Payne had agreed, but Ali was all set to light the cauldron, and we just needed the secret to stay that way. As for logistics, Don Mischer had ingeniously designed the staging for the climactic moment, with a five-story ramp connecting to the track in the brand-new Olympic Stadium (the future Turner Field; construction had just been finished days earlier) for the athletes to walk up and down leading to the Parade of Nations. Initially, the placement of the cauldron—high atop a tower beyond the ramp—seemed like it would be a problem for Ali if he was going to light it. But then someone on Mischer's team had brainstormed a solution: he could light a fuse on a rocket, and the lit fuse would travel up on a wire to the cauldron.

Still, there was a lot of uncertainty as Friday night, July 19, approached. There'd only been one rehearsal with Ali a few evenings earlier, and it had been completed in darkness, after midnight, with only a few people on Mischer's team present, and without the lighting fuel—because the stadium was immediately adjacent to a national interstate highway, nobody wanted to take any risk that people would see a flame being lit and start wondering what was going on as they drove by. The magic of the moment was dependent on the element of total surprise. No one could be expecting to see Ali at the end of the ceremony.

It was a hot, clear night, and the show, as always, was a few hours long, with an artistic component followed by nearly two hundred delegations of athletes marching into the stadium up and down the ramp in the Parade of Nations. Then the moment built from there. Evander Holyfield did end up getting a big part—he jogged the Olympic Torch into the stadium, and then handed it off to Janet Evans, the Olympic swimmer. Janet took half a lap around the track, and then headed up the ramp, where a figure emerged out of the shadows. The Greatest.

Eighty-five thousand people gasped at once. President Clinton, who was in the stadium that night, told me a few days later on a visit to the IBC that the reaction to the sight of Ali—and the recognition—resulted in "the loudest hush" he'd ever heard in his life. Ali, dressed in all white, holding the torch with his right hand, his left hand shaking wildly from his Parkinson's. Once the most gifted fighter in the world, still, despite everything else, exuding a remarkable presence. There was a stunning dignity to it that made it all the more poignant, more striking than any of us could have imagined.

On our broadcast, I'd made sure for weeks that Bob Costas and Dick Enberg hadn't had a clue about what was coming—I wanted their reactions of shock and surprise to be pure and genuine, completely in the moment.

Bob, as ever, immediately sensed the significance of what was happening.

"Look who gets it next!" he exclaimed as Janet passed the torch to Ali.

"The Greatest!" Enberg added. "Oh my!"

With hundreds of millions watching around the world, Ali took the flame from Evans, held the torch aloft for a moment, and then turned and held it downward to light the rocket.

And it wouldn't light.

In our production truck, it felt like the perfect moment was breaking apart. Without a true rehearsal, no one knew how hard the fuel would be to light. There was an ample amount of fuel to be lit, but the mechanism to get the cauldron to light moved slower than anyone expected. And so Muhammad stood there holding the torch, with the flames flaring back at him, seeming like they were about to burn his arms, for what felt like an eternity. But he stood there patiently, even bravely, and waited those few extra beats—which felt like hours to the rest of us—until it finally lit.

The hush turned to a roar, with parts of the crowd breaking out in a chant of

"Ali, Ali, Ali." It was nothing short of glorious, simply a magnificent way to start the Centennial Olympic Games.

Ali would stay in Atlanta for the Olympics and attend a whole series of events throughout the Games. The day after the ceremony, I called Samaranch in his room in Atlanta; he was also thrilled with how it had gone. But I had another idea to talk to him about. The story that had long been told was that Muhammad had thrown his gold medal in the Ohio River when he'd gotten home from Rome, after getting turned away at a Louisville restaurant because he was Black. The truth, however, as Muhammad had told me himself in a conversation before the Games, was that he'd simply lost the medal. Now, talking to Samaranch, I asked him what he thought of giving Ali a recast medal (the IOC keeps all the castings of medals from every Games). Sure enough, at halftime of the gold medal game in men's basketball between Team USA and Yugoslavia, the IOC presented Ali with a new medal. It was another moment to savor.

Maybe the best part, though, came a couple weeks after the Olympics, when I got a call from Lonnie, Muhammad's wife. They'd just gotten back to their home in Louisville from a day at the PGA Championship at nearby Valhalla Golf Club.

"For so long," she told me, "Muhammad hasn't wanted to go out in public anymore. He's just so embarrassed by his condition. But after Atlanta, he agreed to go to this tournament.

"And when all these admirers surrounded him"—I almost felt her beaming over the phone—"it was like he was himself again!"

And with that, Muhammad Ali returned to public life, and began again to thrill people all over the world by simply showing up places. He didn't speak much, but somehow, even in silence, he emitted an otherworldly presence wherever he went. And it all began in Atlanta.

At any Olympics, there's nothing more important in terms of ratings than getting off to a good start. Swimming and gymnastics are the two most popular sports with viewers, and there's nothing better than a great story to grab their attention, and give them a case of Olympic fever that will sustain for two weeks.

In Atlanta, that story unfolded spectacularly for us on the first Tuesday of the competition, when the U.S. women's gymnastics team captured a gold medal in Hollywood fashion, with Kerri Strug capping off the victory with her unforgettable vault on a broken ankle. The drama all unfolded in prime time, and the story inspired a generation of gymnasts to come. With the United States by far the deepest team in the swimming competition, winning thirteen gold medals, our momentum only grew through the first week.

As with every Olympics, there was attention on every aspect of the proceedings, and that included plenty of praise and some criticism. It was almost inevitable that writers would find something wrong with our coverage—that we were too dramatic, or too jingoistic, or we were putting the wrong sports in prime time. But when our public relations head, Ed Markey, came into my office early every morning with the press clippings and a very long face, I'd happily make a show of dumping all the clippings into the trash, and picking up off my desk another pile of papers to wave at him: the ratings. We were setting records every night. The first week, we averaged over 35 million viewers a night, topping off at around 42 million with the gymnastics coverage. Those ratings were not just making us money, they were also unassailable proof of how much America was enjoying the show. When they were over, the Games would conclude as the most-watched Olympics in history.

In the IBC, the work was as thrilling as ever. After Barcelona, our production group had learned plenty of lessons, and it felt like we were part of a powerhouse team. Every night, I'd wander over to the truck at gymnastics to talk to David Michaels, our terrific producer there, to go over the stories we were going to cover. Then, back at the IBC as the show began, I'd situate myself in the control room, with all the feeds coming into the wall of monitors in front of us. At other networks, that control room would have been a popular stop on tours of visitors. But not at our shop—I didn't even allow Bob Wright, or Susan for that matter, to come inside. I didn't want our producers and directors to feel like they were on display. It was a sanctuary where work was being done, and they deserved to do it in a strictly business environment.

One week into the Games, we'd had more than 102 million viewers. And that middle Friday night, one week after the Opening Ceremony, I left the broadcast center at about 1:00 a.m., still riding high after watching the U.S. win three swimming gold medals, and the prime-time production team put on a fast-paced, fun

Left: Coming out of our house in Torrington, Connecticut, ready to go to work.

Author Collection

Below: With my fellow class officers in my junior year at Litchfield High. A year later, I'd be in France, discovering how much of a bigger world was out there.

Author Collection

Below: With Frank Sinatra and Roone Arledge at the 1973 Muhammad Ali–Ken Norton fight. Later that night, I'd find myself at Sinatra's house, talking about our favorite books.

Photo by American Broadcasting Companies via Getty Images

In Bel Air with the great Burt Sugarman and a friend.

Author Collection

Talking to Lorne Michaels, with *Saturday Night Live* about to launch.

Author Collection

6

Above: I couldn't get Richard Pryor to star in my original idea for an NBC show, but we still became friends. Here we are at a reception for the Special Olympics on the White House lawn.

Author Collection

Below: With Brandon Tartikoff at a press conference for *SNL*. He was the greatest friend I ever had in television.

Author Collection

"Saturday Night Live"
The Tradition Continues!

Saturday night, April 11th, 1981, SATURDAY NIGHT LIVE returned with the first of a new series of originals. Due to the strike by the Writers Guild of America the rest of our new shows have been delayed. But don't worry. We left 'em laughing, and we'll be back!

"SATURDAY NIGHT LIVE," in its new incarnation, hit the tube late last Saturday to critical approval."

KENNETH CLARK/UPI

"Consistently entertaining...A nifty 90 minutes of entertaining nuttiness."

MIKE DUFFY/Detroit Free Press

"The new SATURDAY NIGHT LIVE was great. It is better tasting and better written. It has bite, crunch and texture now. Everything seemed to work."

MARVIN KITMAN/Long Island Newsday

"SATURDAY NIGHT LIVE came back to the land of the living over the weekend!"

MICHAEL HILL/Baltimore Evening Sun

"The revamped SNL was an excellent program, crammed full of tough humor, the bizarre situations and the splendid acting that characterized the first four years of the program. In short, SNL was both successful and inspirational. There's no doubt that Dick Ebersol, the new SNL producer, has done virtually everything right."

GARY DEEB/Chicago Sun Times

"There was a lot to laugh at in the revamped SATURDAY NIGHT LIVE!"

JACK DEMPSEY/Variety

"A distinct improvement over others this year! They have taken a big step in the right direction...very funny sequences."

JANET MASLIN/New York Times

"...week one of SATURDAY NIGHT LIVE REBORN. Noticeably better than t previous version...making the whole package a happily reminiscent look to the show's glorious past."

BILL CARTER/Baltimore Sun

8

After I returned to *SNL* for one episode as its producer, the critics were pleased. But I knew we still had a lot of work to do.

National Broadcasting Company

9

Susan and I met on October 4, 1981. We were married exactly forty-eight days later.

Photo by Ron Galella, Ltd./Ron Galella Collection via Getty Images

Above: With Vince McMahon and the WWF's biggest star, Hulk Hogan. Maybe not the best two guys to stand next to while flexing.

Author Collection

Below: With André the Giant and a young Willie. At a party after my last WWF event, André picked me up and put me headfirst into a giant cake. Jesse Ventura later told me it was the ultimate sign of his affection.

Author Collection

11

12

Above: With Jesse Ventura and Vince McMahon on our way to see Arnold Schwarzenegger in Mexico, all decked out in University of Michigan maize and blue.

Author Collection

Below: With the one and only Johnny Carson and his wife, Alex.

Sylvan Mason Photographs

13

14

For my fortieth birthday, Susan surprised me with a party on a boat (that thanks to engine failure stayed docked in the East River). It was a great night with Roone, Don Ohlmeyer, and others.

Author Collection

15

When Magic Johnson announced he was HIV-positive, it felt like a tragedy. Less than a year later, he led the Dream Team to gold in Barcelona, and more than thirty years later, he's still alive and well.

Author Collection

Above: With Russ Granik, David Stern, and Ken Schanzer. The NBA on NBC remains as great of a partnership between a league and a network as there's ever been.

Chuck Solomon/NBA Entertainment via Getty Images

Below: I never ran out of questions to ask Juan Antonio Samaranch—at our first dinner together, or in all our years working side by side.

International Olympic Committee/Giulio Locatelli

Above: For my fiftieth birthday, Susan outdid herself—a massive celebration full of guest stars, highlighted by "the Greatest" himself, reenacting his great Olympic torch moment with the boys looking on.

Author Collection

Below: President Clinton offering a high five to Teddy while his brothers and the First Lady look on at a White House Christmas party.

Author Collection

Above: Charlie, me, Teddy, Harmony, Sunshine, Willie, Susan's mom, and Susan at Teddy's eighth-grade graduation from his Montessori school in June 2004.

Author Collection

Below: Teddy Ebersol's Red Sox Fields were dedicated in June of 2005, complete with a replica of the scoreboard on Fenway Park's Green Monster.

Author Collection

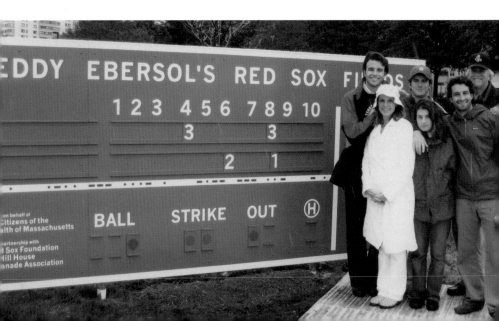

Mike Wallace's show *Biography* inspired the idea for *Later . . . with Bob Costas.* Then an interview with Mike on the show proved just how appealing the format could be.

Scott Rudd/Patrick McMullan via Getty Images

22

With an American hero, Neil Armstrong. The first man to walk on the moon was our neighbor in Telluride for years, not to mention an ace at charades.

Author Collection

23

John Madden was like a favorite uncle, a beloved college professor, and the smartest, most influential guy in every room he ever walked into.

Photo by Frederick M. Brown/Getty Images

With Madden's fellow stars on the *Sunday Night Football* team: Al Michaels, John's partner in the booth; Bob Costas, who was the perfect host for *Football Night in America*; and Cris Collinsworth, who would start in the studio and ultimately replace Madden in the booth in 2009 in what John himself termed "the perfect succession plan."

Photo by Kevin Winter/Getty Images

Left: Michael Phelps pulled off the greatest feat in Olympic history. Along the way, he also became a terrific friend.

Photo by Gary Gershoff/WireImage via Getty Images

Below: With George W. Bush— president and Yale classmate— and our wives at the Daytona 500.

Photo by Eric Draper/Courtesy of the George W. Bush Presidential Library and Museum

With Susie when she got her star on the Hollywood Walk of Fame.

Michael Tran/FilmMagic via Getty Images

28

29

There may be no funnier human being on earth to share a stage with than Bob Uecker.

Rick Scuteri/AP Images for WWE

Above: Almost fifty years after we first went for coffee, Lorne and I are still keeping the conversation going.

Photo by Fernando Leon/Getty Images

Below: Receiving the Lifetime Achievement Award at the Sports Emmys in 2009, presented by Roger Goodell, Gary Bettman, David Stern, Tim Finchem, Bud Selig, and Brian France. It was said to be the only time the commissioners of every major televised sport were in the same building at one time.

Marc Bryan-Brown/Getty Images

show around it all. I went back to my hotel the same way I had all week: on the back of a large motorcycle, driven by a police officer we'd hired, winding through the Olympic Park that had been built as the central gathering spot of the Games. Knowing that traffic to get around the park would be brutal, this was my way of cutting through the congestion and saving time where I could. But on this night, halfway back to the hotel, I heard an unmistakable boom elsewhere in the park. I wasn't sure what it was, but told the driver to keep going, and get us to the hotel as soon as he could.

When I got inside, I called the broadcast center to confirm what had happened: a bomb had been set off in the park. I immediately sent Tom Brokaw, who'd been doing the evening news each night from Atlanta, from the hotel back to the studio on my motorcycle; getting our network's news anchor on the air to handle the coverage was most important. By the time the motorcycle came back for me, Brokaw had taken over, and I'd gotten Jeff Zucker—who by then had been the *Today* show's producer for several years—to lead us in the control room. We'd be on the air through the night, with Brokaw staying on through the late morning, when he passed the desk off to Bob Costas. I flashed back many times that night to twenty-four years earlier in Munich, when we'd covered the terror attack there. This time, like then, the Olympics would resume once everything was deemed safe. As the story would continue to unfold over the next several weeks and months, Richard Jewell, the security guard who spotted the bomb and tried to warn bystanders about it, would be wrongly and sadly pinned as a suspect. Two people died in the attack—one directly from the bomb, as well as a European cameraman who had a heart attack while running to the scene. And the bomber, eventually identified as Eric Rudolph, would stage other bombings over the next several years before he was caught. Looking back at the Atlanta bombing, as much as anything else, it feels like a relic of another time, five years before September 11 changed the idea of security at an event like the Olympics forever.

As for the rest of the Games, they went on, scarred by the terror, but the spotlight would gradually return to where it belonged: the athletes. On the final Thursday night of the Olympics, Michael Johnson, one of the breakout American stars of the Games, in his custom-made golden track shoes, shattered the record he'd set in the Olympic trials a few weeks earlier in the 200 meters, capping off a legendary performance that had seen him win gold in the 400 meters as well. Then, the final day of the Games, the U.S. women's basketball team won gold, a dominating performance by a breakout team that had toured the country for months beforehand, building up a following before the Games. It was another brilliant marketing stroke by David Stern and the NBA, putting together a group of former college superstars like Lisa Leslie and Rebecca Lobo with the idea that they could serve as the foundation for the launch of a women's professional league after the Olympics. We'd worked alongside the league, and worked with the organizing committee to schedule the gold medal game right before the Closing Ceremony—always a highly rated spot. A year later, when the league launched, we'd cover the WNBA with the same production values as the NBA, with games scheduled late in the afternoon during its summer schedule to maximize viewership.

The Atlanta Games had been an event enjoyed by the entire nation, and it was a massive financial success for everyone involved. The revenue-sharing plan that we'd proposed to the IOC and the Atlanta Organizing Committee a few years before when we closed the deal earned them close to another $100 million when it was all said and done.

And as a side story, there was also this: a few months before the Games, WNBC, the largest owned-and-operated affiliate in NBC's network family, had needed a new general manager. I'd had the perfect recommendation: a former station manager in Chicago whose greatest claim to fame was discovering Oprah Winfrey, and then had gone on to run ABC Sports, before departing late in 1995. The executive's name was Dennis Swanson. Sure enough, my old friend Dennis would get the job, and during the Olympics, he'd make WNBC New York's top-rated station for the first time ever, a position the station would hold for years thereafter.

At the Closing Ceremony, Stevie Wonder, Gloria Estefan, and Little Richard performed, and once the final credits had rolled, we all stayed up much of the night celebrating at our wrap party on the roof of our hotel. Forty-eight hours later, I'd be home in Litchfield. There was a lot of sleep to catch up on. Even if the truth was that it would take several more days, if not weeks, to get the Olympic adrenaline to stop pulsing through my body.

CHAPTER 20

Outside the Box

The Atlanta Olympics were a highlight of a historic peak of success for us at NBC Sports. They were the culmination of a stretch that saw us broadcast the World Series, the Super Bowl, the NBA Finals, and the Summer Olympics—the first and only time in television history that one network has ever been the home of all four of those singular events in the span of a year. From the return of baseball after the '94 players strike, to the Steelers and Cowboys squaring off in a classic battle for the NFL title, to Michael Jordan's return to glory from retirement, to the Olympics, it really was an unforgettable run. Along the way, there was also Notre Dame football, the French Open and Wimbledon in tennis, and the U.S. Open and PGA Tour in golf—all of which made our slogan at the time, "America's Sports Leader," undeniably well earned.

By the end of 1996, I'd been in the job for seven and a half years, and had never been happier or more satisfied professionally. But around all the success we were having, over those seven and a half years, the truth is, not everything went perfectly, and a few of the lessons I learned went down harder than others.

The first learning experience unfolded within my first year on the job, and was based, maybe more than anything else, in a measure of hubris I had as I made my original deal with Bob Wright and Jack Welch. Because as excited as I was to return to sports in 1989, I also had it in my head that sports wouldn't quite be enough for me. Having spent years balancing multiple projects in the independent production world, I felt like I could handle other work at the company as well. And I had a specific challenge in mind.

"Let me have a shot at fixing *Today*," I told Welch and Wright as I negotiated my deal. "I really think I can solve your problem."

The problem at the time on the *Today* show was a feud between the host, Bryant Gumbel, and America's favorite weatherman, Willard Scott. A memo that Gumbel had written to the show's producer with ideas to improve the show, criticizing Scott along the way, had been leaked. Gumbel had said the weatherman held the show "hostage" to his "bad taste." Willard, in turn, had said the criticism "cut like a knife," and the controversy and bad PR was overshadowing the most important thing: the show was still tops in the ratings, above *Good Morning America* on ABC. It all left NBC's leadership eager to find a path to peace as soon as possible, and happy to take me up on my offer. So, when I was hired, I would not just be the president of NBC Sports but also a senior vice president at NBC News as the executive in charge of *Today*. That meant that as I chased David Stern and the NBA and found my bearings back in the sports world, my days actually began early before dawn on the third floor of 30 Rock, where the *Today* show was produced.

The president of NBC News at the time was Michael Gartner, a man who would become a great friend in the years to come. Michael was an Iowa native, a lifelong newspaperman in the Midwest rarely seen without a bow tie who'd worked at a number of papers, including *USA Today* and the *Wall Street Journal*. He'd been recruited to NBC by Bob Wright and Jack Welch to rein in out-of-control costs in the news division, which he'd quickly managed to do. Michael knew the business of journalism better than just about anyone, but he also had little interest in the soap opera sagas that could inevitably unfold around on-camera talent. I, on the other hand, reasoned that my years at ABC Sports and *Saturday Night Live* had taught me how to handle talent, and I could help quell the controversy at *Today*.

Like I said, I wasn't lacking for hubris.

To use a baseball analogy, I ultimately went one for two in the talent wars. Repairing the friction between Gumbel and Scott proved to be not that hard. I invited them both over for lunch at my apartment, and speaking face-to-face, the bruised feelings were smoothed over. But as I looked at ways to improve the show from there, I ran into trouble.

Deborah Norville was a bright, appealing talent who'd become popular as the anchor of *NBC News at Sunrise*, which aired before the *Today* show. Deborah was thirty-one, a summa cum laude graduate of the University of Georgia who'd worked in Atlanta and Chicago before coming to the network and becoming a rising star. So in the fall of 1989, I decided to bring her in as the show's full-time news anchor, replacing the staid veteran John Palmer. The goal was to make the show younger, an attribute that was clearly helping *Good Morning America* as ABC's ratings ticked upward with cohosts Charlie Gibson and Joan Lunden. I discussed the move at length with Bryant and Jane Pauley, the show's cohost, and they were completely on board with what I was trying to do.

But it all went sideways when a *USA Today* story headlined "Norville: A Rising Morning Star at NBC" began with the line "Watch out, Jane Pauley. *Today's* woman of the '90s has been chosen." I later heard that Jane saw the article, which was based largely on innuendo and speculation, in the Salt Lake City airport, and was stunned. We'd never had any intention of replacing Jane with Deborah, but Jane felt threatened, and the headlines continued from there. It all spiraled out of control quickly, and just a few weeks after Deborah started at *Today* as the news anchor, Jane preemptively announced her intention to leave the show.

Much like the Bryant-Willard feud, the discord resulting from the Deborah and Jane situation was pretty much the worst thing that could happen to a show like *Today*, which has succeeded through all its iterations by giving viewers the sense that the cast is *the* happy family America wants to wake up with every morning. The controversy was big news at the time, filling the newspaper gossip pages and magazine covers. "Kiss *Today* Goodbye," read the cover of *People* magazine, with a large photo of a smiling Jane saying she "felt awkward" and a quote from Deborah saying she "cried buckets." Despite all my overtures to assuage her—in lunches, meetings, phone calls, and more—Jane refused to reconsider and left the show, and with Deborah now cohosting with Bryant, the ratings took a dive. Through absolutely no fault of her own, the talent that Deborah brought to the role was overshadowed by the sense that she'd pushed out Jane, who'd cohosted the show for more than a decade. It didn't matter that the narrative couldn't have been further from the truth. By the spring of 1990, the show was in crisis.

Everyone around me—from Gartner to Bob Wright to Jack Welch—remained supportive of me. But as the crisis became a matter that even the GE board grew concerned with, we had to figure something out. Even if I'd touched all my bases before making the move, the situation had nonetheless gone haywire, and it had happened on my watch. I felt like coming up with a fix was most incumbent on me. And at some point, an unconventional but perfect solution occurred to me. It would take the pressure off of the talent, and give a new story for the press to focus on.

So I called Bob Wright from my office.

"Just put it all on me," I told him on the phone. "I'm going to resign from NBC News, and put all my focus on sports. I'll take the full blame for what happened, take the heat for a few days, and then the story will fade, and you guys can move forward."

Wright thought the idea was crazy; in his mind, no executive should ever admit a mistake so publicly. Gartner—who had been a wonderful partner throughout, and remains as honest, stand-up, and forthright of a human being as I've ever met—encouraged me to stay. But the most important figure, Jack Welch, loved the idea. Jack liked out-of-the-box thinking, and he also liked fearlessness. And so we went with it. In the middle of May, the company put out a press release explaining my departure, and I gave a series of interviews explaining that the whole situation was my fault, and stepping away to concentrate just on my job in sports with the NBA contract beginning would give the show a chance to start fresh.

It would take some time, but improbably, everyone would find some version of a happy ending out of the fiasco. Jane would move from *Today* to *Dateline*, the evening newsmagazine, and remain the face of that show for years. Within a year, Deborah would end up getting pregnant and taking maternity leave, ultimately leaving the show after that, but resurfacing a few years later as the host of the syndicated newsmagazine *Inside Edition*, a job she still has today, nearly three decades later. And as for the *Today* show itself, a new anchor would replace Norville and lead the show back to the top of the ratings for decades to come. Her name was Katie Couric.

Meanwhile, I had been given one of the best lessons of my career: If you find a job you love, don't try to satiate your ego by trying to find something else. Just realize how lucky you are, and have a great time working your ass off from there.

That lesson came in handy again two years later, when, after the Barcelona Olympics, Wright and Welch came to me with another offer. Sports was going so well, why not now take advantage of the full breadth of experience I'd brought to the job, and take over news as well as NBC's West Coast operation, too? Michael Gartner was already intending to leave the news division in a matter of months and return home to his native Iowa, and Brandon had finally left the company in 1991 to become the head of Paramount Pictures. But my quick answer to Bob and Jack surprised them: I wasn't interested at all.

First off, it was hard enough balancing my work life in New York with my family in Connecticut; adding a minimum of bimonthly trips out to the West Coast would put an even bigger strain on spending as much time as I wanted to with Susan and the kids. Then, also, I had no interest in trying the news thing again. And with regard to the entertainment part of the offer, if there was one thing that my return to sports had shown me, it was how much more I liked live television than the pace of the drama- and comedy-scripted TV entertainment world. Brandon may have loved it, but to me, having to wait months, if not years, for projects like sitcoms and dramas to come together was an often frustrating, maddening process where so many different things could go off the rails. Producing football games and basketball games and the Olympics—the rush of adrenaline was, I'd come to realize, one of my favorite things about my job. Really, on any given day of the week, whether I was in my office at 30 Rock or on the road at an event, I wasn't blind to how ridiculously fortunate I was to be able to say with certainty that there was no place else I'd rather be, nowhere else I'd rather be working.

For a while after that, Welch was miffed at my rejection of the offer; what I heard was that no one at GE had ever turned down a high-level executive promotion like this. Also, the company badly needed to fill the position; the foundation of NBC's success as a network was its ratings in prime time, and after Brandon's departure, the numbers had fallen off. But who Bob and Jack ended up hiring for the entertainment job instead worked out phenomenally, as my old pal Don Ohlmeyer became head of all programming on the West Coast. With the rise of the comedies *Seinfeld*, *Friends*, and *Frasier*, and *ER* and the *Law & Order* franchise on the drama side, NBC would soon get back to the top of the ratings ladder. All these years after starting just a month apart at ABC Sports, and later nearly becoming Roone's top two executive lieutenants, Don and I were now back together, if on opposite coasts, at NBC.

For me, turning down the job was not only the ultimate crystallization of what the *Today* experience had laid bare but also the perfect confirmation of exactly what I wanted to do at NBC. Like anyone, early in my career, I'd been driven by ambition—a thirst to continue to get better jobs, more responsibility, and more opportunity. But now, in my mid-forties, after all the things I'd been remarkably fortunate to already do, and after the realization that I was doing exactly what I wanted, my ambitious thirst was quenched.

Don't get me wrong—I still wanted to work as hard as ever, but only in the sense of doing my job, not in pursuit of something bigger. The result of it all was ironic: as someone who didn't want anyone else's job, or have any interest in intruding on anyone else's turf, my role, at least informally, actually expanded. I became something of an executive-at-large within the corporate suite at NBC—someone frequently brought in for advice or help in all different situations, with people knowing that whatever I said was going to come with complete honesty, and no hidden agendas.

That went for my bosses, like Bob and Jack, with whom I developed a wonderful trust, at least after Jack got over my decision. It also went for my peers, like Don, who every year would invite me out to California for a few days to screen the pilots that had come in and offer my thoughts. Don knew that if he asked my opinion about a show, good or bad, he'd get it. I also remained close with Gartner in the remaining years we overlapped. One of my favorite stories involving Michael took place on a day in 1991 when I knew he was arriving late to a GE meeting in Princeton, New Jersey, on account of a lunch meeting he was having with a correspondent—the purpose of which was to fire the individual. But when Michael arrived even later than expected, and I asked him how the firing had gone, he confessed he'd found the guy just too fascinating to let him go. Actually, at that lunch, Michael had ended up promoting Tim Russert to become the host of *Meet the Press*.

The closest relationship I developed at NBC, meanwhile, was with Jeff Zucker, who, as another Michael Gartner out-of-the-box hire, took over the *Today* show when he was just twenty-six years old, in 1992. Jeff and I had originally met in the mid-eighties, when he was fresh out of college and hired by NBC Sports to be the

Olympic researcher leading into the Seoul Games. I was producing *Friday Night Videos* and *Saturday Night's Main Event* at the time, but heard good things about Jeff and took him to lunch to trade Olympic research stories. After those Games, Jeff had moved to the news department, and quickly moved up through the ranks at *Today*. When he got the top job, I was working in Sports, and was happy to be a consigliere and mentor whenever he needed it, certainly knowing how tricky the morning-show business could get. Jeff, however, was the best producer *Today* has ever had, responsible not just for top ratings every year but innovating on top of his success, bringing the show outside onto Rockefeller Plaza, and creating morning concerts that would become staples of the show's summer programming for years to come.

As an aside, years later, in 2000, Jeff was asked, just as I had been eight years earlier, to run NBC Entertainment. He called and told me about the offer, and asked me what I thought, telling me to take a few days to think about my advice. When he then came by my office to get my thoughts, I counseled him not to take it—knowing that he was like me, and he wouldn't enjoy the process of making shows in Hollywood, because really nothing made him happier than producing live TV. Well, Jeff didn't listen to me, taking the job and finding plenty of success, eventually rising to become CEO of the whole network when Bob Wright retired. But I don't think Jeff was ever really happy again professionally until he went to run CNN, where he could be back in live control rooms, covering the news as it broke.

The result, of course, was that Jeff single-handedly revived CNN, putting it back atop the cable news world.

The area I got brought in to consult most prominently was my old stomping grounds of late night. In the spring of 1991, I was sitting backstage at an annual meeting of NBC's affiliates at Carnegie Hall next to Johnny Carson when he turned to me just before going out onstage to talk to the press.

"This will be interesting," he said matter-of-factly. "I'm about to tell everyone I'm going to retire."

I wouldn't have any chance to warn Wright and Welch; a few minutes later, he was out front onstage telling the world. The announcement was a huge surprise for everyone, stunning a crowd that had been laughing at Johnny's onstage jokes one moment and dropping their jaws the next. Over the next several months, Carson's departure set off a fervor of debate over the two logical candidates to replace him, Jay Leno, the stand-up comic who'd been Johnny's regular guest host for years, or David Letterman, who'd long hosted the late night show that aired after *Tonight*. The executives running the West Coast operation in the wake of Brandon's departure had promised the job to Leno, but Letterman, who was closer to Carson and idolized him, desperately wanted it as well. The drama played out in real time, a Hollywood gossip blockbuster if there ever was one, with CBS lurking as a potential home for whoever didn't get the job. Everyone in the company seemed to take sides, and the drama had so many twists and turns that it eventually was adapted into a book and HBO movie. All throughout, I found myself in the middle of the "comedy drama," brought in to give the other executives plagued with the tough decision any counsel I could provide.

Honestly, my position on the big question at the time, in retrospect, was the wrong one: I liked Letterman over Leno. I knew Dave well, going back to my time in 30 Rock at *SNL* when *Late Night* taped a few floors beneath us. He'd introduced me to Vince McMahon, and he'd vouched for talent like Bob Costas, who'd called "elevator races" for him as a gag when he'd started out at Sports. I thought Dave was funnier than Jay, and thought the audience would follow him and keep him the more relevant, more beloved comic for years to come.

The situation was further complicated by contracts—a guarantee in Jay's that he'd get *Tonight* when Carson retired, and the fact that Dave's deal didn't expire for a year after the transition. The West Coast execs tried in vain to please all parties when Johnny left in 1992, giving Jay the show and trying to convince Dave he was part of their plans, but it all just seemed to make the situation worse. While Dave entertained potential offers from ABC and CBS, Jay struggled to flourish in Johnny's deep shadow and amid so much negative press. It all came to a head, at least behind the scenes, in early 1993, at a GE senior management meeting in Boca Raton, Florida, where Bob Wright brought a group of executives together late one night after all the official company business to debate what to do: stay the course with Jay, or abandon ship and try to get Dave to stay and take over the show. The arguments on both sides were heated, and I got especially annoyed when someone tried to compare the situation to Jane Pauley and Deborah Norville. The supposed argument was that if Jay was removed, the public and media would rally behind him the way they did for Pauley—which made no sense, since the public and media had already done that for Dave.

The meeting went on for a few hours, well past midnight on the East Coast, with pretty much every senior entertainment executive at the company—most in the hotel suite in Florida, and a few by conference call back in Burbank—laying out for Wright (and at one point Welch, who stopped by) which side they were on. When it was time for final statements, I certainly made clear my position.

"The company should go with the host who we think will have a more successful show," I said. "That'll always be the most important thing. The show that tops the ratings—ultimately the most important part of Johnny's legacy—can make hundreds of millions of dollars for this company just like he did. Everything else is details."

No decision was made, but that seemed beside the point when, the next day, Leno began talking to some of the people in the meeting and giddily quoting what they'd said in the room. Jay later claimed that he had snuck into the corporate offices at Burbank and hid in a side room on executive row, eavesdropping on the whole meeting while it unfolded on speakerphone a few doors away. Knowing the layout of those offices, and where Jay said he'd hid, I've never seen his story as plausible—I don't think he could have heard even a loud speakerphone. But I suppose it made for a great story regardless.

In the end, the network went with Jay, and Dave went to CBS. Whether or not Jay had eavesdropped on me vouching for Dave in that Boca Raton summit, I felt like it was important to let Jay hear my opinion directly. So once the issue was settled, I called Jay and explained myself.

"I don't know what you heard or didn't hear," I told him. "The truth is that I thought the company should go with Dave. But that doesn't mean that I don't think you're talented, because you are, and you can absolutely host a terrific show. I'll do whatever I can to help, and you have my support here on out."

He appreciated the truth and my straightforwardness, and the conversation solidified a warm relationship that continues to this day.

But the punch line to the whole affair is another incontrovertible truth: I was wrong. Jay Leno was in fact the right choice.

Why? Well, first, he was willing to do what Dave certainly would not: go across the country to visit the fifty top NBC affiliate markets, and do promos and appearances and the like to give the local stations ways to promote him in late night. Usually Jay would work in his trips alongside his relentless stand-up comedy touring schedule; occasionally he'd even fly out in the morning for a meeting with an affiliate before heading back to tape the show that night in L.A. To get Letterman to do that at NBC—for executives he resented, in places he didn't want to go—would have been all but impossible.

Then there was also the lesson that Johnny himself had imparted to me all those years earlier: to succeed in late night, the audience that you had to resound with was "between Trenton and Reno"; the viewers in the middle of America who were mostly watching the show at 10:30 p.m. local, and were consumers of the broad humor that Jay specialized in, and Dave loathed. (And the truth was, for all of Dave's deification of Carson, Johnny's humor was much broader than his as well.) In any event, while Dave would be the favorite of critics on either coast for the next few decades, it was Jay who would wrest control of the top ratings spot within a year of their long battle, and stay on top for decades. The audience always lets you know what the right decision is with who they laugh for—and in this case, the audience was the whole country. As I'd said in that suite in Boca Raton, having the most successful show was paramount—and that's what Jay had.

And as for the greatest of all the late night hosts, late in 1992, a few months after he'd retired, NBC asked me to head out west to have lunch with him. I'd known Johnny longer than anyone else had at NBC, and the relationship had continued when I'd come to Sports, and Johnny—a tennis junkie—was a regular user of the network's Wimbledon tickets. As for the purpose of the get-together in L.A., it was to lightly inquire if there was any chance that he might come back—not for *The Tonight Show*, but to host occasional specials. We had a great lunch, and I approached the issue as lightly as I could. But the answer was unequivocal.

"C'mon, Dick," he said as he poured himself another glass of his beloved red wine. "I've done my last show."

There'd be another troubled transition years later with Conan O'Brien's brief tenure as the host of *Tonight*. In 2004, in an effort to keep everyone happy (always a difficult proposition), Jeff Zucker, as head of the network, negotiated deals for Jay and Conan that guaranteed that Conan, hosting in Letterman's old 12:30 a.m. slot, would take over for Jay five years later. But when five years were up, Jay was still going strong, printing money in late night, and NBC didn't want to lose him. The creative solution in 2009 was to give Jay a nightly show in prime time, with Conan taking over *Tonight*. But the concept failed on both sides. Jay's new show didn't rate well in prime time; it was just too tough to try to get a comedy talk show to compete with hit prime-time dramas. Then, beyond that, the *Tonight Show* audience—particularly people "between Trenton and Reno"—didn't respond to Conan's often quirky, even arcane brand of humor.

As usual, whatever role I had in the whole scenario was completely unofficial. But with Jeff's blessing, I'd gone out to L.A. to meet with Conan, who I liked very much personally, before he'd taken over *Tonight*. The meeting was on the lot where Conan's new studio was being built, and the message there, in his office, was simple: to pass along to him what Johnny had taught me. He had to keep in mind how particular the audience at the start of late night was, how different it was from the audience an hour later, where he'd been performing for years. He also had to remember all the people between Trenton and Reno; the America he had to win over. Conan seemed receptive that day to the advice, but he didn't change his humor even a little bit when he moved to the new stage, and his new 11:30 p.m. audience didn't take to it.

So after years of domination in *The Tonight Show* slot, NBC had a major problem. Jeff was doing his best to fix the problem—at one point, he tried to give Jay a half-hour show at 11:30 p.m., with Conan starting at midnight, but Conan and his people rejected it. The story got messier and messier by the day, and as I watched it unfold, I only got more angry, not just for Jay, but for Jeff. By that time, I'd been around long enough to truly not worry who I pissed off or offended, and when the story blew up, I decided on my own to call the *New York Times* and let them know what I thought of the situation. I told the paper's media reporter Bill Carter, who I'd known for years, how weak I thought it was that Conan was blaming Jay for his struggles, and that whatever anyone thought of the difficulty of the situation, Conan had to be accountable for the continuing ratings failure on his watch. He just didn't attract viewers. Was it a shame that Conan ended up having to leave? Absolutely. But the prejudices of the media notwithstanding, Jay was who the audience wanted to see.

From Saturday Night to Sunday Night

My quotes became a big story for Carter; it wasn't every day an executive just called up a reporter with some candid, even controversial, opinions. Letterman would spout off about it on his show that night, which was fine—it was better for the heat to be on me than Jay or Jeff. For my part, I was glad to pick up the phone, and then go right back to sports, and the team of people I'd come to love working with.

CHAPTER 21

Human Resources

Just before the NBA All-Star Game in February of 1996, the night before I was supposed to fly to San Antonio for the weekend, I walked back to my apartment in New York after a dinner and felt some tightness in my chest. The next morning, back at work, I felt it again, and went to see the NBC and GE doctor who was always on call at 30 Rock. He gave me an EKG and told me in no uncertain terms that I should not go to the game. My response was that Bob Wright and David Stern were already on their way to Teterboro Airport in New Jersey and expecting me to fly to Texas with them; I was going.

I was fine on the plane, but that night when Bob and I took a walk by the Alamo in San Antonio, the discomfort came back much worse—like an anvil pressing down on my chest. I didn't say anything, but a few minutes later when we walked into a bar to have a drink, I did something that as a real light drinker I never do: I ordered two double scotches without water. As self-medication, it worked at least for a little while.

About an hour and a half later, I got back to my room and called my assistant, Aimee Leone, who was for the first time traveling with me on a trip like this. I asked her to come to my room, which, as she told me later, she thought was really odd, considering it was almost midnight. But when she came, I told her what was going on, and asked her to find out the best medical facility in San Antonio—we could go there in the morning. She argued with me that we should go immediately; again, I won the argument, and I'm lucky that I lived to shake my head at my own stupidity.

The next morning, Aimee and I went down to the lobby, said hi to Ken Schanzer and a group of executives getting ready to play golf with some clients, and then got into a car and drove to University Hospital, a tremendous medical institution. I walked inside and told them I wanted to see a specific doctor; they said it would be about two hours. I returned to the car and told Aimee this wasn't worth it—let's go back to the hotel. But by this point, she'd had enough of my nonsense.

"We're not going anywhere," she said. "I'm going inside, and I'm dealing with this."

Two minutes later, I was on my back in the emergency room being hooked up to a collection of monitors. Ten minutes after that, I was being wheeled into the operating room. At forty-eight years old, I was having a heart attack.

Doctors installed a stent in an artery that was almost totally blocked. I'd watch the All-Star Game from my hospital bed, and eventually head for a little more rest with my family in Florida early the next week. I was about as lucky as someone could be; after a bit of rehab, I wouldn't feel the effects of the issue again. And while I'd be lying if I claimed that the incident completely changed my life, there was one thing I thought about during those few days in the hospital bed that I could take care of. Right from there, I called Schanzer, who by now was back in New York.

"Everything with my heart is going great," I updated him. "And really, everything is great in the office—we're in the middle of the best year any network sports group has ever had. But I think we need to make a few changes."

NBC Sports was filled with dedicated, passionate, hardworking staffers who quite literally gave over their lives to their work. Every weekend, they were on the road at an NBA game, a golf tournament, an NFL game, or the like. And they loved every minute of it. But in their midst, there were—I knew and Kenny knew—a few assholes in our group. Producers who screamed in trucks just because they could, who abused assistants and coordinators and technicians, who didn't appreciate how lucky they were to work in our business, at our company. And it was time for them to go.

Ken got it done in two days. Without those members of our department, NBC Sports was better off, and our defining rule of hiring people—as christened by someone on our staff—was born: the "No Assholes" policy. And while it's true that for as long as I was at NBC, there would be no more assholes allowed inside our group, the "No Assholes" rule was bigger than just that. It was a statement about the kind of culture we wanted to have, the kind of culture people would want to work in. I'd never forgotten the time at ABC when I'd asked a senior producer if there was anything I could do for him, and he'd responded nastily, saying I could take a piss for him. I wanted to be part of the kind of place where every producer we had would embrace every chance they could get to teach something to someone, and do it with interest and empathy.

"No Assholes" was, looking back, even more than a realization in a sobering moment about what really matters. It was a culminating lesson in one of my best years as a leader, and would serve for years as one of our defining standards at NBC Sports. The good news was that, in the most important positions, we already had outstanding people in place. From Schanzer to Falco to Swindler, on the business side, I had some of the greatest partners I'd ever worked with. On the creative end, Tommy Roy had been our executive producer since 1993. The day we promoted Tommy, I'll never forget Kevin Monahan, our head of PR, poking his head into my office to tell me that I was a hero with the production staff, who'd just been told of the news. Talk to people at NBC Sports today, where Tommy still masterfully oversees all the golf coverage, and you'll find dozens of talented producers who he mentored in production trucks and compounds all across the country, and even the world.

Tommy's importance—as a great producer, and a great person—was so paramount because, at NBC Sports, our production team was paramount. That is to say, much like ABC Sports had been under Roone, I wanted my production people to know that their jobs were the most important of anyone in the department. I knew from being in enough places how often the business side of a creative operation controlled what happened. But I also knew the most successful places gave the creative people freedom and support to do their jobs. The creative people are the people who feed any show business enterprise; who put asses in seats, or eyeballs in front of television sets. Yes, it's right to respect accountants and controllers, but they can't be in charge—because they can't build the most important asset: *the audience*.

It helped, of course, that I was a production person, and I loved creating stuff—being in trucks or edit rooms with creative people leading conversations about what ideas we could make possible. But beyond that, ultimately I knew that it was our production people who made our coverage of the NBA, the Olympics, the NFL, college football, tennis, golf, and beyond shine. So I wanted us to do everything we could to treat our staff well.

One of the angriest moments I ever had at NBC was at an Olympics, when someone on the penny-pinching side had cut the catering budget significantly, against my wishes, without me knowing. For the entire Olympics, our commissary had to feed hundreds of people, many of them freelancers who were there for their love of the work more than anything else, working long shifts with no breaks. The chow was important—an army moves on its stomach, as the saying goes. Usually, the food service at an Olympics was a quality operation, but at these Games, it was just terrible. You get what you pay for. And one night, eating some awful dish from the commissary in my office, I just had enough. I walked outside into the outer area of executive offices in our compound, said something about the food, and threw the plate against the wall. And—for extra emphasis—instructed the staff not to clean up the mess. It may have been a bit much, but my point was made. For the final several days we were there, we supplemented the rotten food in the commissary by bringing in mass amounts of takeout from local restaurants.

Even more than just feeding the staff, I also believed in rewarding them—and rewarding the best of them with increased salaries and bonuses. Just like at *SNL*, where the most productive writers got paid the most, at NBC Sports, the best producers were paid the most; I never believed in everyone getting paid the same. One of the best things about working an Olympics, in fact, would be finding the dozen or so people who had worked the hardest and contributed the most to the coverage, and telling them that they'd be seeing a bonus in their next paycheck when they got home.

I cared about the staff, and always wanted them to feel lucky about being part of the NBC Sports team. At the beginning of my career, I'd ghostwritten letters from Roone to his ABC staffers to thank them for their work. Now, in the job myself, I wanted to find ways to be a more authentic leader; to have real relationships with my staff. My goal was that everyone working for NBC Sports always felt like they were working somewhere special, and at a place that cared about them. At an Olympics, besides the bonuses, one small thing I liked to do toward the end of a Games was personally invite people into my office to give them gifts and let them know how much I appreciated their hard work. Literally hundreds of people would come by over the last few days of the event, one at a time, all exchanging a handshake or a hug. They'd know they had a boss who knew who *they* were, and who recognized their individual contributions. And they'd leave the office with a goody bag containing an NBC Olympics fleece or jacket, for good measure.

The approach went for our talent, too. Julius Erving was a great analyst for us on the NBA. But one year during the playoffs, I got word that Dr. J. had skipped his son's high school graduation because he had to work. I called him immediately, beside myself that Julius would think he couldn't be excused for that kind of occasion. And from there, I made sure the word got out that as much as we were about hard work and dedication, there were exceptions that everyone—from NBA Hall of Famers to production assistants—could use, with support from the department's highest perches.

More regularly, I also was religious about my most important daily routine back at 30 Rock. On days I was in New York, sometime after lunch, I would try to leave my office on the fifteenth floor and just roam the halls of the sports department's three floors. Sometimes it would be for ten minutes, sometimes it would be for a half hour or longer, but the idea was to duck my head in every office, every cubicle, and every conference room on our sports floors just to say hi to people in their space, and get a sense of what they were doing and any issues they were having. I also had an amazing asset in Aimee Leone, who was my eyes and ears in the department, flagging everything from minor issues and squabbles to birthdays and anniversaries for me. Aimee understood as much as anyone that creating the community I wanted at NBC Sports was about forging emotional connections, and making people feel seen and part of something where their role was valued. I'd like to think that approach, as much as anything else I did as an executive, fostered our culture at NBC Sports; a culture where no one was ever afraid to ask a question, where everyone was encouraged to be curious and creative, and, with some work, there were no assholes anywhere to be found. When people like working with each other, and even just being with each other, the work is just better, and the audiences are the better for it.

I was so proud to be the leader of my group. And that pride was only enhanced by knowing the kind of guy I worked for.

Early in my time at NBC, Jack Welch called me up. He wanted to talk about one of our golf commentators; he wasn't sure he liked him. My response was unequivocal.

"Okay, Jack," I said. "And while we're throwing around suggestions, I don't think the guy running GE's locomotive division is really the right man for the job, either."

He roared with laughter—and got the message. I really wasn't trying to be impertinent; I was only reminding him of his own treasured style of management. Jack had made his reputation on hiring experts to run GE's many businesses—and leaving them alone to let them run them the way they saw fit. Now, he'd realized in an instant, here he was breaking that way of management.

It was from Welch's confidence in me that the original NBA deal came to be, and as I've hopefully made clear, how the Olympic deals came to be. Jack loved risk, and he loved taking big swings. He trusted me and my team to make the right, smart deals, and savored them paying off with big ratings and big profits. Sometimes he'd call just to talk about some piece of gossip in the sports world, or wanting to hear how a broadcast of a big game went. He loved sports, and he loved hearing reports from behind the scenes.

While Jack was always willing to foot the bill when I asked him to, there were occasionally times when I was able to save him a few dollars. After former Laker head coach Pat Riley cohosted *NBA Showtime* for our first season covering the league, the Knicks wanted to hire him as their coach. Dick Evans of Madison Square Garden called me up to ask permission to interview Pat, and make sure he could get out of his TV contract. On the phone with Evans, I had a thought. Not more than a few months earlier, Jack had been complaining to me about a luxury box at MSG that someone at GE had purchased or leased without Jack's knowledge for several hundred thousand dollars a year; way too much money, in his opinion. Maybe I could make Jack happy in this deal. So the next day, I told Evans that we would release Riley from his contract with no penalty—if MSG agreed to let GE off the hook for the box. When I later told Jack this, he loved it.

Still, I didn't always listen to what he wanted. We were once at a management retreat with a series of Six Sigma seminars—the arcane management technique that Jack was in love with and made all GE employees train in. It never made sense to me; as much as it might help somewhere in a factory, there was no legitimate application to sports production. So, one afternoon, rather than go into an auditorium to sit in a lecture I wouldn't listen to, I took a seat outside on a lawn of the retreat center to catch up on my mail and paperwork for an upcoming deal. Sure enough, just a few minutes after I sat down, there came Jack.

"Ebersol," he said, looking down at me on the ground with a smile, "you think you can just sit outside and read while everyone else goes inside to the workshop?"

"Jack, you know that I'm not going to listen, and you know that the Six Sigma jargon isn't going to help me when I'm in a production truck looking at a wall of monitors filled with Michael Jordan and Charles Barkley. C'mon, let me just work on something useful."

"That's fine," he said, smiling. "But you've got to pay for it. Tonight, you're gonna talk to the whole group after dinner. And whatever you say better be interesting."

Jack knew it was hardly something I'd object to. GE directors were always happy to hear stories from the sports and entertainment world all night long. I spoke off-the-cuff for almost an hour. I think Jack loved it the most.

But my favorite Jack Welch story took place a few months after my heart attack, when Schanzer and I had a big annual budget review with Jack at 30 Rock. It was a warm spring day, and I walked into the conference in khaki cargo shorts and a sweater vest; everyone else there, including Ken, was wearing a suit. Ken thought I was crazy; yes, everyone knew I didn't like wearing ties, but this was a big meeting.

When Welch walked in, he took a quick look at me and then turned to Ken.

"What's the matter, Schanzer? Ebersol's the only one with balls around here?"

And the real punch line: Eventually my disinclination for formality led to the long-standing dress code at NBC being loosened. No ties, no high heels, no problem.

CHAPTER 22

Adventures in Negotiation

The most important asset I had in my relationship with Jack Welch and Bob Wright was their trust. If there was a deal I wanted to chase, I could do it with the confidence that my bosses would support my investments, and believe in the calls I wanted to make.

That confidence infused every negotiating adventure that we went through in my first decade on the job. That included the big early deals like the NBA and the Olympics, of course, but also every other one as well. We looked at every chase and every courtship as their own little sagas, with plots and characters that were all part of the adventure. And every one of them started the same way: getting everyone in the company connected to the deal, from the advertising execs to the finance personnel, to realize they, themselves, were part of the story. You couldn't bullshit them, but you could inspire them to want to be part of our success.

One great example was the agreement we made with the United States Golf Association to start broadcasting the U.S. Open in 1995. Looking at the first three Opens we'd potentially have on our slate, we realized they were in New York, Detroit, and Washington. The country's media capital, its automotive capital, and its political capital. Each of those three locales could set up their own narrative for the ad sales team to sell to their clients, from commercial buys to sponsorship tents. That notion excited the business side of the company—it showed them they would be just as critical to the success of the shows as our production teams. They bought in from day one of the effort to make the agreement. And sure enough, that deal paid for itself the day it was signed.

That sense of teamwork was a central defining factor in the path we took to making NBC the top sports network in the 1990s. Everyone believing in each other, everyone feeling they had a stake in our performance—that was all an unseen foundation of our success. Meanwhile, out front, I continued to manage the most important relationships we had, with Juan Antonio Samaranch and the IOC and David Stern and the NBA, in very personal ways. That went for other major partnerships we had as well; chief among them the National Football League.

About a year after I started at NBC, in the spring of 1990, we renewed our deal to broadcast the NFL's AFC package, which had been part of the network's portfolio for decades. The NFC package, always on CBS, was considered the superior group of games because the NFC had the more desirable markets: New York, Philadelphia, Washington, Dallas, Chicago, San Francisco, Los Angeles—all the homes of iconic teams whose games typically rated the highest. But NBC had long been content to be the network of the AFC, which not only guaranteed steady sports ratings every Sunday during the fall but also a Super Bowl—and the advertising bonanza it begat—every three years.

Negotiations in 1990 went pretty smoothly; the NFL network television landscape had been a portrait of constancy for decades, with CBS and NBC splitting Sundays, and ABC carrying Monday nights. But in 1993, when it came time for another round of renewals, offered a different outlook for a few reasons. First, the league's ownership corps had undergone a change, with some new team owners looking to shake up the way the NFL had always done business. That was absolutely felt on the television negotiating committee, with longtime Browns owner Art Modell's influence usurped by a pair of newer, younger owners, Pat Bowlen of the Broncos and Jerry Jones of the Cowboys. Pat and Jerry weren't going to do business the way the league had always done it, and that made the atmosphere ripe for change.

In those first few years of the nineties, I did everything I could to build relationships with the new power players through the dealings we were having with them as part of our ongoing coverage. Jerry Jones and I clicked quickly when he came into the league by buying the Cowboys, but Pat took longer to connect with. As it turned out, in an unlikely twist, the reason was rooted in the way NBC let me do business. At one point, I asked a mutual acquaintance, the head of our NBC station in Denver, if he could shed any light on why Pat seemed kind of cold in our meetings. The answer I got back was that Pat couldn't figure out why NBC was showing up at negotiations without the head of the company at the table to be involved, like the other two networks did. My solution was to bring Bob Wright along to our next meeting. While it was good for him to meet Pat and some other owners face-to-face, Bob stayed quiet at the table, letting me and Schanzer take the lead. In the process, Pat saw for himself the way business was done at NBC Sports. We weren't insulting the NFL by not bringing Bob; I had the authority to craft the deals. Soon after, Pat and I started having dinners whenever I was out west, or he was out east, and the friendship grew from there.

But the changes in the ownership ranks were hardly the only changes heading into the 1993 negotiations. There was also the matter of Rupert Murdoch, who was interested in using the NFL to increase the profile of his fledgling Fox network. He'd tried to make inroads in 1990, but gotten nowhere; now, this time, he was even hungrier, and willing to spend whatever was necessary to get the attention of the league. And that aggressiveness was a dramatic contrast from what we and CBS were hoping for: in an advertising market shrinking thanks to a struggling economy, we were actually hoping to negotiate lower fees for the new rights package. We'd been negotiating with the NFL for weeks, hoping to modestly reduce the $188 million a year we were paying for the AFC rights. We had heard that, at some point in the fall, Fox had made a presentation to the NFL in Dallas, but not much more. Then, everything went down in a stunning, whirlwind forty-eight hours in mid-December.

Fox's offer, which came in on December 13, 1993, was an absolute earthquake to the television landscape: a stunning $400 million a year. The good news for us, as it turned out, was that Murdoch wanted his splash to be as big as possible; and so, while he would have taken either package, the offer was for NFC games only—CBS's package, not ours. For comparison, CBS had been paying $265 million, and, just like us, they were hoping to lower that number, not raise it by more than 50 percent!

The NFL, obviously delighted, called us in on that afternoon of December 13. The message, essentially, was: The game has changed. Fox may not be coming for you, but you need to raise your offer for your own games. We were still, at least theoretically, in a competitive situation; I knew that CBS could, as a consolation prize, turn to the AFC instead. The league's message was to get in a new offer as soon as possible; I took that to be the next morning.

Immediately, I went to Wright's office, got Welch on the phone, and worked to figure out how high we could go. It was about calculating multiple variables: What number could allow us to break even on the deal, and also, how high did we think CBS might go? On the second point, I felt like I had an informed sense. Five years earlier, Larry Tisch, the head of CBS, had spoken to me and Bob Pittman, my neighbor in Litchfield and the MTV CEO, about coming in to run the entertainment side of his network. I hadn't seriously considered the offer, but felt like it was worth going to his office to talk about it. We spent a few hours together that day, and I'd never forgotten what Tisch had said in passing about sports rights deals—how the money was getting out of hand even then, making them bad investments. It was hardly likely that five years later, in a shrinking sports sales economy, he'd changed his mind. If we could make an improved offer, and make it quickly, we could ensure CBS wouldn't match us.

Still, the economy was what it was, and adding money to the deal was tough. Then I came up with another idea. Because the deals being set up were for four years, there were going to be four Super Bowls up for grabs for three presumed network partners. So what if we included in our offer that we would be the network to get two Super Bowls rather than one?

I was taking no chances—I called up Commissioner Paul Tagliabue late that day and asked him and his top executives to come to 30 Rock the next morning at seven o'clock. The deal we presented to them was an offer for four years of AFC rights—and two Super Bowls—for $217 million a year. As far as the Super Bowls went, Fox wouldn't be in a position to complain; as they'd shown, they were desperate to just get in the game. I later found out that Tagliabue called Dan Burke, the head of Capital Cities, the owner of ABC, which had already quietly renewed *Monday Night Football* weeks before, to ask if he was all right with us getting the bonus Super Bowl. Dan's response was phenomenally gracious: "If it helps NBC, and helps the NFL, I'm all for it."

Tagliabue and I shook hands on the deal on the afternoon of December 14. Once again, a massive deal had come together extremely quickly; having the confidence of my bosses, and the buy-in of every other part of the company, made that kind of speed possible. And it was hugely important. A few hours after our meeting, CBS Sports executives finally convinced Tisch what a disaster losing the NFL would be for their network; the league was the bedrock of CBS Sports, and a huge moneymaker for affiliates. So they called Tagliabue, and told him that a bigger offer for the AFC rights was forthcoming.

As I learned later, Tagliabue said he'd get back to them. He then went over to see Leon Hess, the venerable founder of Hess Oil and the owner of the New York Jets; they had been scheduled to have dinner that night. Hess had owned the Jets since their days in the AFL, and, in a quiet, understated way, was one of the more powerful and influential owners in the league. As Tagliabue arrived to pick up Hess at his office, he updated him on the wild day it had been, and confessed he didn't know what to do about the CBS offer after shaking hands with me. Hess looked at him calmly and said he had one question.

"Did you give Ebersol your word?"

He had, Tagliabue said.

"Then there's nothing to talk about," Hess said. "Let's go to dinner."

And just like that, we were in business with the NFL for another four years.

If NFL games had been a consistent staple of network television sports from the beginning, there was at least one corner of the football universe that was long thought to be unconquerable. Going all the way back to when college football had become one of America's most beloved sports in the 1920s, the one team that attracted a truly national following had been the Fighting Irish of Notre Dame. Yes, there was Alabama in the South and USC in the West, but Notre Dame, even in years when they weren't contending for the national title (which back then came few and far between) was in a class of its own.

The NCAA had long controlled the whole of college football rights, but in 1984 came a landmark decision by the Supreme Court that voided that arrangement. In response, sixty of the top college football programs, including Notre Dame, had formed a body called the College Football Association, which had negotiated a deal with CBS to broadcast their games through 1990. But even though Notre Dame had a whole different scope of popularity from all the other programs, there was still no way to break off their games in an exclusive package. That is, until Ken Schanzer found a way.

Just like Wright and Welch did for me, I tried to be a boss for Ken who gave him freedom to work on the projects he wanted to work on. So while I certainly was highly involved in the NBA and the Olympics, he built his own close contacts in other places. For years, even before I'd gotten to NBC, Ken had had his heart set on working with Notre Dame, and he'd regularly gone to South Bend for games, cultivating a relationship with the school's athletic director, Dick Rosenthal. That meant that while the CFA negotiated a deal with ABC Sports in 1990, represent-ing its pool of more than sixty schools, Ken knew Notre Dame was dissatisfied by the way the deal was going, emphasizing regional games that didn't take into ac-count the school's broader national appeal. And in 1991, Ken was able to convince Rosenthal and Father Bill Beauchamp, the school's number two leader in charge of sports, to go off on their own, and quietly negotiated a historic deal that stunned the rest of college football, getting Notre Dame to break away from the CFA for $38 million, and making NBC the exclusive home of all Notre Dame home games every season. Every game would be nationally televised, of course, and every one would be on NBC.

Beano Cook, the colorful longtime analyst for ESPN, called the deal "like get-ting the rights to *Casablanca.*" As for others, much of the rest of the college football establishment, particularly the people running the CFA, were upset by the deal, but with the Big Ten and the (then) Pac-10 already negotiating their own deals successfully, it was the direction the sport was heading. Now, thirty years later, long after the departures of both Ken and myself, Notre Dame and NBC are still a pair, with Irish games anchoring Saturday afternoons in the fall on the network.

Though I came to NBC just after we'd given up Major League Baseball rights, I certainly never lost my passion for my original favorite game as a kid. We were something of a lame-duck broadcaster in 1989 when I first took the job, knowing it was our last season, but I still had fun with the chance to get close to the sport for the first time as a producer; ABC hadn't had baseball when I was there in the seventies. At some point between taking the job in the spring and taking charge of our plans to broadcast the All-Star Game in Anaheim in the summer, I read an article that gave me an idea.

The article was a profile of Ronald Reagan, who just a few months earlier had left the White House to return home to California. It recalled Reagan's start in entertainment in the 1930s, even before he was an actor, when he'd lived in Des Moines working at radio station WHO. Reagan's specialty was doing "play-by-play" for Cubs games—and I put the "play-by-play" in quotes because in reality, he wasn't watching the games at all, but rather calling the action off of a batter-by-batter account from the Western Union newswire. So then, what he was really doing was a real-time re-creation of the play-by-play, complete with made-up pitch counts, and sound effects like banging a stick on the table to simulate a bat hitting the ball.

All these years later, Reagan's popularity was through the roof, which led to my idea: inviting the former president to join Vin Scully in the NBC booth for a few innings during the All-Star Game right near his home. To gauge his interest, I used a connection—a producer who'd worked for me at *Later . . . with Bob Costas* named Michael Weinberg, whose brother had been on Reagan's White House staff. The response was favorable, and so I flew to Los Angeles, and after having breakfast with Scully, we both went to the former president's office in the Century Plaza Towers to meet with him. He couldn't have been more charming, and regaled us with stories of his Des Moines days. We explained our idea, and sure enough—helped in no small part by his affection for Scully—he agreed to do it.

And so, a few weeks after that meeting, on the afternoon of Tuesday, July 11, we met Reagan before the game, under the stands, where the batting practice cage was stored. We'd been a little concerned a couple of weeks earlier when news had broken that he'd fallen off a horse at his ranch in Santa Barbara, but he looked stout when we greeted him. He wanted to clarify (as he would on air a few hours later) that he hadn't fallen off the horse—he'd been bucked; but he also noted that it had taken some arm-twisting to allow him to keep his commitment.

"Mommy really didn't want me to come," he said of his devoted wife, Nancy, "but I told her I'd given you fellas my word, and I wasn't going to break it."

When the game started, color analyst Tom Seaver gladly made way for the former president, and Scully had perhaps his most famous broadcast partner of all time. Not to mention, it turned out, one of his more nervous ones. But Reagan worked through the nerves to talk about the enduring magic of the All-Star Game, and even recalled playing Grover Cleveland Alexander in *The Winning Team* nearly forty years earlier. He also dutifully offered some thoughts on players like Tony Gwynn, Will Clark, and Kevin Mitchell as the National League put up two runs in the top of the first, with Scully happily guiding him along. Then, in the bottom half of the inning, with Reagan pithily noting that the American League leadoff hitter "had a pretty interesting hobby for his vacation," the part-time NFL phenom Bo Jackson hit an absolute moon shot to dead center, way over the wall. Scully, not wanting to interrupt the president, barely got in enough time to finish the call. A moment later, with poor Reagan starting to delve into a story about calling games in Des Moines, Wade Boggs hit a ball nearly as far. It was the most action anyone had seen the first inning of an All-Star Game in years. And it kept interrupting the president!

Afterward, I went downstairs in the tunnels beneath the stadium to thank the president in person. When he apologized for being nervous, I laughed and assured him that the reviews would be some of the best of his career. Sure enough, America was happy to see and hear from him; in those days, Democrats and Republicans could still respectfully appreciate someone from the other side. A few days later, I got a lovely note in the mail back at 30 Rock—the former president thanking me, unnecessarily, for the opportunity to get back in the broadcast booth.

Three years later, in response to the catastrophe of CBS's MLB deal, the network took what might have been the biggest write-down in network sports history on it, upward of half a billion dollars. So in the aftermath of that disaster, in 1993, baseball, now led by new commissioner Bud Selig, the former owner of the Brewers, began looking for a different kind of arrangement, one in which they would have more direct control of the games. Working primarily with the trio of owners who constituted baseball's television committee—Eddie Einhorn (who had made his money in the TV business) of the White Sox, Bill Giles of the Phillies, and Tom Werner (then) of the Padres—a new type of deal was hatched before the 1994 season. CBS was out, and we were back in: NBC and ABC would be the joint homes of "The Baseball Network," a venture run by Major League Baseball that would produce its own games to air on our networks.

Neither network would put up any money; instead, it was a revenue-sharing deal, the first of its kind in major league sports. The productions would be produced by a team of people working for the "network," with twelve weeks of regular season games airing regionally late in the season. The production operation would be based out of ESPN in Connecticut; even though ESPN wouldn't actually air the games, doing a deal to use their facilities to produce highlights and manage the broadcasts made sense. It was all a complex agreement that took a lot of chances, and as it was ironed out, the question of who was going to lead the undertaking became very important. The best answer, it became evident to everyone, was Ken Schanzer. It was a great opportunity for Kenny to try something new, so at the end of 1993, he took a leave from NBC and moved his office a few blocks north of 30 Rock into the new offices of the Baseball Network.

Though the network was launched in concert with some exciting changes in baseball—namely realignment and the institution of the wild card—it ended up being all but cursed when the first season of the agreement was cut short by the 1994 players' strike. All the money in the deal was tied up in the playoffs, the World Series, and September baseball; the idea was that with more teams in contention later in the season, the wild card would "win back September" for MLB with big, exciting games that mattered all month long shown to regional audiences. Instead, all those games, and then of course the playoffs, were wiped out by the work stoppage. So with no money coming in, Major League Baseball quickly began to see the wisdom in having a more traditional rights deal, with money guaranteed to flow in from a partner. In 1995, knowing that the deal was doomed, we collectively decided to disband it after two years, and go back to a traditional rights-holder structure, splitting the '95 postseason down the middle with ABC—even the World Series—in an effort to salvage as much of the situation as we could.

But as ever, just because a deal went south didn't mean the relationship had to blow up. Both Ken and I had grown close to Bud Selig during our time together, and we were able to work out a limited agreement to broadcast postseason games over the next several years. Predictably, eager to take any opening they could get, Fox became baseball's primary television home, and after 2000, they'd become the sole network broadcaster of the World Series. But before that point, we'd broadcast a wonderful seven-game series between the Marlins and the Indians in 1997 that ended on an eleventh inning, Game 7 walk-off single, and also one of the Yankee dynasty's championships in 1999.

Being part of those broadcasts were a reminder—not that I needed it—of just how fun it was, even in my forties and fifties, to be able to say going to the World Series was my job. Not to mention work up close with one of my oldest friends in television.

I first met Bob Uecker in the late 1970s hanging around *The Tonight Show*, where he was long one of Johnny Carson's favorite guests. Johnny always said that Uecker, the former fringe major leaguer turned Milwaukee Brewers broadcaster and actor, was one of the funniest people he ever knew, cracking him up in more than a hundred appearances without the benefit of any writer slipping him jokes on the side. Getting to know him backstage, it was great fun to confirm "Ueck" was just as hilarious when the cameras were off.

I'd also spend time in those years going to Angels games in Anaheim, where I'd sit in the booth with the local broadcast team of Dick Enberg—who, of course, I'd later work with at NBC—and Don Drysdale, the former star Dodgers pitcher who'd first become a friend when we'd crossed paths at ABC Sports. In any event, on a night when Milwaukee was in town, Uecker poked his head in Drysdale's broadcast booth and invited me to come next door to the Brewers' visiting team booth. I thought nothing of it, figuring we'd get some laughs in during commercial breaks, but then, just as I was looking out onto the field and half listening to Ueck's call of the game, he went off on a tangent.

"Folks, we've got a great game going on here," he said to his sleepy radio audience two thousand miles away in the Midwest, where it was well after midnight, "but we've also got a special treat here in the booth for you. Admiral Ebersol of the Second Fleet, Task Force 20, is currently docked off the coast here, and he's brought some of his sailors with him to the park tonight. That's a strike on the outside corner to the Angels' Don Baylor. . . ."

And so he went on as only Uecker could. But the night was just getting started. After the game, we hung out in Angels owner Gene Autry's suite, at which point Uecker wanted me to go to the bar in the hotel where he was staying. I protested softly, saying that as a lightweight, I had already had too much to drink. But Ueck wouldn't be denied, saying he'd be happy to drive my car to the hotel. So off we went with Drysdale and Angels manager Gene Mauch. And then it was 2:00 a.m. and last call and there was no way I was driving the fifty miles home to my house in Mandeville Canyon. I told Ueck, hazily, that I was going to the front desk to get a room. Again, he wouldn't hear of it.

"That's ridiculous, Richie," he said, fully and joyously uninterested in the fact that my given name wasn't Richard. "I've got two king beds in my room—we'll sleep together!"

Ueck has gotten mileage out of that story for years. And I grew fortunate to call one of the funniest people on earth one of my closest friends. With Susan having grown up in Rockford, Illinois, which isn't too far from Milwaukee, we've long made yearly family trips there to spend a few days with Bob and his wife, Judy. He also became a regular special-guest commentator at WrestleManias, and served as the "guest ring announcer" for the Hulk Hogan–André the Giant main event in Pontiac, Michigan, in 1987. I'm hardly the only person who will tell you this, but one of the funniest things I've ever seen is Uecker in a broadcast booth, where, like he did years ago on my first visit, he puts on a show for any visitors, pressing the "cough" button (which silences him for the radio audience) fearlessly, and doing a hilarious alternative commentary of the game. And some of the best memories of the Baseball Network and NBC's coverage was getting the chance to work with Ueck, as he was our color commentator alongside Joe Morgan and Bob Costas for postseason games.

Uecker, of course, was a star long before he worked at NBC. There were others who came to us to start their broadcasting careers, and who developed into big stars. Following a brief tour at ESPN, Phil Simms came not long after his retirement from the Giants to do games for us, and we liked him so much we put him straight on our top team alongside Enberg and Paul Maguire. People forget this, but he also worked as a sideline reporter on some NBA games, and even did Olympic weight-lifting commentary in Atlanta. Cris Collinsworth was another future broadcasting star who joined our coverage soon after retiring, in what turned out to be only his first stint at NBC.

One of the biggest NBC Sports stars who almost left the stage before he became a broadcasting institution was golfer Johnny Miller, a two-time major winner. We hired Johnny off of nothing more than a tape not long after I got to NBC; he'd played in an exhibition that aired on ABC, and was interviewed in a tower on the course, and seemed like a natural when it came to the unique combination of skills you need to be a golfing analyst—sharp observation, fearless analysis, and storytelling ability. The very first broadcast Johnny worked was the Bob Hope Classic in 1990, and he didn't waste any time with the honesty part. Working alongside Bryant Gumbel, and calling Peter Jacobsen's second shot on eighteen on Sunday, Johnny used a word that might not ever have been heard on a national golf broadcast ever before.

"This is the kind of shot Peter has to be careful on," Miller said about his good friend. "It's the kind of shot you can choke on."

The comment immediately ricocheted around the golf world. Though Jacobsen—a future broadcaster himself—would make the shot, and win the tournament, he and Johnny didn't talk for six months after that event.

"Choke is a bad word," Jacobsen said afterward at the time. "I think Johnny will do a good job [announcing], but it could get difficult to get along with his peers."

A year later, a similar controversy would arise at the Ryder Cup on Kiawah Island in South Carolina, the so-called War on the Shore, when Johnny called a Paul Azinger shot "terrible," and Azinger called Johnny "the biggest moron in the booth" in the next day's paper. Having a whole group of his former rivals and friends erupt at him took the discomfort to another level, and a few days after the event, we got a call from Johnny's lawyer; he had no interest in all the criticism—he was quitting, and his mind was made up.

Knowing Johnny, rather than call him directly to try to talk him out of it, I decided to reach out to someone else: his wife, Linda, at their home in California. I explained the situation, and then told her my plan.

"This is what I'm going to do," I said. "I'm getting on a flight to San Francisco that leaves in about two hours. I need you to make a reservation for three at your favorite Italian restaurant. And I'll meet you and Johnny there tonight."

At dinner, face-to-face, with the help of Linda, I was able to convince him to stay on the job. And over the next three decades, he continued on his path to becoming the best analyst in TV golf history. Not to mention becoming a close mentor to both Jacobsen and Azinger, who eventually joined him on the

NBC Sports broadcasting team, with Azinger taking his place as lead analyst when Johnny retired in 2019.

It's easy to reminisce about the relationships I had with announcers like Johnny and Ueck, and so many others. But it's not so easy to reflect on a man who far and away was the most charismatic person I've ever crossed paths with in TV sports—O. J. Simpson.

It's easy to forget now, but in the 1970s and '80s, there really was no one more popular than O.J. His fans were young and old, male and female, representing every identity and background. You'd figure football fanatics would want to shake his hand and talk to him, but the people who you'd least expect—from grandmothers to small kids—would be just as excited to recognize him when they saw him. And the fact that O.J. was unfailingly gracious and kind and warm to admirers ensured his fan base was always growing, past his days on the field and well into his acting and broadcasting career.

In 1989, my first football season at NBC Sports, I hired O.J., who'd last worked in television on *Monday Night Football* for ABC Sports in 1985, to work alongside Bob Costas on our *NFL Live* pregame show. My reasoning at the time was simple: we'd run a survey, and found that even ten years after he'd retired from playing the game, O.J. was still the most recognizable football personality in the country.

Behind the scenes, though, I was aware of the marital problems that O.J. and his wife, Nicole, were already having, though at the time, they were working through them. Don Ohlmeyer had long been a close friend of O.J.'s, and Susan had actually known him going all the way back to his USC days, when he'd had a summer job on the Universal lot and she was starring in *McMillan & Wife*. So as we were talking about the job, I invited both O.J. and Nicole to come to dinner with me and Susan and Bill Walsh, the legendary coach I'd just hired to be our top game analyst, and who'd coached O.J. at the end of his career with the 49ers.

My message that night was clear: If any of this was going to work, I didn't think their family situation could survive with O.J. working in New York every weekend and Nicole and their young children in Los Angeles. So they agreed to move as a family to New York for the school year, renting an apartment on the East

Side and sending their kids to school in the city. The arrangement worked well, but by the next year, they were having problems again, and split up.

Any of us who knew O.J. and Nicole well have long wondered what we could have done differently in the years to come. That week in June of 1994, when we were covering the Knicks-Rockets NBA Finals, was almost surreal—the news of Nicole's murder, and the increasing clarity for all of us that O.J. was the main suspect.

It all came to a head on that fateful Friday, June 17—when O.J. went missing in the afternoon, and then turned up in a Bronco on the L.A. freeways as Game 5 of the finals began. That day at the Garden, everyone on our staff who knew O.J. was shaken up, none more than Ahmad Rashad, who no one could find just before tip-off. I found him myself in the tunnel beneath the stands, totally distraught.

"Hey, buddy," I said, "no one knows how this night is going to unfold, but there's not much we can do here. And we've got a job to do. So do the job, and we'll worry about everything later."

Ahmad was a pro, and he was on the air moments later.

For the game, I was sitting in the second row at midcourt next to David Stern, with a monitor at our feet in front of us showing the broadcast feed, and a phone next to me that provided a direct line to the production truck. I'd spend much of the game with one eye on the action and one ear on the phone talking to our producers and also to folks at 30 Rock who were controlling the master national feed of NBC, with the news department lobbying to cut away from the game and cover the chase.

"Stay with us!" I pleaded. I could see by flipping channels on the television in front of us that all the other networks were covering the chase; if viewers wanted to see what was going on, they could flip over, but we were the only place they could see the basketball game. It's antiquated to think about it now, considering that a channel like MSNBC could give our news folks an outlet. But it didn't exist back then. NBC was the only place for NBC News.

O.J.'s arrest and everything surrounding it was first and foremost a tragedy, but it was also unavoidably a massive problem for NBC. O.J. had long been a regular at client meetings and dinners; one of the faces of the company in that way. Obviously I'd known him for years, and Don was even closer to him. It wasn't a difficult decision at all to cancel his contract after he was charged, but I still felt like I needed to do it in person. So a couple of months after the Bronco chase, in August of 1994, I flew from the world basketball championships in Toronto to Los Angeles. I arrived on a Saturday morning, and Bobby Kardashian, O.J.'s friend who I knew from our days in the music business together when I was producing *The Midnight Special*, picked me up at the airport. Once we got to the jail downtown, the plaza blanketed with paparazzi, it was clear what a circus the whole case was already becoming.

Inside, seeing O.J. in prison garb, sitting across from me through a glass partition, his hands and forearms handcuffed to the table, was yet another dose of the surreal. As I sat down, I asked him how he was. I'd barely get a word in edgewise over the next two hours, as, unsolicited, he went on and on about how he hadn't done this, he couldn't have done this, and he wouldn't have done this. I listened, and didn't say much, except to give him the news that Ahmad would be replacing him on the NFL in the fall. Though some people had told me it would upset him, he didn't seem to pay it much heed.

I haven't spoken with O.J. since that day. It's still tough to think about the man I thought I knew. It's still sad to think about Nicole and her family, and the family of Ron Goldman, the other victim in the murder. The whole story is nothing short of an American tragedy.

On a cold night in December of 1995, at the outset of that incredible year ahead for NBC Sports, I had dinner with a writer named Sally Jenkins at Nanni il Valletto, a restaurant on Manhattan's East Side. The purpose of the meal was to talk about the deals I'd been making, particularly our Olympic agreements, for a big year-end profile in *Sports Illustrated*. As it happened, without Sally even knowing, I'd had to excuse myself while we talked in my office before heading to dinner to seal the final pieces of our extension for the 2004, 2006, and 2008 Games. It had to stay top secret until finalized; she'd find out about it with the rest of the world a week later. Meanwhile, when we sat down at one of the two booths at the front of the restaurant, I realized a familiar face was already ensconced in the booth across from us. It was Roone Arledge.

We greeted each other warmly; by then, Roone had moved on from sports, but was still the president of ABC News. As Sally stood there, he talked about how proud he was of me, as well as how irritated it made him that ABC Sports—where he was no longer involved—had fallen out of the hunt for the biggest sports properties, especially the Olympics. As Sally and I returned to the table, the symbolism of another encounter with my mentor struck me. Years earlier, I'd run into Roone on my first night out with Lorne Michaels in Beverly Hills. Now here I was back in New York, talking about the department that I'd built that in many ways emulated the department he'd built. In the sixties and seventies, ABC Sports had reigned atop the industry as the standard; Roone had built the template for the rest of us to follow. In the nineties, I felt like we at NBC Sports had become the heirs to Roone's approach, covering the biggest events and telling the best stories along the way.

From the World Series in Cleveland and Atlanta to the Super Bowl in Tempe to the NBA Finals in Chicago and Seattle to the Olympics in Atlanta, it would be an incredible year. Even so, as proud as I was of our team, our network, and our company, the truth was I knew even then that whatever dominance we were enjoying wasn't meant to last. The television business was on the verge of massive change, upending how money was made, and how much money could be made. To stay in the game at all, we'd have to swallow our pride and adjust our approach in the years to come.

CHAPTER 23

New Century, New Landscape

On January 25, 1998, in San Diego, California, NBC Sports broadcast Super Bowl XXXII between the Packers and the Broncos. The game was a major turning point for the company, and its people. NBC had televised NFL games for thirty-three straight years, and pro football had been a central part of the sports department's identity, not to mention a huge component of people's jobs. But as much as the NFL continued to be the highest-rated sport on television, the reality that we'd been reckoning with soon after signing that extension in 1993 was that the math just couldn't add up anymore. And so the Super Bowl was going to be our last game with the NFL.

In making the deal in 1993, we'd calculated the $217 million that we had agreed to as an annual rights fee as a number that would give us a chance to merely break even. And remember, that whole negotiation had been a fire drill; when Fox had made their massive offer to get in on pro football, our instinct had been to maintain our own status quo and stay in business with the league. But in the years since, an uncomfortable reality had set in: we were actually losing money on the deal. Regardless of the ratings, and the continued popularity of the NFL, at the time, $217 million a year was just too much to ask our sales team to cover in advertising. It seemed almost sacrilege to say it, but the NFL wasn't good business anymore for NBC.

Now, for as long as I'd been at NBC Sports, Bob Wright and Jack Welch had essentially given me everything I wanted to chase properties that put NBC at the top of the sports television ladder. But there was a tacit understanding built in with the freedom they gave me: if at some point the deals stopped making sense financially, I'd have to back off. As exciting as it was to complete deals, and as much pride as I took in the idea that I was someone who got deals done, I could never lose sight of the basis of the trust they had in me—the sense that I'd maintain my responsibility to the company. And while the economy was humming along in the mid- and late nineties, with Fox willing to invest whatever was necessary to grow their network, the rights fees got out of hand. Remember, Fox and NBC were in very different places in those days. They were still trying to build a network. In prime time, we were number one, meaning that we couldn't think of sports partnerships such as our NFL deal like they did: as a loss leader—that is, an investment that lost money but provided less calculable benefits like promotion. Which meant to NBC, pro football just wasn't a worthwhile investment anymore.

And by the way, football wasn't the only sport that needed to be judged on that kind of harsh rubric. In the fall of 1997, just before we broadcast our first of two World Series under a new deal, post–Baseball Network, that carved out limited postseason coverage for us alongside Fox, Don Ohlmeyer had been asked about the Series by the press in the context of it preempting the start of his dominant prime-time schedule.

"We're looking for four and out," Don said, referring to the possibility of a four-game sweep. "Either way, that's what we want. The faster it's over with, the better it is."

Maybe Don could have been a little easier with words to avoid offending our good friends at Major League Baseball, but that's never the way he was—and all I could do was laugh. Because the truth was, Don was right—NBC would get a much bigger audience from *Friends* and *Seinfeld* than the Indians and Marlins. Unfortunately for him, that year the Series went seven. And even then, with three more years on our contract, I knew that our days in business with baseball were numbered.

With baseball, bowing out wouldn't be particularly difficult; Fox was still in growth mode and eager to meet baseball's price to take over the full network package and be a partner for the long term. (More than twenty years later, their partnership is still going.) With football in 1997, the situation was a little different.

Everyone knew that CBS was desperate to get back into business with the NFL; losing the NFC package had been just as calamitous as their executives feared when it happened; they'd lost a number of key affiliates in big markets, and their overall ratings had taken a significant hit. But if we made a public display of letting the world know that we were done with pro football when it came time to negotiate, then it would undoubtedly make CBS's path to returning all that easier; they'd know they basically had an open slot, and the league wouldn't have any leverage.

It's not the kind of consideration you might immediately think about when it comes to a big deal, but over our years in business with the NFL, I'd grown close to Pat Bowlen and Jerry Jones, as well as Patriots owner Robert Kraft, not to mention Paul Tagliabue in New York. To me, the right thing to do was to help out a partner who'd been great to us over the years. And so we kept our intentions to leave extremely quiet as it came time to begin negotiations for a new deal. The league knew we weren't going to put in any kind of real bid to stay in the game, but they appreciated us sticking around as something of a red herring and participating in the process. CBS ended up having to pay full market value to become the network of the AFC, and we bid adieu to the NFL as mutually admiring former partners. We never knew when we might need to revive that relationship.

So Super Bowl XXXII became, as I called it, our "last dance"—coincidentally, the same year that Phil Jackson gave the Bulls' final season together the same moniker. There was no chance of us half-assing our effort—we were going to go out as strongly as we came in, to make sure the league knew how much we still cared, and would remember how first-rate our work was. The game was also a last hurrah for our staff, and emotional for many of them. And a few weeks before that Super Bowl kickoff, I had an idea that would provide an appropriate send-off behind the scenes. I looked at our production format of the game and created a new sixty-second spot that our ad sales team could sell, above and beyond what we'd budgeted. When that new commercial spot sold for somewhere in the range of $100,000, I had enough money to treat our staff to the send-off they deserved. I went deep into my Rolodex and back to my days in music, and booked the only act I wanted to have play at our wrap party. It wasn't the way most executives would finance a party, but it was what our production team deserved after all their years of work on the NFL, and the disappointment of losing football. And so at our San Diego hotel, a few hours after John Elway had helicoptered his way into the end zone, leading his Broncos to an upset win over Brett Favre and the Packers, Donna Summer was on a stage singing "Last Dance" to the good people of NBC Sports, a private concert to bid farewell to the NFL on NBC.

It ended up being only one of the major sports we'd be saying goodbye to—as a new century, and a new era in sports television, was dawning.

The reason we parted ways with the NFL in 1998 was simple: other networks were willing to pay more than us—so much more that the deals would lose money for them. But the reason we walked away from the NBA, the partnership that had defined NBC Sports in the nineties more than any other sport, was a little more complicated, and based in the changing landscape of sports TV as a new century approached.

When ESPN first launched in the early 1980s, it was a curiosity as much as anything else. To sports fans, it sounded like a dream—a network covering sports, all the time—though it took some years to emerge as a true powerhouse in terms of what it televised. Early on, alongside *SportsCenter*, there was a lot of aerobics, rodeos, hunting and fishing, and cheerleading competitions. The early milestones for the network were events like the NFL Draft, and college basketball games that largely held regional appeal more than anything else. It took a long time for cable to grow across the country. I mentioned how *Friday Night Videos* just took what MTV was doing and brought it to more people—that was possible when MTV was only in 20 to 30 percent of homes. For years, ESPN was in the same category.

But as the nineties went on, and cable became more of a ubiquitous presence in homes across America, it was evident that the implications for sports were potentially huge. As ESPN steadily picked up more game coverage—from NFL games on Sunday nights to baseball and hockey games to more college football and basketball—its value also skyrocketed. Unlike network TV, which was free to anyone who bought a television and put up an antenna, cable was based on monthly subscriptions. And the more popular a channel was, the more a company could charge for it every month. As you might guess, on cable packages all across America, ESPN became one of the most popular channels—and thus, one of the most lucrative.

When Disney bought Capital Cities in 1995, ABC was pitched as the centerpiece of the deal. But within just a few years, because of the economics of cable, it turned out that ESPN was really the crown jewel. It was also a beast that needed constant feeding. To keep ESPN growing and becoming more profitable, the network had to continually add value to its programming so it could justify raising its rates—known as "sub fees"—to the cable companies. The best products it could provide for customers were live games—and with the NBA rights coming up for renewal just after the turn of the century, they would provide a great match.

And as often happens in business, the financial trends fed themselves. ESPN was flush with cash, with the sub fees continually adding to its coffers, all but printing money every month—money that could be spent on a huge rights package. In network television, the only moneymaking tool we had was advertising. Yes, our superior viewership numbers across a wide scope of programming—morning, daytime, prime time, late night, news, entertainment, sports—still made us a viable business, but there was still no contest when it came to profitability.

By the year 2000, the writing was on the wall. As successful as our partnership with the NBA had been for both sides, I knew that when our deal expired, after the 2001–02 season, there was no way we would be able to pay the kind of money ESPN could. During the NBA Finals in Los Angeles in 2001, David Stern and I took a long walk on a misty foggy morning along the water in Marina del Rey to talk it over. A decade earlier, making his biggest partner a cable network would have been a nonstarter for David; the NBA had needed the visibility and broad reach of a network. But as much as putting nearly all the playoffs on cable would be a risk for his league, David couldn't turn his back on the enormous amount of cash ESPN would be able to pour into his owners' pockets. It was a changing world, and we both knew it. There were no hard feelings, just a bit of sadness that as close to a perfect partnership as there ever was between network and league was coming to an end.

ESPN would make a six-year, $2.4 billion deal to become the league's main partner—Turner would keep its deal as the other cable partner for another $2.2 billion. Even for the contract we had been working on, with the ratings decline of games following Michael Jordan's second retirement and the labor stoppage in 1999, we lost money on our last few years of the deal. As with the NFL, it was no longer the right thing business-wise to broadcast the NBA on NBC.

At our last big production dinner, an emotional gathering during the '02 finals with the staffs of both sides in attendance, I presented David with a parting gift that cracked him up: a giant wheel of a hundred yards of coaxial cable.

"You'll find this necessary," I proclaimed to him dramatically with a big smile, "when you're home and can't watch the games on over-the-air TV. You can just 'hook up the cable.'"

He was entering a brave new world, a world that would bring with it new challenges of how to keep his sport feeling big enough as a "cable league." As for NBC Sports, thanks to the deal we'd made years before, we knew the foundation of our identity would remain the Olympics for the foreseeable future. Filling in the gaps from there would require a little creative thinking.

Long before the economics of broadcasting the NFL got out of hand, the idea of creating another football league was tantalizing to television executives. In the early 1980s, there was the USFL, a league that attracted some serious talent (Jim Kelly, Herschel Walker, Warren Moon, and others) before flaming out in 1985. But as we were getting set to part ways with the NFL, a wild idea came out of our weekly meetings with the NBA: What if the basketball league and the network partnered on starting a new league to play football in the spring?

The rough concept was that the league would feature teams in secondary markets—that is, cities not big enough for NFL teams, but areas where football was incredibly popular, like the South. The conversation soon expanded to include Turner as a partner on the cable side, as they had been on the sidelines for football after televising Sunday night cable games for a few years, and were eager to capitalize on sports to increase their own sub fees. The idea got far enough that, at one point, there was a meeting of titans in the GE conference room on the fifty-second floor of 30 Rock, with Jack Welch and Ted Turner, long considered massive rivals, getting together at a table for the first time in years. There was a lot of concern about how they'd get along, but within minutes, they were laughing and joking with one another. Nonetheless, the idea for the football league never came to fruition; the NBA decided to keep the focus on their main business, and the money was just never going to work enough for us or Turner to get it off the ground.

Still, I didn't completely discount the idea of an alternative football league, particularly as we went into "NFL exile" in 1998 and beyond. Yes, I knew I'd absolutely made the right business decision by not renewing our contract. But still, as the head of NBC Sports, with a number of people in my department having lost their jobs, not to mention as a sports fan, it still was difficult to follow the league and not be a part of it.

Then came a Thursday afternoon in February of 2000, just a few days after the Super Bowl. I was working in my office when Aimee Leone alerted me to a press conference that had just begun down the street in Times Square. I turned on the television in my office to see a familiar face at the podium: my old buddy Vince McMahon. And what Vince was talking about was a new football league he was launching. As Vince put it onstage, if the rigidly ruled National Football League was the "No Fun League," then his new league, the XFL, would be the "Extra Fun League." It was typical Vince; bombastic, fearless salesmanship. He wasn't actually challenging the NFL—he was launching a spring league that—beneath all the swagger—would complement it. Still, he wasn't going to let that reality get in the way of the show.

The instant response of many in the media was that he had no idea what he was getting into. My immediate reaction, on the other hand, was to tell Aimee to get Vince on the phone as soon as possible. I wanted in.

In a lot of ways, it was a dream come true. First, the opportunity to get back in business with Vince, who'd been one of my favorite partners ever, was appealing. I really, truly admired him as much as I admired David Stern and Juan Antonio Samaranch. Then there was also the notion that while, yes, I'd taken plenty of risks since coming to NBC Sports, this was totally different. This was truly another long shot—another wild idea akin to *Saturday Night's Main Event* or even *Saturday Night Live* with Lorne.

Just like we had years earlier, Vince and I worked out a deal quickly and easily, though this time we did sign a contract on top of the handshake. NBC and World Wrestling Entertainment, as it was now called, would be fifty-fifty partners on the XFL; the deal was announced just about six weeks after Vince's original press conference. What we were selling was clear: a new football league that would embrace a version of the game that was even more smashmouth than the NFL, spotlighting the personalities of its players—the more colorful, the better. Plus, just as important, on TV would be a production that would take fans closer to the action than they'd ever been before. It would be a combination of the best of NBC Sports and the WWE: a top-notch sports television product with storytelling and a heavy dose of humor that would capture the passion of an audience eager for more of their favorite sport. Play would begin immediately after the Super Bowl in 2001, aiming to pick up off the NFL's momentum with a whole new spring season—an idea I'd always believed in. Now the race was on to put it all together.

Over the next eleven months, the league would take shape at breakneck speed. It was bold, and maybe too ambitious, but we felt momentum was important in terms of capturing the public's attention, and probably the best joint asset of NBC and the WWE was the capability of our marketing teams to jump into the project. John Miller was the head of NBC's award-winning marketing team; the man behind "Must See TV" on Thursday nights. For the XFL, John and his team put together a collection of some of the best promotional spots I've honestly ever seen. And the spots, funny and outlandish—from players lifting trucks in training to the Hall of Famer (and future Chicago Enforcers coach) Dick Butkus screaming at the camera as he introduced the league's official ball to, yes, introductions of the league's cheerleaders—all found a way to cut through the crowded media landscape, in no small part because they were airing on the country's top-rated network during Must See TV and the 2000 Olympics, as well as throughout WWE telecasts, which had one of the most devoted audiences in television.

So the hype was real, and growing every time a new spot was released. There would be eight teams—in big markets like New York, Chicago, San Francisco, and Los Angeles, and smaller cities like Birmingham and Memphis. Ken Schanzer and I would go up to Stamford twice a month for meetings with Vince and his team—where it was clear particularly to Kenny how much remained up in the air as the spring of 2000 turned into summer and then fall. But my faith in Vince was unshakable—after what I'd seen him pull off in our years together in wrestling, I just believed he would find a way to get this thing off the ground. I knew the quality of play was a big concern. But I reasoned that college and high school football were compelling products with huge followings, and the World League of American Football—later renamed NFL Europe—had been a modest success. So if the XFL could meet that level with former college players and NFL hopefuls, I felt like the excitement of the games and the massive awareness factor that would kick-start the league would go far in carrying the audience's interest, even before you added in all the flourishes that the league's attitude would bring.

The problem, however, at least with that assumption, was that the focus wasn't where it needed to be: on the football. The people who'd been hired to manage the game side of it weren't capable. Plus, training camps didn't begin until about a month before the season started—and with the players not even meeting one another until practice began, the football wasn't just destined to be lower quality than the NFL. It was going to be a mess. No matter how many good ideas we were developing on the production end, and with some tweaks to rules to make the games more exciting, like an "opening scramble" instead of a coin toss, no point-after-touchdown kick conversions, and a shorter play clock, the football itself was being overlooked.

On February 3, 2001, exactly a year after Vince's original press conference, the league launched in Las Vegas. All the promotion, all the anticipation, all the excitement we'd generated completely paid off: that first Saturday night game blew away our greatest expectations, with a rating over ten, higher than many of baseball's playoff games the previous October, and the highest rating that prime-time slot had seen on NBC in years. But for all the success of the marketing, what people watched was a very sloppy football game, filled with wayward and dropped passes, sloppy tackling, missed field goals, and more. What fans read the next day in newspapers and on websites were reviews from writers aghast not just at the quality of play, but also at the focus on the cheerleaders, the players with the nicknames on their jerseys, and Vince coming to the fifty-yard line when the game started to welcome everyone, in his biggest WWE-style growl, to the start of the league.

Ratings tanked from there, and when, a week later, a technical failure caused the game we were broadcasting nationwide to have to be paused midway, it felt like the league was undeniably doomed. By the end of the season, we'd gone from those record-high ratings to minuscule numbers. The weekly XFL games on Saturday nights became the lowest-rated show in all of prime time, which the press delighted in sharing with the public. And who could blame them—from the start, we'd overpromised and under delivered.

Looking back, the media's sharp teeth all throughout the season was a reaction not just to Vince's brash confidence in its success but also a reflection of a discomfort with all the standards that the XFL was upending. To them, adding the XFL to NBC's portfolio, with the Olympics and *The West Wing* and *Friends*, was a strange, uncomfortable marriage. But going back to my original days in wrestling, I had never looked down on the brand of entertainment that Vince sold. There was clearly an audience for it, and my opinion was that that audience very much overlapped with people who wanted to watch a new brand of football, at a time of year when the sport went away. For all the press's posturing, none of the packaging or the image of the XFL was the problem. It was simply the football.

As I looked at the financial losses piling up after that season, and also the improbability of turning things around, I knew we had to get out. The audience had spoken; the project had been a failure. Still, we'd signed an ironclad contract that clearly stated NBC would guarantee funding for two seasons. There was only one way to handle it: go straight to Vince and be honest about the situation. It wasn't easy, but never for a moment did the relationship even come close to breaking down. Vince trusted me, and he understood that NBC just couldn't go on. As much as it pained him, after all his proclamations guaranteeing success, we agreed to rip up the contract and shut the league down after that one season.

To me, though, as much as I'm absolutely willing to own the failure, the story can't be rightly told without some postscripts. First, the NFL would end up using many of the XFL's production innovations, most notably the sky cam, which became the standard in NFL and college football coverage within a year or two. There'd be more cameras, more sound, and more access on the sidelines as well. Also, while the XFL had teams on both coasts, the Las Vegas Outlaws had been something of its signature team; the idea of putting a team in Vegas was looked at as a rebel act at the time. Well, in 2020, the NFL's rebels themselves, the Raiders, moved to Vegas.

I still look back on the whole experience with a smile. In a closet in my office at home, you'll find every XFL team jacket hung up next to one another on a rack. Even more of a lesson to me, though, came a year or so after the league folded and I was at a meeting of senior GE directors. It was just a few months after Jack Welch had retired from the company at the mandatory age of sixty-five, and one of our first meetings being run by his successor, Jeff Immelt. Sitting in the back of the room with Jeff Zucker, I listened to Immelt talk about the way he wanted his businesses run, and then unexpectedly heard my name and Jeff's called out.

"We at GE need to take risks," Immelt was saying. "Not a lot of people would think of this as a model to follow, but I want to take note of our friend Dick Ebersol's most infamous experiment, the XFL. Which our friend Jeff Zucker so strongly supported and believed in as well. Did it work? No, it did not. But it was a risk worth taking. Whatever money we lost, we could handle, and Dick and Jeff knew that. Because if that thing had taken off, a new spring football league that people would watch? The rewards would have been extraordinary. Not every risk is going to pay off. But that doesn't mean you don't take them."

CHAPTER 24

The Games Go On

There was certainly an element of risk in the 2000 Games in Sydney. The combination of the late start—mid-September, to account for the reversal of seasons in the southern hemisphere—as well as the extreme time difference, making live marquee events in prime time infeasible, set up Sydney as a very different kind of event to produce than Atlanta four years earlier.

There were, though, reasons to think that the Sydney Games, as far away as they were taking place, could resonate with the American audience. Australia was kind of a mystical place, where very few Americans had ever been, or even dreamed of going. These Olympics could be a way to take them there; and focusing on the exotic scenery, not to mention fun-loving culture, of Australia could capture our audience's imagination. Sydney also, candidly, offered a much more picturesque panorama than Atlanta; in 1996, I'd explicitly instructed our directors not to show any shots of downtown during the day in our coverage because it was so unappealing, having been blanketed with giant advertising banners. The goal with an Olympics was to make the audience feel like they were watching something truly singular—like they were being taken to somewhere almost magical, a destination on their ultimate bucket list. Sydney definitely offered that potential.

Still, on one of my first trips down under after we'd made the deal, I'd been disappointed to learn that one of the main filming locations the organizing committee spotlighted for us, with a beautiful view from the stadium all the way back to the skyline of downtown Sydney, was blighted by some power lines right in the middle of our potential best camera shot. Talking to reporters at the site, I offhandedly compared the issue to a "pimple on the face of a beautiful woman." Today, I'd probably get mauled for that comment. In the mid-1990s, the headlines that resulted spurred the Australians to spend 40 million Australian dollars to move the power lines.

In both the U.S. and Australia leading up to the Games, the anticipation grew; in Sydney, reporters took to calling me the "billion-dollar man," a reference to the billion Australian dollars ($700 million in the U.S.) that we'd paid for the Games. Arriving down under almost a month before the start, we worked for weeks to prepare for a stunning Opening Ceremony set to be highlighted, once again, by the cauldron lighting. If Muhammad Ali had been a tremendously symbolic choice in the United States and the world in 1996, Cathy Freeman—a track star with Aboriginal heritage—was just as significant of a choice for the Australians.

And yet, eight thousand miles away back in the U.S., it all didn't quite resonate. No, we certainly weren't completely surprised when the ratings went down; we knew the time difference, and prime-time shows airing tape-delayed competition would have an impact, as would the fact that the Games didn't start until mid-September, with kids back in school, the other networks' new shows in prime time beginning, and also football back in action. But to me, all of that could have been overcome had something else, totally not in our control, gone our way: the stories.

On the first weekend of competition, the first big event in swimming was the men's 4x100-meter freestyle relay—an event Team USA had never lost at an Olympics. But swimming is one of the most popular sports in Australia, and the Aussies came in hungry to upset the Americans. There was some trash talk, which made the narrative all the more interesting—but also disappointing to the audience back home when the Aussies prevailed in the event. Then, the first week, the U.S. women's gymnastics team—the heroines of Atlanta—failed to win a single medal (though years later, they'd be awarded a bronze in the team all around when it was revealed that China was competing with underage gymnasts).

Going all the way back to the Olympics on ABC with Roone in charge, the most popular sports for the Olympic audience—that wide, predominantly female audience—were swimming and gymnastics. But the American stories in both of these arenas had essentially laid an egg. Part of me couldn't blame the audience for not getting excited about it, even when the swim team ultimately won more medals than any other country, and even when, in the second week, sprinters Maurice Greene and Michael Johnson were the stars of track and field. In the broadcast center, I tried to stay measured about the disappointment. Just like me, the hundreds of people working day and night on the event were competitive and followed the ratings closely, even the freelancers. To keep their spirits up, I wrote them daily notes extolling the best of our coverage, making sure they knew how proud we were of their work. We'd done our best, and it just hadn't worked out.

Still, there may have been a few more tweaks to make. When we got home, we had a week of debriefing meetings in New York, with all the top executives reviewing what we'd done right and wrong. At one point, as we talked about the format of our shows, Randy Falco spoke up. Now, mind you, Randy was a finance guy; the focus of his job was always on the business side of things. But sometimes, you actually need someone who's not so close to a problem to identify it, and I've never worked with anyone better at identifying problems and solving them than Randy Falco.

"I just think the features were too long," he interjected.

My instinct was to disagree. The features—the "up-close and personal" profiles of athletes—were one of the signatures of our coverage. They were how we set up our stories, the stories that the audience could get behind, as they learned about the athletes they were rooting for. Many of them were produced like short films, with artistry and creativity. They were to me the strength of the theory that Roone had espoused a few decades earlier.

"But they're just too long," countered Randy. "They slow the momentum of the show. People want to watch the competition. They need to know the stories, yes, but they also want to see the competition. I think you've got to figure out a better way to strike a balance."

It was a criticism that cut at the heart of my whole approach to broadcasting the Olympics. And yet, it made sense. Watching back our shows, I could see what Randy saw: regardless of the disappointment in swimming and gymnastics, our profile films were cutting into the flow of the shows, and it felt like they were almost getting in the way of the races and routines. The solution, though, was not to cut back on storytelling. Rather, it was to change how we told the stories. In the years ahead, there would be fewer Olympic profiles, and the pieces themselves would be shorter. But more than that, we'd lean more on our announcers to tell the stories in the course of the competition. In the tradition of Jim McKay, we'd teach them to integrate an anecdote or brief capsule of their biography as they introduced the athletes.

"And here's Jane Doe," an announcer could say during live coverage. "She's the nineteen-year-old from Chicago who's worked two jobs for the last five years to support herself while training as a fencer." Just a few details could draw the audience in, as much as a five-minute feature.

The adjustment was a reminder of a couple of fundamental concepts. First, the importance of encouraging an environment where everyone could speak their mind; Randy had to know that raising a criticism wouldn't get everyone on the production side resentful of him. There was too much at stake to take things personally, too many smart people in our group to ignore. Then, also, it underscored the whole venture of broadcasting the Olympics for nearly the rest of the decade. Taking place only for a few weeks every two years, changing our approach wasn't quite as simple as it would be for a property where we were broadcasting weekly, every year. The Olympics were a bit more of a risky business.

And considering the hot water the International Olympic Committee had gotten itself into, I'd have to be proactive to make sure the ten-figure investment General Electric had made in my idea didn't go sideways.

It was late November of 1998 when a Salt Lake City television station broke the story that started one of the biggest scandals in the history of the Olympic movement. The original Salt Lake Organizing Committee—the group that was in charge of putting on the 2002 Winter Olympics in Utah—had paid for a "scholarship" for the daughter of an IOC member from Cameroon to attend college in the U.S. Over the next few weeks, it became clear that not only was the story true but it was just one of several payments that looked suspiciously like bribes that had been made to IOC members in the years leading up to the vote to give Salt Lake City the Games.

By the middle of December, Juan Antonio Samaranch had announced an internal probe to explore what appeared to be a problem that went well beyond the Salt Lake bid, as for years, cities campaigning to host the Olympics had evidently made all kinds of payments and done all kinds of favors to secure votes of support for their bids. It confirmed the worst of perceptions about the Olympic movement—that it was run by a bunch of aristocrats whose commitment to the athletes and the benefits of the Games were cover for their own personal amusement and gain. And because the purported collection of bribery and fraud had taken place on American soil, very quickly, investigations were also opened by the U.S. Olympic Committee as well as the FBI and the Department of Justice.

The crimes were bad enough, a stain on the whole idea and ideals of the Olympics. But anyone could also see that the spiral might just be starting. At worst, the near-term problem would be that the Games would be taken away from Salt Lake City, and even if that didn't ultimately happen, sponsorships for the committee, not to mention our advertising, could go in the tank. There was also another punishment the American government could wield—taking away the IOC's tax-exempt status, which would be a killer blow to the finances of Olympic sports in the country, hurting young athletes—who'd lose out on development programs, training opportunities, access to top-level facilities, and so on—more than anyone else.

As the media reports of the controversy continued to spill out, there was a distinction to be made between perception and reality. The perception was that Samaranch was the crux of the problem; that he had openly encouraged a culture of glad-handing and bribery, and kicking him out of the IOC would be the only way to create a new, cleaner culture at the organization. But the reality, a reality I'd come to know from my decade immersed in the Olympics, was much different. The International Olympic Committee was a vast collection of figures from all over the world—all with competing and conflicting agendas, some corrupt and problematic. Samaranch had taken all those agendas, wrangled everyone together, and turned the Olympics from a flailing, financially struggling enterprise into a powerful, profitable entity. It was true that he'd been in the post for a long time, and that his time was coming to an end. But to kick him to the curb abruptly would risk throwing the IOC into even more chaos.

As the investigations began, the Senate formed its own committee to look into the scandal, and named John McCain as its chair. This was good news; McCain was one of the most effective, honorable public figures this country has known in modern history. Meanwhile, the committee appointed by the USOC was chaired by George Mitchell, the former senator and peace envoy in Northern Ireland who'd been nominated for the Nobel Peace Prize. Working alongside Mitchell as the vice chair of that commission was Ken Duberstein, a former White House chief of staff for Ronald Reagan.

The stakes were sky-high; these were major players with the potential to create serious issues for the IOC—and, with ten years left on our Olympic deal, NBC. It wasn't a time for me to sit idly by. I knew these men and their aides had no real relationship with Samaranch or anyone in the IOC; all the understanding they were bringing to their work was from what they'd heard, or what others said. Maybe if I could work behind the scenes to bridge the gap between Lausanne and Washington, we could find a solution that would satisfy all parties, and truly fix the IOC's problem.

So one day in early March of 1999, with the scandal still gaining headlines even after the resignation of a handful of IOC members, I called Alex Gilady and told him I was coming to Lausanne to have dinner with Juan Antonio. After all these years, I hoped he'd trust me, and agree with my idea for a plan going forward. He hadn't spoken to the press, and was losing the PR battle; articles were swirling about the furtive ways Samaranch ran the IOC, caricaturing him as an emperor who used his post for an extravagant lifestyle and vast collection of perks. The problem was, little or none of it was true. To take just one example, the "penthouse" suite that Samaranch was reported to live in while he stayed in Lausanne was actually a small room, and of the times I visited him there, the only notable extravagance in the room I'd seen was a chin-up bar that the septuagenarian had hung for his daily workouts.

At dinner that night, I was candid with Juan Antonio. He had a big problem, and the American lawmakers threatening to pull the IOC's tax-exempt status could make it much bigger. I started with a simple question: Did he want to stay president of the IOC? Resigning immediately, and leaving his successor to clean up the mess, was theoretically an option. But he wanted to stay—as I expected.

"Okay," I said. "But you have a problem. And you have to solve it, or someone else will make this decision for you."

I went ahead and outlined the kind of PR strategy that I thought could work. Over the course of our relationship, I typically hadn't been so bold; the respect I had for him typically guided my reserve. But the time had passed for gentle diplomacy.

"You need to make a simple statement to start," I said. "No interviews, just a statement. And it can outline a number of reforms you're going to propose."

He listened, quietly seeing where I was going.

We talked through the reforms that made sense, and the kind of panel that the IOC could set up to work together to put together serious reforms. The reforms could be locked in by year's end, and apply to the IOC and all individual national Olympic committees. It was another dinner that went past ninety minutes without his objections. And another productive one at that.

A few weeks later, GE's top lobbyist in Washington, a smart guy named Bob Okun, scheduled me a meeting with John McCain. My conversation with the senator started on the right foot when I mentioned my older brother, Si, who'd made a name for himself after serving as an army officer in Vietnam when he'd written a scathing novel about the experience. Si had since gone on to academia, becoming the superintendent of the Virginia Military Institute—all of which McCain knew; he was a huge admirer of my brother. From there, we talked about the scandal and the investigation. My pitch was pretty simple: Samaranch was a leader who managed a lot of different interests in a complex organization, but he wasn't a corrupt figure who'd orchestrated some culture of fraud and bribes. If you looked at who had taken bribes, it was almost uniformly IOC members from poorer nations—taking every chance they could to pad their own wallets in ways they couldn't back home. The dishonest figures needed to be eliminated for sure, but the best way to do it would be for Samaranch to lead the reforms, and included among them would be a map to his own retirement.

McCain listened, and asked smart questions. At the end of the meeting, it seemed like he was satisfied.

"If you can convince Mitchell and Duberstein," he said, referring to the USOC-appointed panel, "then I'm good with this plan."

Over the next several months, not many days would go by without a conversation with Ken Duberstein on the phone. Ken was firm in his desire to effect change in what had clearly become a broken element of IOC business, but also eminently rational and deliberate in trying to understand the byzantine ways of the organization. Ken once called me his "Sherpa" as he worked through the USOC panel report. Through our frequent back-and-forth, we became good friends. He might not quite have trusted Samaranch, and Samaranch might not quite have trusted the Americans investigating the IOC, but their shared trust in me bridged the gap.

If the whole affair sounds like a diplomatic mission, in the middle of it all, I would get a master class in the art from one of its giants. Among the American representatives to the reform commission that the IOC appointed was none other than Henry Kissinger. Which is how on a spring morning in 1999, I went over to Kissinger's apartment overlooking the East River in Manhattan to walk him through what had happened, who the players were, and so forth. My "briefing" lasted a little over an hour, and then I headed for the door—only to hear his distinctive voice call me back.

"Dick," he said. "Are you sure you want to leave these here?"

He pointed down to the table where I'd been sitting; I'd left behind a pile of cards on which I'd written notes to use in the meeting, with my candid thoughts on the various characters he'd be meeting on the panel. He was grinning.

"Do you know what I could do with these?"

I didn't miss a beat.

"Dr. Kissinger," I said. "The trust has to start somewhere."

His grin got even wider, and we both roared with laughter.

A couple of months later, at the start of June, Kissinger and I would be in Lausanne for two days of meetings as part of the IOC Reform Commission. The group included senior IOC members, including Samaranch's eventual successor, Jacques Rogge, the Austrian skiing legend Jean-Claude Killy, and Peter Ueberroth, who after he'd headed the '84 Los Angeles Games had become the commissioner of Major League Baseball and a good friend. Just before lunch, I made a presentation, talking about my pride in being an "Olympic storyteller," and trying to impart the value of changing the story that the public was hearing about the Olympic movement. There was definitely work to be done: in the afternoon, in a working group dedicated to the future of the IOC, Sepp Blatter, the Swiss head of FIFA who was also a committee member, noted openly that the IOC would have been better off dealing with its members the way FIFA did; just giving them thousands of dollars in cash to do with whatever they wished—in essence, a ridiculously large per diem. That, he said, was a simple way to avoid bribery. It's safe to say that wasn't adopted in the reforms (and no surprise that he would be tied up in a corruption probe with FIFA years later that forced him out of his job).

At the beginning of July 1999, Duberstein and Mitchell came to London in the middle of Wimbledon and had their one face-to-face meeting with Samaranch in my hotel room—with me downstairs waiting in the lobby. When Duberstein and Mitchell came down after the meeting, I anxiously asked how it went. Rather than answer, Ken pulled out a leather-bound book and handed it to me. I still remember the thick, poster-board-like pages filled with typewritten copy—all the commitments to the reforms that Samaranch intended to present to the full IOC assembly. He'd presented them the book at the start of the meeting, showing that he'd agreed to everything the American panel wanted, and was also committed to retiring when his term ended, in 2001.

In December of 1999, Samaranch would get the full IOC to approve the reforms, including adding active athlete members to the committee; implementing term limits, reelection processes, and age limits for members (Samaranch was in essence "age- and term-limiting" himself); and, of course, instituting new policies for the host city bidding process. From now on, only small, handpicked panels would visit potential host cities; no more "anyone could fly in or out" recklessness.

That IOC assembly took place shortly after Samaranch came to Washington to testify in front of a House of Representatives committee. Predictably, the hearing in Washington had its requisite moments of politicians trying to make a scene for show, but little else. The IOC didn't lose its tax-exempt status; and the U.S. would remain a huge part of the Olympic movement, starting with the Salt Lake Games little more than a year away.

In addition to the reforms that the IOC bid scandal brought about, there was another more serendipitous benefit. After the heads of the Salt Lake Organizing Committee resigned, the city had to find someone new to lead the Games, and quickly. By February of 1999, they found just about the perfect person: Mitt Romney. At the time, Romney was best known as the former head of Bain Capital who'd unsuccessfully challenged Ted Kennedy for the Senate in Massachusetts a few years earlier. He was also a Utah native eager for a new challenge. The combination of his business acumen and political experience made him an ideal fit, particularly when the Games had to grapple with the additional challenge of security, taking place just five months after 9/11.

I was in my office at 30 Rock that Tuesday morning in September, watching the *Today* show, where Jack Welch, recently retired, was set to promote his newly published memoir. Then the news reports started coming in about a plane that had crashed into the World Trade Center. The next hour seemed to unfold in slow motion: seeing a second plane hit the second tower, coming to the realization that it was a terror attack, and then the further realization that 30 Rock was another iconic New York City location that could be a target. As the building evacuated, Ken Schanzer and I went around to every office in the sports department—he took the high floors, I took the low ones—to make sure people were on their way out. One secretary refused to go; her boss wasn't in yet, and she didn't want to leave unless she had his permission. I made it clear to her that I wasn't just giving her permission—I was ordering her to go.

As the next few days and weeks unfolded, it became clear that while the Salt Lake Games would go on, their significance—as a uniting world event, and also as a test of security—would be amplified. And if we needed any reminder of just how tense the situation could get, it came in November, when we were in Utah for our regular three-day production seminar a few months before the Games. I set out to fly back to New York with a group of my senior staff on a GE private plane, a convenience that turned into a scare when just about sixty miles outside Salt Lake City, we heard a zoom, and suddenly fighter jets were on either side of us. It turned out our plane's communications equipment had stopped working, alarming the authorities, and the jets had quickly been scrambled to escort us down to nearby Provo, where things could get fixed.

From start to finish, working alongside Romney and his top lieutenant, the organizing committee's COO, Fraser Bullock, was tremendous. I recommended that they hire Don Mischer to produce the Opening Ceremony, and just like he'd done in Atlanta, Don did a wonderful job, with the 1980 "Miracle on Ice" hockey team lighting the cauldron. With President Bush in attendance, the most heartwrenching moment in the ceremony came when a tattered American flag rescued from the World Trade Center was carried around the track; a reminder of all that had been lost, and all that was still alive and possible.

Another emotional piece of the Salt Lake experience for me was bringing back Jim McKay, now eighty years old, to be a contributor to our coverage. It wasn't easy; though Jim was largely retired at the time, ABC previously hadn't been willing to "loan" him anywhere else. Fortunately, Howard Katz, the president of ABC Sports and an old friend, saw how special the idea could be, and it ended up being a great way for Jim to be part of one final Olympics, joining Bob Costas, who had succeeded him as "America's Olympic host," in the studio.

Dating back to when we'd made the deal seven years earlier for the rights to the Games, we knew the ratings in Salt Lake would be great. Even with the shadow of the bid scandal, the audience was excited for an American Games, and Romney and the organizing committee worked closely with us to map out the perfect schedule for the audience. Then Team USA took it from there—putting forth the best showing for an American team at a Winter Olympics ever. A host of snowboarders and freestyle skiers dominated those new events. Jimmy Shea, a third-generation Olympian, won the first Olympic skeleton gold medal in more than fifty years at a Games in the return of that sport to the Olympics, just a few weeks after his grandfather Jack, a speed skating gold medalist seventy years earlier, had died in a car accident. And in figure skating, always the marquee sport in the winter, Sarah Hughes, a seventeen-year-old from Long Island, stunned the world with a gold medal in the ladies' competition, while a judging scandal led to the Canadian and Russian pairs teams sharing gold, our audiences enthralled by every twist and turn in the drama.

Another two years later, the Athens Games, with another time difference making live coverage in prime time impossible, was expected by many people in television to be much less successful. If tape delay in Sydney had been a concern, four years later, the information revolution had only progressed exponentially. Everyone in America found out news, and the results of sports in particular, in real time. That wasn't a problem for the rest of sports television; just about everything could be shown live, with leagues and networks working together to maximize audience size, to boot. But an Olympics in Europe, where evening events would be taking place in the early afternoon back in the States, just didn't line up that way.

From Saturday Night to Sunday Night

There were critics who wrote that we should broadcast the events live, as they happened, regardless of the time. But they were ignoring two big factors. First, you can't forget that NBC was in the Olympic business to make money. For all the ratings woes of Sydney, the Games had still been profitable, thanks to the wealth of advertising revenue we sold. But more than that, I went back to a notion that had guided me all the way back to my days in late night: you have to give the audience what they want. Our research—and we did a ton of it—overwhelmingly told us that Americans wanted to watch the Olympics at night in prime time, together with their families. The critics could claim that viewers wanted to watch the competition live, and surely there were a few diehards who did, but the vast majority wanted it delivered to them when they could watch it. Even in 2002, we'd showed tape-delayed coverage to the West Coast audience, and gotten our biggest ratings from that slice of the country. They loved the Olympics, but they wanted to watch the story of the Games unfold at the time most convenient to them.

And in Athens, what a remarkable story we were ready to tell. Four years earlier, the youngest member of the U.S. swim team had been a fifteen-year-old kid from Baltimore who our experts were already touting as the next big star of the sport. Michael Phelps had finished fifth in his one event in Australia, but soon after that, had begun dominating just about every race he entered. Michael's story was compelling in so many ways. The son of a divorced single mother who worked as an award-winning public school principal, his competitiveness and motivation were matched by the wonder of how ideal his anatomy was for his sport: he was six foot four, with his height coming from an extra-long torso, and he had large hands and feet, almost like flippers. Even better, Michael didn't swim in just one or two events—he was a master of multiple strokes, making him a medal favorite or contender in five different individual races in Greece. Combine that with the relays, and Michael came to Athens with a shot at winning a medal in eight events. As the Olympics approached, I met Michael and his family several times and couldn't have been more impressed by his poise and focus—particularly for a nineteen-year-old who was the centerpiece of the marketing effort for one of the biggest sports events of the year.

The romance of the Games taking place in the home of the ancient Olympics was another enticing narrative to wrap our stories around. At the age of fifty-seven, I was just as excited for these Olympics as I'd been for my first Games when I was twenty. Along with our nightly prime-time shows, we'd have more coverage than any Olympics ever, with shows airing around the clock on NBC's cable networks, MSNBC, CNBC, and Bravo—much of them showing live competition, by the way.

To manage everything, at some point before the Games, I had an idea. Rather than take a car every day to our hotel twenty miles away to catch a few hours of sleep, what if I could just put a bed in my office at the International Broadcast Center and sleep there? There was no place I'd rather be than near the control room, nothing else I'd rather be doing than heading our coverage, and it also ensured I'd be there if news broke that needed to be dealt with immediately; security was still a major concern.

Our logistics staff was able to build a bathroom right off my office so I could shower every day, and I was always around at a moment's notice to deal with a potential crisis. That turned out to be important late in those Games, when a surprising run by the Iraqi soccer team—just a year after the U.S. had taken out Saddam Hussein—led to a flammable political situation, with some Iraqi players speaking out against the Bush administration. Then, right as the final weekend began, Greece's communist party unfurled a large anti-American banner aimed at then secretary of state Colin Powell, who was set to arrive for the Closing Ceremony. As soon as we got word of that protest, I was able to speak directly on the phone to President Bush's top aide for counterterrorism, Frances Townsend.

"If you're looking for my advice," I told her, "I don't think the secretary should come. There's just too much risk of an incident. I'm not sure what kind of incident, but something could happen."

A few hours later, Powell canceled his visit.

Having the large bedroom office had a much less serious bonus: when medal-winning athletes came to our compound to sit for on-camera interviews with our hosts after their victories—athletes like Phelps—they would see we were just as devoted to our work as they were to theirs. We would cue up the tapes of their performances, and often with their families next to them, they'd be able to quietly watch the greatest moments of their lives on-screen, and fully process the wonder of what they'd achieved. Michael's visit was particularly celebratory; when his competition was over, he'd not just gotten on the podium in eight races as people hoped—he'd won six golds, more than fulfilling the potential everyone had seen in him. And to think, he was still just nineteen years old. Adding to the success of Phelps and the swim team was U.S. gymnastics, which won golds on both the men's and women's side. Even in a new age, the formula could still be the same: you earned ratings by telling great stories that went right to the audience's heart.

Flying home at the end of August, I had a familiar post-Olympics high. It felt like our success was a harbinger for another rise for NBC Sports. Another idea—a huge risk with huge reward—was brewing in my head, and it seemed like we had a real shot at pulling it off. I couldn't wait to get back to work.

There was no way to know how much my life was about to change forever.

Part Four

CHAPTER 25

Family

I always embraced how exciting and unpredictable life in television production can be. From my first trip to Winnipeg barely a week after getting hired at ABC, the idea of the constant travel all over felt like a guarantee that the world would never stop feeling like a playground for adventure. Through all my jobs, in and out of sports, there was something appealing about not just going all over the globe, but doing it through unusual, sometimes crazy means. Working the Pro Bowlers Tour and the NBA at the same time as a college student, and figuring out a way to spend twelve hours at a bowling alley in Southern California before rushing off to make a flight to get to a basketball game in Philadelphia the next afternoon—I loved the sense of wild chase that created. Years later, from heading to the Mexican jungle to chase down Arnold Schwarzenegger for a WrestleMania booking, to dashing off to Sweden on the GE jet with two hours' notice and then veering back to Montreal to jump-start a megadeal with the IOC, the travel remained one of the most exciting—and constant—parts of my job.

On the road, in any city, and in any country, one of my favorite things to do was simple: walk around. Head out of the hotel, maybe get a lay of the land from the concierge if I needed it, and then just explore. Once cell phones came around, I'd sometimes make calls during my walks, but for the most part, walking was just a chance to get a little exercise, clear my head, and keep the world in full color, offering small adventures to quench my curiosity. I walked a lot in New York City when I was there as well; pretty much always during a "normal" workweek, all I had to go home to was an empty apartment. So I'd walk from Rock Center back to my apartment in the East Sixties, or vice versa, or just set off to go on what the Australians would call a "walkabout," anywhere and everywhere my feet would take me.

Now, for all the unpredictability and adventure that defined my work life, what's ironic is that anyone who knows me well would also tell you how much I love familiarity and routine in the rest of my life. My favorite restaurant in New York? Right across the street from my apartment, an Italian joint called Isle of Capri. Why go somewhere else when you have the perfect bowl of pasta or veal chop right out the door? I've eaten there thousands of times over the last forty years. My wardrobe, my haircut, my cigars, my coffee place—I like what I know, and I find comfort in what I can count on. And most important of all, throughout my career and my life, in New York City, or in hotel rooms across the globe—I always knew my days would all start and end the same way: with a call home to Litchfield. At seven thirty in the morning, the kids would be heading off to school, and at five thirty, they'd be in the midst of homework or dinner, but they still recall today one of their defining shared memories of that time: lining up at the phone to take turns to talk to me.

It wasn't ideal, but the duality that developed in our home life came out of the resolution that Susan and I made as soon as we started our family—we didn't want to raise the kids in the city. Harmony and Sunshine had spent the beginning of their childhood with their mom in Los Angeles, and then had gotten used to a new life when we moved east to Connecticut. Charlie was born in 1982, and Willie in 1986, which meant a lot of back-and-forth for everyone when I was producing *SNL* and *Friday Night Videos* and Susan was on *Kate & Allie*. There were a lot of weekdays when I would be the parent at home with the kids while Susan was filming. And when I was at *SNL*, I'd sometimes bring the kids into the city for a visit, spend the morning taking them somewhere while Susan worked, and then once she wrapped shooting at 5:00 p.m., I'd drop them off at the Ed Sullivan Theater, where they filmed, and head off to 30 Rock. Then, as the family grew, and *Kate & Allie* went off the air just as she was pregnant with Teddy, Susan made the transition from sitcom star to full-time mom right as I took the job at NBC Sports.

From then on, I pretty much spent weekdays in New York, coming home as often as I could on weekends when I wasn't at a sporting event. For Susan, it was an even more seismic change, a kind rarely seen so absolutely in the entertainment business. But much like her first career, she took to her new one with passion and, honestly, brilliance. With her parents moving back to Connecticut, and my parents still living only a few streets away in my childhood home, there were many nights where she hosted all four of them, along with three, four, or five kids, for dinner—all this with me in the city. Susan remained active in causes close to her heart, like the Special Olympics, but her number one priority was our family. For both of us, it was a trade-off, though the separation of work and home did have a benefit for me: when I'd return to Litchfield, sure, there would be phone calls to make, but I'd also be away from the office, and in an age before email and smartphones, that could mean *really* being away. As ever, there was peace to be found in routine: regular Saturday afternoon trips to the movies before or after a Notre Dame game on TV, some Sunday morning sports activity in the backyard with the kids before the NBA games started, and so forth.

Taking vacations was just as absolute—when we'd go away, I'd be completely away. In Telluride every winter, we made great memories all together on ski trips, where another bonus was a neighbor who just happened to be the first man in history to walk on the moon—though Neil Armstrong couldn't have been more delightful and, well, down-to-earth. A little-known fact: Neil was a song-and-dance man at Purdue who wrote and directed college musicals, and when our families took up a tradition of playing an annual game of charades at our house, Neil would frequently make up all kinds of hysterically funny songs and lyrics that earned him plenty of victories in the games.

Our family would spend summers at Martha's Vineyard, with me coming up as much as I could when work allowed, at a house directly across the water from none other than the legendary Walter Cronkite. Every year, Walter would invite us to go sailing on his boat, and every year in response, I'd make up every excuse not to go; I didn't want America's newsman to see me—terribly prone to seasickness—throwing up off the side of the deck. Finally, one night at a dinner party, he cornered us and got Susan and me to agree to go out with him the next day. On the harbor, I was relieved at how smooth the ride was, though still nervous about what might come next. But two hours later, as he enthralled us with stories of World War II and his work as one of Murrow's Boys, I didn't even notice how bumpy it had gotten until we were heading safely back to shore.

Though, while Walter, Mike Wallace, and Vernon Jordan—who shared a birthday with Susan, and who I once gifted with one of our garish NBC Sports leather jackets at the height of the Lewinsky scandal, to make sure he knew he was boldly supported by a friend—were all great Vineyard friends, no relationship I had there ever got quite the press as one that had its own fifteen minutes of fame in early August of 2003. It all started as Susan and I exited a restaurant one night and ran into the singer Carly Simon, who we knew fairly well. As we exchanged greetings, I couldn't help but notice something seemed a bit off, and asked her if everything was all right.

"Oh, I don't know," she said. "Art Buchwald talked me into this thing tomorrow night, and I'm just not sure I want to do it."

Art Buchwald was the longtime columnist for the *Washington Post* who was something of an institution on Martha's Vineyard as a longtime resident. The next night was his annual Possible Dreams Auction, an event that was always a fun highlight of summer to raise money for a community service group on the island. The premise of the event was that there were no objects auctioned off, only experiences and adventures involving some of the celebrities who lived nearby. And apparently this year, Art had managed to convince Carly to not just participate but share a secret—and one of the most famous secrets in music history at that: who the subject was of her classic song "You're So Vain." For decades, people had speculated—was the song about Warren Beatty, Kris Kristofferson, Mick Jagger, James Taylor? Now, the eve of the auction, she was having second thoughts about telling a stranger.

I told her not to worry about it—sometimes these problems take care of themselves.

The next afternoon at the auction, when Carly's "prize" came up for bid, I immediately raised my paddle from my table and shouted out a large dollar figure that took the air out of the room. Certainly there was plenty of wealth scattered across the guests, but it wasn't the kind of number that was typically heard at the event. No one tried to outbid me, though afterward, more than one friend came up to me to try to buy into the opportunity and learn the secret alongside us. Sorry, I told them—it wasn't for sale.

A few days later, Susan and I went over to Carly's house, where she served peanut butter and jelly sandwiches and shared with us the answer to one of music's greatest mysteries. Carly has dropped hints in the years since of who she was singing about, confirming the second verse is about Warren Beatty, but I can tell you there's more to the story. A story that continues to be hers to tell.

Our family also enjoyed some big benefits of my job. Starting with Barcelona, they came to every Olympics we broadcast—keeping a healthy distance from the madness of the broadcast center, but going to events and enjoying the celebration that surrounded the Games. My parents loved Wimbledon, and made an annual trip out of it. Harmony's favorite sport was hockey, but probably his favorite event to attend was WrestleMania, which we of course continued to get tickets to years after I stopped working with Vince. And Sunshine's love of baseball eventually led her to a job with the Red Sox.

The two older kids, Harm and Sunshine, came of age largely before I got the job at NBC; Charlie and Willie, on the other hand, were eight and four, making for essentially perfect timing. They loved sports from virtually the time they could talk, and they certainly were happy to benefit from their connection. While I grew up nursing my obsession with sports through books, newspapers, the radio, and television, they enjoyed something much closer to a dream world for young sports fanatics. Several times a year, they'd come to a game or a tournament or an event with me, and get to meet the stars they usually watched from home. Charlie might be the only kid ever to go to all four Super Bowls that the Bills lost in the 1990s— and he sat in owner's boxes for all of them, fruitlessly rooting for Buffalo. As he sat crying in the fourth quarter of the Bills' final loss, a rout to the Cowboys, none other than Jerry Jones walked up to him and tenderly put a hand on his shoulder.

"You know, son, you could just join the winning team," he said, genuinely meaning it.

My favorite Willie story comes out of the time I took him and Charlie to an NBA All-Star Game. I took them to a room where NBA players were coming through, and while I went over to say hello to a league executive, Willie drank one of the many cans of Sprite that were sitting on the table, going on and on to the man seated on the next couch about how much he loved Sprite. When the man got up, Charlie turned to his brother and said, "Do you realize that you just pitched Sprite to Grant Hill, the official face of Sprite?"

For his part, Teddy—four years younger than Willie and eight years younger than Charlie—was a different case. Born a year after I took the job at NBC, he was too young to go along with his brothers and sister to a lot of the events when they were of prime age, and he didn't naturally come to a love of sports the way they did. When he was five, we took him to a golf tournament in Palm Springs, where he had little interest in the action, and even less when a wayward iron shot took two bounces and hit him in the back. As he wailed in tears, a well-meaning attendant came over and said, "Little boy, little boy, don't worry—I'm going to have Yogi Berra come over here to give you an autograph." Teddy immediately stopped crying—but as soon as good ol' Yogi showed up, he started sobbing again. He didn't care about the Yankee legend. He was expecting Yogi Bear.

As the youngest of five, Teddy's childhood personality was really probably best defined by his penchant for mischief, and a sense of humor that belied his age. When he was seven, I turned fifty, and Susan threw a huge party for me—an incredible celebration in a theater in Manhattan that had a *This Is Your Life* theme, complete with Bob Costas hosting and Muhammad Ali walking onstage as a culminating surprise. But Teddy's favorite part was the hats that were handed out as party favors, embroidered with my first name and the phrase "Head of NBC Sports." Young Teddy got the joke—the juxtaposition of "Dick" and "Head," and it cracked him up for weeks.

It wasn't long after that when we identified the source of the troubles Teddy was having at the Montessori school he was attending—a language sequencing problem. And so it was that one fall, he actually spent several weeks living with me in New York. Susan—as was her way—had found the absolute best school to deal with his issues in the city. So, every weekday that fall, he'd go to school downtown, and then would be dropped off at 30 Rock in the afternoon, where he'd hang out in the area outside my office getting some homework done and laughing with the staff, including my assistant Rob Sawyer, who quickly became a close pal of Teddy's, and later my son-in-law. Then we'd go to dinner, usually across the street at Isle of Capri. It was a fun few months, and the only time I got to spend that kind of quality time with any of my kids when they were that young.

While that brought me and Teddy closer together, there was certainly no one closer to him than Susan. When Teddy was ten, with Harmony and Sunshine already out of the house, Charlie headed off to Notre Dame, and Willie also moved away to live at Hotchkiss, a boarding school about a half hour away, meaning it was just the two of them, Susan and Teddy, at home full-time. Over the next few years was when Teddy really turned the corner on his learning issues and began flourishing at school. The kid who'd often been frustrated by trying to do homework was now confident, clever, funny, and thriving. With all their time together, Susan started getting Teddy involved in her work with the Special Olympics. A lot of kids might have been uncomfortable dealing with the scenarios that entailed, but Teddy was a natural—and never more so than one afternoon when Susan took him to a group home to do an activity with some adult residents. As Teddy walked in, a mentally disabled man who was well known at the home for being irritable and unfriendly glared at him.

"Hey, you got any smokes?" he barked at Teddy.

Without missing a beat, my son patted the pockets of his coat, and then his pants.

"Sorry, man," he said. "I must have left mine in the car."

The guy looked at him quizzically, and then cracked up laughing at the idea of a thirteen-year-old kid leaving his Marlboros in his car. And from that day on, Teddy was the one volunteer who that man was always friendly toward.

As Teddy began to grow up, something else happened, too: he became an absolute Boston Red Sox fanatic. It began when he started spending some time with his older sister, Sunshine, when she lived in Boston and started rooting for the Sox. The kid who had had trouble reading for years suddenly had no problem motoring through a five-hundred-page Ted Williams biography. He knew the team's roster up and down, the weaknesses in the pitching staff, the batting orders that produced the most runs, the next three months of the schedule. He even listened for weeks with his mother to the audiobook of *The Girl Who Loved Tom Gordon*, Stephen King's horror novel that featured a plot involving the Red Sox star relief pitcher and was published by Scribner, where Sunshine was working. And then, of course, the perfect capper on it all, if you understood Teddy's personality as a youthful contrarian: being a Red Sox fan meant he could now converse in the family language, yes, but being a Sox fan also meant that he could stand in contrast to the family team, the Yankees.

Decades earlier, I'd loved having conversations and good-spirited arguments with my dad, a lifelong Pirates fan, about our teams. Now Teddy was happy to square off with me (and everyone else in the family) about the New York–Boston rivalry, which, as fate would have it, was headed toward peak intensity in the early 2000s. In 2003, when the Sox challenged the Yanks for the division title, Teddy spent all summer in Martha's Vineyard watching his team on TV. We went to games at Fenway, where Teddy was thrilled to get to know Tom Werner, the team's co-owner who Susan and I had known since the eighties and his days in television, as well as John Henry, his partner. Like his brothers before him, he'd fearlessly engage in conversation and debate with these top executives, offering unsolicited advice on everything from lineups and batting orders to contract negotiations.

For Teddy, the 2003 playoffs were a brutal introduction to the heartbreak that October baseball can bring, as the Yankees' Aaron Boone hit an extra-innings home run off Boston knuckleballer Tim Wakefield to beat the Sox in seven games in an unforgettable playoff series. But within a few days, Teddy was already looking forward to another shot for his team in 2004, a year when he'd graduate from the Montessori school and begin his freshman year at the Gunnery, a boarding school not far from our home.

For the second straight year that fall, the Yankees and Red Sox were again facing off in the playoffs for the American League pennant. In 2003, the series had gone down to that epic extra-innings Game 7. But the rematch looked to be one-sided from the start. The Yanks beat up on the Sox in Game 1, outpitched them in Game 2, and then annihilated them in Game 3 by a score of 19–8. By Sunday night, October 17, when the Yankees took a one-run lead into the ninth and brought in the greatest relief pitcher of all time, Mariano Rivera, it looked to pretty much everyone that another Red Sox season was coming to a disappointing ending. Everyone, that is, except fourteen-year-old Teddy Ebersol in his freshman dorm at the Gunnery School in Washington, Connecticut.

Just after Kevin Millar worked out a walk against Rivera, and Dave Roberts pinch-ran and stole second base, the teacher in charge of Teddy's dorm came into the rec room where he and his friends were watching the game on a small TV and told them that it was already long past bedtime, and they had to turn in for the night.

But Teddy, who was never shy—though always polite—about challenging adults on their rules, protested.

"You can't do that to us," he said. "Roberts is on second, and he's the tying run!"

The teacher was unmoved. So Teddy tried another tact. And there were multiple witnesses to this who have attested to its accuracy.

"How about this—let's make a bet. You let us keep watching, but if the Yankees win, I have to buy the entire dorm pizza for a party. The entire dorm."

The teacher didn't immediately say no, so apparently Teddy decided to keep going.

"Actually, here's the bet. The Red Sox will win tonight, and they'll win the next three. They're gonna come all the way back to win the series, and then they're gonna go to the World Series and sweep it. If they don't, I will absolutely buy the entire dorm pizza. All you have to do is let us keep watching tonight."

The teacher, maybe just speechless at the kid's confidence, sheepishly agreed.

And as history will tell you, everything Teddy swore would happen did indeed unfold, in one of the greatest miracles in baseball history.

When I came home to Litchfield Halloween weekend, Susan and I drove the half hour southwest to see Teddy and take him for a haircut. That Sunday night, his teacher bought the entire dorm pizza in what turned out to be a Red Sox victory party—the perfect feast to celebrate a championship title.

CHAPTER 26

Follow the Living

A few weeks after that 2004 World Series, we did Thanksgiving not in Litchfield as we usually did, but in Los Angeles. We had looked at the calendar that summer and realized that on the holiday weekend, USC—poised to be the best college football team in the country, and where Willie was starting his freshman year—would be playing Notre Dame, where Charlie was a senior. By now, with the NBC connection, everyone in our family were huge Notre Dame fans, and Susan had the idea that we'd all fly out to have our turkey there, and then have a great weekend in L.A., capped off by the game on Saturday night.

The smallest details of those days in Los Angeles will forever stay with me. I flew in separately from the rest of the family, arriving late Monday afternoon, getting a key to our suite in the Century Plaza Hotel, and taking a shower when I settled in. Teddy and Susan had been out with Sunshine, who'd come in from Boston, and when they all returned to the hotel, Teddy greeted me as I was getting dressed.

"You know," he said as he opened the bathroom door, "cologne is *supposed* to be something that's welcoming to both women and men alike. What *is* that you have on?"

He was grinning as he said it; he knew full well that Ken Schanzer had given it to me as a present, and had needled me about it before.

The next day, though it was chilly, Teddy wanted to go swimming; the hotel had a nice outdoor pool. While I sat on the deck in a lounge chair watching him swim, my cell phone rang; it was David Stern returning a call. A few days earlier, he'd levied the punishments on the players involved in the infamous "Malice in the Palace" brawl between the Pacers and the Pistons. Though we'd been out of the NBA for two years, David and I still spoke frequently. While we caught up, Teddy realized who I was talking to.

"Tell Mr. Stern . . . Tell Mr. Stern . . . Tell Mr. Stern!" he panted as he swam up to the side of the pool.

"Tell him what, Teddy?" I asked as David laughed in the background.

"Tell him everything will be okay with the league!"

We took up almost an entire floor at the hotel. Susan and I were in a suite with Teddy and Willie in the other bedroom. The rest of our large party extended down the hall. Thanksgiving dinner, accordingly, set up in a room downstairs at the hotel, was huge; it included not just us and our five kids but Susan's first husband, Tom, and his wife, Rebecca, a longtime friend of Susan's; Rebecca's daughter; Tom's sister; and some other friends of ours—the point is, the table and the turkey were both massive, our group was, as ever, a sprawling collection of loved ones, and dinner was a lot of fun.

The rest of the weekend was spent in the ways so many of our weekends together were spent. Harmony, living in L.A., brought over his hot-off-the-shelves copy of *Halo 2*, and on the Xbox that Teddy had lugged all the way from Connecticut, Harm, Teddy, and Willie played the game for hours each night. We went to the nearby outdoor mall a few blocks away to see movies, including *Christmas with the Kranks* and *The Incredibles*. To this day, I still have a memory—one of the most distinct memories of my life—of walking back from the movies to the hotel and placing my hand on the small of Teddy's back as we crossed a large boulevard in Century City. He was too old for me to hold his hand; he'd just turned fourteen and was suddenly five eight or five nine, taller than his older sister and his mother, and so in control of himself as a young man.

That young man and his mother also found time on the Black Friday shopping sale day to spend a few hours in the mall picking out Christmas presents for everyone, Susan reasoning to her son that he wouldn't have a chance to do shopping when he was back at school, and Teddy happily obliging and enjoying a few hours of time with his mom. When Saturday turned out to be the rarest of Los Angeles events—a cold, rainy day—only Charlie and Willie decided to go to the

USC–Notre Dame game that night, with the rest of us gathering in our suite to watch another movie, *Love Actually*. Later that night, Willie and Teddy hung out in their room with their video game, while Susan and I turned in early, knowing we had an early wake-up call for our flight out on Sunday.

The plan was for me, Charlie, Teddy, Susan, and Rebecca to fly out at 8:00 a.m. on a leased private plane from Van Nuys Airport. It would be about a two-hour flight to Colorado to drop off Susan and Rebecca so they could head to the new house we'd just bought in Telluride to do some decorating before Christmas. Then Charlie, Teddy, and I would fly to South Bend, where we'd drop off Charlie back at school, and then ultimately land in Connecticut at day's end.

The call we'd gotten the night before—that we couldn't fly to Telluride, where the snow was going to be too severe, and would instead make our first stop in Montrose—hadn't changed our schedule much at all. It just meant a longer drive south for Susan and Rebecca to our house.

Willie never awakened when we quietly got Teddy up and tiptoed out of the hotel suite. The ride to the airport was quick. The plane was ready, and soon Teddy and I were in our seats toward the front of the small cabin alongside the women, with Charlie dozing on the long couch-like seat in the back. The pilots boarded, and then the single flight attendant, an engaging man whose name was Warren, greeted us warmly. We took off a few moments later and had an uneventful flight to Montrose.

A few hours later, Teddy was still full of cheerful angst about the Red Sox, now speculating hopefully about how Édgar Rentería, a free agent, would be a great replacement for the outgoing Orlando Cabrera as shortstop.

We were on the plane, sitting on the ground in Montrose. We'd had no trouble landing in the snowy conditions, and Susan and Rebecca had gotten in the car at least a half hour earlier. Now a maintenance crew worked to fix a small problem with the plane's bathroom, and the flight attendant told us we'd be taking off again shortly. In the back, Charlie was reading a newspaper. Teddy, meanwhile, now positioned directly across the aisle from me to my left in the front of the cabin, had turned back to his personal DVD player; with headphones on, he was watching the Red Sox World Series highlight video yet again.

As I'd later learn, when the pilot, Luis Polanco, had radioed with the air traffic controller back at the tiny airport, he'd been told he'd have to wait a bit for a snow-plow to complete its work before we could go on the main runway. He'd radioed back that he'd take off instead from the airport's other, shorter runway. We taxied out there, accelerated, and took off.

It didn't take very long to know there was a problem. No more than a couple hundred feet off the ground, the plane lurched dramatically to the left, clearly out of control. I instinctively screamed. Teddy looked over at me, alarmed.

"Dad, I'm scared."

My memory gets scattered from there. The plane's left wing hit the ground first, then the right wing, and as we skidded on dirt still accelerating, we hit a road, which gave us a massively violent jolt. Then the plane skidded on its nose for a long while—nearly a thousand feet, as the investigation would show—ultimately crashing through a fence and hitting an embankment, stopping just short of an ar-royo with a fifty-foot drop-off. The left wing was gone, and the right wing was hanging off; another few feet, and the plane would have slid completely down the arroyo, and no one would have had a prayer of survival. The crew of three in the cockpit had been ejected from the plane from that jolt. Inside, it was just quiet.

Charlie, lying on the couch in the back without a seat belt, had been vio-lently thrown through the cabin, but improbably hadn't lost consciousness. As he got his bearings, he looked around him. Teddy's seat was just gone. Where I had been was a mound of debris. But next to it, the plane's kitchen galley—which had been located between the passenger cabin and the cockpit—had collapsed and lay horizontal. And underneath it, Charlie could see a swath of grayish, blondish hair. My hair.

He managed to get the galley off of me, and drag me to an upright position, positioning my back against the now-empty pilot's seat. I remember kind of being propped up, and being aware that there was no seat, and no door, and I could see right outside, with blue flames starting to rise atop the kerosene from the plane's nearly full tank of gas. I lost consciousness again a moment later as he dragged me off the plane, which was on its belly. Leaving me no more than five or ten feet from the plane, my twenty-one-year-old son went back to the wreckage to look for his fourteen-year-old brother.

A moment later—and this is what I was told afterward, as I was semiconscious at best—two men in a pickup truck coming back from a church service who had seen the smoke rising from the crash pulled in. The men got out and screamed at Charlie to get away from the plane, knowing it was about to explode. One of them actually pulled him out, and then together they dragged me about thirty or forty feet from the wreckage, propping me up against a pile of railroad ties and mud that separated the airport property from a nearby cattle farm. I have a vague memory of looking up, seeing the cows in their pens, and looking back at the plane, in flames. A few moments later, there was a pop, and then a blast—the plane had exploded. Two minutes and fifty seconds had passed since we'd crashed.

The fire and smoke were visible from the nearby highway, and soon a police jeep and ambulance were on the scene. Charlie was running on complete adrenaline, but his hand had been shattered in the crash, and he had to ask one of the men to get his phone out of his pocket. He dialed his mother, but had trouble reaching her, as she was driving high in the mountains, where cell service was spotty. Finally, he reached her.

"The plane crashed," my son told his mom. "I have Dad, we're going to the hospital, but I can't find Teddy."

The bad connection prevented much more from being said, and the call disconnected soon after. I can only imagine the fear and agony Susan was feeling as she turned her car around and headed back north to Montrose. She had no phone service; she couldn't get Charlie back on the line.

They loaded me into the wide-body ambulance—again, I was semiconscious and in complete physical agony. Charlie tried to climb up the steps, and instantly stumbled; the adrenaline had given out, and the pain from the vertebrae he'd broken in his back was too much. They loaded him into another ambulance that would trail mine. Fortunately, it was just a short, eight-minute ride to the Montrose hospital.

Meanwhile, for Susan, her disbelief was only heightened when she pulled up in the tiny airport parking lot, ran into the lobby, and breathlessly asked the attendant at the desk about the crash.

"What crash?" was the answer.

Somehow, the attendant didn't even know; the runway was so far from the terminal that no one had heard anything, and the rescuers had shown up on their own. Still, through the fog of the snow coming down, Susan could see smoke billowing in the distance from the window. Left with an impossible decision—run out to the crash site or head to the hospital—Susan, as she later said, "followed the living." She asked where the hospital was, and sped off there immediately. When she got there, she was able to see me in the emergency room. There was real concern for my life, because I was having a hard time breathing, and the doctors were preparing to send me and Charlie to a larger hospital in Grand Junction, an hour away.

I was briefly lucid as Susan exclaimed to me that they couldn't find Teddy. Just as the doctors began sedating me, the only emotion I could summon was honesty.

"We have to be thankful that we had fourteen good years with him," I said.

My next memory is waking up in St. Mary's Medical Center in Grand Junction at seven o'clock the next morning. I had broken my back in six places, and fractured three ribs, my pelvis, coccyx, and sternum. I was heavily sedated, and in a body cast—any slight movement would be excruciatingly painful. Charlie was in a room down the hall. He'd broken his back, shattered his hand, and sustained burns on his arm as well as an eye injury. It was hard to grasp the fact that, twenty-four hours earlier, we'd been celebrating a wonderful holiday weekend, and getting set to go back to work. Now our entire world had been shattered.

News of the crash had quickly spread across the newswire over the course of Sunday afternoon, and like all plane crashes, had quickly become front-page news. By Monday, midmorning, the rest of the family had come to Colorado. Bob and Suzanne Wright, Randy Falco, and Lorne Michaels flew out on a GE plane on Monday morning, and Jeff Zucker and Ron Meyer would be on another plane a day later. Aimee Leone was, of course, there as well, working alongside Suzanne Wright to make sure that meals, cars, and all kinds of logistics for the family were taken care of. Even if I was in no condition to even speak much to them all, I'd never forget that they came, and did everything they could to help make the situation as comfortable as possible. There are very few bosses who would go as far as Wright (and his wife) did to be so caring and attentive. And Lorne's presence, too, was particularly meaningful—a sign of the lasting depth of our bond.

That Monday afternoon, Randy flew back to Montrose with a man named

Howard Winkler, who was GE's top corporate pilot. There, our good friend Bobby Landry was already pushing officials to get a crane to lift the wreckage of the plane. When they finally did that, late that day, they at last found Teddy, underneath. Randy identified him for us; nobody in the family ever saw the body. The bodies of Luis Polanco, the pilot, and Warren Richardson, the flight attendant, were also found. The copilot, Eric Wicksell, had survived, but was badly burned. We were told that, in all likelihood, Teddy died immediately, from the force of the crash. It made virtually no sense that sitting less than eighteen inches apart, I had lived and he had died. But then again, what made sense about any of it?

I was out of intensive care by late Monday, but stayed at St. Mary's for ten days before GE flew us home on their biggest plane, with me still in a hospital bed, on December 8. Still in a body cast, I couldn't move at all without bursting with extreme pain; and in a cruel twist, crying was one of the most painful things I could do. The plan when we got home was for me to recuperate in our bedroom; our bed had been moved out and replaced with a hospital bed for me and a small cot for Susan to sleep next to me at night. During the days, the kids would come up, find a comfortable spot, and we'd just watch movies all day long, getting intermittent distraction from the pain and sadness.

As anyone who's ever mourned knows, there was really no escape from the heartbreak. The emotions were constant, and constantly shifting—from despair to disbelief and back again. But amid her own agony, from the start, Susan somehow resolved that she was going to guide our family through it; she wasn't going to let this break us. Part of it, she would tell people, was her instincts as a mother; through her immeasurable sadness, she still felt an obligation to make everyone around her feel better. Then there was her mantra, simple but incisive: It was okay to cry, it was okay to be sad—okay, even, to be sad for the rest of our lives. But we couldn't be mad. Anger would cloud our ability to mourn and to find some improbable path to healing. And as Susan made sure, we would do that by clinging to the one thing we had left: each other.

The whole family had come back to Litchfield, and we were all back in the house. For fifteen years, life had been defined by a whirlwind schedule, but now, under the same roof, we were trying to grapple with the awful reality that our youngest piece was missing. In our family, the truth was that "together" had always come with an asterisk, because I was always on my way out, heading back to the city, or to an event. Now, though, I couldn't go anywhere, I wasn't able to disappear into work, or find any distractions. Like our entire family, I had to take the time to heal, and heal alongside everyone else in the house. I'd been so lucky for so long, and never really doubted the path I was on and the way I lived, giving so much of it over to work, and compelling my family to bend their lives for the sake of that work. But now, the thoughts were impossible to escape. How many more days could I have spent with Teddy if I hadn't been off working? How many more games could I have gone to with him? How many more movies? Those feelings, combined with the massive physical pain, made those days and nights, undeniably, the hardest of my life.

Outside the confines of home, Susan also gracefully became our family's voice over those first days and weeks of mourning. After thousands of letters poured into NBC, she spoke to Tim Russert on the *Today* show to relay our thanks, and to tell the world about Teddy, and why he'd be so missed. It wasn't easy, but Susan found a way to be brave in the face of losing, as she told Tim, what felt like her best friend. In that interview, Tim also found a way to put the loss in a way that somehow made sense and even offered a little comfort.

"If someone came to you and said, 'Susan, this is the grand design. We're going to give you young Teddy for fourteen years, and then we're going to take him home, you would have signed up for that deal, right?'"

Of course the answer was "Absolutely," as hard as it was to say goodbye.

There was so much to plan, and in a family of producers, Susan and Sunshine somehow guided everyone through it. About a week after getting home, the night before Teddy's funeral, we held a memorial service in the gym at his old Montessori school. More than a thousand people—from the local area, and from NBC and all over the sports world—showed up, and the service lasted nearly three hours. Susan's idea was to run it like a Quaker meeting; anyone who wanted to was given a chance to speak for a few minutes. Dozens and dozens of kids, teachers, and neighbors who'd known Teddy took the opportunity to do so. Still unable to walk, I was brought in on a large gurney, and greeted everyone who came through the procession. Then I lay there in the corner of the gym, listening to it all.

The next day, December 17, a little less than three weeks after the crash, was the funeral, at our local church, St. Anthony's. Five hundred people were crammed into the pews, and this time, I was wheeled in from the back. The first people I locked eyes on from my bed were Michael Phelps and his mom, Debbie. In Athens, when Michael had visited my office-slash-bedroom in the broadcast center, he'd spotted a photo of Teddy by the bed, and signed a picture for him. Now, here he was, just a few months later, sitting at Teddy's funeral, and the sight of him, having come up from Baltimore, brought the tears immediately. And from there, everyone I made eye contact with—from David and Diane Stern, to Bill Walton, to so many friends from NBC and beyond, brought their own emotional connection. So many relationships I'd forged through work—so clearly revealing themselves to be about much more than the job.

We'd debated as a family what kind of music we should play at the service. At one point Charlie suggested that Teddy would have liked the Notre Dame fight song to be part of the program. And so, for perhaps the first time ever, the congregation sang a slow, ballad version of "Victory March" as people went up, one by one, to take communion. And then Paul Simon, sitting on a stool at the front of the church, played "Citizen of the Planet," a song we'd used in our coverage of the Athens Olympics a few months earlier. Paul was wonderful, though he later told me that it was the toughest gig he ever had, including playing at Joe DiMaggio's funeral. The air was almost dried out, he said, by the sadness in the room, and he had trouble summoning his voice.

The most important thing that day, though, for our family, was what Susan insisted upon: that every child get up and say something about Teddy.

Willie went first, and somehow found the poise to lead with humor.

"I don't know how many people knew Teddy actually really well," he said, "or well enough to have seen that he had a small birthmark right above his right ankle.

"He liked to say it looked like an angel—kind of like a snow angel. And he had this—thus, he was an angel. And I said, 'Teddy, you can't be this annoying and possibly be an angel.'"

After the crowd laughed, Willie went on to talk about how grateful he was that in those last few years, he and Teddy had gone from constant foes to close friends.

Sunshine talked about how much she and Teddy had shared: a love of the Red Sox, and a love of writing, reading from an "autobiography" Teddy had written just a year earlier. It was a beautiful remembrance full of light laughs and deep meaning, a powerful reflection of all the life Teddy had lived, and all the life he'd never be able to live.

Harmony was next; as a schoolteacher, he'd carved his own special connection with Teddy, teaching him how to ride a bike years earlier and playing video games together when his youngest brother became a teenager. He read "A Child of Mine," a poem by Edgar Guest that's long been a source of comfort to families of children who've died young.

Charlie began his speech as the most emotional of the group, fighting through tears to talk about the final moments on the plane, and then years of memories with Teddy, before pivoting and joyously leading the church in a rendition of "Take Me Out to the Ball Game" as he gently placed his hands on the casket.

And then, a few moments later, Susan spoke.

"I keep thinking that the phone is going to ring," she said as she looked out onto the church, "and someone is going to say, 'Susan, there's been a terrible mistake.'

"But I can tell you what *would* be a terrible mistake."

And she paused, and rather than repeat all the wonderful things that had been said about Teddy, or talk about her own relationship with the boy she called her best friend, she spoke to us—her family. And she went straight for our darkest thoughts—our guilt, imploring us to realize what would be that terrible mistake. One by one, she implored our kids not to feel guilty about any times they were thinking about when they might not have had enough time, or enough patience, or enough energy, or even enough love for their youngest brother. That, she said, was nonsense. What they should remember were all the many wonderful memories they had shared, from watching movies together to playing video games together to listening to music together to wrestling and talking baseball and so much more.

She saved me for last.

"It would be a terrible mistake if you, Dick, were to ever entertain any thought such as 'I should have been home more,' or 'I worked too much and that was bad.' Because your passion and creativity and vision and successes and devotion to the details of your work and all the joy that you got from that was a pulse of our house. The heartbeat—we all thrived on it and learned from it and it rubbed off on us and once we were able to teach you to 'check your crown at the door on the weekends,' we also owned a part of it. You had, in fact, worked very hard at making that whole conundrum work—humungous job versus family. And Teddy jumped in with both feet once he learned the lingo. And the only bad counsel I ever remember you giving him was 'Son, why choose the Red Sox as your team and condemn yourself to a life of misery?'"

The audience laughed through their tears. My brother Si—who'd served stints in the army, the marines, and as the superintendent of the Virginia Military Institute—later told me Susan's speech was the bravest thing he ever saw.

The burial was at our local cemetery, about a mile down the road. Teddy was laid to rest next to our neighbor and good friend Michael Mortara, a partner at Goldman Sachs who'd died four years earlier from a brain aneurysm at the age of fifty-one. There would be no headstone; Susan felt like a boy shouldn't have one, his life forever incomplete.

We all stayed together at the house through New Year's. There would be nights of almost unbearable emotion, like Christmas, when the presents that Teddy had bought everyone that day over Thanksgiving weekend with his mom in Los Angeles were brought out to open; his final gifts. He had gotten me a gag gift—an ashtray for my cigars labeled "Ash-Hole." He was a little rascal until the very end.

So through the tears, there were some smiles, and some laughs, like Charlie's reaction when Susan bought us all Red Sox gear to wear—"No way, Teddy never would have wanted us to change sides." Every day, just a bit, the new normal settled in. As I started making more contact with the outside world, it felt like people just wrapped their arms around us, physically and emotionally. There were some poignant conversations I'll always remember with great friends who knew loss all too well, like Lilly Tartikoff, who'd buried Brandon when he'd succumbed to his lymphoma in 1997, and also Michael Gartner, our old friend from NBC News who'd lost his son Christopher to a sudden illness when he was eighteen. Even Johnny Carson reached out; he'd lost his son Ricky in a car accident decades earlier. Johnny, just a few months from his own passing, was honest—he said it was going to hurt like hell for a while, and there never really would be any answers to be found. Maybe there weren't answers, but there was solace in the feeling that I wasn't alone.

Susan's speech and her attitude of looking out for the rest of us at home helped life start to move again in January. The kids went back to their lives, and I started making more and more phone calls, including a fateful one with Pat Bowlen in mid-January that kick-started talks we'd been having with the NFL throughout the previous fall. I would never pretend it was anything close to flipping a switch, but gradually, day by day, I started to remember who I was, and started to be okay with the idea that work could be a distraction for me.

A little more than two months after the crash, the day before the Super Bowl in February 2005, Susan and I left Connecticut to head to Palm Springs, California, where I'd continue my recovery. The agenda was simple—to walk every day, and keep getting my body back into shape. One of my favorite daily routines was a path to getting better. Don Ohlmeyer, who lived nearby, joined me on the walks many afternoons, and was patient with my glacially slow pace. Our joke was that you could always trace where we were from the smell. One of the world's last great smokers, Don would smoke at least five to seven cigarettes on every walk. Aided by a cane, outside in the desert air, every day my body healed a bit more. And after two weeks in Palm Springs, we began a journey east that would be the next part of that process.

With Susan driving, we headed out from Palm Springs on February 21. We spent a night in Green Valley, Utah, and then went on to Grand Junction, Colorado, where we wanted to present a check to the children's wing of the hospital that had taken such phenomenal care of me, St. Mary's Medical Center. From there, it was a two-and-a-half-hour drive to our house in Telluride, where we'd stay for three weeks, with one central item on the agenda. We had gotten thousands of letters, cards, and emails from people since Thanksgiving weekend. Sitting at our dining room table, Susan and I sorted through every one of them, answering them all, and writing personal notes to the people who we knew best.

At the end of our stay in Colorado, near our house, a ceremony was held, where the trailhead leading down the mountain was officially named "Teddy's Way." It was small, but meaningful, and the start of what would be a year of commemorating Teddy's life in ways that we couldn't have ever expected. For years, we had been fortunate to be able to give to causes we felt passionately about. But to be on the other side of it, with people wanting to contribute gifts in memory of our son, was gratifying in a whole new way. What was most profound, in retrospect, is the message the gifts sent. For all the unfinished nature of Teddy's fourteen years, we were able to glimpse that his short life had in fact had an arc—a beginning, middle, and end—and the impact that the tributes had reflected that idea. At the Montessori school, where Teddy had gone from struggling youngster to flourishing graduate, the gym was named in his honor. At the Gunnery, where he'd spent just a few months but become a popular freshman, we spearheaded an effort to build a new dormitory in his name; the NFL and the NFLPA would be instrumental in bringing that idea to life. But the biggest gift of all was one first raised in a phone call to us just a few days after the crash—from Tom Werner, the Red Sox co-owner.

Tom's idea, immediately fully formed out of his own grief over the kid who'd talked his ear off about the Sox in their handful of meetings, was to raise money to renovate a state-owned park along the Charles River in downtown Boston, put a series of baseball diamonds in it, and rename it for Teddy. Tom made the founding gift, and from there, donations flooded in, to rebuild a park that would now house three baseball diamonds, and have space for soccer fields and other sports as well. So many amazing friends followed suit, including Robert Kraft and his family, who'd known our kids for years, and always supplied them with Patriots tickets and gear they could use to be auctioned off at school functions and the like.

The groundbreaking ceremony would be on a Saturday in June of 2005, and many friends flew to Boston for the occasion. The night before, we went to dinner with Tom, his partner John Henry, and Larry Lucchino, the team's president. The last time Larry had seen Teddy had been at a game the previous summer, when Teddy had talked to him for nearly the entire nine innings about the importance of signing the Sox catcher and captain, Jason Varitek, when he became a free agent. Teddy, Larry remembered, had said that it would take a four-year, $40 million deal to keep Varitek in Boston. Larry had signed him to a contract to exactly those terms.

That night, we went to Fenway to catch the Sox and Angels, Varitek scored the first run of the game, and Boston won it in a comeback, 7–4. The next day, Bob Costas was the perfect emcee for the groundbreaking ceremony of Teddy Ebersol's Red Sox Fields. Werner, Henry, and Lucchino were all there representing the team. Robert Kraft and his family were there, including son Jonathan, who a few days before had driven by the fields after a rainstorm, seen them saturated with water, and immediately made a call to bring over the field covering they used for concerts at Gillette Stadium for the ceremony. Senator Ted Kennedy and his wife,

Vicky, longtime friends of Susan's from her involvement in the Special Olympics, were there, with Kennedy among the speakers. Mitt Romney, who'd gone on from running the Salt Lake Olympics to become the governor of Massachusetts, and who had played a key role in freeing up the land to be used for the fields, was also there, as well as Joe Buck, Katie Couric, and a host of other close friends from sports and NBC.

What was most satisfying was that the fields would be a living memorial—that the fields would be used by generations of kids and their families. And when they were completed the next year, among the special tributes to Teddy were a hand-operated scoreboard in one of the outfields, a replica of the scoreboard on the Green Monster in Fenway, and a granite bench behind the backstop on one of the ball fields, with the words "Curse Reversed . . . 2004" engraved on its side, and a bronze replica of Teddy's baseball glove resting on top.

It still rests there today.

Eventually, you come to a certain acceptance of the idea that the sadness will never go away. And the truth was, as I returned to work in the spring of 2005, I pretty much immersed myself in the job as much as ever before. It was, frankly, a bit of an escape, and it was still something that invigorated me, especially considering the fact that I was chasing something as big as *Sunday Night Football* at the time. But there were still changes. Some were very small; my regular phone calls with my kids would forever always end with a very purposeful "I love you." For a long time, crying continued to come easily, and unexpectedly, whether in meetings with colleagues, my staff, or even interviews with the press—and for someone who had often put up a pretty stoic shield, that was definitely something to get used to, and accept.

More than anything else I think, I learned to be even more grateful for all the wonderful things our family had in our life, and how to be thankful for the fourteen years we'd had with Teddy, even if we wanted, and he deserved, so much more. In my case in particular, I'll forever be grateful for those last few years, when Teddy found his way, on his own, to sports—the passion that has defined my life, and how we were able to connect and bond over that, and how, as fate would have it, his romance with the Red Sox coincided with such a joyous pinnacle in the team's history.

Some summer night in 2003 or 2004, Teddy was watching a game on television with Sunshine, and his sister turned and asked, point-blank, why he cared so much about the game; why he'd become such a passionate fan so quickly.

His answer is something I'll cherish forever.

"I wanted to have something in common with Dad," he said thoughtfully. "I wanted to be able to speak his language. He loves baseball. So I wanted to love baseball."

There was much more to Teddy Ebersol's life than the Red Sox. But in the very last moments of his time on earth, just one month after they'd at long last won a championship, as he rewatched that World Series DVD, the Sox gave him joy. I'm glad that he got to see that, and could feel that joy. A boy's joy, for my son, who will always be forever young.

CHAPTER 27

Football Night in America

At 7:00 p.m. eastern time on Sunday, September 10, 2006, a new theme song—composed by our old friend from the Olympics, the legendary John Williams—chimed through televisions all across the country. Then the familiar voice of Bob Costas welcomed the audience of millions of fans to "Football Night in America," their gateway from the National Football League's slate of afternoon games to the featured matchup of the night an hour and twenty minutes away. About ten miles away from Bob in 30 Rock, I was in a production truck outside Giants Stadium in East Rutherford, New Jersey, working with a new producer, new director, and the most exciting new show on NBC that I'd been involved with since we'd gotten the NBA a decade and a half earlier. Soon, Bob and Cris Collinsworth would check in for a preview of the game with the broadcast booth—Al Michaels and John Madden. It was a legendary football foursome. And it was the culmination of a deal and a dream years in the making.

To understand how *Sunday Night Football* came to be, and why it mattered so much, you really have to go back to the turn of the century. From a personal vantage point, of course, I'd missed working on pro football since we'd pulled out of the NFL in 1998, and I knew our staff did, too. But from a business perspective, for General Electric and NBC, flourishing in so many other ways, electing not to hang on to pro football was absolutely the right strategy. Yet the television business, and the entertainment business, are never static objects, and as a new century began, the changes afoot were impossible to ignore. And some of the most eye-opening changes in sports TV were coming on *Monday Night Football.*

After three decades on the air, the show was no longer the powerhouse it had been for so long after Roone and Pete Rozelle had created it on ABC. The show's ratings actually peaked in 1989, and over the course of the next decade, the numbers dipped gradually but steadily. In response, ABC began tweaking their production, luring my old buddy Don Ohlmeyer out of retirement to take over the broadcast in 2000. Don had left NBC the year before, and the challenge of re-invigorating the show where he'd gotten his start was alluring. As ever, Don went big, bringing in comedian Dennis Miller as a third commentator in the booth, looking to capture some of the magic that Howard Cosell had had decades earlier. While Dennis had his moments with some funny one-liners, the ratings just continued to sink.

Regardless of my feelings for Don or Dennis, the problem, as I and anyone paying close attention could see, was something much bigger: the games themselves. On Sundays on Fox and CBS, the games that got the biggest ratings were always the same: the best matchups featuring the most popular teams. And yet on Mondays, those matchups—scheduled months in advance before the season started—simply weren't showing up. All you had to do was look at the facts to see the significance. Every season, the ratings would generally slide downward as the schedule moved along. At least in one sense, that was counterintuitive, since the stakes of the big games theoretically mattered more as the playoffs drew closer. The problem was, the big games that mattered late in the season weren't airing on Monday nights. And with cable television growing, and people with more options than ever before, bad football games just weren't going to cut it.

Observing all this, my mind started to swirl with thoughts, and I asked our research department at NBC to look into the *Monday Night Football* ratings to get some data to back up my analysis. The researchers came back to me with a figure that said it all. Over six years of *Monday Night Football* on ABC, looking at the last six games of each of those seasons (that is, thirty-six late-season games in total) only one—*one*—of those games featured a matchup between two teams with winning records. That is to say, thirty-five of what should have been the most important and most profitable thirty-six pro football games on prime-time television featured at least one losing team. Bad games were the problem.

The obvious solution was to get better games onto Monday night. But that wasn't so simple: often the games that sounded like they'd be competitive when they were scheduled before the season actually ended up being duds once November and December came along. It wasn't anyone's fault, necessarily; the NFL schedulers certainly weren't trying to put bad games in prime time. But if that issue couldn't be rectified, the ratings weren't going to get better.

It wasn't good for the NFL, and as far as ABC was concerned, I actually didn't have to speculate how nervous the network was about the decline. Not long after we'd walked away from our Sunday package, ABC executives had quietly approached NBC—without telling the NFL—to ask if we'd ever consider buying the Monday night package from them; essentially subletting the broadcast deal. I was immediately skeptical that the NFL would ever even permit that kind of transaction, considering how bad it might look for the league to have a partner bail on them like that. But even if I had been interested, I also knew *Monday Night Football* on NBC wouldn't be the right deal for our network before we could even get to the issue of the inferior schedule of games. NBC's late night lineup, Jay Leno and Conan O'Brien, was a massive, lucrative moneymaker for us. If once a week, late night was pushed a half hour or hour later, thanks to a (potentially bad) football game and then the late local news, the result would be terrible for ratings, and thus a costly decrease in ad money. The idea of *Monday Night Football* on NBC was never going to happen.

Knowing all of ABC's consternation about its package—not to mention the NFL's disappointment with the sinking ratings—and knowing that a new negotiating window for the rights to all those games was approaching in 2005, the basis of a new idea for NFL games in prime time started to take shape in my head around that time. What if there was a way to guarantee that, all season long, the NFL could air premier games, always featuring premier teams, in prime time? It would be complicated, but maybe, just maybe, it was possible.

What if we could create *Sunday* night football on NBC?

For years, a weekly Sunday night game had been something of an afterthought for the league. Mostly airing on ESPN (with a period on TNT), Sunday night had been the home of typically underwhelming games—but games that were, all the same, critical to the cable channels airing them. I mentioned before how cable channels like ESPN were cash cows for companies with the "sub fees" they could charge; well, having a weekly NFL game, even if it wasn't a marquee game, was a huge asset for ESPN when it came time to negotiate those fees with cable carriers. Oddly then, for Disney—the parent company of both ABC and ESPN—the secondary, less important telecast on cable, because it was part of their fastest-growing business, had arguably become more critical than their signature network broadcast. And by 2004, *Monday Night Football* presented an even bigger dilemma when you factored in the growing success ABC was having with the rest of its prime-time lineup, with new hit shows like *Desperate Housewives* and *Lost*. ABC Entertainment executives in Los Angeles looked at football's sinking ratings and stewed, feeling like they could do better with more scripted dramas or reality shows than a series that only lasted through December anyway.

So then, what if I could thread a needle through that tumult? What if I could convince the NFL to make a deal to move the premier, network package of prime-time games from Monday on ABC to Sunday on NBC? It would mean upending the more than three-decade-old network TV institution of *Monday Night Football*—but it also could create a much stronger product. Why? Because with the biggest games on Sundays, a flexible schedule would be possible. That is to say, a Sunday night matchup that looked good when the schedule was put out in the spring but turned out to feature poor teams could be swapped out for a better afternoon game. And that game could move into prime time without significantly hindering prep time for the teams impacted. The idea of moving a Sunday afternoon game to Monday night was just too challenging logistically, even several weeks out. But while moving Sunday afternoon games to nighttime wasn't nothing, it was a much more viable concept.

Of course, the NFL wasn't the only entity I had to convince. There was also the matter of getting my colleagues at NBC on board. And I thought I had a good argument. The fact was, our rivals had made major inroads on our longtime dominance in the overall prime-time ratings, thanks to the phenomenon of *American Idol* on Fox and the steady diet of appealing dramas on CBS and ABC. Airing football on Sunday nights would potentially be a huge boost for the network, considering Sunday had become the most-watched night of the week on television. And it also wouldn't get in the way of late night programming during the week.

Yes, investing potentially a few billion dollars back in the NFL would be a huge about-face from our departure out of football a few years earlier, and there was no guarantee that better games on Sunday nights would be a ratings hit. It was absolutely a huge bet to make. But as with any risk, the payoff could also be just as massive.

There were a lot of people to sell on the idea—at both the NFL and NBC. But as 2004 began, I was ready to convince anyone and everyone I had to that *Sunday Night Football* on NBC could become a reality.

It wasn't going to be a simple process. But week after week in those early months of 2004, well before I could have ever known the hellish turn that year would later take for me and my family, I started, over the course of many meetings and calls, introducing the idea to the key players at the NFL, and also inside NBC. The conversations were spent talking and also listening to people, getting input and exploring options, figuring out what might work and what wouldn't work, and, as much as anything else, getting a firmer sense for myself about what the deal could look like.

Absolutely not surprisingly, from the start, I met a healthy dose of skepticism in a wide variety of points at GE and NBC. Some of my most trusted colleagues on the financial side—like NBC's head of ad sales, Keith Turner, as well as Randy Falco, who was now the business head of the entire NBC network—just didn't think that the money it would cost to bring a Sunday night football package to NBC would draw enough viewers to make the ad dollars work. Randy and Keith knew the space better than anyone, and just didn't think that ad agencies would buy into the idea that fans, after two Sunday afternoon games, would have the appetite to turn a third game into a big ratings hit. My argument was that great matchups could overcome that problem, but in our many discussions, I knew that if I were in their roles, I'd probably have the same instincts. Randy and Keith always listened, though, and our conversations made the plans I was forming much stronger.

As for the upper levels of management, the feedback was mixed. In the ultimate role of decision maker, Jeff Immelt wasn't the swashbuckler that Jack Welch had been, but I knew that he appreciated risk and big bets, and thus was willing to listen. Bob Wright, though, was definitely skeptical. If the network took a big risk like this while struggling in the ratings and failed, the public fallout could be brutal. But just underneath him, I had a strong asset in a great friend: Jeff Zucker. In May of 2004, Jeff was promoted from president of NBC Entertainment to president of the entire organization, working directly under Bob as his heir apparent. Through his path across news, comedy, and drama, and now all network business, Jeff—the former Olympic researcher—had remained a huge sports fan, and saw my vision for *Sunday Night Football* immediately. Not to mention, he knew it could be a way to win the biggest night in prime time—Sunday—for his entertainment group.

As for the leadership of the NFL, lobbying would also require getting a wide group of people on board. Fortunately, I knew them all well, and had stayed in pretty close contact with my friends at the league since our last Super Bowl six years earlier. That started at the top, with Commissioner Paul Tagliabue, who needed no reminder how much I loved football. Late in our final season of covering the AFC in 1997, I'd had dinner at an Italian restaurant on the East Side of Manhattan with Paul. As we finished up, I let him know once more how hard it was to end our partnership—and then added one more thought.

"We'll be back," I said with a smile. "I'm not sure how or when, but NBC will be back in business with the NFL at some point."

Six years later, it was time to convince Paul that I'd figured out the how and the when. In the league office, I began speaking more frequently to his top lieutenants. One was Steve Bornstein, the former president of ESPN and ABC Sports who was now the league's top broadcasting executive. No one in the league office had more experience on the television side, or more insight into what the data and research said about viewing patterns of NFL games. It also didn't hurt, I figured, that Steve had had a less-than-happy parting with Disney, and might be disposed to another network stepping in to, at least in part, replace it. Every little edge could help.

The other key voice at league headquarters was a man named Roger Goodell, who I'd gotten to know years earlier when he was a rising executive in the league office. We'd worked on a number of projects together and gotten along well. Now Roger had risen all the way from intern to the NFL's chief operating officer—Tagliabue's top deputy and likely heir apparent.

The league executives in New York were only half the equation when it came to the NFL; while they handled the operational business side, it was the owners on the broadcast committee who approved the deals. If they didn't buy into the vision, then we had no shot. And here again, I felt like I had the inside track, considering the great relationships I had with the three owners who composed the committee: Jerry Jones of the Cowboys, Robert Kraft of the Patriots, and Pat Bowlen of the Broncos.

Even when we'd been out of football, I'd stayed in touch with Jerry, a great character and brilliant businessman. As little as you might have thought an oilman from Arkansas and a TV producer from New England would have in common, Jerry and I both loved taking risks, and there was a great deal of mutual respect and admiration.

As New Englanders, Kraft and I had shared roots, and crossed paths frequently; I'd actually first met Robert and his wife, Myra, when we were introduced at a charity event hosted by David Stern. He'd impressed me as he turned the Patriots into one of the NFL's powerhouse franchises, and on top of that, he'd since been great every time he met my sons, at games or elsewhere, and had become a wonderful friend, there for us when we built Teddy's fields in Boston, just as we'd be there for him years later when Myra passed away. So our relationship transcended football—though there was that one time in the early nineties when Kraft had hired away one of my employees, wooing Bill Parcells away from our studio to become his coach. Parcells had told me the news over the phone as he drove over the Tappan Zee Bridge from his home in New Jersey, heading to New England to sign the deal. I wished him and Robert only the best.

As for Pat, both Ken Schanzer and I had maintained our friendships with him; it helped that both of us frequently took our families out west to ski in Colorado, giving us ample occasion to spend time with him on stopovers in Denver. Even when we were out of the league, Pat was never shy on those get-togethers about sharing his opinions about TV matters. Which was significant, because Pat was the broadcast committee chairman, working with Robert and Jerry to determine how the league put its product on television.

And for all the value of those personal relationships, Pat's take on the state of NFL broadcasting in 2004 was maybe the most significant thing I had going for me. For years, he'd quietly been questioning the direction of *Monday Night Football*. He'd already been part of conversations within the NFL about flexible scheduling; the league had, maybe not surprisingly, actually explored the idea on their own. And so when I started sharing with Pat my idea for *Sunday Night Football*, he got it. He saw the potential of reinvigorating the NFL in prime time on the most-watched TV night of the week. And when we got into the details of my plans, he also saw the potential of working again with NBC. More than most owners, Pat had an innate sense of how top-notch production could make events feel bigger. He saw my vision for the kind of presentation *Sunday Night Football* could be, and also some of my ancillary ideas, like an extended pregame show before kickoff hosted by Bob Costas that could serve as the first "paper of record" on all the games that day. He lit up when I told him the name I had brainstormed: *Football Night in America.*

After months of conversations with all these different figures, across the country and in New York, it really seemed evident that the league was open to changing up the status quo of its rights deals. A clue came at one point when I suggested that Tagliabue and his executives come over to the executive dining room at 30 Rock, where we'd have plenty of privacy to talk about what kind of deal we could make. They said lunch would be great, but wanted to do it instead in a private room at the 21 Club—the same place that, decades earlier, Pete Rozelle and Roone Arledge had hashed out the original *Monday Night Football.* The next day, a report appeared in the media: NBC was in the mix to get back in the NFL TV game. The league—not us—had leaked the news of our lunch to serve notice that change could be afoot.

It was one of many signs of small progress, even as the fact remained we were on the outside looking in. As the current rights holder to the Monday and Sunday night games, Disney had absolute renewal rights on both, and the inside edge on making a deal before we could even formally get to the table. Despite all their consternation, they theoretically controlled the destiny of both nights. If in the end they decided they wanted to keep both packages, and made an offer the NFL couldn't refuse, we'd never actually officially get to the bargaining table to make an offer.

All through a busy spring and summer prepping and then producing the Athens Olympics, as well as negotiating new deals for the PGA Tour and NHL, football stayed on the agenda. In early November, I was with my staff in Beijing, for meetings regarding the Olympics to be held there in 2008, when the NFL announced new six-year deals with Fox and CBS for Sunday afternoons. Neither had been a threat to enter the prime-time negotiations; their Sunday packages were a huge part of each network's identity, and that of course was great for us. A few weeks later, the weekend before Thanksgiving, Ken Schanzer and I flew on a GE jet from the season-ending NASCAR race in Homestead, Florida, to Denver for a big meeting with Pat about the deal. Disney, it was now clear, despite its deep pockets, was dragging its heels. Their priority was ESPN, and with the issues they had at ABC, the company even seemed willing—if not eager—to move *Monday Night Football* to the cable network. We couldn't have asked for a better opening, and since the NFL knew that it could get almost whatever it wanted dollarwise for that to happen, they were happy to focus that way.

Things really felt like they were progressing, and at the meeting in Colorado, we discussed dollars with Pat for the first time, as he mentioned a target of $700 million a season to broadcast *Sunday Night Football* on NBC. It was more than I knew I could ever get from GE, but it was also within a range to begin a negotiation. We knew Pat believed in our vision, and Goodell and Bornstein also seemed to be warming to it as well. Only Tagliabue—the most critical voice in the room—still needed to be convinced.

There was no one single point when I felt like I was recovered from the plane crash. It just doesn't work that way. But looking back at those horrible few months in the wake of November 28, 2004, one moment that I will never forget came on a night in the middle of January 2005. I was lying in the hospital bed that had been installed in my room. By that point, I had begun to tolerate sitting up easier, and walking the few steps to the bathroom with a bit less pain, and had started to check in with the long list of treasured friends with whom I hadn't spoken since the crash. And among the first calls I decided to make from my bed on this particular early evening in mid-January, as the rest of my family ate dinner downstairs, was to Pat Bowlen.

For Pat, the crash had been all the more stunning, given that we'd had that meeting just a few days prior. On top of that, Pat had actually been one of the first people in America to hear about the crash. He'd been on the sidelines before kickoff at a Broncos game, about to watch his team play the Raiders when the state policeman who served as his security guard had whispered to him that he'd heard on his radio that there'd been a crash at Montrose a few hundred miles west, and my family had been on the plane.

Now, a month and a half later, almost as soon as he picked up the phone and we began to talk, I broke down. I was still just finding out how much I'd cry when I talked about Teddy with family and friends over the months and years to come. Quietly, I could hear Pat—a father of seven children himself—weeping, too. Then, eventually, in his understated style, he found a way to change the subject.

"Well, I do have one piece of good news."

He paused.

"I've got another vote."

Another pause.

"And it's Paul."

Sitting in that hospital bed, still barely able to move, I immediately grasped the significance of what he said.

Over the six weeks since our meeting, Pat had gotten Paul Tagliabue to come around on the idea of *Sunday Night Football* on NBC. We now had the NFL's support for a deal, assuming Disney gave us the opening to negotiate. Then and now, it's impossible to calculate how much the crash, and my relationship with Pat, Jerry, Robert, Paul, Roger, and everyone else figured into what the league wanted to do. There was a lot more pain for me to deal with, a lot more healing for me to do, a lot more unanswerable questions in my life to make sense of—including, first and foremost, whether it was okay to even think about work while mourning Teddy's loss. It would take a long while for that notion of guilt to find an appropriate place in my consciousness. But as I sat up gingerly in bed, and the adrenaline started pumping a bit for the first time in a long time, I saw, at the minimum, a path forward to some distraction.

As my recovery continued, I gradually began focusing on work more, bit by bit. That included calling Jeff Immelt from the passenger seat of the rental car that Susan drove from Palm Springs to Colorado in February, catching him up on what Bowlen had shared with me. Immelt was definitely intrigued, and over the next few weeks from Telluride, as we replied to the thousands of cards, letters, and emails we'd gotten from people, I continued getting on more and more calls. I actually made a habit of calling Immelt weekly, on Sunday mornings, when I discovered he went into the office to get work done. Outside of the pressures of his week-day schedule, the conversations were more relaxed, and I could start laying the groundwork for what had become the biggest priority: getting the approval for the ten-figure fee I was going to need to produce a multiyear agreement, should the process get to that point. One huge development in my favor: I could tell Immelt that Jeff Zucker had agreed to something extraordinary: handing over 25 percent of NBC's annual prime-time development money for the deal. For Jeff, it was worth it: investing in a show that he believed would be a hit—as opposed to taking a chance on an unknown pilot—and that would air on the most-viewed television night of the week.

I returned to the office on March 29, almost four months to the day after the crash. I eased in, with a meeting or two each day that first week. The next week, I started doing full days, and the schedule, almost inevitably, quickly grew packed. On Monday, April 4, Pat Bowlen, Paul Tagliabue, and Roger Goodell came to my office for a 4:00 p.m. meeting. It was the first time I'd seen them since before the crash, and like every meeting I had in those first weeks, it was tinged with plenty of emotion. Business was business, but it was impossible for any of us to separate the friendships we had built for so long. Meanwhile, as always, Pat—the man of few words—had also been a man of his word. It was evident Paul was now definitely on board with the idea of *Sunday Night Football*. The sense, they told me, was that the Disney negotiations would be wrapped within a few weeks. Nothing was set in stone, but I could read what they thought was the most likely scenario: *Monday Night Football* going to ESPN, and Sunday night up for grabs.

Over the next week, I continued to monitor the situation on both sides. Immelt's one request of me was to make sure I got all the other NBC executives who'd been skeptical of the idea, and whose questions had made us all think harder and find ways to make our plans stronger, on our side, and by now, Randy Falco, Keith Turner, and Bob Wright were all on board. I had never been much for signs, but on April 11, I got a call out of the blue from John Madden. He said he was calling for no particular reason—just to check on me, and see how I was doing back in the office. But John was more tapped into the NFL than anyone I knew, and I figured he had a sense that we were close.

Then, that Friday, April 15, my phone rang around 1:30 p.m. It was Roger Goodell. He asked me how quickly I could get over to the NFL offices on Park Avenue. Twenty minutes, I told him. He paused. "Is it really going to take you twenty minutes to walk four blocks?"

I had to remind him with a laugh that I was still walking with a cane.

A half hour later, I was sitting alone in the league's Gene Upshaw conference room, waiting to be joined. I'd been brought in through a back entrance, and had the sense that maybe representatives from another network might still be in the building. When the door opened, Pat Bowlen, Robert Kraft, Paul Tagliabue, and Roger Goodell walked in, and they had the news I'd been waiting to hear. Just minutes before, Disney had closed the deal to put *Monday Night Football* on ESPN, and they were dropping Sunday nights. The package was up for grabs. But more than that, the Disney executives had done the deal knowing that top-quality games regularly scheduled on Monday nights were a thing of the past, and Sunday nights would potentially have the flexibility to switch into even better games as the season went on.

It was everything I'd hoped the opportunity would be; now we just needed to negotiate a deal for a few billion dollars. Believe it or not, the foundation of the agreement would take just five minutes to reach. They asked if I was willing to make a six-year deal. I was, and said I was good for $600 million a year. I looked briefly at Pat, who of course had thrown out $700 million, but $600 million was what I was going to get from GE. They nodded. It was time to get to work.

As ever, the efficiency was no accident. The hard work had been about getting so many different people to buy in to the idea; having done that right, the money was not going to be a complicated issue. Beyond that, Immelt, just like Welch prior, had set me up with the trust to make the agreement on my own.

Slowly walking back to NBC, I called my colleagues—Zucker, Immelt, Wright, Falco, and Schanzer. The NFL was available, I told them all, and the league was ready to make a deal. Immelt had just one priority left: to negotiate a number of opportunities and benefits for GE into the deal. Just like we'd done with our most recent extension with the Olympics, GE could add all kinds of value to our relationship with the NFL. Everything from GE lighting in stadiums to GE MRI machines at practice facilities to GE metal detectors and other security equipment at special events to loans from GE Capital—General Electric could be a preferred partner and negotiate any number of extra deals over the life of the contract. It was an all but guaranteed way to bake more value into the deal, and solidify a bigger relationship that would go beyond just football on television.

By 4:30 p.m., I was back at the NFL, in the same Gene Upshaw conference room, this time with Schanzer and Ed Swindler by my side, opposite Goodell and

Bornstein on the other side of the table. Even with the basic terms of the deal settled, there were still various points to work out—a range of elements that had been growing, living parts of the plans for months. One was the GE partnership, and all the different ways that our parent company and the league could work together. Another was much more connected to the coverage: our *Football Night in America* pregame show. With the game starting sometime around 8:15 p.m., the plan would be to come on the air at 7:00 p.m. eastern, recapping the NFL day. ESPN had long controlled the space with *NFL Primetime* hosted by Chris Berman, but now, we wanted exclusivity—to be the only network that could show extended highlights on Sunday night.

The NFL's concern was that by starting the show at seven o'clock, we'd poach viewers from the late game on CBS or Fox. That really wasn't my plan at all—if there was a good game on, I knew most football fans wouldn't tune away from it to see highlights from the earlier games. That said, there would be an audience, and I knew I could offer the first half hour of the show to our affiliates for local commercial time. It would give them something to sell advertisers, thus justifying their contribution to the $600 million a year we were paying for the package. It took a few hours, but I was able to hash that point out with Bornstein over a dinner across the street from my apartment at Isle of Capri and then even later that night on the phone after we'd parted ways. The next day would be another marathon meeting focused on details like the payment schedule, and by the late afternoon, everything had pretty much been settled. Sixteen Sunday night games (in those years, the league didn't want to go up against a World Series game; that would change in the future), along with the pregame show, and maybe most critical, that flexible scheduling scenario that would take hold as the season went along. We'd also get the Thursday night NFL season opener featuring the defending Super Bowl champion. And then a day of Wild Card playoff games every year, and two Super Bowls over the life of the six-year deal.

In less than forty-eight hours, we'd made one of the most monumental deals in NFL broadcasting history—even as the foundation had been quietly laid long before it.

Late that afternoon, still relying on my cane, I decided to walk the ten-odd blocks back to my apartment. The feeling was hard to describe. There was the exhilaration of success, still measured by the hole in my heart that would never disappear. I thought a lot about Teddy during that walk, and when I got to the corner of East Sixty-First Street and Park Avenue, I'll never forget walking right past Roone Arledge's old building. Thirty-five years earlier, I'd watched him launch the biggest sports show in prime-time history. Now *Monday Night Football* as he'd envisioned it would cease to exist. I knew Roone, who had died in 2002, would be disappointed by that—disappointed that the ABC Sports he'd built, and where I'd started my career, was all but gone. My plan, though, was that *Sunday Night Football* would be a worthy heir.

Our first kickoff was a little less than seventeen months away.

CHAPTER 28

Sunday Night Is Football Night

From the beginning, at the center of the vision for *Sunday Night Football* was the idea that the game would feel special. It wouldn't just be a third game on Sunday for fans to enjoy, and it certainly wouldn't be the afterthought that Sunday night games had been on cable prior. It would be the premier game—the game everyone looked forward to as the pinnacle of the NFL week. Fans and observers of the league take that for granted these days. But then, it was an idea that we had to create.

Being that we were still more than a year away from our first kickoff, the biggest factor—scheduling the best games into the Sunday night slot—wouldn't be determined just yet. But there was still a massive amount of work for everyone involved to do—work that could start immediately. On the league side, Roger Goodell and Steve Bornstein were totally committed to our success, and making sure everyone in the Park Avenue offices knew that *Sunday Night Football* was going to be a whole new kind of showcase for the NFL. Meanwhile, Pat Bowlen, Robert Kraft, and Jerry Jones were tremendous in terms of selling to their fellow owners just how important these prime-time games were going to be to the league. Then there was the job I had to do:

figure out what the broadcast would look like, how it would be produced, and who the talent would be.

It was an exciting scenario—and my expectations were sky-high. One, because I saw our talent as the single best way to signal to the audience that this was the premier football game of the week, and two, because I felt like I had the relationships to secure the most important pieces. In my early meetings with Pat, I'd laid out to him my ideal targets. Now it was time to go get them. And that started with the biggest name of all in football broadcasting. Indeed, the phone call I'd gotten from John Madden just before we'd closed the deal with the NFL was hardly just a harbinger that we were getting the contract. It was also a reminder from an old friend that we'd also both said that if the chance ever arose, it would be a dream come true to work together.

John and I had first met in 1982, four years after he'd retired from coaching and become an instant television star on CBS. From the very beginnings of his iconic partnership with Pat Summerall, John had become the greatest football analyst television had ever seen. No one was as insightful, no one was as entertaining, no one was as much of a natural at making a football game better to watch. And while John effortlessly projected the image of a larger-than-life cartoon character whose only cares in the world were whether a lineman hit his gaps correctly and a quarterback went through his progressions smartly, the truth was that John was an incredibly savvy performer. I found that out firsthand when he hosted *Saturday Night Live* at the end of January in 1982. It was right after the Super Bowl, and John couldn't have been better to work with. We followed him with a camera as he took the train (this was in the days before his Madden Cruiser bus, when he crisscrossed the country via Amtrak) from the big game in Detroit to New York. Once he arrived, he was great all week in meetings with the writers, and then the dress rehearsal seemed to go smoothly enough. At least, I thought so, until just before the end, when John called out to me, with the entire rehearsal crowd listening in.

"Where's Ebersol?" he said. "Get him out here!"

I popped out from where I'd been, under the bleachers monitoring the show.

"Listen," he said to me, looking gravely serious. "I'm going to stay here for these people and finish this dress rehearsal, but when it's over, I'm out. I'm done. I'm leaving. This has been a total fiasco."

I'm not too often speechless, but the specter of losing a host minutes before air was a nightmare I'd never encountered. Plus, I was also confused, because the rehearsal had seemingly gone well, even if the giant bear of a man talking to me didn't look happy at all.

John waited until presumably every bit of color drained from my face, and then spoke again.

"Gotcha," he said, breaking into a massive smile. The audience exploded into laughter. "I thought you might keel over!"

Needless to say, even if I lost a couple days off my life from John's little gag, the show went off without a hitch, and a great friendship was blossoming.

Over the next two decades, John's stardom only grew, in no small part due to the phenomenal success of his video game, which still ensures that young kids know his name today. Meanwhile, in the broadcast booth, when Fox took the NFC from CBS in the mid-1990s, hiring John became the new network's quickest path to legitimacy. At the time, I had looked into hiring John for NBC; Jack Welch even wanted to offer him his own train, built by GE, the largest locomotive manufacturer in the world, that he could use to travel to games in place of the famous bus. But like a lot of things with Fox, when we found out just how much money Rupert Murdoch was offering him, train or not, I knew John had an offer he couldn't refuse. John would spend several years at Fox, and then when Summerall retired, he seamlessly moved to ABC and *Monday Night Football*, where he formed another Hall of Fame pair with Al Michaels. Now though, at long last, the stars were aligned for the perfect final chapter of John's career, and I don't know who was more excited, me or him.

About a month after the *Sunday Night Football* deal was announced, I flew to Pleasanton, California, the town south of San Francisco where John lived and had his production facility, Goal Line Productions. I stayed a night at the hotel he owned, the Rose, and we spent a great day together talking about what the show could be. A few weeks later, negotiations with Sandy Montag, John's veteran agent and a good friend, were wrapped. We were off to a terrific start.

The next piece I was after was another person who I'd known for years, with a relationship that transcended the business. Cris Collinsworth had been thirty-one, two years out of retirement from the NFL when we'd hired him to do a few lower-tier games. He'd shown up at his first game completely green, with the entirety of his research on the back of an envelope. His producer, David Michaels (the brother of Al), quickly taught him how to prep, and Cris turned out to be a natural; within a few years, he was our analyst for Notre Dame games. He'd eventually transitioned to our studio show, and then arrived at a crossroads with many other talented people when we parted ways with the NFL in 1998.

Not surprisingly, both Fox and CBS wanted Cris for their pregame shows, and by Super Bowl week, he had both offers in hand. In San Diego that Wednesday, Cris came to my room to lay out both scenarios and ask my advice, making clear he was leaning toward CBS. Their show was going to be shot in New York, which was closer to his home in Cincinnati and also where he taped his weekly HBO show, *Inside the NFL*. Fox, on the other hand, was based in Los Angeles. He wanted to get my blessing. I couldn't give it to him.

"You've got to go with Fox," I'd told him.

Fox had done a lot of things right since they'd begun their NFL coverage, and I'd come to have a ton of respect and affection for their leader, David Hill, and his partner, Ed Goren. "Hilly" had been fearless in the way he innovated, including creating the now commonplace but then revolutionary permanent score box in game coverage. To me, if people came across a game, you didn't want them to know the score immediately; if it was a blowout, they'd change the channel. But thank goodness, Hilly knew better, and that's why every game in every sport you turn on today has a score box in a corner of the screen. As an executive, it's embarrassing to admit how against it I was. As a fan, I'm glad Hilly would have never listened to me.

Fox also revolutionized the pregame show in their coverage, though in a subtler way. Terry Bradshaw, Howie Long, and Jimmy Johnson were all Hall of Famers, yes, but their show wasn't really about football. It was about laughing and having a good time talking about football—and the cast had become football's answer to cartoon characters, beloved by their audience. And so it was a much better idea for Cris Collinsworth to join that cast than it was to become part of an unproven entity at CBS. Cris was able to work out some scheduling things with Fox to get to some of his kids' games, and the deal he signed with them worked out great for both sides. Then, eventually, Cris transitioned back to games, becoming part of Fox's top broadcast team alongside Joe Buck and Troy Aikman.

Now, seven years later, in the spring of 2005, it was time to cash back in the chip I'd laid with our rivals. First, I called Cris and let him know I was interested in bringing him back to NBC. He was a little confused—if John Madden was coming to be the game analyst, then where would he go? I explained to him my vision of creating *Football Night in America* as a studio show that would be a worthy rival for Fox, the concept that it would be the NFL's "first paper of record," airing after the afternoon games every Sunday evening before our game. Costas would be the perfect host, and Cris could be alongside him as the star analyst. There might come a point where John, who had reached his seventies, might want to retire, but for the time being, this was the role I had for him.

Even though Cris's first choice wasn't the studio, he didn't hesitate to say yes—years later, he would quip that he's entrusted me with every major life decision he's ever made with the exception of marrying his wonderful wife, Holly (who predates our friendship). The problem was, he had another year left on his Fox contract. I told him I didn't think it would be a problem. I called Hilly and Ed and didn't have to remind them that, without me, they wouldn't have had Cris in the first place. Cris really wanted to come back, and this was better for his family; at last, his weekly trips could be shorter. Hilly generously agreed to let Cris out of his deal, and our agreement was announced in July.

So in two months, we'd gotten who in my view were the two most talented football analysts in TV. Costas, Madden, and Collinsworth were three massive stars, giving our coverage a sense of prestige more than a year before our first game. But there was one more big fish I wanted to catch: Al Michaels. Having Costas and Collinsworth toss the coverage to Michaels and Madden every Sunday night would be a weekly foursome of legends. Though I'd never actually worked with Al, we knew each other well, and there was a lot of mutual respect—from football to baseball to the Olympics and more, Al had solidly established himself as the greatest play-by-play man of his generation. The problem was, when we met in the spring, he was hesitant to switch teams, even though his company's NFL coverage was moving from ABC to ESPN. A year earlier, after David Stern had been unhappy with how ABC aired the NBA Finals, he'd smartly had them move Al into their broadcast team. That had resulted in a significant raise for Al, and when we began discussing a deal, I wasn't going to match his new salary; he'd just be doing football for us. Disney pressured Al to make a call quickly, and torn between staying and going, Al decided to stick with Monday nights.

It was a bit of a disappointing finish to the summer, and left a hole in our broadcast booth. But we still had a little more than a year before our first game. And I was just as excited about the team I'd recruited behind the scenes.

Along with the talent, from the beginning of our lead-up, just as big a priority was making sure that our production team would be top-notch. The producer of the games, I'd decided quickly, would be Tommy Roy. Tommy had produced three Super Bowls for us in the nineties, and though he'd left the job of our overall executive producer to move to Florida, he produced all our golf coverage, as well as swimming and speed skating at the Olympics. As for a director, Don Ohlmeyer had raved to me about Drew Esocoff, who he'd worked with in his one year back at *Monday Night Football*. Drew had continued to direct that show after Don left, but ESPN had quickly decided that their new version would be helmed by the team that had worked on their old Sunday night games. That made Drew a free agent, and he was excited to commit to moving over to our game when we spoke in the summer.

Meanwhile, Sandy Montag, Madden's agent, had been pushing me to meet the man who had been Drew's partner in the *Monday Night* production truck, the show's producer, Fred Gaudelli. Madden also spoke very highly of him. It was nice to hear, but I was especially comfortable going with Tommy as my producer—I knew how talented he was, and he would be a familiar link in a chain of a lot of new challenges. Still, pushed strongly by Sandy even though there was no job opening, in October, Fred came on a Tuesday, right after a game, to 30 Rock to meet. He was definitely impressive, and our hour-long conversation focused mostly on what it was like to work with the NFL, and the different challenges of producing games. The next day, a package arrived: Fred had sent a copy of his collection of production manuals—the notebooks he compiled every year that detailed how he covered his games, from camera assignments to framings to replay sequencing and much more. It was generous, and again, perusing the books, very impressive.

A few weeks later, Ken Schanzer and I arrived in Florida for an affiliate meeting when some news that we'd been tipped off about finally broke. ESPN was walking away from its coverage of the PGA Tour, and that meant a series of tournaments were now up for grabs. We'd been in touch with the PGA, and let them know our interest in picking up the rights to these events; they were attractive properties because Tiger Woods played in them every year, making them all but guaranteed to attract high ratings. Within less than an hour of the news breaking, Kenny spoke to his contacts at the PGA, and essentially locked up the rights to the events. And right there, I saw an opening for an audible to my plans, and called Tommy Roy to fill him in.

"So let me ask you a question," I said after I told him about the new tournaments. "Do you want to stay with golf and produce the extra events, or do you still want to do *Sunday Night Football*?"

Yes, the NFL was the NFL, but golf ran in Tommy's blood; his father had been a longtime club professional in Arizona, it had always been his dream to work in the sport, and he is the finest producer of golf on television that the business has ever known. He said he wanted to talk it over with his wife, but called me back within fifteen minutes to thank me and lock himself into golf.

Next, I called up Sandy.

"Do you think Fred would still be interested in producing *Sunday Night Football*?"

He wasn't just interested; he was thrilled.

Two weeks later, we were all in Baltimore—me, Tommy, Kenny, Cris, and Sandy, for a Ravens-Packers *Monday Night* game. ESPN's president, George Bodenheimer, had long ago offered me a standing invitation to observe their production, and this was the perfect time to take him up on it. We ducked into the truck in the second quarter, and I was struck by how calm and quiet it was. (In the years to come, I'd find that it wasn't *always* so calm and quiet.) In the front row during a time-out, Fred and Drew stood to greet us. We didn't stay long—I knew how much I hated interlopers in a truck and control room—and went back to our hotel. Not that I needed much confirmation, but I was feeling better than ever about what my gut was now telling me to do, and asked Sandy if he thought we could close a deal.

After the game, we invited Fred up to my suite, shook on the agreement, and then headed down to the lobby to celebrate. When Drew walked in a few moments later, Tommy was the first to greet him.

"It was great working with you," Drew said with a laugh to the producer who he'd never actually gotten to work with.

So if you're keeping score at home, now we had hired the producer, director, and analyst from ABC's *Monday Night Football* for Sunday nights. Only Al Michaels was left back at Disney, and he wasn't happy about it. In truth, it wasn't a good situation for anyone—Al wanted to keep working with Fred, Drew, and John, and ESPN was looking for a fresh start to their production. But the problem now was that the ink was barely dry on Al's new contract. Yes, both sides probably wanted the same thing, but with lawyers, agents, and PR people involved, it was a complicated predicament, and we weren't sure how it would play out. We had to start making contingency plans.

Fox and CBS had all their top play-by-play announcers locked up in contracts, and there weren't any options of young up-and-comers that I could put alongside John. So late that season, I quietly had Cris begin a crash course in learning how to be a play-by-play announcer. He thought I'd lost my mind when I told him my plan, but he was willing to try it. In Cincinnati for a series of games, Sean McManus, the head of CBS Sports, gave us access to their production feed, and Cris sat in a truck with his friend Merril Hoge, the ESPN announcer, and they practice-called the action. Then, in early January, we had a whole group fly out to Pleasanton, where at John's production facility we set up a mock broadcast booth and communications system on his soundstage, and put the live feed of a playoff game between the Patriots and Broncos on a big monitor for an experiment: Madden working with Collinsworth as his play-by-play announcer. Maybe having these two natural talents—even with one playing out of position—could actually work. Though it started off really rough, as the game got going, I felt like the lineup could work as a possibility; that the audience would enjoy these two football geniuses in conversation.

But sometime in the second half, my PR chief, Mike McCarley, pulled me aside. A reporter had called him requesting comment about a report that Disney had decided to let Al out of his new contract after all—he was back in play. On the plane on the way back east, I pulled Cris aside.

"I honestly think there's potential here," I said to him. "You'd have to work at it, but this could be something different. That said, I want to ask you something. If I told you that there was still a chance I could sign Al to do play-by-play, and you'd go back to the studio, what would you say?"

Cris didn't hesitate.

"Go get him, man!"

A few weeks later, we'd wrapped up negotiations with Al. ESPN did ask for a few trade-offs, including the opportunity to bid for the first few days of Ryder Cup coverage, and, in a twist that the press ended up focusing on, the rights to a little-known cartoon character called Oswald the Lucky Rabbit, which had been Walt Disney's first character, before he'd conceived of Mickey Mouse. It was the only character of Walt's that Disney didn't own—and lucky for us, the owner was Universal Studios, which the year before had become our corporate partner in a merger. When I called up my old friend Ron Meyer, running Universal, to ask if it was possible to give up the rights, he'd laughed and said absolutely—they'd been essentially lying dormant for decades, not making any money for the company. Again, the "trade" of Oswald for Al was really nothing at all, but if the press wanted to feast on it, that was fine with me.

The real headline was that our new show had the kind of superstar lineup— in the broadcast booth, the production truck, and the studio—that I'd fantasized about when I'd first started working up the idea for *Sunday Night Football*. Costas and Collinsworth teeing up the games for Madden and Michaels.

Now we needed the games to measure up.

The idea behind flexible scheduling was, of course, that the schedule wouldn't be locked in stone; the final six weeks of the season, we would be able to "flex" out of bad matchups and replace them with better games, more attractive to the audience. But that wasn't the whole story—I also wanted all seventeen of our games to be as strong as possible. And beginning months before the schedule even came out in our first season, 2006, I knew that my approach to dealing with the league on the issue had to be, in its own way, just as flexible.

This was a new circumstance for everyone—us, the NFL, and also the other networks. Fox and CBS had been longtime league partners, and to expect them to just give us all the best games for Sunday nights wasn't just unfair—it was misguided. They had protections in terms of limits on how many times we could have the defending Super Bowl champions in prime time (three), and they also had the opportunity, once the flexible portion of the schedule began, to block a number of games that they didn't want to give up. But beyond even that, going into that first season, and continuing beyond, my mindset was that if I was going to be able to influence the process at all, I needed to keep in mind the priorities of those other partners. I couldn't go into a meeting with the NFL with the best game of the week circled for seventeen weeks. That didn't make sense for anyone.

In this case, as I figured out the best way to go about things with the league, I had two relationships on my side. The first was with John Madden. John's role as a partner for me in the construction of *SNF* began with our very first meetings, when we talked about him coming aboard. As I laid out my vision to John, the most impressive element of our deal in his view was that we'd have a chance to have a say in the process of allocating which games went to prime time. "A seat at the table," as I called it. No network had ever had that before.

In the lead-up to that first season, as the television schedule was worked out, John and Fred and I pored over the matchups together, so I could present our preferences to the league.

"The games have to *sound* like *big* football games," was John's biggest mantra. "Never forget that." Green Bay versus Chicago. Dallas versus New York. Denver versus New England. These were matchups and traditional rivalries that evoked a feeling in fans that two major teams were playing, and the event wasn't something they wanted to miss.

That philosophy, as much as anything else, guided me in my meetings with the league—meetings that I very quickly began looking forward to because of who was on the other side of the table. Howard Katz had been hired as a production assistant at ABC Sports in 1971 when I was working as Roone's assistant. He'd later worked with Don Ohlmeyer in California before returning to ABC Sports, and eventually becoming the department's president. In 2003, he'd gone to work at NFL Films, where he ran the business side of the company alongside the legendary Steve Sabol. Then, just as we signed our deal for *SNF*, he got the call to come work at the league office and be the overseer of the television schedule.

From the start, Howard and I were on the same page about what the Sunday night package needed to be. He knew that I fully understood that NBC couldn't get every game we wanted. I also knew that it was most helpful to him if I didn't approach our conversations as negotiations, but rather just a running dialogue, bolstered by the most detailed and most realistic plans we could propose. The more prepared I was, the better. In some cases, John or Fred may have calculated that a player like Brett Favre was going to be likely on track to break a record in a given week, so we wanted the game. Being that specific with our ideas helped Howard, and shaped a running dialogue that in many ways went year-round. Howard and I hadn't spoken much in the years before he got the job, but as was the case with some longtime friends, we'd reconnected when he'd written me a letter after the plane crash. As we became business partners, our friendship quickly grew, and pretty soon, we were having dinner every Monday night at Isle of Capri, talking football, yes, but also life.

When the schedule was announced for our inaugural season, we couldn't have had a better matchup for our first game: it was the Colts and the Giants—the first time ever that Peyton and Eli Manning were matching up. The next week would be Washington and Dallas—a classic rivalry; and the week after that, Pat Bowlen's Denver Broncos and Robert Kraft's New England Patriots, a rematch of playoff rivals from the year before.

Getting the schedule set, of course, was just a slice of the preparation. A few years earlier, John Williams, the iconic composer, had called to tell me that CBS had asked him to compose a theme for their sports coverage, and he'd turned them down—feeling like NBC was his home after his Olympic theme had been part of our presentation for so long. Now I was thrilled to pick up the phone and ask him to compose another theme for us. We also needed a massive promotional campaign to get fans excited. Fred enlisted the pop star Pink to sing the show's original anthem, "Waiting All Day for Sunday Night," a takeoff on Joan Jett's "I Hate Myself for Loving You." Meanwhile, John Miller, NBC's marketing wizard, oversaw a million-dollar two-day shoot at Madden's facility with all our talent months before the season began. The day after the shoot, Mike McCarley, my young, bright PR chief, came to my office to give me the recap. He raved about how great it went, and how great it looked, but seemed to be holding something back as he related the story. Finally, when he was done, he paused, and then spoke again.

"The thing is, it was great," he said, "but on the plane ride home, I kind of had another idea. It just hit me, you know. I think we should be saying something definitive. A line like 'Sunday night is football night.'"

I looked at him for maybe a second and said, "Yup, you're right."

Sunday night football had really had no meaning to fans for years. Now we had to change that—and this was the perfect tagline.

Back up went the sets, and we filmed for another day to get our guys to deliver the new addition to our campaign. The reshoot would pay for itself down the line. Everything had to be as perfect as possible.

The Manning Bowl, as it was called, was an exciting game—Peyton got the best of his little brother, with the Colts winning, 26–21, the first victory of what would be a Super Bowl championship season for Peyton and his coach, Tony Dungy. But in a lot of ways, the game was just the icing on a rollout that revealed the blueprint of how *Sunday Night Football* could be successful.

Because it wasn't just ESPN and sports shows that were focusing on the matchup of the Mannings. It was also the *Today* show, through a feature that our production team put together interviewing Archie and Olivia Manning, Peyton and Eli's famous parents, that aired the Friday before the game in the show's most-watched 8:00 a.m. hour. What mother could sit and watch that and not empathize with Olivia when she talked about being torn over who to root for?

That story line remained the center of our pregame show, *Football Night in America*, and of course throughout the broadcast of the game, with Fred and Drew repeatedly cutting to the suite where Archie and Olivia were sitting, and John hitting the story line again and again—particularly focusing on Olivia, and what it was like for the mom to watch her sons. It was like John had a sixth sense for what the audience—men and women—would be keying in on. And that night was the start of a trend for *SNF*—that our audience wasn't just men who'd been watching football all day but women who joined them, caught up in the storytelling of our presentation, whatever it was. Every week from then on out, from everything from features about players to cooking segments, *Today*, *Weekend Today*, and plenty of other NBC programs would focus on football and the *SNF* story line of the week to keep interest high in the game for potential fans from all over the demographic map. As much as the Olympics, *Sunday Night Football* became part of NBC's DNA, and its very identity as a network.

Maybe my favorite instance of that approach came in 2009, when the second week of the season featured the first game ever in Jerry Jones's brand-new Cowboys Stadium. Construction had begun on the site in the spring of 2006—before our first season—and I'll never forget flying down to Dallas to see Jerry, and him being so excited to show me the site where construction had just begun. In his Cadillac, he'd insisted on personally driving me from his office to a tour of the stadium—and then had to call his assistant with a laugh when we got lost trying to find it.

Three years later, as the opening finally approached, I went to Jerry with an idea. Before the first game, we would blow out our coverage of the new stadium, with even *Today* coming on the air that Friday morning from Dallas, giving our audience a tour of the place and mounting the anticipation for the Sunday night game. The stadium was every bit the marvel that Jones wanted it to be, complete with the largest high-definition screen in the world at the time hanging above the field. Fascination with it was high, and Jerry loved what we did showing off his building on TV. The only thing that went wrong, at least to Jerry, was that the Cowboys lost the game in a thriller to the Giants, 33–31.

That kind of commitment got the word out to all the other teams and their owners what kind of partner we could be. And back at league headquarters, we couldn't have asked for more support, in large part thanks to a new man in charge. A few weeks before our first season on the air, Roger Goodell had been elected to succeed Paul Tagliabue as the new NFL commissioner. His tenure had officially begun right before week 1; we'd have our rookie seasons together. It couldn't have been more fitting, or more rewarding, to work even more closely with such a longtime friend. Roger was invested in our success, and would stay deeply involved in the conversations I had with Howard as we figured out flex games that season, and in all the seasons to come.

But for all the excitement of the business side of the deal, it was secondary to the experience of being a part of it all every Sunday night.

———

As we'd gotten closer to our debut season, I'd made a decision: I was going to go to every game. And not just show up ceremoniously—I was going to be there, alongside Al and John, Fred and Drew, every week, from Thursday through Sunday night. It wasn't something the head of a network sports department had ever done before—showing up for the home team's Friday practice, for the meetings that broadcasters had with coaches and players, and for all the production meetings behind the scenes. Almost forty years earlier, I'd realized the value of just "being there" when I stayed late in the ABC Sports offices. Now going to games every week was another example of the same ethos.

For starters, being there was the best way to show the league how committed we were to our coverage. At one point that first season, John walked over to me at a practice and pointed out a team owner standing on the sideline.

"You don't get it," he said. "These guys never used to come to practice. They're only showing up because they know you're showing up."

Even behind the scenes, they could see that we were raising our game, treating every week as our own mini Super Bowl. So they felt compelled to step up as well.

The same, even more impactfully, went for players and coaches. Being there, going to the games, was the only way to really get to know the league. I was almost sixty, but truthfully, I was just as big a fan as I'd been when I was a little kid. It was still a thrill to talk to the biggest stars and the best coaches. And it was rewarding to discover how many fantastic human beings there were among them. One week, I got to Baltimore before the rest of the crew, and just walked into the Ravens facility by myself, soon finding my way to head coach John Harbaugh's office. Two days before game night, he welcomed me inside and started peppering me with questions about the NBA on NBC, the Olympics, *Saturday Night Live*, and more. I went right back, asking about his dad and his brother and growing up in a coaching family. It was a fantastic conversation with a terrific man.

The last game of our first season on the air was a New Year's Eve matchup in Chicago—the Packers and the Bears. Week 17 was always an automatic "flex" game—to ensure the last Sunday night of the season was meaningful—and we'd gotten the ultimate "football game that sounded like a football game" to boot. It was a rainy, cold weekend, and on Saturday afternoon, John, Al, Fred, Drew, and I all left our hotel to go across the street for our meetings with the Packers in their hotel. We'd sit in a conference room, and players and coaches would come in for what were essentially interview sessions on background to give us insight into the game, and talk about their own personal stories.

Brett Favre was, of course, the biggest star on the Packers, and for a half hour, he talked openly with John—one of his biggest admirers—about the game and the season. Then, afterward, he looked over at me.

"Well," he said. "How did I do?"

"What do you mean?" I replied.

"I mean, if the boss is here, that means you're auditioning me to be an announcer, right?"

Before I could speak, John jumped in.

"Brett, no! Dick comes to all of these. He's come to every one of them this season. This is how we do things over here. The boss wants to know everything. And he does."

I couldn't have gotten a more resounding endorsement. All through that season and the years to follow, to players like Brett, to coaches, to general managers and owners as well, there was no bigger star of our operation behind the scenes than John Madden. People would say things to John that they wouldn't tell anyone else; they'd want his opinions on their play, their game plans, their prospects. Until the day he passed away in late 2021, throughout the league, John was singularly beloved and admired, respected and listened to—still deeply connected to the game, even in retirement. The outpouring of grief and appreciation that followed his death was overwhelming. To millions of fans, he was the embodiment of everything great about the NFL—the passion it stokes in people, the significance it's had on American culture, the joy it's brought.

Meanwhile, for those of us who were blessed enough to get to call John our friend, we knew him as our favorite uncle, our best college professor, and the smartest, most influential guy in every room we ever shared with him. In his years on *Sunday Night Football*, every week started the same on Thursdays. Everyone would fly in, except for John, who, with his flying phobia, of course traveled in his luxury bus. Thursday night dinners would be three-hour Madden storytelling bonanzas, always at one of the nicest steakhouses in the city, at a big round table with Fred, Drew, the peerless do-everything-magician production coordinator Vinny Rao, John's close friend and traveling mate nicknamed "Junk," and also, more often than not, one more guest: Susan.

From Saturday Night to Sunday Night

After all the years of keeping television and family separate, with the children out of the house, and us relying on one another more than ever to grapple with the emotions of the loss of Teddy, *SNF* became the show that switched it up. Susan loved traveling to different cities every week, she loved football, and she loved hanging out with John (even though he would never let her order the petite filet at dinner—it was always full filet or bust). And as an unexpected coda, before dinner sometimes, when she'd come to a team facility to meet up with us, there were players who would stop her in the hallways with a strange look.

"I know you from somewhere," they'd say. "Where do I know you from?"

The answer was that fifteen or twenty years earlier, as kids, they had watched *Kate & Allie* growing up. Many of them shared that they'd had single moms who would put the show on in their house to show their sons that there were other family units like theirs out there.

So every week was a football adventure somewhere in America, and each one ended in the same place: our production truck on Sunday night, where in my opinion, the finest television producer and director in football history went to work. The role that Fred Gaudelli and Drew Esocoff have played in entertaining millions and millions of Americans over the last few decades is immeasurable. My instinct, as I told you, was not to hire Fred, but stick with what I knew in Tommy Roy. Instead, thanks in large part to the initiative that Sandy Montag took, I ended up with Tommy—the greatest golf producer in TV history—doing what he loved, and Fred doing the same on Sunday nights.

As soon as I began working with them, I realized there was no great secret to what made Fred and Drew so great. It was like anything else—they simply worked incredibly hard, and demanded the most of themselves and their crews. Fred's preparation was the stuff of legend, and was part of why John Madden fell in love with him. Production meetings were hours-long trips through teams' playbooks; and for Super Bowls, Fred pioneered the idea of bringing in local high school teams to come on the field and run each team's specific signature plays so his camera crews could practice their coverage.

Drew was similarly prepared, but also the yin to Fred's intense yang; if you walked into a trailer near the production truck a few hours before the game, the figure who looked more relaxed than anyone else in the compound was Drew. He was relaxed, I discovered, because he knew he was prepared, and ready for whatever the game might present. And while the pair's personalities might have been a bit different, ultimately, they understood the biggest key to producing a football game, which you might note is also the biggest key to producing anything in sports: telling a story. From that first season, that sense of story was always the biggest thing about what I felt set our broadcasts apart. Whether it was something off the field, like a player's life story, or a narrative like an offensive line play, even the most casual fans could watch *Sunday Night Football* and be seized by the story that Fred and Drew and Al and John were telling.

Every week, sitting behind them in the production truck, I felt like I had a front-row seat to two virtuoso orchestra conductors. Just like the Olympic control room, we treated the truck as a sanctuary; only essential personnel were allowed inside. Fred and Drew had told me the horror story of an ABC executive who once brought his young son into a truck during a game, and the kid wandering up to the front deck and coming within inches of pressing buttons that would have taken them off the air. There would be no such visitor tours on *Sunday Night Football*. As for my role, I mostly just watched the monitors, trying to keep an eye on what might be coming five, ten, or fifteen minutes down the line. But essentially without fail, Fred was prepared for any contingency, and Drew was ready for whatever surprises might crop up. And as you might imagine, the unheralded team around them—editors, producers, camerapersons, researchers, and more—were an all-star group of performers in their own right.

All those ingredients—the flexible scheduling, the promotional muscle, the best talent and production team in the business—combined to do exactly what all of us at NBC and the NFL were aiming for when we had begun discussing the show in 2004: transform football in prime time. Early in that first season, it was clear that fans were not just willing to watch a third game on Sunday—they were excited to do it. With all due respect to our friends at ESPN, Sunday night became football night, and has remained so ever since. It had become exactly what I dreamed *Sunday Night Football* could be. Our first season averaged over a million viewers more per week than *Monday Night* had, and the most in prime-time football since 2000. To the press, I had predicted that we'd be in the top ten or twelve in the year-end ratings—we ended up eleventh, which made it NBC's highest-rated show. But it was just the start of steady momentum for the series. The next year, we were tenth, then eighth, then fifth, then fourth, and in the final year of that first contract, *SNF* became, improbably, the number one show in all of prime-time television—the first and only time a sports show has achieved that distinction. Somehow, we'd exceeded our expectations. We'd proven that I'd been right to dream about transforming the NFL on television, and completely changed the narrative about football in prime time.

And while lifting ratings on Sunday night did what Jeff Zucker and I had hoped for NBC in prime time, it also was a catalyst for the company beyond that. Broadly speaking, the deals the NFL had with GE netted millions for the company in security and equipment and technology contracts. The NFL even used the GE learning center for important off-site executive meetings; the deal between the Jets and Giants owners over sharing what would become MetLife Stadium was ironed out there.

It was great to help the company in that way, but also great to see the results of the deal much closer to home. The return of football gave our sports department a new signature series to be proud of, after a few years of contraction. Our staff knew that *Sunday Night Football*, along with the Olympic Games, were our two major contributions to the identity of NBC. And with regard to the Olympics, two years after the premiere of *SNF*, the most significant installment of the Games maybe ever was set to take hold of the world's consciousness. Globally, it would be the most significant sports event in decades. Not to mention a venue for one of the most incredible athletes I've ever seen to pull off an achievement that still gives me goose bumps to think about.

CHAPTER 29

Olympic Diplomacy

On Saturday, August 9, 2008, in the National Aquatics Center in Beijing, China, a stunning new venue better known as "The Water Cube," Michael Phelps walked onto the pool deck for his first race of the Olympics. At age twenty-three, this was Michael's third trip to the Olympic stage, and he'd come to it set on accomplishing what I still think is the most ambitious challenge by an Olympic athlete in history. It was a challenge that would rivet tens of millions of Americans watching back home over the next several nights to come, and the central attraction of the most fascinating, exciting, and significant Olympics that I'd been a part of, dating back to my days at ABC. But the story of those Games, and their success on television, began long, long before the Opening Ceremony torch was lit at the "Bird's Nest" stadium.

Really, the tale of the Beijing Games has to begin in Moscow, of all places, a little more than seven years prior, in the middle of July of 2001. That was when the IOC held what was officially known as its 112th session, one with a number of important items on the agenda. The first, and most anticipated around the world, was determining where the Games of the XXIX Olympiad, then seven years away, would be held. Five cities were bidding to be host: Beijing, Toronto, Paris, Istanbul, and Osaka, Japan, and the sense was Beijing and Toronto were the top candidates among voters to win. As with all IOC sessions, I'd be flying in to represent our company as an observer; the sessions were a gathering of IOC members from all over the world, and there would be any number of meetings and opportunities to connect with different figures of significance. But when I left New York on the night of July 11, set to fly to Paris and then on to Moscow, there was a measure of more urgency than usual.

A few weeks earlier, I'd gotten a call from Jay Kriegel, an old friend and long-time New York lawyer and political adviser who'd done consulting work in the national and international media space over the years. Jay had taken a business trip to China, where he'd found himself in a meeting at the mayor's office in Beijing and learned something he thought I should know. As the Chinese were navigating the bid process, he told me, they had the perception that NBC didn't want Beijing to get the Games; that our company preferred Toronto as the candidate city, and that using our sway as the TV rights holder in the world's most important market, we were lobbying IOC members to vote that way.

There were a number of problems with this. For starters, it was certainly no good for one of the leading contenders for the bid to think that we, as a broadcast partner, were against them winning. But beyond that, the rumor wasn't the least bit true. First, while we did pay hundreds of millions of dollars in rights fees, that didn't get us a seat at the table for the host city bidding process; its hundreds of members from around the world weren't going to listen to us when it came down to making their decisions. And even if we had ever tried to influence the process, we would never risk the exact scenario that was potentially playing out—that a bid city would get word of it. Anyone who understood managing relationships would understand that wasn't the way to go about our business. Then, the last point was the most crucial to communicate to the Chinese: we actually didn't prefer Toronto. Yes, there might be some observers who would think that having the Games in North America, in the eastern time zone, would allow for live coverage of events just like Atlanta had. But for all the benefits that would bring, I also knew that for General Electric—really paying the bills as our parent company—the opportunity to be part of such a huge event in the capital city of a huge emerging market like China would be even more attractive.

The only other possible explanation that I could think of went back to Sydney the year prior, when I'd spoken to Juan Antonio Samaranch about the Chinese bid, and told him that the only thing that concerned me was that their plan was to hold the Games in September of 2008. A huge reason the ratings for the Sydney

Games were off was because the U.S. pro and college football seasons had already started; and in Europe, ratings were affected by their football season—i.e., soccer—having begun as well. So, figuring it would benefit European rights holders as well as us, I'd suggested to Juan Antonio that he talk to the Chinese about moving their proposal to August. And they'd soon revised their plans to do just that. Yet, maybe signals had gotten crossed somewhere in the meantime. Which meant it was on me to remedy the relationship as soon as possible, and certainly before the 2008 host city was decided.

So, with some behind-the-scenes work from our ace Olympic insider Alex Gilady, I'd secured a meeting with the leader of the Chinese delegation the night before the vote. The problem was, my flight was delayed in Paris several hours, and I only got to Moscow a little before 9:00 p.m. I went over to the hotel as fast as I could, checked in, and by ten thirty, I found myself alone in a small hotel room with Liu Qi, the mayor of Beijing, a translator, and his two security guards.

Liu had been put in charge of the Olympic bid committee by the Chinese government, and would go on to be the president of their organizing committee. The hotel we were all staying in for the IOC session was certainly nice, but the rooms were small; this was no spacious suite. So with nowhere else really to go, I sat down on one of the twin beds in the room, with Liu sitting in a chair at the foot of the bed, and a translator next to him. One security guard stood by the door, the other was by the window. Outside, we could see the lights of the Kremlin. As Liu and I spoke, we drank hot, clear tea someone had ordered from room service.

My message was simple—in part because the language barrier necessitated it, and also because the situation called for it. NBC, I told him, not only never tried to interfere with or lobby the process, but as we anticipated the vote the next day from the sidelines, we actually would be thrilled if Beijing won the bid. To make the meeting even more surreal, as we spoke, our area of the city had a power outage. Everywhere we looked out the window, lights were out. But by that point, we'd established enough of a rapport that it didn't really deter us, and sitting there in the dark, we reached what seemed like an amicable understanding. NBC had no influence in the bid, had no interest in influencing the bid, and for GE, one of the world's most powerful and successful companies, getting a foothold in this massive emerging international market would be enthusiastically embraced.

I thanked Mr. Liu, and went downstairs, where Alex, Randy Falco, and a few others from our team were eagerly awaiting a recap. I told them that I felt like the meeting had gone well, and we resolved to wait for the next day to see just how relevant the whole issue was. At two thirty the following afternoon, after I'd slept off the jet lag in the morning, our team went to observe the voting in a large auditorium attached to the hotel. We sat in the back while each of the five cities went through their presentations, and then, the voting began, every member holding a small apparatus in their hand that allowed them to register their choice electronically. The process went quickly; each round, the city with the lowest vote total would be eliminated until one city had a majority of the vote. Well, after the first round, Beijing was impressively close to that majority, with forty-four votes, and Osaka eliminated. Then, when voters punched in for a second round, the final results were announced. The Games of the XXIX Olympiad were awarded to the Chinese.

It was a historic moment for sure—the Chinese had long had a fraught history with the Olympic movement. Due to the long-running conflict between China and Taiwan, and specifically its objection to Taiwan competing independently, China had boycotted the Games for three decades before coming to a resolution of the issue and returning in 1984 in Los Angeles. Then, as the nation began to open up its economy, and underwent skyrocketing growth in the 1990s, hosting an Olympics had become an objective that served as a way to proclaim its arrival on the world stage as a global power. Beijing's first Olympic bid, for the 2000 Games, had fallen short, but now, less than a year after those Sydney Games, the overwhelming victory set the stage for a seminal event seven years down the road.

There was a lot to digest, and no small measure of controversy ahead with regards to China's bid. Though the climate wasn't nearly as toxic then as it is now between the U.S. and China, I was quite aware of our country's questions about China's human rights record and its ultimate objectives as a world power. But in that moment, watching the Chinese delegation happily celebrate their win wildly onstage, the idealism of the Olympic movement—the idea that a sporting event could actually bring the world closer together—felt laid bare for everyone to see. As I made my way down to the front of the auditorium to talk to some members I hadn't seen yet on my visit, I was able to make eye contact with Liu Qi. With a giant grin on his face, he came toward me, bounded down the few steps of the stage, and shook my hand excitedly, even enveloping me in a half embrace.

It was going to be a fascinating seven years of anticipation. And I was already thinking about the best ways to get our country just as excited about it as me.

Being that the Beijing vote was, as I've said, less than a year after the Sydney Games, the idea of another Olympics taking place far from U.S. shores—and thus with a massive time difference—was definitely on my mind as China got the Games. The problem with the time difference, as Australia had of course shown, was that it made it impossible to show the premier sports, typically taking place at night in an Olympic city, live in prime time back home. I firmly believed, at least in 2001, that live coverage in prime time wasn't essential to a successful Olympics on television—great stories were great stories. But obviously being live helped, and helped a lot. And as I thought about it a bit more, it began to dawn on me that with some creativity, and some help from our partners at the top of the IOC, maybe we could find a solution to the time zone problem.

As far as the leadership of the IOC went, there was news on that front just a few days after Beijing's selection as the committee's meetings continued to play out in Moscow. After twenty-one years atop the organization, Juan Antonio Samaranch was finally retiring, and the intrigue over who would take his place was definitely palpable. When Juan Antonio had taken the job, the Olympic committee was near bankruptcy and plagued by boycotts, the entire movement in danger of falling apart. Now, it was a multibillion-dollar organization, and though the fallout of the Salt Lake City bid scandal was still to be dealt with, the future of the Olympics looked bright, with its financial future assured—largely, I might add, by our American television deals. There were three leading contenders for the president's job: Dick Pound, the Canadian head of the IOC's broadcasting committee who we'd worked closely with for years; Kim Un Yong of South Korea, another longtime IOC member; and Jacques Rogge, a former gold medal–winning Olympic sailor from Belgium who was now a doctor and best known at the IOC for his work as a point person for host cities, including Sydney. I knew Pound the best, though I'd also met Rogge several times and respected him.

Given that this was the first presidential election at an IOC session in more than two decades, the intrigue over the election dominated the three days between the Beijing vote and the presidential vote. There was plenty for our NBC crew to do in the meantime; while we snuck in a tour of the Kremlin, our schedule also included meetings with senior representatives of the upcoming Athens and Torino Games, and, the night before the vote for president, a dinner honoring Juan Antonio in a massive venue next to the Kremlin. At the cocktail hour, with about thirty minutes notice, an IOC representative approached me and told me that Samaranch had requested that I give the only speech of the evening, to say a few words about him. I was happy to speak to the room about our shared history together; and the fact that the honor wasn't going to someone from Coca-Cola or Visa, or even in the IOC, was just one more sign of the depth of our partnership. A relationship that had started with a warning that dinner could last only ninety minutes was culminating with me speaking about my friend at a dinner for 2,500 people. I focused my remarks on the ever-youthful energy of a man who, even past eighty years of age, maintained the same passion for his work as ever.

Early the next morning, the voting went in fashion similar to the bid city balloting—it took just two rounds to elect Jacques Rogge as the new IOC president. I got a chance to briefly congratulate him at a press conference that afternoon, and then left Alex Gilady, still the insider of insiders, to try to arrange what I wanted to do next. Knowing from Mitt Romney that Rogge would soon be coming to the United States for his first inspection of the setup for the Salt Lake Games that coming February, my proposal was for him to make a one-night stop at our summer home in Martha's Vineyard. It could be a nice way to get acquainted, and maybe the opportunity for the former Olympic sailor to get out on the bay off Chappaquiddick would be an alluring enticement. (And, yes, my lifelong aversion to boats made that last idea nauseating to me—that's how much I wanted to make the right impression.) Sure enough, Rogge agreed.

And so it was that three weeks later, early on a Tuesday evening at the small airport on Martha's Vineyard, I met the new president of the IOC when his flight landed, along with Alex and a Rogge aide. We went back to our house, and all enjoyed some wine on the porch, talking mostly about the Salt Lake Games. Then, early the next morning, Jacques and I headed over to the Charlotte Inn, one of the best restaurants and places to stay on the island, to talk some and get to know each other some more. Observing him from a distance over the years, my sense was that he was an honest man, and certainly well-versed through experience in the ins and outs of setting up a Games. Now, as it was time to start a relationship as partners, I was happy to learn he was exactly what I thought he was, mild-mannered but clearly sharp, and aware of the challenges he was taking up in his new job.

After breakfast, we walked along the water, and I brought up the topic I'd been waiting to broach for months. We hadn't had long to build a connection, but I knew face-to-face was really the only way to bring this up.

"However long we work together as partners," I said to him, "I'm going to promise—I'm only going to put to you this one request. One big thing I'm asking for, and I promise, it will be the only ask of its sort."

He nodded, curious.

"In Beijing, right now, it's nighttime—they're twelve hours ahead of us here on the East Coast. That means that tonight, at, say, ten p.m. here on Martha's Vineyard, it'll be ten a.m. tomorrow morning in China. What we at NBC would like to ask is that swimming—as you know, the event that means the most to us—be held in the morning in Beijing, so we can air the races live in prime time back home."

It was a big ask, I knew, but not an impossible one. International swimming competitions always have morning and evening sessions; typically, the qualifying heats are held in the morning, with semifinals and finals held at night. This would merely be flipping the schedule, to put the finals—when the medals were awarded—in the morning. It wouldn't be typical, but it wouldn't be totally impractical; in fact, it had previously been done in some international meets in South America.

Rogge nodded as I laid it out for him; he knew everything I was saying was true. Asking the athletes to compete in the morning wasn't a totally foreign concept. The bigger issue was what it meant for other countries—and their TV broadcasters. They wouldn't benefit in the same way. None of them, however, made as much of a commitment to the Games and the Olympic movement as NBC. Rogge knew that, he knew how important it was for us to have strong programming and high ratings in prime time, and he understood how much of an extra boost live competition could give us. After I laid everything out to him, Jacques was clear in his response—he would do what he could to make it happen. He couldn't promise success, but he could promise to do his best.

When we got back to the house, there was one more activity on the agenda— the trip I'd promised him out on the water. We took a group of people, including

Susan and Alex, on Susan's friend Sharon's boat. With Sharon's twelve-year-old son piloting the boat for what I'd learn years later was the first time, Jacques was a patient guest, particularly when the weather didn't cooperate, with virtually no wind on the bay. In the end, the old Olympic sailor was able to give us a lesson in resourcefulness, showing us that it was possible, at least a bit, to sail without wind. (Which, by the way, I preferred much to the seasickness I'd get on a normal breezy day.)

When we got back to land, I drove Rogge to the airport so he could head out on the next leg of his trip, to Salt Lake City. It was August 8, 2001. Exactly seven years to the day until the Opening Ceremony of the Beijing Games.

Over the next year or two, I had plenty to talk about with Rogge as we moved from Salt Lake onto Athens and beyond. Keeping Beijing in the back of my mind, my confidence in the pledge he had made to me on the Vineyard remained high, and the next time we spoke about it, the only concern he expressed was actually not about any issues internationally, but rather in the United States. If he was going to make this happen on our behalf, he said, by working with FINA, the international swimming federation, and the Beijing Organizing Committee, the one thing he couldn't afford would be for any dissenting voices in the U.S. swimming community. He wanted to make sure there wouldn't be an outcry by American coaches, some of the most powerful voices in the sport, over having morning finals. He could deal with other big countries where swimming was popular, namely Australia; Channel 7 there had just enjoyed an Olympics where virtually everything they wanted was live in prime time. But he couldn't have Americans objecting to a maneuver engineered by American television.

To keep things simple, I went right to the top, calling Chuck Wielgus, the top executive for USA Swimming, based in Colorado Springs. I didn't know Chuck well, but knew he was a smart, affable guy, and when I laid out my plan for him, he couldn't have been more excited. He understood the potential of what it would mean for American swimming—if the country could watch the medal races live, they'd be more enthralled by what they saw. After a disappointing showing in Sydney, the next generation of talent was promising hope for a turnaround, and in Wielgus's eyes, the more attention that was paid to that potential success, the better it was.

The headliner of all that American talent, of course, turned out to be more compelling than I would have even dared imagine: the sensational Michael Phelps, who originally announced himself as swimming's next superstar at the 2003 World Championships, breaking five world records, before winning those incredible eight Olympic medals the next year in Athens. Michael's emergence not just as a headliner but as a star who would be in the water virtually every night, his story unfolding as the first week of the Games went on, was unprecedented in Olympic competition, and a television programmer's dream—driving our ratings success even with a tape delay. Plus, on a personal level, it was great getting to know him when he visited our compound in the broadcast center afterward.

A few months after those Olympics, just about two weeks before the crash, I saw Michael in New York, for the inaugural Golden Goggle Awards, an awards show put on by Chuck Wielgus and USA Swimming. Just a few weeks prior to the ceremony, Michael had been arrested for drunk driving near his home in Maryland. He took the occasion of receiving one of his awards that night to apologize to everyone in attendance. I also was presented an award that night—the event's Impact Award, for raising swimming's awareness—and in my remarks, I looked right at Michael and did everything I could to let him know that, despite his mistake, we were still in his corner.

"There was no American in Greece who we as a country had more reason to be proud of than Michael Phelps," I said. "There's great cynicism in our country about people who have big goals. In Athens, Michael was a winner not only in the pool but in life, and he still is today."

I was definitely emotional up on the stage that night; I was really upset at the fact that, after all Michael had done to serve as the face of the American team, it felt like that team—and its community—had abandoned him, remaining silent in the wake of the news. I was speaking directly to the assembled crowd, letting them know in no uncertain terms that I hoped they embraced him more after his mistake, and that I honored his friendship. As I spoke, with Michael and his mother sitting directly in front of me, thirty feet away, I could see tears flowing down Debbie Phelps's cheeks.

The next time I saw him would be a month later—in St. Anthony's church in Litchfield, when he and his mother flew up for Teddy's funeral, and they were the first people I laid eyes on as I was wheeled on the hospital gurney up the center aisle. I'd later find out they'd been so nervous about finding the church after flying up from Baltimore that they'd arrived more than two hours early.

Bookending my recovery, my first full day back in the office the following April—who was my first meeting with? None other than Michael and Debbie Phelps.

"We wanted to be here to see you," Michael said. "We wanted to be here for you on your first morning back."

We did a little more crying, and a little more reminiscing about Teddy, and then, I was happy to tell them, I had some news.

Swearing them to secrecy, I told them for the first time about the plan for Beijing. This time, all of his races would be unfolding live on television back home in prime time. As soon as I told him, Michael's eyes absolutely lit up. He understood the power that would have on the drama of his pursuit, and was all for it.

"My only real goal in all of this," he told me, "is to leave the sport bigger and better than I was lucky enough to find it."

There was zero trepidation about the traditional schedule being flipped and swimming for medals in the mornings. If anything, Michael walked out of my office that day hungrier to train for an Olympics still more than three years away; hungrier than ever to succeed. He didn't say it that day, but it wasn't hard to read his mind: in Beijing, he'd be going for not just eight medals again—but eight gold medals.

From the day that the 2008 Games were awarded to Beijing, it was clear that the diplomatic dance surrounding this Olympics was going to be as complex as any I'd been involved in. Every Olympics we'd broadcast had its own challenges in terms of engaging with the host nation and organizing committee; even Atlanta and Salt Lake, as domestic Olympics, had, as I've described, their own complications. Athens in 2004 was a different story; with all the concerns about readiness, some of them merited, I tried to make sure NBC did whatever we could to help and advise the organizing committee, and the president of the committee, Gianna Angelopoulos, became a trusted partner. Regardless of what the media said in the run-up to the Games about preparation and security issues—and the media surely has a predilection for predictions of doom when it comes to the Olympics—Gianna was a terrific leader, and those Games were a success because of her.

With Beijing, the concerns were different. This was China, a mysterious, far-off locale to much of the world. It's hard to remember now, with so much attention focused on our adversarial differences, but as 2008 approached, China had a real innate appeal to the curious American audience. And yet, the year leading up to the Games was filled with all kinds of land mines that led me to think, several months out, that for all my optimism for their possibilities, the Olympics would lose us money. The economy took a downturn, with the beginnings of the financial crisis, and advertisers were cutting budgets, putting our sales team way behind where they should have been. Add to that the major concerns even then from Americans about China's government, its approach toward human rights, and the various disputes with which it was engaged—and controversy began to bubble up. The torch relay going around the world had been met with protests starting in Europe, and in the U.S., even prominent politicians had begun raising the specter of a potential American boycott. Even if that was never going to happen, it wasn't something we wanted to hear.

In the spring of that year, the Chinese Congress met and elected a new vice president of the country, a man named Xi Jinping. The election made Xi the heir apparent to become the president of China, but more immediately, the appointment meant he'd be overseeing the final preparations for the Games. Soon after the news was announced, his office reached out to me to schedule a meeting. No one on the world stage had met with Xi; I would essentially be the first foreigner to connect with him. We set up a visit to Beijing in April.

As it happened, a few years before, my head of PR, Kevin "Sully" Sullivan, had left NBC to take an amazing opportunity at the White House to work for the Bush administration. Mike McCarley, Sully's former deputy who'd replaced him, was still close with his old boss, and mentioned to him after Xi reached out that I'd be going to meet with him. When Sully mentioned it to the president, with whom I had a friendly acquaintance dating all the way back to our college days, it was determined that I'd carry a letter from President Bush to China to hand to Xi Jinping. The letter became an essential piece of my mission—as it stated not only that the United States had no intention of boycotting the Olympics but the president also reaffirmed that he fully intended to be in the stadium for the Opening Ceremony in August.

I got to Beijing on April 21, meeting Alex Gilady at the airport, and soon after took a walk with him in cool, rainy weather to discuss all the different things I needed to accomplish on the visit. As we walked, I couldn't help reflecting on my first visit to Beijing, eighteen years earlier, in 1990. That trip was truly a journey to what might as well have been a whole different world. It was as if everything was built to fade into a larger background; there were tall white walls everywhere, blocking the view from the road in from the airport. Then in downtown Beijing, virtually everyone seemed to be on a bicycle, and wearing the traditional Mao tunic suits. Now, all these years later, walking with Alex, everywhere I looked was massive change: the now-visible streets dotted with different businesses, from clothing shops to chain stores to car dealerships for Rolls-Royces, Bentleys, and Maseratis. The people, meanwhile, were all wearing different, colorful clothing, a stark contrast from the drab suits of the earlier era. China, it struck me, was a fundamentally singular place now, still apart from the rest of the world, but also poised to become a global economic power.

It would be a busy and productive three days in Beijing. There would be several meetings with the members of our NBC team already on the ground, to discuss everything from visa and customs issues for our several hundred employees, to finding the best vantage points for our cameras. I also toured the IBC and the National Stadium, construction of which had been completed. Already, it was being called the "Bird's Nest" for its striking design of intersecting bars all throughout, and it was among the most impressive Olympic venues I'd ever seen— as much a sculpture as it was a stadium. And there was also a great meeting with Ma Guoli, an engaging man who was the head of the "host broadcaster"; that is, the host country's television services that provided the world feed coverage to the rest of the globe. Mr. Ma, as we called him, had become a trusted collaborator for our production team on the ground, and was playing a central role in our ongoing efforts to get permission to film in some historic areas as part of our production. As Mr. Ma and I walked together through the streets of Beijing, I tried to get as much insight as I could on the man I was meeting with the next day, anything that might make our interaction easier. Ma's advice, ultimately, was just to trust my experience, and remember that Xi was the one who'd actually asked for the meeting.

For all the explosive growth their nation had undergone, the Chinese had never hosted an event like this, with so many people—including twenty-five thousand journalists—coming from all over the world. They were looking for whatever counsel they could get.

On the afternoon of Wednesday the twenty-third, the final day of my trip, I went over with Alex and Gary Zenkel, another of our top executives, to meet with Xi at the Great Hall of the People on the edge of Tiananmen Square. Walking into a large office named for Zhou Enlai, China's famous former premier, we were introduced, and sat side by side. Off to his left were four important leading Olympic officials I knew already, including my old friend from Moscow seven years earlier, Liu Qi. To my right were Alex and Gary. As the meeting started, I pulled out the letter from my coat pocket and handed it to him. A translator read it aloud in Mandarin, and he certainly seemed to appreciate the message, which set an agreeable tone for the rest of the meeting. There was no sense of hostility or tension. The main reason he'd asked to meet with me, it seemed, was because I'd been identified as a central figure with the Olympics, and it made sense to connect. Even across the world, in what felt in a lot of ways like another world, relationships still mattered.

As we spoke, and discussed different challenges of hosting a Games, my biggest message was some media advice. Pointing to the aides seated next to him, I told him I thought the most important move he could make was to as soon as possible appoint one of them to be the designated liaison to the world press. The best determining factor, I said, might well be which of his deputies spoke English the best; so much of the Olympic world knew the language, making communication simplest. The value of a spokesman was that if any controversy or crisis arose, even a small one, the organizing committee would be in position to offer its public statements efficiently and in an organized manner. As an example, however harrowing it was, I offered the story of the Atlanta bombing tragedy; the organizers had quickly determined that the Centennial Park bombing wouldn't derail those Games, and by the morning, the world knew that they would continue. Xi seemed to appreciate the advice; he clearly wanted to make a good impression on outsiders for China's big global coming-out moment.

When we returned to the States, we passed along the message to President Bush that Xi had enthusiastically received the letter. The clock was ticking until we were all together in Beijing on the eighth of August.

CHAPTER 30

Keeping America Awake

For all the many moving parts of the lead-up to the Beijing Games, one source of support that I was able to count on at every turn was the figure with perhaps more pressure on him than anyone else involved with those Olympics. But whenever we needed Michael Phelps, he was there—from the "upfront" sales presentation for advertisers we held in the spring of 2007, to the one-year-out commemoration a few months later in August, when he traveled to Beijing to appear on the *Today* show and film some spots with our marketing team. Even if he didn't like talking about it publicly, Michael was singularly focused on winning eight gold medals, which would break the record of seven that Mark Spitz had set in Munich in 1972. To get there, every training session would be a critical part of the program put together by Michael's unrelenting coach, Bob Bowman. Yet, he was also true to what he had said in my office when I'd told him about the morning finals—that he wanted to grow his sport, and would do what was necessary to promote the Olympics, and get people's attention on Beijing come August.

By the time I arrived back in China in late July, our ad sales had caught up, and we were optimistic about turning a profit for the Games. Still, as always, to me, the Olympics were a lot bigger than that, and reason for more excitement came when we started attending rehearsals for the ambitious Opening Ceremony, being directed by the celebrated Chinese filmmaker Zhang Yimou. The show would feature an unprecedented fifteen thousand performers, a tribute to Chinese history that carried the theme "One World, One Dream."

There was an innate challenge in broadcasting an opening ceremony like this one; as appealing as the artistic portion was visually, explaining it to an American audience in a way that would resonate was another thing entirely. Bob Costas and Matt Lauer would be the hosts of the ceremony, but as much as they could do research and preparation, we needed someone who could really explain the culture, and give context to our viewers. Fortunately, I'd found our answer about nine months before the Games in the most unlikely way, when I got a letter from a woman named Roberta Cooper Ramo. Roberta was a prominent attorney in New Mexico and the first woman ever to head the American Bar Association; we'd met when we'd served together on the panel to reform the USOC after the Salt Lake bid scandal. Roberta was writing to let me know that if I was looking for resources or a consultant on Beijing, her son, Joshua, lived there, and I might want to look him up. It was the first recruiting letter I ever got from a mother, but also one I wasn't going to take lightly when I found out her son worked for Henry Kissinger's consulting company as its vice chairman. When I met Joshua on my next trip to China, I was blown away, and realized he could do a lot more than answer a few questions over lunch. I hired him as a commentator, and his first appearance would be at the Opening Ceremony alongside Costas and Lauer.

With any Olympic Opening Ceremony, it often feels like you can't prepare enough. There are multiple rehearsals that the television partners can watch, and meetings with the creative team, but to keep the most important parts a surprise, not everything is completely run through before the night itself. (If you remember, that's how Muhammad Ali almost got burned in Atlanta.) Our best asset in Beijing was the connection we built with Zhang Yimou and his team. With multiple meetings and inside looks along with the rehearsals in the days and weeks prior, our production team got an intimate feel for the rhythm and themes of the show. Along the way, we gained Zhang's trust with our dedication and attention to detail. In fact, in one conversation, we offered him a suggestion: The sheer scale of the show was so impressive, it was actually intimidating. And never more so than the portion when exactly 2,008 performers beat drums to the same beat in complete unison. Considering the idea was to welcome the world, what if he directed his massive contingent of drummers to change their expressions from intense focus to welcoming smiles as they finished their performance?

On the night of August 8, 2008—8/8/08—there were definitely some nerves in our production truck leading up to 8:00 p.m. local time. That said, I knew we were in the absolute best hands possible, given who was directing our production of the show. Bucky Gunts had been the lead studio director of NBC Sports for decades, and this after a long tenure as the director of the *Today* show. Bucky, who's retired now, had the perfect demeanor for a director: always in control, never outwardly nervous, with the complete faith and trust of his crew, and the total affection of his peers. Camerapersons, graphics operators, producers—all of them respected Bucky completely, and would do anything for him. The Beijing Opening Ceremony would be Bucky's tour de force in a great career; so great in fact that Zhang would later say the American broadcast of his work was better than his own nation's. With Bucky orchestrating the mesmerizing broadcast featuring fifteen thousand performers—including those 2,008 drummers breaking out into bright smiles—the show ultimately culminated with the legendary gymnast Li Ning suspended high above the stadium, appearing to run horizontally along the walls toward the cauldron, followed by one of the greatest fireworks displays the world has ever seen. All in all, it was a simply unparalleled visual spectacle.

Now, with the show taking place at night in Beijing, the only way we could have shown it live would have been to air it at eight o'clock in the morning back home. It wasn't anything I ever considered. The next night, the American audience would be able to start enjoying the competition live; however, for this first night, the only choice was to hold it for as large an audience as possible, twelve hours later in prime time. There would be those in the media who criticized that decision, but any way you looked at it, it would have been inexcusable to put it on in the morning. First, I can't deny that, as a business decision, we owed it to the company to get the biggest audience, which would reap the biggest advertising dollars. But more than that, there's a reason that prime time would get us the biggest audience: prime time was when our audience wanted to watch. For many years before the Olympics, our research department had canvassed viewers all across the country, asking them when they wanted to turn on their TVs for the event. Overwhelmingly, the answer was after dinner, in prime time. That research informed putting the Opening in prime time; and it also informed us putting swimming on a three-hour delay on the West Coast. Viewers in California were some of the biggest Olympic fans our country had, but they also told us that they didn't want to watch the Games at 5:00 p.m.; they wanted to wait until they could be together as families, and watch later. Whether it was late night television or the Olympics, the answer was always the same: listen to the audience.

The half-day delay for the Opening Ceremony actually benefited us that first Friday night in 2008 in an unexpected way. On the internet, the media reports on the ceremony that came out over the course of that day in the U.S. were raves; of a show unlike any that had ever been staged. It was the greatest promotion we could have gotten, and by the time 8:00 p.m. arrived, the anticipation led tens of millions to their TVs. What they watched was a terrific three-and-a-half-hour show that would win Bucky an Emmy Award for directing, and our team a prestigious Peabody Award. Joshua Cooper Ramo was a phenomenal addition to the booth, walking the audience through the artistic portion of the show clearly and colorfully, and serving as a touchstone to explain Chinese customs in a way Americans could understand.

When the ratings came in, they were massive—34.2 million people had watched, the most since Atlanta in 1996. But the show was just getting started.

I woke up in the bed in the corner of my office in the broadcast center that Saturday with the adrenaline still coursing through my veins from the ceremony the night before. Michael's first race, the heats of the 400-meter individual medley, wasn't until that night, and his first race for a gold medal wouldn't come until Sunday morning (Saturday night in prime time back home), but there was still a huge broadcast ahead that afternoon: the cycling road race.

That at first may not sound like one of the most popular Olympic events, but experienced viewers might note that it's always on the first Saturday of the Games, and for good reason, as it typically serves as a travelogue to introduce the world to the host city. With the cyclists often riding through historic places, it's a great early way to get the audience excited about where the Olympics are taking place. And for these Games, exactly where they were going was a triumph of the relationship we'd built with the hosts. Going back years, with the help of Ma Guoli and others, we'd pushed the Chinese to open up Tiananmen Square for our cameras. It would be a striking backdrop for cyclists that first day to ride past the Forbidden City. Any concerns about references to the history of the location, particularly the deadly protests that had taken place there in 1989, were shortsighted; those references would come up regardless. Eventually, the organizers agreed, and the result was a backdrop for the road race as striking as any I'd ever seen. Our relationship with the Chinese also earned us the privilege of opening our broadcast on Sunday morning from the location as well, with Bob Costas standing in an empty square, welcoming our audience back to China, and setting up a Saturday prime-time schedule highlighted by Michael Phelps swimming live for his first gold medal in the pool.

Michael would earn that gold in the 400-meter individual medley in what looked like relatively routine fashion—even if it was anything but that. He broke his own world record by a second and a half, and was more than two seconds ahead of the field. Early returns indicated that swimming finals in the morning wouldn't have a negative impact on performance; Michael's world record was one of an incredible twenty-five that would fall during the meet. But as impressive as all those were, for the millions of American families getting together every night, the records were just part of the fun of cheering on the kid from Baltimore who was swimming for history. History that almost didn't happen.

Monday morning, August 11, was always going to be one of the critical points of Michael's path to eight golds. He'd be busy, swimming the semifinals of the 200-meter freestyle, but the spotlight would definitely be on his second race that day, the finals of the 4x100-meter freestyle relay. This was the first major hurdle for Michael's goal. In a relay, he'd only be one of four parts for the American team. And further, the Americans weren't favored; in fact, our analyst, Rowdy Gaines, had run the numbers every which way, and concluded that there was little to no chance that the U.S. could defeat the French, whose four swimmers had better times cumulatively than the Americans.

As always, we did our best to set up the story for the viewers; and the idea that the U.S. was the underdog in the race was just the start. The Americans had once been dominant in this event, but in both 2000 and 2004 had come up short, winning the silver. And the day before, our research room had produced the translation of a headline in a French newspaper, in which the French swimmers were saying they were going to "smash" the Americans in the event. Add all that to the biggest narrative—that Michael needed the U.S. to pull off an upset to keep his hope of eight golds alive—and we had a tremendous Sunday night of television for America.

Like virtually every race in Beijing, it would be extraordinarily fast, with the top six teams—yes, six teams—coming in under the previous world-record time. Michael swam the first lap well, and halfway through the race, the U.S. was leading. But then the French got the upper hand, and by the time the anchor legs began, the Americans were trailing, with Phelps's hope seemingly slipping away with every stroke. By the halfway point of the last lap, Jason Lezak, Michael's thirty-two-year-old veteran teammate, was trailing by almost a full body length to the Frenchman Alain Bernard. But then, somehow, some way, Lezak started closing in. And closing in more. And more. On our live broadcast, Gaines and Dan Hicks, our play-by-play announcer, were sensing a miracle, starting to shout into the microphones. In our broadcast center control room, people were instinctively screaming, too. And back home, millions of Americans were no doubt doing the same.

Wouldn't you know it, by eight one-hundredths of a second, Lezak touched the wall first.

Our production team at the compound—led by none other than Tommy Roy and Drew Esocoff, working together at last—captured the ecstasy of the moment brilliantly: Phelps leading the celebration on the pool deck with his exhausted teammates; his mother and sisters in the stands in sheer disbelief; even President Bush, sticking around to watch the biggest events of the first weekend of the Games, cheering on these American heroes. It was incredible television, and our team pulled it off seamlessly. And most important, I knew, was that the story that could carry our audience all week long was off and running.

The next morning, Michael set another world record, and got his third straight gold, in the 200-meter freestyle. After that came a tough day: swimming two finals in the span of less than two hours. First came the 200-meter butterfly, which he won even as his goggles got water inside them, fogged up, and rendered him virtually blind for the back half of the race. After just a brief rest, he swam the fastest opening leg ever in a 4x200-meter freestyle relay, setting his team up for another gold and world record. Five down, and three to go, with the whole saga playing out like a movie for all of America to savor.

In the broadcast center, we were all carried by the emotion of Michael's quest.

Coming live on the air at eight o'clock every morning meant wild hours for our prime-time crew, even for an Olympics. Folks would stream into their edit rooms and offices in the dead of night, our production meetings would be at 6:00 a.m., and then we'd grind on the air into the early afternoon. By then, it was a combination of elation and exhaustion, with our team hanging around to watch other events and cheer on their colleagues working on our other shows. In addition to our prime-time telecast, our Beijing coverage would ultimately total more than 3,600 hours—on NBC, USA, MSNBC, CNBC, Oxygen, Telemundo, Universal HD, and streaming on the NBC Olympics website. Years earlier, I'd pitched Juan Antonio Samaranch on turning NBC into America's Olympic network. Now we'd become America's Olympic family of networks, and with GE using the occasion to grow its business in China, these Games were a massive moment for the company. Every night, just before catching a few hours of sleep in my office—my bed once again just a few feet from my desk—the ratings report would come in. And while it was clear that across all our shows, America had Olympic fever, nothing was better than seeing the prime-time ratings, as high as any numbers we'd seen since Atlanta. A record 200 million people in all would watch our coverage, and our profits would eventually soar past $100 million.

Michael easily won gold in another world-record-setting performance in the 200-meter individual medley on Friday morning of the fifteenth, making him six-for-six. Then came his final challenge: his hardest individual race, the 100-meter butterfly. As a slow starter, 100 meters gave him less room for error than his 200-meter races. Plus, the competition in this event was particularly fierce, including Phelps's teammate Ian Crocker, the world-record holder, and a swimmer from Serbia named Milorad Čavić, who, before the race, got some attention by telling the media he thought it would be better for swimming if he beat Michael. And then there was the fact that a week into the meet, Michael had swum more than any other competitor, and now had to summon whatever he had left to find a way to touch the wall first.

As expected, when the gun went off, Cavic and Crocker got out ahead in the first half of the race, with Michael seventh out of eight swimmers. But then Michael started making up ground as the wall came into view ever closer. At the last instant, rather than cruise into the finish in rhythm, Michael on instinct took an extra half stroke and, almost unfathomably, he touched the wall first by the absolute slimmest of margins: one one-hundredth of a second. Even on slow-motion replay, it was hardly visible to the naked eye—but Michael had indeed pulled it off.

On Sunday morning in Beijing, Saturday night back home, Michael looked to wrap it up with his final relay, the 4x100-meter medley. An eighth gold medal would accomplish his goal, and break Spitz's record of seven. The U.S. was favored; and the race felt like a coronation. The afternoon before, Jeff Zucker had been in my office, and I mused to him about maybe changing my plans so the West Coast would watch the race live, earlier in the day.

"No way," the former Olympic researcher turned CEO said. "Everything you've done for years has been working perfectly. The ratings on the West Coast are higher than anywhere else in the country. Families want to watch it in prime time, don't mess with it now."

I listened to my friend and stuck with the plan. The U.S. was in third place in the race when Michael dove into the pool for his butterfly leg, but a hundred meters later, he'd handed Lezak—swimming freestyle in the anchor leg—a big edge. The U.S. set another world record, and another thirty-odd million Americans watched on television as an exhausted Phelps raised his arms in celebration, shouting "Let's go! Let's go!" repeatedly as his teammates embraced and high-fived him. He'd done it—eight golds in eight races.

The next day, Michael came to the broadcast center to be interviewed, and the entire NBC compound broke out in applause when he walked in. Afterward, we sat in my office, reflecting on the path he'd traveled. He was exhausted but exhilarated. Back home, how many kids were asking their moms to sign up for swim lessons now? How many of them were measuring their own dreams of all kinds, using Michael Phelps as inspiration to become the next great ballplayer, or ballerina, or even doctor or lawyer?

It had been a long, long time since the Olympics had first captured my imagination that way. And it was amazing to think how, for all the ways the world had changed, that was still exactly the same.

Michael Phelps was the biggest star of one of the most anticipated, most watched, most consequential television events of all time, but that's not the only reason Beijing was so seminal. In terms of competition, it also served as the global coming-out party for another phenomenon, Usain Bolt, who picked up where Michael left off over the second week of the Games, with two stunning world-record performances in the 100-meter and 200-meter sprints. For our American audience, Nastia Liukin and Shawn Johnson were great costars for Phelps, as the two dueled for gold in the all-around gymnastics competition, while Misty May-Treanor and Kerri Walsh Jennings made their way through the beach volleyball tournament to win their second straight gold medal in that sport. At every venue, and back in the IBC, all the thousands of hours of coverage made for our most technically challenging Olympics ever by far. But from Bucky Gunts to our engineering czar, Dave Mazza, the broadcast—and the massive internet stream—was a big success.

Mix that success with the significance of China and its emerging role on the global stage, and it just felt like we were all part of something bigger. My philosophy was always that families tuned into the Olympics to follow the stories we were telling them; we weren't covering a political convention. Still, President Bush's presence was certainly news, and as he remained in Beijing for the first several days of the Games, I invited him to come by the broadcast center and join Bob Costas for a live interview in prime time. The interview covered all the relevant issues, and the exchanges were in many ways prescient, considering all that's unfolded since.

"In the long run," Bob asked him, "is China's rise irreconcilable with America's interests?"

"No," replied the president. "In the long run, America better remain engaged with China."

Historians can debate whether that was the right philosophy, and whether the way that Bush and his successors handled China had a tangible impact on the path that China has taken in the years since. Certainly it was hard to find as much hope in the 2022 Winter Olympics in Beijing as the original, with the pandemic preventing fans—and even most of NBC's production team—from going to China, and the competition overshadowed by the diplomatic boycott in response to China's human rights record and the U.S. government's declaration that the Chinese government was committing genocide on its Uyghur Muslim population. But I still firmly believe holding the Olympics in Beijing in 2008 was a worthy effort, like President Bush said, to engage China.

And in 2008 in particular, the way the Olympics brought so many people together in front of their television for such an extended time was a hugely important fact on its own. In our increasingly fractured culture, any time the nation can come together for anything is a good thing. And Michael Phelps, Usain Bolt, and so many great moments around them were just so compelling, and so entertaining, they couldn't stay away. In fact, at one point during those 2008 Games, one newspaper headline called me "The Man Who Keeps America Awake," referring to all the late nights our viewers spent watching our prime-time coverage as we stretched it later and later, often live past midnight.

It was a moniker I accepted with pride.

CHAPTER 31

Larger Than Life

I was in Scottsdale, Arizona, the last weekend of September 2009 when I got a call from Jeff Zucker. It was the Friday night before a Sunday night game between Kurt Warner's Cardinals and Peyton Manning's Colts, and Susan and I were at dinner with our son Willie and his girlfriend (later to be his wife), Lauren. I stepped outside to take the call.

"Are you alone?" Jeff said to me.

"Yeah, I'm halfway out into the parking lot of a restaurant," I said. "What's going on?"

He paused.

"Immelt told me I could tell one person—you," he said. "This deal is really, really close. It's gonna happen."

He didn't have to say much more.

For months, General Electric had been exploring the sale of NBCUniversal to Comcast, the giant cable company based in Philadelphia. Rumors had been flying on Wall Street, and I knew firsthand how true they were. I'd been pulled into a dog and pony show a few months earlier with a consulting firm for Comcast to walk them through the economics of how our Olympic and NFL deals worked. They were clearly parsing every part of the business to make sure it was sound.

The business of Comcast, of course, was booming. Cable was by now well into the third decade of its boom—almost every home in America had cable television,

326

and raising the sub fees on channels even just fractions of a cent every year could net a company like Comcast millions and millions of dollars in profit. Executives there had been eyeing a play to expand into the content-making business for years, and after some near misses, had finally found a willing partner.

At GE, things had changed. It had been eight years since Jeff Immelt had taken over for Jack Welch. Jeff had been a supportive boss and, beyond that, a real believer in what we did. And not just with *Sunday Night Football*. In 2003, he'd also been willing to invest in the Olympics, when we'd extended our deal past Beijing for two more Games, in 2010 and 2012, for a little more than a combined $2 billion. But despite that, there was no doubt Immelt didn't have the same passion for sports; the same love of the game and the media business that Welch did. Immelt was a tried-and-true GE man who'd come out of the company's plastics, appliances, and health care business. The recession had inflicted a huge impact on the company, and Wall Street was full of analysts insisting that GE needed to off-load its television and movie properties (the merger with Universal had been a few years earlier) to stay afloat. It had only been a matter of time before Immelt listened to them.

When I got off the phone with Zucker, I returned to dinner with my family. There was nothing to say, really—and not just because Jeff had sworn me to secrecy. As a media company, Comcast's purchase (technically, at first, of 51 percent of NBCUniversal) was going to be tied up in Washington with antitrust regulators for months. For the foreseeable future, it would be business as usual at NBC Sports. And there was still plenty of business to tend to.

The biggest thing we'd done in the year since Beijing was our first Super Bowl telecast of the *Sunday Night Football* era. The first two seasons of our deal with the NFL, our only postseason coverage was Wild Card Saturday, and it had been exciting to finish our third year by finally producing the most-watched show of the year in television. The game was in Tampa, and was as exciting as any Super Bowl in history, with the James Harrison one-hundred-yard interception return for a touchdown just before halftime, and then Warner and Larry Fitzgerald leading the Cardinals to a second-half comeback—only to have Ben Roethlisberger march the Steelers down the field in the final two minutes to offer a resounding final answer. Al Michaels and John Madden were at their best during that drive, their excitement a perfect match for the moment. And when Santonio Holmes stretched for the winning touchdown reception in the corner of the end zone, somehow keeping his toes inches inside the sideline, John's guttural response—"Unbelievable!"—spoke for the millions of people watching all over the country.

Afterward, the mood outside our production trucks in the stadium parking lot was celebratory. Fred Gaudelli, Drew Esocoff, and their crew were spent but satisfied, and a spread of champagne, cold beer, and some food was attacked with a vengeance. Bruce Springsteen and the E Street Band had played the halftime show, and you could hear some engineers playing the set back out of a speaker. It took a while for Al and John to make their way down from the booth, but when they arrived, it felt like the party was complete. Al was buzzing, still on the high of calling the game, and congratulating everyone in sight—he couldn't stop talking about what a team effort it all was. Meanwhile, sitting in the front seat of a golf cart, as everyone flocked around him, clutching a bottle of beer in one giant hand, John, a few months away from his seventy-third birthday, was like a king holding court. It was the eleventh Super Bowl he'd broadcast, and he'd become the first announcer to call the biggest game in the world for four different networks.

He was the only one who knew it was the last game he'd ever call.

A few months later, John told me he was retiring, over the phone one night as I talked to him from my apartment.

"It's just time," he said. "Simple as that."

Even though I hopped on a plane the next day to try to see if I could change his mind, I knew the effort would be fruitless. John's biggest point was that he wanted to retire while he was still at the top of his game, before anyone thought he was slipping even just a bit. It made sense, even if, more than anything, I was just sad as it sunk in that I wouldn't be able to spend eighteen straight weekends with him on the road anymore. Though John, as always, aware of everything around him, reminded me that I was lucky about something else.

"C'mon, Dick," he said, "you're gonna be more than fine. You've got the perfect succession plan in place."

And sure enough, when Cris Collinsworth stepped into John's massive shoes in September of 2009, it might have represented the smoothest transition in the history of sports television. From his earliest days on NBC more than a decade prior, Cris had always been a natural in front of the camera (later, his smooth, casual "slide in" to the opening on-camera shot would become an internet cult sensation), but his success in this role would be more than about just sounding and looking good. Cris got what made John great: preparation and respect around the league. In fact, Cris would eventually turn his prep into something even bigger—buying a start-up company called Pro Football Focus (based in Great Britain of all places) that did customized advanced analysis and breakdowns of the game.

Even before that, though, the respect that Cris engendered throughout the league—from coaches, players, and executives—meant that, just like John, they'd step up when he came to town, always going out of their way to try to give him real insight in broadcaster meetings. Like millions of others, they watched Al and Cris every Sunday night, and understood how they could help the telecast—talking about the minutiae of strategy or small adjustments that Cris could use, working in tandem with Fred and the production truck, to educate viewers as the game played out.

Cris's departure from the studio also was the impetus for us to rearrange the chairs on *Football Night in America,* and the result was, I think, the best lineup the show's ever had. We decided to move Bob Costas on the road, and have him host the show from the game site each week. The idea was that the countdown to the game would feel bigger with Bob on the sideline, and as always, he was a perfect fit. Then, back at our studio at 30 Rock, there was plenty of talent still on the floor. Former ESPN stars Dan Patrick and Keith Olbermann continued the successful reunion we'd staged for them a year earlier, doing the highlights as only they could, and now they were joined by two rookie analysts, both recently retired from the field, Tony Dungy and Rodney Harrison.

Tony had become one of the most respected figures in the league during his time leading the Bucs and the Colts, but, soft-spoken and religious, no one pegged him for the TV type when he retired in just his mid-fifties to focus on endeavors like his prison ministry work. But I'd seen something when we'd met for Sunday night games, and offered him a guest slot on our pregame show for Super Bowl XLIII. Tony didn't have the same kind of energy as most studio analysts, but the same quiet charisma that had made him such a great leader in the locker room came through in a unique way on camera. Also, as one of the smartest people I've ever worked with, Tony was a quick study into the nuances of the job, plus—not surprisingly—he became a leader in our own *FNIA* locker room.

Among the new teammates who looked up to him was Rodney, who, like Tony, had wowed me with his guest spot in that Super Bowl pregame show in

Tampa. In a lot of ways, Rodney was the opposite of Tony: one of the toughest players in the league who took pride in his reputation, and once admitted to setting aside $50,000 for fines every season he knew he'd rack up for hard hits. Rodney's quick fuse and intensity came through with his emotional reactions to the drama of each week we recapped on the show; if the former Patriot was a vision of intensity as a player, he knew only one way to speak—honestly—with his new tool, the microphone. Together, Tony and Rodney were a unique complement, and eventually would be key voices in putting the heat on the football community to make the game safer for players, speaking out week after week as they commented on highlights of players exiting games with concussions. With them at the studio table, our Sunday night coverage was better than ever.

As a new decade dawned, I'd just celebrated my twentieth anniversary at NBC Sports. Sure, the Comcast deal, with its review by regulators beginning over the course of that season, signaled change was coming. But I loved the job as much as ever. That had always trumped all else—there was no reason at that point to think anything was different this time.

About a month after his first year partnering with Cris Collinsworth had ended, Al Michaels was sitting in my office at the International Broadcast Center in Vancouver.

"It's amazing how familiar it is, and how different it is, at the same time," Al was saying.

I'm not sure there was anyone in Vancouver besides Al who'd worked an Olympics for Roone Arledge, and now also worked one with me. Al's new contract extension that we'd negotiated had included a new feature: in addition to calling *Sunday Night Football*, he'd come to the Olympics as the host of a studio show. Initially, people had talked about Al returning to do play-by-play of hockey games, reprising the role that had given him his signature call from the 1980 Olympics, "Do you believe in miracles?" But he graciously though firmly refused, explaining—correctly—that there was no one better in the universe at calling hockey games than the great Mike "Doc" Emrick. Al would be perfectly content in the studio, throwing to Doc for game coverage. And now, a week into his first Olympics in more than twenty-five years, he was having a ball.

"In some ways, it feels totally the same," Al said. "But you do run things differently than Roone did. Yeah, you've got the big office and everyone knows the buck stops with you, but it also feels like you delegate a lot more. Maybe because there's just a lot more coverage. Or maybe because you just trust your people. But it feels like there's a vision for everything at all times, and everyone knows what it is."

Vancouver was my eighth Olympics for NBC, dating back to Barcelona in 1992. After some disappointment with the ratings in the prior Winter Games in Torino, we had roared back with fantastic numbers. We still had the momentum of Beijing eighteen months earlier, with Americans again eager to feel the Olympic fever Michael Phelps had given them. Stars like Shaun White, winning his second straight snowboarding gold medal in the half-pipe; Lindsey Vonn, who was the first American woman skier to ever win gold in the downhill; and Apolo Ohno, who won an American record eighth medal, were among the most popular names. Even Comedy Central's Stephen Colbert got in the act, airing *The Colbert Report* from Canada, complete with an on-set pet stuffed moose he named "Ebersol." Most important for our ratings: all the figure skating was live in prime time, and the stories all captured the American audience night after night. The top U.S. performance came with the first American men's gold in the sport since the eighties, won in an upset by Evan Lysacek, whose elegance on the ice was only eclipsed by the dazzle of his costumes. In fact, to lighten the mood in the control room, I had our wardrobe department quickly work up a replica of one of Evan's performing suits, and strolled in one night in full competition attire, leaving the whole front deck of the production operation roaring with laughter. Fortunately, I had the foresight to come in during a commercial, so no television was harmed by the gag.

Vancouver did mark a few other small changes in my approach: I didn't live in the IBC, considering our hotel was right next door, my room a two-minute walk from my office. And for the first time since Sydney 2000, Susan joined me for several days. She'd always said the Olympics were "my mistress," but after all our family had been through, we weren't going to take any happy memories we could make together for granted. And on the first Saturday evening of competition, after the prime-time show ended at 9:00 p.m. local time, she joined me for a brief appearance at a surprise seventieth birthday party for Tom Brokaw that Jeff was throwing. It was the first time I'd ever done anything like that at a Games, and with a guest list that included Olympic tourist friends from Roger Goodell to Lorne Michaels, it felt like the brief break was worth it.

Working so hard at an Olympics had never been a performance thing; there was just nowhere else I wanted to be during those two weeks. Whether it was a news story like the tragic death of the Georgian luger Nodar Kumaritashvili in a training accident on the first day of the Games, or something much brighter, like the Canadian hockey team's thrilling overtime win over the U.S. just before the Closing Ceremony two weeks later, I always felt like I needed to be there, and more than that, wanted to be there. Everyone around me knew how authentic my passion was, and they fed off that energy with their own enthusiasm and ingenuity, which coursed through every part of our own ever-expanding coverage—in prime time, on our cable stations, even our Spanish-language coverage on Telemundo.

Maybe no one better understood how much the Olympics meant to me than a visitor I invited to Vancouver during that fortnight. Don Ohlmeyer hadn't been to an Olympics since the seventies, but flew up from California to go to some events and relive some memories. One night during his trip, he toured the broadcast center, amazed at all the advances in technology that allowed us to broadcast on multiple networks and the internet at once, virtually all day and night. Then I suggested he sit behind me during the show in the back of the control room. After an hour or so, I got so caught up in the show that I forgot he was there, only to remember and turn around to see something surprising: Don was crying. They weren't tears of sadness, but, as he explained it later, overwhelming joy.

"It was the passage of time," he told me later that night in my office. "Bucky [Gunts, the director], Brian [Orentreich, the associate director]—those guys were kids when I hired them. Now they're directing and producing.

"And us, too. We were Roone's kids. And now, we're the oldest people in this joint."

All in, the success and high ratings of Vancouver, on the heels of the success of the same for Beijing, was something I was tremendously proud of, and took tremendously personally. Which was why I was so upset, not to mention confused, when reports started coming out shortly before the Opening Ceremony that for the first time since Barcelona, and its ill-fated Triplecast, NBC wouldn't make money on the Vancouver Games. Our ad sales were strong. Plus, like in years past, money from the sub fees of MSNBC, CNBC, and USA, where we aired coverage, counted for earnings, as did the sizable dollars that GE could claim from all the ancillary contracts they had with the IOC as the result of our deal, for GE-manufactured security, lighting, electronics, and the like.

When I looked into it, the explanation I got was telling, and eye-opening. People deep at GE had pushed out the story publicly that the Games had lost money to advance the narrative that NBC Olympics was a poor business. The deal with Comcast was out in the news now, with regulators beginning their review, and the company wanted to win the public-image battle with the message that they'd been smart to rid themselves of NBC. We'd paid almost a billion dollars for the Vancouver Games. The complex accounting on it all, plus that massive rights fee that our profits ran against, made it hard for anyone to dispute their claims—even if they weren't true.

It was an unmistakable early sign of how much was going to change with the Comcast deal. Maybe business as usual was no longer.

I'd known and liked Brian Roberts, the president of Comcast, for years prior to his company buying NBC. And I still like him today. Brian has a house on Martha's Vineyard, and we got to know each other by crossing paths in the summer. A few years before talks between Comcast and GE heated up, I actually stepped in as an intermediary between the NFL and the company, trying to bring together Roger Goodell and Brian for a compromise to end a years-long carriage dispute that kept the NFL Network out of Comcast homes. And when regulators began reviewing the deal between GE and Comcast over the course of 2010, Brian and I spoke frequently, as the idea of what NBC could look like under new management took shape.

It was during those conversations that I first met Steve Burke, Brian's lieutenant and the COO of Comcast. Like Brian, whose father, Ralph, had founded Comcast, Burke was a second-generation media executive; his father, Dan, had been the owner of Capital Cities, a first-rate guy who had been the man who'd told Paul Tagliabue to give us the second Super Bowl that justified us hanging onto the NFL in the nineties. Steve, though, was harder to get a measure of, particularly when he showed little interest in the biggest point I tried to make with him as he evaluated the company before Comcast formally took over: keep Jeff Zucker in the fold, if not as CEO, then at least as president of the company's news operation. Jeff had been at NBC his whole career, news was his first love, and he'd been the best news executive of his time. I really felt like there was a path to keeping him at the company. But Jeff was let go in late 2010; Burke himself would be stepping into the CEO role at NBC.

As for sports, the merger was creating a department that would combine network and cable assets into a package that rivaled Disney and ESPN and Fox and their cable channels. NBC, of course, had the biggest properties in sports, *Sunday Night Football* and the Olympics, as well as rights deals with the NHL and NASCAR, plus tennis, golf, and horse racing. But Comcast wasn't coming empty-handed, and once the deal was finalized in early 2011, a new, larger, and more complex collection of channels and properties took shape, under what the new company decided to call the NBC Sports Group. There were a lot of parts of the new landscape that were exciting, and chief among them was that the merger brought us together with the Golf Channel, which had been cofounded years earlier by none other than the king himself, Arnold Palmer.

My friendship with Arnold went back years, honed every March when we broadcast his annual tournament at Bay Hill outside Orlando, Florida. Susan would often come for the trip, and we'd watch the action unfold from one of his houses right on the course. On one of those visits Arnold once served a young and delighted Charlie Ebersol the first-ever Coca-Cola of his life. Though, my favorite Palmer story involved a young Tiger Woods as we watched him play one day from his porch.

"He's obviously a great player," Arnold remarked. "I just think he could do a better job of connecting with the gallery while he plays."

"So have you spoken to him about it?" I asked.

"Of course I have," he replied.

"Well, what did you say?"

"I told him it's simple," he said. "When you're walking up the fairway, just *look* at the crowd—once for a few seconds to one side, and once to the other. All you have to do is look, kid."

Arnold was a great storyteller, and on top of being a golf legend, he was also a great businessman. Golf Channel had been started in the nineties, and then, in

2001, Comcast had bought a controlling interest. Now, another ten years later, we were all merging, and the opportunity to bridge our long-standing coverage of the U.S. Open, the Ryder Cup, and a portion of the PGA Tour with Golf Channel was a major part of what made the deal so attractive to Comcast.

The addition of Golf Channel, plus the eight or so regional sports networks that Comcast owned, plus its cable sports network Versus (eventually to be renamed the NBC Sports Network), meant our leadership would have to grow as well. I was under no illusions that I had any experience on the cable side in sports. Burke suggested I bring in someone to handle that part of the business, and my first thought was Mark Lazarus, a former Turner executive who I'd met when we'd flirted with starting that spring football league with the NBA years earlier. Ken Schanzer spoke to Mark and got the sense that he'd be willing to relocate from Atlanta to New York, and we were able to bring him in.

There were also opportunities to promote some of my best executives into new positions. Mike McCarley had always been much more than a PR assistant to me, and he'd been at my side everywhere from Beijing to the Super Bowl for years. Now it was time to let him go, and reward him, and Mike happily moved to Orlando with his family to become the new president of Golf Channel. Going with him would be another of my favorites, Molly Solomon. Molly had started at NBC as an Olympic researcher in 1992, and eventually risen to become one of my top producers on Olympic coverage. She was also a golf nut, and married to an editor at *Golf Digest*, Geoff Russell. I was proud to make her the channel's executive producer, the first-ever woman to hold that title at a national sports network, even if I was sad to say goodbye to her on the Olympics.

The appointments were announced in February of 2011, and were a great joy for me to make. But there was something more complex fast approaching on the horizon. My own contract was up a few months later, and it was the next item of business for Burke and me to discuss.

If you got off the main elevator on the sixth floor of 30 Rockefeller Plaza sometime after the Vancouver Olympics, you were greeted by an odd sight: a giant stuffed moose, standing in front of a display of the history of NBC and RCA.

The plaque next to the moose identified it as "Ebersol"; we had gotten it as a gift from *The Colbert Report* after the Games, with the understanding that it would be displayed for posterity—and laughs—when we came home.

Was it silly? Of course. But it also made a point: NBC may have been a huge company, but we were a company of people—and people unafraid to laugh at ourselves. There was something meaningful about the fact that my history at NBC went back almost forty years; that members of the technical crew, sales teams, marketing group, and more—engineers and executives on both coasts—knew my name, and I knew theirs. The same went for Lorne, and also for Jeff. We'd all grown up at 30 Rock, started there as kids, and made our careers there, intertwining our stories with the story of the network. And I really think that knowing us, the company's leaders, and the kind of people we were, helped make NBC not a faceless monolith, but something that, as much as a public company could, resembled a big family.

All that undoubtedly and abruptly changed when Steve Burke took over the company.

In every which way, it was clear from the start of his time as CEO that he had no interest in institutional memory. If anything, he was afraid of it. To Burke, the way to take over NBC, and mold it in Comcast's image, as he saw it, was to eliminate all the soft edges. To paint over the identity that had defined the company for decades. To ignore the relationships that made the place special; a place to care about, not just a place to work. And if I bemoaned all the ways I thought that was the wrong path to go down, I also couldn't deny what it would mean for me.

My initial response was the same as ever: try to cultivate a relationship with him. But I knew from the start it wouldn't be easy. First off, he just saw the business of television differently than I did. My favorite part of the job was the Super Bowls and the Olympics—all the joy of the creativity that went into planning them, and the excitement of the production as we put them on. His favorite part was the earnings calls. And then, more than that, from our very first meeting, it was apparent how he viewed me.

"You're just larger than life, Dick," he said continually as we talked about how he saw my role at NBC Sports and Olympics going forward. "Larger than life!"

It was, I suppose, his way of saluting what I'd accomplished. But at the same time, it felt like he was saying he didn't know what to do with me. That he didn't understand how I could fit into his team with the reputation that I had.

"He's afraid of having strong people around him," a close friend said to me early on in 2011. "He doesn't see how that can be an asset."

And the more he said I was "larger than life"—over and over again, like an inside joke he'd written—the more it began not just to bother me a bit, but confound me. It was like he didn't get that people like me, and Lorne for that matter, had succeeded not because we cultivated some image, but because we worked harder than everyone else, and had earned whatever status and following that got us at the company. In my case, having the influence I did went back to the relationships I'd built; relationships I'd worked long and hard to build over years and years. His own boss, Brian, had seen that firsthand a few years earlier when I was the one the NFL called to try to resolve that carriage dispute. How did Burke not see that the foundation of who I was had nothing to do with some "larger than life" bullshit, but actual work I'd put in?

It was in those same conversations and early meetings with Burke and the senior staff that he informed us of something else. As we negotiated our next personal service contracts, he didn't want us working through lawyers or agents. He wanted us to be negotiating directly with him and him alone. It was a demand that was unheard of, and, as I thought about it more at one point, almost inexplicable coming from the son of Dan Burke—an executive who'd been known for always handling every negotiation with grace and skill. The whole scenario wasn't necessarily something that scared me; I'd been in plenty of negotiations. Though what came next would reveal just what kind of negotiator Steve Burke would be.

We worked through my deal on and off through the spring, Burke and I talking, and then me bringing in my longtime lawyer, Mike Rudell, to look at the contracts that Comcast was proposing. On May 9, the Monday after the Kentucky Derby, I got a call from Mike, who'd been reviewing the latest deal offer.

"Didn't you say that you and Burke were talking about different money in Olympic years?" he asked me.

"Right, exactly, that's what we agreed on," I told him.

The idea was, in a new five-year deal that would potentially cover three Olympics—2012, 2014, and 2016—I'd make a larger salary in those years than I did in the non-Olympic years, owing to the particular value I brought to the Games as not only their producer but the key member of their negotiating team with the IOC. Those were both things that Comcast had no experience with. This, of course, was all assuming that we had the Olympics in 2014 and 2016; the negotiations for those rights were coming up in just a few months.

"Well, that's not what it says here," Mike told me. "All the compensation is the same, each year."

It was strange. Burke and I had clearly talked about the Olympic-year pay being different. We'd shaken hands on it in our last meeting, and Burke had told me that he'd gone to the Comcast board to review it, and the board had approved.

So maybe it was an oversight.

Or, maybe it wasn't.

I thanked Mike and told him I'd call him in a few days when I figured out what I was going to do next.

I kept my thoughts to myself over the next few days. But I couldn't get out of my head the idea that Burke hadn't lived up to what we'd talked about. It wasn't about the money. It was about the idea that we'd agreed on something, and he'd potentially decided on his own that he would offer something else.

That Thursday, Susan flew with me down to Florida for the Players Championship. After a day of meetings and calls, we met for dinner in the hotel, just the two of us.

"I'm starting to think this deal might not work out," I said to her, saying it out loud for the first time. "Maybe it's just not meant to be."

She was surprised, but less so than I thought she'd be. She'd been reading the signs that maybe I'd been avoiding, and as ever, knew the right questions to ask.

"If you find out there's no mistake, and he didn't live up to what you agreed on, you won't regret overreacting?" she said.

"It won't be overreacting," I said. "It'll just be my honest feelings about where this thing is headed."

Back in New York the following week, I had Aimee Leone set up a meeting for Burke and me, which took place that Wednesday in his office. I got right to the point after I sat down.

"That deal isn't what we agreed on," I told him. And I laid out the terms we'd talked about in our last negotiation.

"How is that possible?" he said. "You shouldn't think I would ever screw you."

"I don't," I said. "But let's solve this."

"Give me a day," Burke said.

I agreed.

When I got back to my office, I called Susan.

"Things look better," I said. "Maybe this will work out."

But I wasn't totally confident. And that night, I called Howard Katz. He was a good person to vent to—a calm sounding board who knew me well, and wasn't going to rile me up further. It wasn't about the money, I told Howard. But if I accept it, then who knows the next time he'll go back on his word? I couldn't work for someone whose word wasn't his bond, particularly after the people I'd been lucky enough to work for over the previous twenty-two years. Susan was in New York at our apartment with me, and when I went to work the next morning after an early coffee with her, I didn't know what the day would bring.

Waiting for me outside my office was Joe Posnanski, the sportswriter then working for *Sports Illustrated*, and at 30 Rock to interview me for an article he was writing about Johnny Miller and our upcoming U.S. Open coverage. I didn't know Joe, but he was smart and curious, and the interview went longer than I expected. So at ten o'clock, I had to excuse myself to head up to Burke's office for our meeting.

"So how about this," Burke said to me when I walked in. "I really want to have a circle of equals on my staff, where everyone's deals line up. But I understand the Olympics and what they mean, and how much work they are. So how about we split the difference on what we talked about?"

Split the difference—between what he'd already agreed on, and what he was saying he now thought of as fair. I didn't hesitate to respond.

"Steve, how about we call it a day?"

There was no more drama than that. No yelling, no tension. The deal was simply off. It had been a great twenty-two years. But it was time to go.

The rest of the day was a blur. I called Susan, and then Schanzer, and then Brian Roberts, which was a conversation full of mutual respect. His guy and I couldn't see eye to eye, and this was the only path forward. I called Roger Goodell, Howard Katz, and a few members of my senior staff. Then, at eleven forty-five, I gathered everyone at NBC Sports who was in 30 Rock at the top of the interior staircase that connected the fourteenth and fifteenth floors outside my office. That was the first time I got emotional, telling my team I wouldn't be leading them any longer.

Pretty much the entire afternoon would be spent on the phone—with more colleagues, including Mark Lazarus, who Burke named as my replacement. I also spoke with old friends like David Stern, and a cavalcade of sportswriters, including Posnanski. Knowing a good story when he saw it, Joe had stuck around 30 Rock all day, and we sat together for a follow-up interview a little before 4:00 p.m.

From Baltimore, where they were stationed to produce and direct the Preakness Stakes, Fred Gaudelli and Drew Esocoff reached out—they wanted to know if they should come back. Of course not, I told them—they had a show to do. I finally left the office after eight o'clock, and met Jeff Zucker for dinner at Isle of Capri. We'd been Olympic researchers twenty years apart. We'd left NBC within months of one another.

My last call of the night was with Al Michaels, out in L.A. Al had put it well just a few hours earlier when he'd spoken to Posnanski for his article.

"I think Dick saw his role as 75 percent creative and 25 percent business," Al told Joe. "And I think things were changing so that [the ratio] was going to be the other way around."

They would be changing from now on without me.

Well, maybe not so fast.

"Let me try to talk to him," Howard Katz said five days later, sitting across from me the following Tuesday night at our regular table at Isle of Capri. "There's got to be a way to work this out."

After the whirlwind drama of Thursday, Susan and I had gone as scheduled for a trip to Boston to catch a few games at Fenway with Tom Werner, before returning to Litchfield. At one of the games, I'd had a great time talking to Louis Zamperini, the subject of the book and movie *Unbroken*, who was sitting in Werner's box after throwing out the first pitch at the age of ninety-four. Meanwhile, all weekend, the calls continued to come in, with everyone curious to know what had happened, and some more emotional than others. Pat Bowlen, Jerry Jones, and Robert Kraft were probably the angriest, while Rodney Harrison—who caught me as we drove to Boston—touched me as he reflected on the kind of leader he thought I was. It was a little bit like hearing my own funeral played out, call by call—even if I had to remind people that I was still alive and well.

Really, the emotions of everyone else were much bigger than my own. People may have been shocked to hear I was leaving, but I'd been mulling it for weeks. As personally as I'd always treated the job, I also had been in it long enough to know how lucky I was that the circumstances around me let me enjoy it so much. I hadn't achieved success alone; I'd been in the right place, with the right people around, above, and below me, to make it all happen. Now circumstances had finally changed. NBC Sports would go on without me. And I would go on without NBC Sports.

That said, if I had to pinpoint what I was bummed about, it was not getting to take part in another Super Bowl season on *Sunday Night Football*, and not being able to take part in one last Olympics in London that we'd been working on for months. Sitting at the restaurant, picking at my veal chop, I could admit that part to Howard.

"It just doesn't make sense to have you walk away like this," he repeated. He knew in particular that his owners were upset, and that football would run a lot smoother with me still in the mix, still working with him and Roger, and Jerry Jones and Robert Kraft and Pat Bowlen.

"Let me try to talk to him."

I wasn't going to stop him, and later that night, Howard called me at my apartment. He'd called Burke and in quintessential Howard fashion had calmly laid out the beginnings of something that made sense for all parties. NBC had too much at stake—with a Super Bowl coming, and the Olympics right after that—to just let me walk away. Plus, these were the two parts of the job that, far above everything else, really meant something to me. Maybe there was an arrangement where I could stay involved in those two properties. Burke listened, and to his credit, saw wisdom in what Howard was pitching. And when he checked with Mark Lazarus, he'd found out that Mark would be more than happy to have me in his corner as he transitioned into the job.

A few weeks later, we finalized the new agreement in Burke's office. It was all amicable, if still a little confounding. As we sat talking, Burke remarked on what he'd observed over the time since my departure had been announced.

"I'll tell you, Dick," said the man who'd so preciously pegged me as larger than life, over and over again. "I expected there to be some emotion with you leaving. But I had no idea how much. I mean, people were still crying days after."

The good news was that I'd be able to work with everyone for the better part of another year. And in a way that kept me engaged with what I was still passionate about: putting on a show.

It would be great working one final season with Mark, Fred, Drew, Al, Cris, and their crew. Anyone who thought I wouldn't be able to let go of control was badly mistaken. After twenty-two years in the job, at the age of sixty-three, just worrying about the fun stuff was incredibly liberating. Consulting with Howard on the schedule, being there for Fred and Drew on the road, guiding Mark through the relationships he needed to develop—it all felt like a natural transition. The Super Bowl that year was in Indianapolis, a rematch between the Patriots and Giants four seasons after Eli Manning had ruined New England's bid for a perfect season. This time out, Tom Brady and the Pats were heavily favored again, and yet Manning and his head coach, Tom Coughlin, prevailed, in a frantic final minute that featured Bill Belichick letting the Giants score a touchdown rather than take more time off the clock, only to see his team fall short in his attempt to lead a drive on the other side. The best part of the season, though, came in a news release weeks after the Super Bowl: this was the year that, for the first time ever, *Sunday Night Football* was the number one show in all of prime-time television. Ten years later, as I write this, in another piece of unprecedented history, it still holds the crown.

The perfect final chapter came in the summer of 2012 in London, for one more Olympic Games. Mark named Jim Bell as the executive producer. Jim had begun his TV career literally carrying Randy Falco all around Barcelona; Randy had torn his Achilles tendon, and with so much of the city only accessible by stairs, Jim, a former Harvard football player, was the only person who could get him places. Jim had gone on to become a coordinating producer on our Olympic team, and then, at my recommendation, the executive producer of the *Today* show. Now he'd run all of NBC's production at the Olympics, and I couldn't have been happier for him.

But I also wanted to stay out of his way. Which was easy because, if this was going to be my last Olympics on the inside, I was going to finally take advantage of the opportunity to go check out some of the action. Dating back to Grenoble in 1968, when I'd watched Peggy Fleming win the gold medal from alongside the ice just before the Closing Ceremony, I'd only seen one Olympic event live—a Team USA basketball game in Sydney that I'd taken Susan and Teddy to, at an hour when we weren't on the air back home in the States. Now, while I was sure to sit in on Jim's format meetings, and be there for anyone else who had questions, I also had a few events on my bucket list—chief among them to watch Michael Phelps swim in person. I went to see him in the 200-meter butterfly the fourth night of competition, and he won silver. The medal ceremony followed, and as Michael walked around toward the podium, he looked up into the stands and our eyes met. He smiled wide.

"What are you doing here?" he shouted. "You never go to events!"

The same reaction followed the next night, when I went to beach volleyball to see Misty May-Treanor and Kerri Walsh Jennings on their way to winning a third straight gold medal.

"Shouldn't you be in your big office?" they joked from down on the sand, before jumping up alongside the wall of the small stadium to say hello and give me a big hug.

The last day of the Games, my last day at NBC Sports, I spent the morning in a conference room with Jim and Mark going over the Closing Ceremony format. The working plan was to cut parts of the show for time, including a sketch from the *Monty Python* stars. Sitting in the corner of the room, I put in my two cents.

"I'd keep that, guys," I said. "They've got a real following back home, and you don't want the headline to be that you cut Britain's greatest comedy export. Plus, they're damn funny."

As they thought about it, I knew they'd gotten the point—and that I shouldn't push any further. This was their show, and it was going to be their show for years to come. So I walked out, met up with Susan, and hopped in a car to watch LeBron James and Kobe Bryant lead the USA men's basketball team to another gold medal. Then, that night, I came back to the broadcast center to watch the Closing Ceremony, quietly sitting behind Jim as the feed came through from the stadium. It was a great show—and the *Monty Python* sketch stayed in. Still, afterward, there were a few hours of editing to do before the ceremony began airing in prime time back in the States.

From Saturday Night to Sunday Night

While half of our compound in the broadcast center was being packed up, and people done with their assignments were celebrating the end of the Games, back in the edit area that we called Central Tape, there was still a frenzy of activity, with segments being cut down, and producers running back and forth, calling out instructions on what to edit, what to keep, and so forth. I spotted John Gilmartin and Carol Larson, two of my favorites who'd run the Central Tape operation for years, and almost out of habit, we started talking about how the final segment would be edited. And then that led to walking in an edit room, and me walking an editor through exactly where to cut, what pictures to replace, how to make it perfect. Johnny and Carol chimed in, and a familiar feeling set in. Time was running out before we had to feed the show to New York, and if I closed my eyes, I could have been in Barcelona or Atlanta or Athens or Beijing, or even Grenoble or Munich.

It was a brand of adrenaline I knew I'd never feel again. But as the final edits were laid down in front of me, and tears welled in my eyes, I knew there was nothing to be sad about.

Because how lucky had I been to be part of it all.

EPILOGUE

Plenty More Story to Tell

About ten days after I broke off negotiations with Steve Burke and resigned from NBC in May of 2011, I found myself in Malibu, California, at a Memorial Day party on the beach at Joel Silver's house. Joel is a movie producer who was behind a ton of hits in the 1980s and '90s, including *48 Hrs.* and the *Lethal Weapon* movies—he's a true Hollywood character who Susan and I have known forever. And the guest list was something out of a movie itself—with stars walking all around the backyard, and none other than Kobe Bryant playing pickup with a group of kids on Silver's driveway hoop.

My departure from NBC Sports had made news in the media pages, and in fact a *Los Angeles Times* piece had been written a few days earlier, suggesting that now that I was free, maybe I could produce the Oscars the next year. It was flattering, but not anything I'd ever consider doing, though people came up to me all afternoon long to talk about it. And eventually, Susan and I got in deep conversation with Barbra Streisand and James Brolin, who lived a few miles away. After a while, Barbra and James invited us back to their house for a tour, which became a running gag, with our friend Ron Meyer, who was also with us, joking that we shouldn't do the tour—it was "just another house," and there was "nothing interesting to see."

Suffice it to say, we took the tour, and the house was amazing.

It was all as fun and surreal as it sounds. And a perfect example of all the improbable turns my life had taken since I was just a kid in Litchfield, Connecticut, worried about playing varsity basketball and running for class president.

I think probably most people expected me to do something else after I left NBC. I was just sixty-three years old, and plenty of calls came in. But I never considered any full-time opportunities seriously at all. I've consulted for many old partners and colleagues, some formally and many informally, but my rule has always been the same: don't pay me, because I don't want to work anymore. As hard as I'd been working the previous forty-plus years, I took to retirement with a vengeance, and have never looked back. I don't know how many books I've read since retiring, but it has to number in the thousands. Crime novels, mostly—Michael Connelly is my favorite—but also plenty of sports books and history, as always.

I'm not going to say I've never missed it. I sometimes miss the action of *Sunday Night Football*, and the exhilaration of the Olympics. But really, the parts that I miss are connected to the people I worked with. In writing this book, I've gone through my personal diary calendars, which I kept meticulously for my entire time at NBC. Each day is filled with not so much what I did but who I talked to—upward of a dozen phone calls every day, plus breakfasts, lunches, dinners, coffees, drinks, and more. It's always been about the people, and always been about the countless relationships I forged.

My last day at NBC I called in one of my assistants, Marissa, as we were packing up all my things. I held out a strange object in my hand, and told her I wasn't leaving until she was able to teach me how it worked. And after some struggle, that's how I learned to text. Not a lot has changed since I used to bribe dorm mates at Yale to type up my stringer reports for the *Times* and *Globe*—I'm still hopeless with a keyboard or a computer. But I can get around all right with a few news and sports apps on my iPad, and thanks to Marissa, I do know how to text. Even if I still prefer picking up the phone and just calling my favorite people, it's an important skill for a septuagenarian making his way through the twenty-first century.

More than a decade after I left, for all the changes in the media landscape since I've left, for all the ways Comcast was going to move its sports business in a different direction after I left, the identity and strategy of NBC Sports is still defined by *Sunday Night Football* and the Olympics. *SNF* is still the top-rated show in all of prime-time TV, and the league is arguably the strongest force in all of television, thanks to the leadership of Roger Goodell in the commissioner's office, and

Robert Kraft and Jerry Jones skillfully leading the broadcast committee from the owners' side. As for the Olympics, when Comcast took over the company, all the headlines with regards to sports were about how the deals I'd negotiated had finally been exposed, with Vancouver supposedly a money-losing proposition. Well, just weeks after I left, Brian Roberts and Steve Burke flew to Lausanne with my old team to make their bid to keep NBC America's Olympic network. The sense was that, without me, they wouldn't have the stomach to pay for the rights. Instead, not only did they make a successful $4 billion–plus bid to get the Games from 2014 to 2020, but three years later history repeated itself, as Comcast forked over $7.75 billion to extend the deal all the way to 2032. It was the exact same strategy we had in the 1990s—just three or four times as many billions.

I don't point this out defiantly, but I do note it proudly. Not just because it was good business then and good business now, but because it's a tribute to the people who came up under me, and who are still working there, and doing such a phenomenal job. Sam Flood was an Olympic researcher with Jeff Zucker in 1988; he's the executive producer and president of NBC Sports today. Molly Solomon was an Olympic researcher in 1992; now she is still not only the executive producer of Golf Channel but also the president and executive producer of NBC Olympics. Mark Lazarus is now the chairman of all of NBCUniversal television and streaming; sports is just one slice of the many different parts of the company he oversees as a popular and respected leader. Fred Gaudelli and Drew Esocoff produced and directed their final season together of *Sunday Night Football* in 2021, capping it off with Super Bowl LVI in Los Angeles. Now Fred's moved over to *Thursday Night Football* on Amazon Prime Video.

If you would have told me, or anyone else, when I walked out of NBC in 2011, that Amazon would someday be producing football games, you would have gotten some strange looks. But the most important fundamentals are the same. Roone Arledge's memo to Edgar Scherick in 1962 laid out how to produce a great football game. Everything he wrote still holds up today. Build up characters. Bring the atmosphere to life. Make people feel like they're in the stadium themselves. Tell a great story.

Has the world changed since I walked into ABC Sports in 1967 as a twenty-year-old kid? Absolutely. And in many ways, for the better. But I don't think any piece of entertainment will ever bring the country together as broadly as *Wide*

World of Sports, or *Monday Night Football*, or for that matter Johnny Carson did half a century ago. There are just too many places for people to turn when they want to be entertained. And it's great that people who love cooking, or traveling, or any number of other niche pursuits have dozens of shows, not to mention websites and apps, to turn to.

But there's still something special about a show like *Saturday Night Live*—how people will stay up late every weekend to see what the anchors say on *Weekend Update*, just the way their parents and grandparents did. Or, if they fell asleep, taking advantage of a twenty-first-century backup plan: checking the internet first thing on Sunday to see what sketches have gone viral.

And even more significantly, there's still something magical about events, and entertainers, that can bring millions, if not billions, together. They show us how much we share, rather than how different we are. How much we have in common, rather than how much we disagree. Sports offer that chance as wonderfully as anything else. That's why the NFL and the Olympics still get the biggest audiences—even if those audiences aren't as big as they used to be. Watching the Super Bowl still gets me excited, and watching the Olympics can still get me to cry. And that's true for people who are fifty, who are thirty, and who are ten.

How many things can you say that about?

I'm still a creature of habit. And one of my most treasured routines is my daily walk—in Maui during the winters, and back home in Litchfield in the spring, summer, and fall. A perfect day begins with a hot cup of coffee with Susan, a conversation about whatever's in the news, and then a walk. I bring my phone and log plenty of hours of conversation with old friends in and out of television, and of course my kids, now scattered across the country with their own families.

But I do plenty of thinking, too. I think about friends I miss, and who I'd love to be able to call, like David Stern and Don Ohlmeyer. I think about all the great visits Susan and I had with John Madden in the years after he retired, none sweeter than our last one, in late 2021, when we had a few more wonderful dinners to savor with John and his wife, Virginia, talking about everything from football to family to leadership to the future of the country. I think, too, about Brandon Tartikoff, who's been gone since 1997. For all the magnetism of Brandon's charm, and all the brilliance he brought to the world, his legacy is still shadowed by the sadness of the cancer that relentlessly attacked his body and took him from Lilly, his family, and all of us before he could reach fifty. I still miss him, and often wonder how many great shows he would have brought into the world with more time. How many more great memories he could have made with his life.

The destination of every walk I take in Litchfield is the same. Out my door to the right, and toward my three-hundred-year-old town, still one of the most beautiful towns in all of America. Down North Street, past the Sheldon Tavern, where George Washington often stayed on trips between New York and Boston. Then South Street, and the first law school in America—where Aaron Burr was one of the first students. Down Gallows Lane, where the Americans would hang British soldiers they'd captured during the Revolutionary War. Then down the short hill, and into the cemetery, where a boy who will forever be fourteen years old is buried in the back.

To me, what's maybe most striking about Teddy Ebersol today is in the ways he's a living figure for our grandchildren. More than anyone else, that's a tribute to Susan, and how much she keeps him alive in our hearts and in our minds and in our stories. Our kids tell their kids about him—the stories of what a rascal he was, what a huge Red Sox fan he was, everything he liked, everything he disliked. And though they'll never meet him, the next generation feels like they know him.

People still write us letters about Teddy. In the Liberty Hotel, which overlooks the Teddy Ebersol Fields on Storrow Drive in Boston, there's a Teddy Ebersol presidential suite on the top floor, with a great view of the fields, and the Charles River and MIT beyond. People stay in that suite, they see a plaque commemorating its name, they read about the boy whose life was just getting started, and they reach out. And we write back, because it makes us feel a little better, even if we know we'll never feel quite whole.

So I stop walking when I get to his grave, and I talk to Teddy. I tell him how the Red Sox are doing, I tell him what his brothers and sisters are up to, and his nieces and nephews. I update him on the news, and tell him about the shows his mom and I have been watching, and the books I've been reading.

I tell him stories for as long as I can, and then I walk back home. Already thinking about the stories I'll tell him tomorrow when I return.

ACKNOWLEDGMENTS

Early in the summer of 2019, I made a phone call to a former colleague at NBC named Aaron Cohen. Aaron had started out his career as a research assistant at the Sydney Olympics and went on to become one of the most respected writers and producers in sports television. We didn't know each other that well, but I was receiving the Pete Rozelle Radio-Television Award later that summer from the Pro Football Hall of Fame and was looking to bounce some thoughts off of another mind as I prepared my acceptance speech. Someone recommended I call Aaron, and I invited him to lunch in Litchfield. I had no idea how wonderful a decision that would turn out to be.

After he helped me with the speech, I mentioned to Aaron how for years I'd flirted with writing a memoir, but had never quite committed to going all the way with it. But over a few lunches and several phone calls, I'd been struck by Aaron's endless flow of questions, and seemingly infinite curiosity about everything we talked about. Maybe now would be a good time to try the book thing again, and maybe he'd be the right person to try it with. Thankfully, he agreed, and that fall we began meeting regularly and figuring out how to tell the story of my life and career.

This book would not have been possible without Aaron. And I couldn't have found a better collaborator. I've always felt like my memory has been one of my greatest strengths, but this book reflects that only because of Aaron's willingness to continually push me to go into more detail about all my experiences, from the laughter to the tears to the touchdowns and more. I am so grateful for his partnership, and his friendship, and now that the book's done, I just hope he's still willing to come up to Litchfield when I call him to have one of our now standard lunchtime burgers with me. He assures me, with the smile and chuckle that I've come to treasure, that he will.

My relationship with Bob Barnett goes back decades, but we hadn't spoken for years when we connected in late 2020. I told him I was working on a book but wasn't sure what kind of interest there would be from a publisher. Bob, an ace lawyer if there ever was one, sold the book to Simon & Schuster within a few weeks of that conversation.

It was great to hear that a company like S&S was excited about the book; things would get even better when I met my editor, Sean Manning. Curious and sharp, kind and patient, Sean quickly became another of my favorite new friends, and he even came up to Litchfield one summer afternoon for a tour of my home office. Once he got his hands on the manuscript, he guided Aaron and me brilliantly, making every single page better with his vision for what this book could be.

My sons Charlie and Willie encouraged me to write a book for years, and, once we started the process, acted as sage advisors and perceptive editors. They, along with their brother Harmony, sister Sunshine, and their mom, read through any number of drafts, making it so much better along the way.

A number of great friends, other family members, and colleagues of mine were generous enough to sit for interviews for this project, and sadly not all of them lived to see it come to light. Their recollections and insights were integral in reconstructing the details and drama of so many of the stories in this book. I could not be more grateful to Barry Blaustein, Steve Bornstein, Cris Collinsworth, Bob Costas, Michael Gartner, Roger Goodell, Fred Gaudelli, Howard Katz, Aimee Leone, Mike McCarley, Al Michaels, Jon Miller, Tommy Roy, Ed Scanlon, Ken Schanzer, Adam Silver, Molly Solomon, Kevin Sullivan, Paul Tagliabue, Bob Tischler, and Jeff Zucker, as well as the late Ken Duberstein, Don Ohlmeyer, David Stern, and Jack Welch for their time and reflections. Thanks also to Randy Falco, Sam Flood, Alex Gilady, Jerry Jones, Phil Knight, Robert Kraft, Mark Lazarus, Sean McManus, Lorne Michaels, Eric Shanks, Ed Swindler, Bob Wright, and Gary Zenkel for their time, assistance, and support with the project. I also want to thank and acknowledge the help of one of my earliest role models and heroes, my brother, Si Bunting. And I want to thank John Ourand of the *Sports Business Journal*, the preeminent chronicler of the sports television industry, whom I got to know well during my final years working at NBC, and who, through our conversations, provided an initial jolt on how to reflect on my career and begin forming the ideas that became the basis for this book.

In Litchfield, our house would simply not run without the devotion and love of Robin Kocsis and Christine Durkin. Thanks also to Barrie Johnson and Galen Quist for all their years working alongside Susan.

Lastly, one of the great blessings of retirement has been to spend it surrounded by our ever-growing and never-boring family, which now includes seven grandkids—Rowena, Vivian, Fielding, Independence, Amara, Voyager, and Kaia. The time that Susie and I get to spend with them, Willie, Lauren, Charlie, Melody, Sunshine, Rob, and Harmony sustains and delights us.

As for the woman to whom this book is dedicated, through forty years now of wonderful highs and unimaginable lows, my wife has been the best friend I've ever had, the love of my life, and a partner who makes every second of every one of my days better. What else could a guy ask for?

INDEX

Index

Index